Novel Perspectives on German-Language Comics Studies

Novel Perspectives on German-Language Comics Studies

History, Pedagogy, Theory

Edited by Lynn Marie Kutch

LEXINGTON BOOKS
Lanham • Boulder • New York • London

Published by Lexington Books
An imprint of The Rowman & Littlefield Publishing Group, Inc.
4501 Forbes Boulevard, Suite 200, Lanham, Maryland 20706
www.rowman.com

Unit A, Whitacre Mews, 26-34 Stannary Street, London SE11 4AB

British Library Cataloguing in Publication Information Available

Library of Congress Cataloging-in-Publication Data

Names: Kutch, Lynn M., 1970– editor.
Title: Novel perspectives on German-language comics studies : history, pedagogy, theory / edited by
    Lynn M. Kutch.
Description: Lanham, Maryland : Lexington Books, [2016] | Includes bibliographical references and
    index.
Identifiers: LCCN 2016015852 (print) | LCCN 2016016270 (ebook) | ISBN 9781498526227 (cloth :
    alk. paper) | ISBN 9781498526234 (Electronic)
Subjects: LCSH: Comic books, strips, etc.--Germany--History and criticism.
Classification: LCC PN6755.N68 2016 (print) | LCC PN6755 (ebook) | DDC 741.5/943--dc23
LC record available at https://lccn.loc.gov/2016015852

Printed in the United States of America

I would like to thank my contributors for their exceptional creativity and patience during the production of this anthology. I also would like to thank Joshua Steinberg for his assistance.

Contents

List of Figures

Introduction

Lynn Marie Kutch

Premiere German literary critic Marcel Reich-Ranicki (1920–2013) was once asked in an interview whether comics count as literature. His response: "nein, nein, nein" ("Fragen Sie"). Although Reich-Ranicki provided this response in 2010, it continues to characterize a popular view toward comics that has persisted in Germany and German-speaking countries for decades. When Ole Frahm writes in a 2004 essay about the "weird status of comics,"[1] he is not referring to the subculture that has been developing since the birth of the "underground comix" movement,[2] or the ritual of "cosplay"[3] that accompanies comics conventions worldwide. Instead, Frahm explains why particularly German-language comics reside in a "strange in-between cultural place:" "they are no longer low culture but, as ephemera, they are not raised to the status of high culture" (2004, 235). The marked distinction between popular culture and high culture still prevalent in Germany today corresponds to basic, generally accepted definitions of each that frequently speak to a work's artistic quality and level of purpose. In terms of quality, products of high culture generally exhibit identifiable aesthetic criteria, such as beauty, creativity, originality, avant-gardism, and sophistication of form (Hecken 11). As concerns objective, those same creations should "stimulate the critical mind of the citizen," while those of popular culture distract from these goals because of a "trivial" and "gratifying" nature that neglects to engage the viewer or consumer critically (Kukkonen 116).[4] The perceived failure of comic art to fulfill these aesthetic and pedagogical criteria has enabled a generalized non-acceptance in German-speaking countries of comics as examples of high art or works of remarkable literary quality.

This delayed process of German cultural acknowledgement stands most notably in contrast to attitudes in neighboring France and Belgium, where "comic strips are particularly highly esteemed," and where they also carry the designation of the "ninth art," which confirms their cultural clout in that they occupy a new category above the classic seven liberal arts (Screech 1).[5] Indeed these European, as well as Asian and American, influences have caused comics critics like Frahm to regard German comics as part of a "globalized culture" with many "local manifestations which should be carefully considered" (2004, 235).[6] Despite

Frahm's assertion above that comics are fixed between high and low culture, the latter observation suggests a slow yet steady change in German attitudes toward comics as specimens of fine art and literature. Thomas Wegmann and Norbert Christian Wolf confirm the positive development that Frahm describes when they write about comics as an "initially 'illegitimate' genre [that] has over the last decades developed an unforeseen dynamic" (in den vergangenen Jahrzehnten als zunächst "illegitimes" Genre eine ungeahnte Dynamik entwickelt hat; 6). Monika Schmitz-Emans, referencing an international canon of graphic novels, asserts "the graphic novel is now broadly accepted in the circle of 'respected' literary art forms" (391). Nonetheless, in September 2013 as part of the *Internationales Literaturfestival Berlin* German comic artists, graphic novelists, and their publishers essentially refuted the broadness of this acceptance and formally acknowledged a persistent ideological schism between low and high culture through a call to action in the *Comic-Manifesto*.

In this document, the above named "demand that the comic be afforded the same respect as literature and the visual arts," and assert that this respect would ideally take tangible form in the allocation of funding to comic artists that is already awarded to other artists ("Das Comic Manifest"). Unfortunately for comic artists, as Karin Kukkonen points out in her explanation of the difference between high culture and low or popular culture, "[t]he medium and the context of a text do not determine the quality of the text, but they do determine our expectations towards the text" (115). Michael Picone describes a dynamic within the current art culture that "underscores the dilemma facing comic art, suspended as it is between the worlds of visual art and textual art, which follow opposing paths to legitimacy, commoditization and greatness" (44). This is an important distinction at which the *Comic-Manifesto* authors subtly hint. By demanding generally that comics garner the same appreciation as literature and the visual arts, they do not maintain that comics hover somewhere between the two art forms. Instead, comic art possesses enough assertive legitimacy to etch out its own cultural space. In this context of cultural legitimacy, it is significant that the *Comic-Manifesto* concludes with two succinct and forceful pronouncements, capitalized and in bold type in the original: "COMIC IS ART. IT'S TIME FOR CULTURAL POLITICS TO UNDERSTAND THIS" (COMIC IST KUNST. DAS MUSS JETZT AUCH DIE KULTURPOLITIK VERSTEHEN). With these statements, the undersigned vehemently address the firm entrenchment in German-speaking countries of *Kulturpolitik* (cultural policy/politics), a term that refers to the policies surrounding "the regulation of public cultural interests" by political bodies (Heinze 304).[7] Artists' collectives may influence decisions, but ensconced beliefs regarding contexts of publication and reception continue to determine value judgments, and thus sway official decisions still influenced by unwritten rules of low and high culture.

In the case of German comics, expectations associated with low and high art evolve from, according to Daniel Stein, a "double lineage" that informs their historical development: "German comics authors have labored not only in the shadow of Wilhelm Busch, but also under the specter of American comics" (303). The classic status assigned to Wilhelm Busch's comics essentially shield them from current debate, meaning that especially the American part of this lineage contributed to those comics "stemming from pulp magazines that were regarded as artistically inferior products of mass culture and as a kind of fast food for readers" (Schmitz-Emans 391). While many citizens and politicians would argue that *Kulturpolitik* still plays a significant role in identifying "artistically inferior products" and literary "fast food," other theorists have predicted a marked decrease in the continued and powerful influence of *Kulturpolitik*. Specifically citing globalization and economic difficulties that impact arts funding, Armin Klein claims the demise of the "euphoric" status that *Kulturpolitik* had enjoyed in the 1970s and 1980s as "the motor of societal development" (der Motor gesellschaftlicher Entwicklung; Klein 218). The authors of the *The Manifest*, however, make the impassioned counterclaim that cultural political decisions still matter for their art and its recognition as such. Desired arts funding and increased scholarly recognition certainly have the potential to contribute to the acceptability of the art form itself, thereby lifting comics and graphic novels out of the weird in-between place.

A volume that treats both comics and graphic novels, and in which contributors even use these designations interchangeably, must contain a brief discussion of the distinction between the terms. Much has been written on the differences between comics and graphic novels, but critics who consult the most respected scholarly works written on the subject may become easily frustrated with the increasing lack of differentiation. The popularization of the term "graphic novel" is often associated with the publication of Will Eisner's *A Contract with God: A Graphic Novel* (1978), and later to Art Spiegelman's *Maus* (1980). In his own pivotal theory on the medium, however, Eisner proposes the term "sequential art" to refer to graphic texts (122); and Spiegelman's more recent *In the Shadow of No Towers* "exemplifies in a splendid manner most of the paradoxes that characterize the graphic novel as an emerging field" (Baetens 1151). Many respected and oft-cited comics theorists, such as Scott McCloud (1993), David Carrier (2000), and Thierry Groensteen (2007), have used the term "comics" as an all-encompassing term for graphic texts. In their seminal work *A Comics Studies Reader*, Jeet Heer and Kent Worcester support a currently dominant trend of both acknowledging and perpetuating the vagueness: "The term 'comics' is itself filled with ambiguity. . . . For our purposes, the term most often refers to comic strips, comic books, manga, and graphic novels, but also encompasses gag cartoons, editorial cartoons, and New Yorker–style cartoons" (xiii). Other critics, frustrated and dissatisfied with the decreased attention to distinguishing between the terms have proposed other systems, such as the organizing concept of "icononical discourse," to name one example, intended to prevent "the problematic confusion produced by the indiscriminate use of the term 'comics'" (Romero-Jódar 118–19). To add to the confusion and frustration, in addition to the misperceptions or mislabelings of graphic texts that can occur when theorists employ generalized terms, cultural critics have also used "comics" and "graphic novels" to designate inferior and superior levels of artistic quality and purpose, respectively.

This has especially been the case in German-speaking countries, where, as discussed above, criteria of quality and purpose determine important differences between low and high art.[8] Bernd Dolle-Weinkauff explains the widespread usage and acceptance of the label "graphic novel," which has established itself internationally as a term that implies literary value as compared to conventional comics (151). German cultural critic Lars von Törne, however, warns against the tendency to use "graphic novel" as a measure of artistic value: "Graphic novel is no criteria for quality!" (Graphic Novel ist kein Qualitätskriterium!; von Törne). He goes on to suggest that the term's popularity has done little more than to create an artificially constructed division between readers and creators of presumably higher quality graphic novels, and consumers and creators of presumably substandard comics (von Törne). Von Törne also chronicles the commonplace use of the English term "graphic novel" in Germany, and its significance for the low and high debates, as well as for marketing. He writes about ways that the term has improved the willingness of large publishers to print these texts because of their increased potential for sales: "Comics, with its negative connotation, is avoided so that publishers can better appeal to a grown-up target audience with picture stories containing serious subject matter" (Man umgeht das oft abschätzig konnotierte "Comic," um sich mit seriös konzipierten Bildgeschichten besser an ein erwachsenes Zielpublikum wenden zu können; von Törne). In the 2011 *Comic Report* Klaus Schikowski notes that "this year too the gap between comic and graphic novel has grown bigger" (Der Spalt zwischen Comic und Graphic Novel ist auch in diesem Jahr größer geworden; 50). Even if that gap has increased, as Heer and Worcester and others have shown, comics scholars and critics are now spending less time differentiating between these two "artificially constructed" categories, and are devoting more time and scholarly energy to analyzing the interaction of visual and verbal aspects that comprise the medium. In the present collection, I leave it up to the contributors to enter this scholarly debate on their own terms and to address differences and definitions on an individual basis in their chapters.

The present volume gathers an international team of contributors from two continents who demonstrate through their innovative scholarship that they have been answering the *Comic-Manifesto*'s call for some time, and that they regard comics and graphic novels as works of art in their own right. Additionally, their essays can serve as scholarly models and prototypes for further research that can continue to define the relationship between comics and other "accepted" high art forms, such as literature and the visual arts. As this collection demonstrates, critics worldwide have begun taking comics and graphic novels seriously, and have increasingly secured the place of German comics and graphic novels in a globalized culture of comics. As indicated above and cited in this introduction, a wealth of secondary literature exists both in German and English that aims to locate comics and graphic novels within contexts of narrative theory, literary theory, and media studies. In addition to those, a number of monographs and anthologies have also appeared in recent years that collect pedagogical studies[9] and literary analyses[10] of graphic texts. To my knowledge, however, *Novel Perspectives on German-language Comics: History, Pedagogy, Theory* is the first English-language anthology that exclusively treats graphic texts of the German-speaking countries. Thus in its breadth, this book functions as an important resource in a to-date limited pool of critical works on German-language comics and graphic novels. The individual contributions in this book differ significantly from one another in methodology, subject matter, and style. Taken together, however, they present a cross-section of comics and graphic novel scholarship being performed in North America and in Europe. The contributors to this volume have directly confronted the challenge to sort out the "E und U"[11] that still often enters public discourse in the German-speaking world today. The intellectual innovations, in which the contributors reorganize and reconfigure conventional prototypes of reading literature and observing visual art, have the potential to create a new critical language within which this rapidly expanding genre can be read and interpreted.

In general, each of the chapters belongs to one of two broad categories of pedagogy or scholarship. And, in fact, I initially envisioned the book being divided more or less in half in that manner. With that division, I did not want to suggest, however, a simplification of the topic as a whole or of two classifications. For example, pedagogy can encompass using comics and graphic novels to teach culture, language, or history as well as literary methods of reading and analyzing graphic texts that tell stories or influence understanding of history. Scholarship can include defining the genre and evaluating the state of current criticism, assessing adaptations of classic literature and art, or viewing graphic novels as vehicles for social comment or activism. Continued and more in-depth editing work in the early stages of the present volume confirmed what I had already known: that the current state of research on graphic novels is multifaceted, nuanced, and does not allow itself to be categorized so easily. Nonetheless, it is important and necessary to supply headings as a way of organizing this volume's extensive and diverse content. Instead of two large categories, I have subdivided the contributions into five sub-headings: Contexts and Histories, German Cultural Education, Graphic Novels: Hands-on, Generations of German History, and Austrian Voices.

CONTEXTS AND HISTORIES

In the first section "Contexts and Histories," Eckhard Kuhn-Osius and Matt Hambro speculate on the trajectories that German-language comics have taken based on cultural and historical factors peculiar to Germany and German-speaking countries. Hambro presents a highly original approach by synthesizing the theories of thinkers throughout the ages; and he analyzes the role that theories dealing with mimesis and abstraction have played in current debates about the perception of a traditional supremacy of text over image. His chapter "German Comics: Form, Content and Production" offers an overview of the history of German-language comics and demonstrates specific ways that German aesthetics, philosophy, and history have interacted with the production and reception of graphic narratives in German-speaking countries and abroad. The chapter first focuses on form in order to demonstrate how the reception of comics in Germany has been influenced by logocentric preferences for text over image, tension between mimesis and abstraction, and notions of medium purity. Next, turning to content, the chapter demonstrates the significance of the folktale and thematic integration with canonized literature to the German tradition. Then, concerning production, the chapter outlines the significance that group production, state sponsorship, and market orientation have had and have in the German tradition. Finally, the chapter concludes with a look into comics production and reception in Germany today: a time in which many of the concerns and preferences of the twentieth century and earlier have diminished or disappeared entirely.

Eckhard Kuhn-Osius frames his reading of the history of German comic art within an *Erwartungshorizont* (horizon of expectations) that addresses genre, style, or form. Kuhn-Osius engages with the low-high debate by tracing a lineage of German pictorial literature in which the discussed comics did not necessarily aspire to be real art. His chapter takes into consideration the most well-known comics, such as *Struwwelpeter* and *Max und Moritz*, but it also introduces readers to lesser known but nonetheless very significant contributors to German graphic art's recent history, such as *Lurchi* and *Jimmy das Gummipferd*. Kuhn-Osius proposes some new organizing terms belonging to an interpretive apparatus with which comics scholars can read various examples of graphic narrative art from the past two centuries. He suggests criteria for a comics aesthetic and its measurable qualities by discussing the extent to which his examples combine the proposed terms that include internal meta-text and illocutionary text. Addressing the low-high debate, Kuhn-Osius posits that a comic exhibits advanced genre characteristics when it expertly integrates image, internal meta-text, and illocutionary language. These combinations not only make it easier to tell a more complicated story with complex characters, but they also allow for a greater economy of expressive means. His detailed analyses and close readings of individual texts contribute to a larger study of the history of German comics that includes both original German products as well as American and French imports. Each of the developments that he traces has influenced the horizon of expectations that contemporary German graphic novelists must understand and navigate when presenting their own creations and assessing where they might fit.

GERMAN CULTURAL EDUCATION

The popularity and professional acceptance of using comics and graphic novels to teach literary skills and culture have grown both in Germany and the United States over the last few decades. Increasingly, comics have entered cultural debates that concern social and cultural education, such as those political discussions that invoke the Bible as supporting evidence, or those that examine the effects of comics on impressionable youth. The contributions in this section provide a valuable complement to existing scholarly articles and instructional materials on public discourse concerning comics and graphic novels. With a particularly original contribution, Jens Kußmann provides an overview of the representation of comics in secondary school textbooks in Bavaria. He embeds his study in a brief historical overview of public opinion on comics in Germany, beginning with the 1950s, when comics had the reputation of inhibiting reading skills and causing illiteracy. He also offers a brief summary and analysis of scholarly work on comics and graphic novels in Germany. The essence of the chapter consists of a detailed and careful assessment of textbook series currently in use in Bavarian academic high schools, and their incorporation of comics, or more accurately non-incorporation, as Kußmann argues in the chapter. Although the analysis is limited to textbook offerings in one federal state, his study introduces important guiding questions and a template for future studies that could consider similar statistics in the remaining German federal states or in other countries.

In another highly original contribution, Jan Alexander van Nahl considers graphic adaptations of biblical texts using the example of *The Book of Revelation*. Set against the backdrop of biblically based cultural or polit-

ical arguments and the popular endeavors in recent years to make biblical material and the meaning of its contents more accessible to the mass
population, van Nahl's article underscores the supreme confrontation
between sacred text and its remake in a popular medium. His chapter
reflects recent discussions that seek to break down ensconced low and
high distinctions. The examination builds upon the premise that scholarship on the subgenre of graphic novels based on the Bible is still in its
early stages. However, adapting biblical narratives raises topical questions regarding how a graphic artist can do justice to religious ideas,
which not only have laid the foundations of Western thought, but also
influence current sociopolitical treatments of phenomena such as interculturality. The chapter scrutinizes how graphic novel adaptations compare to classical readings of biblical texts and whether they can serve
similar didactic purposes. The chapter is divided into four parts, the first
of which comprises the wider sociocultural background, with a particular
focus on Germany in early 2015. The second part centers on the examined
graphic novel's formal appearance, including remarks on its intended
readership. The third part provides a close reading of important passages. The graphic adaptation's possible impact on its readership, especially the emotive character, is addressed in the concluding part. Notions
of hybridity and heterogeneousness that often accompany pop art correspond to one of van Nahl's central questions of whether aesthetics and
didactic demands can work in synergy. As the author demonstrates
through his analysis, the entertaining style combines with the power to
incite dialogue about the eternal human condition.

THE GRAPHIC NOVEL: HANDS-ON

The two chapters in this section take a hands-on approach to teaching
with graphic novels by showing how instructors can implement the medium in order to teach language, culture, and history. In her chapter, Julia
Ludewig introduces the Basel city reportage *Operation Läckerli* and outlines pedagogical units for two stories of the collection: Ulli Lust's "Ein
Platz in Mitteleuropa" and Jens Harder's "Schnell, Schuss." These two
vignettes are suitable for beginning and intermediate/advanced learners,
respectively. Emphasizing the peculiar mixture of documentary and aes-
theticized elements characteristic of the comics journalism genre, Ludewig details how the instructor can use *Operation Läckerli* to develop students' visual and multimodal, historical and cultural, transcultural, as
well as literary analytical skills. For example, students hone their visual
and multimodal competence by contrasting realistic and abstracted
drawing styles or identifying types of panel transitions. If the instructor
wants to teach historical and cultural knowledge (*Landeskunde*), *Operation
Läckerli* is fertile ground for discussing religion and secularism or the

sports fan culture in a city. The comics also allow for transcultural lesson units as they present but also problematize the ethnic diversity in Basel and Switzerland today. Finally, Ludewig suggests literary analytical prompts that target verbal and visual metaphors or invite comparisons between the city reportage and the long tradition of big city poetry.

Antje Krueger intensifies the focus on the pedagogy of German history, and specifically East German history, with her chapter on teaching about the former German Democratic Republic (GDR) using three disparate examples of graphic novels. This article identifies three graphic novels (*Tunnel 57*, 2013; *Grenzfall*, 2011; *drüben!*, 2009) that allow novice and intermediate German students to engage with GDR history. Many graphic novels about the GDR exist, but these three texts are particlarly engaging for students of German. *Tunnel 57* and *Grenzfall* offer extraordinary stories in the sense of a sensational escape or a remarkable case of resistance against the GDR regime, while *drüben!* is an autobiographical text that portrays how ordinary people were surveiled and oppressed in the GDR. The author gives insights into the history of the medium and discusses how an instructor could capitalize on the specific content, but also on the verbal and visual structure that is typical for graphic novels. The article describes exemplary teaching units for each graphic novel that demonstrate how these texts aid vocabulary development, and improve reading and writing practices. The particular teaching outcomes for these units are based on skill sets suggested by the National Council of State Supervisors for Languages (NCSSFL) and the American Council on the Teaching of Foreign Languages (ACTFL) Standards for the Novice Low to High level (Can-Do Statements). In addition, the units also show how graphic novels can be used to expand students' literary literacy and cultural knowledge. The chapter argues that implementing *Tunnel 57, Grenzfall,* and *drüben!* will make GDR history more accessible, as well as increase students' linguistic, literary, and cultural competencies.

GENERATIONS OF GERMAN HISTORY

In her article on Line Hoven's graphic novel *Liebe schaut weg* (*Love looks away*), Bernadette Raedler picks up on the theme that Krueger had discussed concerning intersections of personal and collective memory. Raedler analyzes this "family story" in which personal life stories from 1940s Germany are closely tied to the historical events of the Second World War. She reads the work within the construct of what she coins "tension art," investigating aspects of the story using different categories of tensions ranging from the technique and style, to autobiography and history, to German-American post-war relations. Raedler examines specifically how the author tells the story about her German-American family history across several generations. As part of her analysis of the com-

ic's "tension art," Raedler scrutinizes factors that contribute to the system
of tensions as presented through oppositions, such as the black-and-
white presentation of the artist's chosen scraperboard medium, autobiography as a narrative of the individual, and contemporary history as a
narrative of the group, or German and American language and culture.
The chapter argues that these tensions collectively create a multipolarity
that discourages a quick or unambiguous reading, despite the comic's
outwardly simple visual style. For example, blank spots in text and image
mirror places where the author has filled in information; and the coexistence of both types of information invites readers' participation. Raedler
explains how Hoven modifies the comic medium to become a reflective
and slow medium that underscores cultural difference, and makes visible
the presence of the narrative tensions that she identifies.

Joshua Kavaloski explores a more current historical theme that relates
to Germany's military involvement. His chapter, however, does not treat
World War II, a theme common for many contemporary graphic novels.
Instead, Kavaloski examines two graphic novels that regard Germany's
active military involvement in Afghanistan. With an informative background on the establishment of the *Bundeswehr* (federal defense force) in
1955, and the nature of its mostly humanitarian missions since 1960, the
chapter shows how this military force had operated within the limitations placed upon the German military after World War II. This chapter
analyzes two 2012 German-language graphic novels that critically explore the evolving role of Germany's *Bundeswehr* (Armed Forces) in the
controversial War in Afghanistan: *Wave and Smile* by Arne Jysch and
*Kriegszeiten: Eine grafische Reportage über Soldaten, Politiker und Opfer in
Afghanistan*, written by David Schraven and illustrated by Vincent Burmeister. Kavaloski addresses criticism of the texts in terms of their portrayals of the military involvement. For example, he labels as misled the
criticism that *Wave and Smile* sought to glorify war and revive Germany's
militaristic past. Instead he develops arguments for a decentralized story
with no overt narrator and a wide range of characters. Indeed, it arguably
employs a pluralistic narrative strategy called polyphony to represent
multiple disparate perspectives. Kavaloski points out that, in contrast to
Wave and Smile, *Kriegszeiten* purports to tell a "true" story about the experiences of the work's writer, journalist David Schraven, who as the first-
person narrator shapes the story about Germany's involvement in Afghanistan. Kavaloski describes the monologic approach that results from
Schraven's including only select voices that share his political position.
The chapter makes the important point that, despite stark differences in
narrative configuration, *Wave and Smile* and *Kriegszeiten* serve an important social function by instigating a public debate about the development
of the *Bundeswehr* into an institution which uses military force to advance
Germany's national interests around the globe.

AUSTRIAN VOICES

In his analysis of Nicolas Mahler's 2003 graphic novel *Kunsttheorie versus Frau Goldgruber*, Vance Byrd confronts the topics of the perceived low culturalism of comics, comics production, and individual development as a cartoonist. Byrd explores in his chapter the ways in which the self-referential nature of autobiographical comics can be used to explore the medium's conventions and the question of cultural legitimacy. In particular, the depiction of absurd situations involving tax authorities, publishers, and the avant-garde suggest that their measures of cultural legitimacy are not suitable for comics and graphic novels. Instead, the book's narrative foregrounds an episode from Mahler's youth—an autograph session with Peter Feigl—as a pivotal moment in the cartoonist's creative development. The act of crafting this tennis player's autograph card sets in motion a narrative in which aesthetic production is used to reflect on the language, purpose, and production of comics. By making cartooning into an observable process, Mahler's practitioner autobiography stages aesthetic production as a useful criterion to consider the value of comics that de-emphasizes arguments based on institutional support, markets, or academic training.

Brett Sterling explores Nicolas Mahler's use of visual techniques to adapt and embody Austrian novelist Thomas Bernhard's iconoclastic novel *Alte Meister* (*Old Masters*). Sterling demonstrates how Mahler takes the central character's critical monologues on art and applies them to the visual material of the novel's setting, Vienna's *Kunsthistorisches Museum* (Art History Museum). Mahler's comic gives shape to the vehement rejection of the value of art found in Bernhard's text, Sterling argues, by reducing the museum's paintings to caricatures and fragments. The result is a gallery of distorted images, here Mahler's signature simplified style is employed to dissipate the aura of veneration surrounding so-called high art Sterling claims further that, in addition to providing a striking visual representation of the novel's aesthetic critique, Mahler's adaptation presents its own argument for the importance of imperfection in artistic production. While Bernhard's main character ultimately clings to a romantic notion of art's possible perfection, Mahler embraces the flaws of human creativity and abandons the notion of a qualitative hierarchy of artworks. As a result, Sterling concludes that Mahler's *Alte Meister* functions as a declaration of the value of comics alongside other—not greater—forms of art.

Rounding out the anthology, Lynn Marie Kutch's article about the Austrian graphic novelist Gerald Hartwig's *Chamäleon* positions contemporary graphic novels within the context of autobiographical literature. The reading combines sources related to cliché and autobiography and responds to these lines of inquiry by examining the text's visual patterns and visual thematic repetition. Kutch argues that Hartwig essentially absorbs clichés of popular art into his innovative artistic gestures. In particular, she analyzes a series of all black pages that break up the dominant sepia-toned pages. She demonstrates specific ways that Hartwig deploys these matte-background pages to present portraitures or caricatures of Jerry, the Americanized first name with which he refers to his protagonist Gerald Hartmann, a pseudonym that Hartwig uses throughout the novel. The chapter reads these renditions within the broader categories of self-portrait, self-reflection through others, or self-reflection through his natural environment. The close reading reveals that when the artist envelops the clichés in these artistic techniques, a multiplicity of identity emerges: that of the aspiring filmmaker, that of the autobiographer, and that of the graphic novelist who prioritizes and foregrounds technique. The chapter discusses and provides evidence for the thesis that any artist's individual style and aesthetics support a non-clichéd presentation of the process of self-examination that accompanies autobiographical writing because it presents a perspective and aesthetic rendering—even if marked by cliché—peculiar to that artist.

In writing about similarities between European pre-modern fine art and contemporary comic art, Paul Duncum observes a "long arc of human history in which human passions and oppressions alike continue unabated and only find new media to explore and exploit" (212). Current research on comics and graphic novels illuminates current comic artists' explorations and exploitations of universal themes through this versatile medium; and the rapidly increasing volume of quality scholarship verifies that comics are taking their rightful place in this long arc of human and art history. Despite the parallel explosion of comics and comics scholarship, however, the research landscape, especially in Germany, remains "less than satisfactory." Eckart Sackmann, publisher of *Deutsche Comicforschung* who lamented this lack of development, defines the comic researcher as one who "does not wax eloquent about what everyone already knows, but instead is always a discoverer of the unknown" (Harmsen). The contributors to this book have both discovered and continued important dialogues about the place, power, and persistence of "weird comics" in German-speaking countries. Similar to the signatories of the *Comic-Manifesto*, the contributors to the current volume demand that the German-language tradition, separate from influential American or Franco-Belgian traditions, be taken seriously at home and abroad.

NOTES

1. Much has been written on the distinction between graphic novels and comics, including the idea that the term "graphic novel" was introduced to raise the literary level of legitimacy of these works above "comics." Most recently, however, scholars have begun using the terms nearly interchangeably and no longer distinguish between

the two. If necessary, contributors address these differences on an individual basis in their chapters.

2. Underground comix were first published as strips in the underground press in the mid-1960s. Often described as an alternative medium, underground comix provided a "vehicle for artistic and journalistic freedom not possible in the above-ground press . . . [T]he underground press advocated opposition to war in Vietnam and the capitalist economy supporting it, sexual freedom and alternative life styles, drug use, support for oppressed minorities and women, and distrust of established political institutions" (Spiggle 101–102).

3. Matthew Hale defines cosplay as a "performative action in which one dons a costume and/or accessories and manipulates his or her posture, gesture, and language in order to generate meaningful correspondences and contrasts between a given body and a set of texts" (8). These "parent texts" can include comics.

4. Some might argue that these principles may be traced back to the Frankfurt school, as Kukkonen does here. It must be mentioned that "the membership is often referred to as the Frankfurt School. But the label is a misleading one; for the work of the Institute's members did not always form a series of tightly woven, complementary projects" (Held 15). Alex Ross details a split within the School on what they called the "culture industry" and traditional forms of culture such as classical music, painting, and literature: "Adorno tended to be protective of them, even as he exposed their ideological underpinnings. Benjamin, in his resonant sentence linking culture and barbarism, saw the treasures of bourgeois Europe as spoils in a victory procession, each work blemished by the suffering of nameless millions" (Ross).

5. Screech explains: "This places *bandes dessinées* [the French term for graphic novels] on a level with the seven liberal arts, the traditional branches of learning: grammar, logic, rhetoric, arithmetic, geometry, astronomy and music." The three new categories are then cinema, photography, and *bandes dessinées* (1).

6. His measured and explanatory tone contrasts a seemingly more irritated one in an article written two years earlier in which he comments on the persistent need for comics scholars to validate the art form and their scholarship of it. See Brett Sterling's article in this volume.

7. The original citation from Heinze is: "Als Kulturpoltik bezeichnen wir den Diskurs zur Regelung öffentlicher kultureller Belange. Dieser Diskurs wird innerhalb und außerhalb politischer Gremien geführt—also unter Einbeziehung von interessierten Gruppen einschließlich der Experten der Verwaltung und der Kulturinstitutionen—aber in den dazu legitimierten Gremien entschieden."

8. This also seems to be the case in Britain, as Giles Coren's article about "comic books" versus "graphic novels" attests.

9. Examples of leading English-language texts are those by Maureen Bakis, Katie Monnin, Stephen Tabachnick, Nancy Frey, and James Bucky Carter. See also Matthew L. Miller's 2015 collection that does include an essay on teaching German graphic novels. There are in general fewer German-language texts. See Anja Ballis and Klaus Maiwald's *Literatur im Unterricht: Texte der Gegenwartsliteratur für die Schule*, or René Mounajed and Stefan Semel's *Begleitmaterial Geschichte* for using graphic novels for teaching history. See also Jens Kußmann's bibliography in this volume for more German-speaking titles.

10. Rather than collections of diverse works, many of the currently available anthologies are organized by theme, for example, autobiography or history. See, for example, El Rafaie and Tolmie. There are also numerous monographs on Art Spiegelman.

11. It is common in German-speaking countries to hear about the "E" and "U" when talking about art in all its forms. The E stands for "ernsthaft," or serious, and the U stands for "unterhaltend," or entertaining.

REFERENCES

Baetens, Jan. "Graphic Novels." *The Cambridge History of the American Novel*. Ed. Leonard Cassuto, Clare Virginia Eby, and Benjamin Reiss. Cambridge: Cambridge University Press, 2011, 1137–153.
Bakis, Maureen, and James Bucky Carter. *The Graphic Novel Classroom: POWerful Teaching and Learning with Images*. New York: Skyhorse Publishing, 2014.
Ballis, Anja and Klaus Maiwald, eds. *Literatur im Unterricht: Texte der Gegenwartsliteratur für die Schule*. Trier: WVT Wissenschaftlicher Verlag, 2014.
Berry, David. *Revisiting the Frankfurt School: Essays on Culture, Media and Theory*. Surrey: Ashgate Publishing Ltd, 2011.
Carrier, David. *The Aesthetics of Comics*. College Park: Penn State University Press, 2000.
"Das Comic Manifest." *Internationales Literaturfestival Berlin*. 2 September 2013. Web. 20 August 2015. www.literaturfestival.com/archiv/sonderprojekte/comic/manifest.
Coren, Giles. "Not graphic and not novel: Literary prizes have no business with comics." *The Spectator*. 1 December 2012. Web. Accessed 6 January 2016. http://www.spectator.co.uk/2012/12/not-graphic-and-not-novel/.
Ditschke, Stephan, Katarina Kroucheva, and Daniel Stein, eds. Comics. *Zur Geschichte und Theorie eines populärkulturellen Mediums*. Bielefield: transcript Verlag, 2009.
Dolle-Weinkauff, Bernd. "Comic, Graphic Novel und Serialität." *Bild ist Text ist Bild*. Eds. Susanne Hochreiter and Ursula Klingenböck. Bielefeld: transcript Verlag, 2014, 151–64.
Duncum, Paul. "Revisioning Premodern Fine Art As Popular Visual Culture." *Studies in Art Education* 55.3 (2014): 203–13.
Eisner, Will. *A Contract with God*. New York: Baronet Books, 1978.
El Refaie, Elisabeth. *Autobiographical Comics: Life Writing in Pictures*. Jackson: University Press of Mississippi, 2012.
"Fragen Sie Reich-Ranicki: Da gibt es nichts zu erklären." *Frankfurter Allgemeine Zeitung*. 30 June 2010. Web. Accessed 6 January 2016. http://www.faz.net/aktuell/feuilleton/buecher/fragen-sie-reich-ranicki/fragen-sie-reich-ranicki-da-gibt-es-nichts-zu-erklaeren-1642978.html.
Frahm, Ole. "Review: Berliner Comic Festival." *Visual Communication* 3.2 (2004): 235–40.
Frahm, Ole. "Weird Signs. Zur parodistischen Ästhetik der Comics." *Ästhetik des Comic*. Ed. Michael Hein, Michael Hüners, and Torsten Michaelsen. Berlin: Schmidt, 2002. 201–16.
Frey, Nancy, and Douglas B Fisher. *Visual Literacy: Using Comic Books, Graphic Novels, Anime, Cartoons, and More to Develop Comprehension and Thinking Skills*. Newbury Park, CA: Corwin, 2008.
Groensteen, Thierry. *The System of Comics*. Jackson, MS: University Press of Mississippi, 2007.
Hale, Matthew. "Cosplay." *Western Folklore* 73.1 (2014): 5–37.
Harmsen, Rieke C. "Alma Mater Comicencis—Comic Studies in Germany." *Deutschsprachige Comics: Goethe Institut*. November 2013. Web. Accessed 12 January 2016. http://www.goethe.de/kue/lit/prj/com/ccs/iuv/en11919135.htm.
Hecken, Thomas. "Bestimmungsgrößen von high und low." *High und Low: Zur Interferenz von Hoch- und Populärkultur in der Gegenwartsliteratur*. Ed. Thomas Wegmann and Norbert Christian Wolf. Berlin: De Gruyter, 2012, 11–25.
Heer, Jeet, and Kent Worcester. *A Comic Studies Reader*. Jackson, MS: University Press of Mississippi, 2009.
Heinze, Thomas, ed. *Kultur und Wirtschaft: Perspektiven Gemeinsamer Innovation*. Wiesbaden: Springer Fachmedien Verlag, 1995.
Held, David. *Introduction to Critical Theory: Horkheimer to Habermas*. Berkeley and Los Angeles: University of California Press, 1980.

Klein, Armin. *Kulturpolitik: Eine Einführung.* Wiesbaden: VS Verlag für Sozialwissenschaften, 2009.

Kukkonen, Karin. *Studying Comics And Graphic Novels.* Malden, MA: Wiley-Blackwell, 2014.

Lanzendörfer, Tim, and Matthias Köhler. "Introduction: Comics Studies and Literary Studies." *ZAA* 59.1 (2011): 1–9.

McCloud, Scott. *Understanding Comics: The Invisible Art.* Northampton, MA: Tundra, 1993.

Monnin, Katie. *Teaching Graphic Novels: Practical Strategies for the Secondary ELA Classroom.* Gainsville, FL: Maupin House, 2013.

Monnin, Katie and Rachel Bowman. *Teaching Reading Comprehension with Graphic Texts: An Illustrated Adventure.* Gainsville, FL: Maupin House, 2013.

Mounajed, René, and Sefan Semel. *Begleitmaterial Geschichte: Comics erzählen Geschichte: Sequenzen aus Comics, Mangas und Graphic Novels für den Geschichtsunterricht.* Bamburg: Buchner, 2010.

Picone, Michael D. "Comic Art in Museums and Museums in Comic Art." *European Comic Art* 6.2 (2013): 40–68.

Romero-Jódar, Andrés. "Comic Books and Graphic Novels in Their Generic Context: Towards a Definition and Classification of Narrative Iconical Texts." *Atlantis* 35.1 (2013): 117–35.

Ross, Alex. "The Naysayers: Walter Benjamin, Theodor Adorno, and the Critique of Pop Culture." *The New Yorker.* 15 September 2014. Accessed 4 January 2016. http://www.newyorker.com/magazine/2014/09/15/naysayers.

Schikowski, Klaus. "Graphic Novels: Die Globalisierung des Comics." *Comic-Report 2011.* Ed. Volker Hamann. Barmstedt: Eidtion Alfons, 2011, 50–57.

Schmitz-Emans, Monika. "Graphic Narrative as World Literature." *From Comic Strips to Graphic Novels: Contributions to the Theory and History of Graphic Narrative.* Berlin: De Gruyter, 2013. 385–406.

Screech, Matthew. *Masters of the Ninth Art: Bandes Dessinées and Franco-Belgian Identity.* Liverpool: Liverpool University Press, 2005.

Spiegelman, Art. *In the Shadow of No Towers.* New York: Pantheon, 2004.

Spiegelman, Art. *Maus.* New York: Pantheon Books, 1980.

Spiggle, Susan. "Measuring Social Values: A Content Analysis of Sunday Comics and Underground Comix." *Journal of Consumer Research* 13.1 (1986): 100–13.

Stein, Daniel. "The Long Shadow of Wilhelm Busch: "Max & Moritz" and German Comics." *International Journal of Comic Art* 12.2/3 (2010): 291–308.

Tabachnick, Stephen. *Teaching the Graphic Novel.* The Modern Language Association of America, 2009.

Thon, Jan-Noël, and Daniel Stein. *From Comic Strips to Graphic Novels: Contributions to the Theory and History of Graphic Narrative.* Berlin: De Gruyter, 2013.

Tolmie, Jane. *Drawing from Life: Memory and Subjectivity in Comic Art.* Jackson, MS: University Press of Mississippi, 2013.

von Törne, Lars. "Vom Türöffner zur Streitaxt." *Der Tagesspiegel.* 4 July 2014. Web. 17. December 2015. http://www.tagesspiegel.de/kultur/comics/graphic-novels-vom-tueroeffner-zur-streitaxt/10144890.html.

Wegmann, Thomas, and Norbert Christian Wolf, eds. *"High" und "Low": Zur Interferenz von Hoch- und Populärkultur in der Gegenwartsliteratur.* Berlin: de Gruyter, 2012.

I

CONTEXTS AND HISTORIES

ONE

German Comics

Form, Content, and Production

Matt Hambro

> This is mad stuff, indeed! . . . [it] all sparkles with talent and intelligence. Some pages could not be excelled. If, for the future, he would choose a less frivolous subject, and restrict himself a little, he would produce things beyond all conception.[1]

After discovering that Swiss teacher Rodolphe Töpffer had made an illustrated parody of his celebrated play *Faust* (1808), Johann Wolfgang von Goethe uttered these words of praise for the illustrator and his work. Goethe's encouragement helped Töpffer to publish his French-language stories, and is one of a few moments in German history when established figures in the literary or visual arts have bestowed such high praise on the comics medium and its creators. This chapter offers an overview of the history of German-language comics and highlights ways that German aesthetics, philosophy, and history have interacted with the production and reception of graphic narratives in German-speaking countries and abroad. The chapter's three main sections focus on the form, content, and creation of comics. First, with regard to form, the chapter demonstrates how the reception of comics has been influenced by logocentric preferences for text over image, tension between mimesis and abstraction, and notions of media purity. Second, in terms of content, the chapter suggests that the folktale and thematic integration with canonized literature are of great importance to the German tradition, which Goethe's remarks above underscore. The third section discusses the significance of group production (which I use here to mean collaborative production involving division of labor and hierarchies of responsibility), state sponsorship, and market orientation in the German tradition. Lastly, the chapter offers a look into comics production and reception in Germany today: a time in which many of the concerns and preferences of the twentieth century and earlier have begun to diminish or even disappear entirely. Overall, the chapter offers a view of comics in Germany as a medium that has, until recently, been stifled by a unique combination of aesthetic and historical factors.

FORM

Comics theorist Thierry Groensteen identifies four main reasons why intellectuals and academics have rejected, and in many cases still reject, comics or graphic narratives: hybridity, non-literary story-telling, connection to caricature, and the connection to childhood experience (35). Perhaps most significant for the German tradition is the notion that comics, as a hybrid medium, has met opposition due to its non-fulfillment of the notion of purity, which, according to Groensteen, has been a dominant criterion since the aesthetics of Gotthold Ephraim Lessing (38). In this sense, purity entails conformity to a singular style and the boundaries of a defined medium. In addition to addressing examples of Groensteen's points, this section also offers a deeper discussion of logocentrism, mimesis, and abstraction in European and German thought.

In the early twentieth century, European thinkers began to reflect on written text and language as epistemologically privileged media. This initiated a process of reinterpreting a long history of devaluing image and other kinds of non-symbolic and non-linguistic media. In his 1929 work *Der Geist als Widersacher der Seele* (*The Spirit as Adversary of the Soul*), German philosopher and psychologist Ludwig Klages[2] uses the word "logocentrism" to describe the European tendency of privileging text and language over other forms of storing and processing information; and strongly criticizes it as reductive and culturally selective (126). The notion of logocentrism also plays a crucial role in Jacques Derrida's philosophy, in which he similarly describes logocentrism as reductive and distinctly Western, connecting it with the West's theological conception of an infinite God as well as its tendency toward mechanization across many aspects of culture. In his discussion of the origins of logocentrism, Derrida writes:

> Within a certain historical epoch, there is a profound unity among infinitist theology, logocentrism, and a certain technicism. The originary and pre- or meta-phonetic writing that I am attempting to conceive of here leads to nothing less than an "overtaking" of speech by the machine. (79)

Klages and Derrida's analyses thus underscore how fundamental logo-centrism is to European and German thought. In the case of visual arts, this entails a certain amount of devaluing; but for comics this proves to be disproportionately true. Whereas visual art, containing little or no text, often passes as an independent form of communication and expression, the juxtaposition of text and image in comics frequently incites logocentric arguments. A common criticism is that comics are for the illiterate, which typifies the fears of "Bildiotismus" (image idiocy) that circulated during a time of increased popularity of American comics in postwar Germany (Dolle-Weinkauff 98).

Another explanation for the disproportionate aesthetic concerns about comics compared to the visual arts may be gained by looking more closely at the relationship between mimesis and abstraction in comics. Mimesis as it relates to knowledge production has been a topic in European philosophy since Plato's *Republic*, which also offers a key example of the origins of logocentric currents in European philosophy. The dialogue that develops Plato's position on art is found in Book X of *Republic* when Socrates reflects on painting in order to highlight the ethical and pedagogical dangers of mimetic art in general. Socrates explains to Glaucon, "A painter can paint a cobbler, a carpenter, or any other craftsman, even though he knows nothing about these crafts" (Plato 268). In this dialogue, Socrates shows how imitations like paintings can produce in the viewer a sense of understanding, yet fail entirely to transmit a truly functional knowledge of a craft. In addition, under Plato's theory of metaphysics, which contends that everything in the world is a copy of an ideal abstract form, mimetic art appears as a copy of a copy. Thus, it appears even further removed from the ideal forms of truth and beauty than objects found in nature or other kinds of functional objects, such as furniture or tools, made by humans. Although Socrates only uses painting as a gateway into the exploration of mimesis generally, it is telling that he begins with the visual arts in his scathing critique, which ultimately results in a ban in the Republic on nearly all forms of mimesis, including visual and narrative types (Plato 262). Comics art, which makes use of both mimesis and abstraction, would likely have been regarded as too mimetic for logocentrists like Plato, but simultaneously too abstract or caricatured for aficionados of the traditional visual arts.

Plato's concerns about mimesis were once again revived in the eighteenth century and influenced German aesthetics just prior to a crucial point in the development of graphic narratives: when Töpffer began publishing in the early nineteenth century. During the early Enlightenment, German Renaissance-Humanist Johann Joachim Winckelmann addressed and modified some of Plato's logocentric and anti-mimetic arguments. His best known work, *Gedanken über die Nachahmung der Griechischen Werke in der Malerei und Bildhauerkunst* (*Thoughts on the Imitation of Greek Works in Painting and Sculpture*), advocates for the combination of ideal forms, mimesis, and allegory in the creation of great visual art. Of central importance is the notion that great art cannot be merely mimetic, simply reporting what the eye sees. Instead it must combine the input of the senses with abstract and ideal forms. Winckelmann writes in section 1: "Connoisseurs and imitators of Greek works find not only the most beautiful aspects of nature in their masterpieces but also much more than nature: that is, certain ideally beautiful aspects of it, which, as an ancient interpreter of Plato teaches us, have been created from images conceived only in the mind" (32). Thus, abstract ideals and forms must play a role in the construction of great and beautiful art. Superficially, this would seem to set the stage for a robust appreciation of comics, which as mentioned combine both mimetic and abstract elements. This was, however, not the case. While inheriting and reinvigorating Plato's logocentric concerns by stressing the importance of allegory and abstraction in the production of visual art, Winckelmann also slips in a new appreciation for mimesis, stressing that mimesis is only negative in isolation, but is of great importance in combination with abstraction. Especially compared to the lush and detailed paintings of the Romantic period, early comics were in danger of appearing much too simplified and raw. Thus, it could be argued that debates from as early as the late eighteenth century and early nineteenth century relate to comics and graphic narratives, which often but not necessarily tend toward greater simplification and abstraction.

As Groensteen's analysis also emphasizes, notions of media purity play a central role in the devaluation of comics and this is especially true in the German tradition. Gotthold Lessing's *Laokoon* [*Laocoon: An Essay on the Limits of Painting and Poetry*] (1766) focuses on the relationship between poetry and painting and affords special attention to the varying conditions that determine success or failure in each medium. In a rebuke of Joseph Spence's *Polymetis*, Lessing suggests the need for a strong distinction between strategies for producing poetry and visual art. Discussing the example of the Greek goddess Venus, Lessing writes, "It is this, that the gods and spiritual beings, such as they are represented by the artist, are not precisely the same as those which the poet employs" (98). Lessing goes on to explain that each medium draws from a different set of resources in order to characterize the figure of Venus and cannot be expected to approach the subject in the same way. Lessing's formulation of purity is relevant to comics in several ways. First, as Groensteen argues, purity poses obvious problems for an allegedly "hybrid" medium, which combines text and image. At a time when no theory of comics as an independent medium existed, this meant that comics could be perceived to fail the criterion of purity as it applied to text and image individually. In addition, comics came into prominence in the United States and Europe during the popularity of abstract art in the early twentieth century: a movement that explicitly declared the value of media purity. Although comics tend toward abstraction, they apply it in varying degrees just as they do with mimesis. This causes a vacillation between aesthetic philosophies that give preference to mimesis, abstraction, or a formally defined relationship between the two.

With the above notions of logocentrism, abstraction, and media purity in mind, it is worthwhile to turn to Töpffer's theory of comics, which departs noticeably from the conclusions of the authors and philosophers discussed thus far. A brief exploration of Töpffer may show how, at the genesis of the comics tradition in the nineteenth century, French and German comics (and their respective theories) were diverging. While Plato's logocentric arguments suggest that visual and mimetic media are not well suited for knowledge production, Töpffer was motivated to create the comics form precisely in order to effectively store and communicate information. Initially, Töpffer wanted to be a painter, but due to an eye disease, he pursued teaching instead, eventually becoming the first chair of rhetoric at the academy of Geneva (Willems 1). As Philippe Willems notes, "Topffer's venture was the outcome of a pursuit of the optimal relationship between verb and icon for efficient methods of information delivery" (2). In a partial confirmation of Plato's views on mimesis, Töpffer's experiments resulted in a shift away from realistic mimetic depictions and toward quick, expressive gestures. Thierry Smolderen summarizes Töpffer's epistemological stance on comics, stating, "He knew that the most elaborate hypotheses and the most comical situations could be clarified by an informal, even awkward doodle" (Smolderen 27). According to Smolderen, comics thus offered a level of efficiency and precision that Töpffer believed text alone could not accomplish. In Smolderen's opinion, however, comics also provided Töpffer an advantage over academic drawings that extends beyond efficiency and has to do with the way we perceive and construct the world. Smolderen paraphrases the core of Töpffer's theory: "academicism imposes rational, and thus external, principles of organization onto the artist. All works of art that derive their unity from the application of rules, measures, or division inevitably cut themselves off from genuine inspiration" (Smolderen 30). Töpffer espoused a theory of comics that praised not only the efficiency but also the reliability of comics to capture and communicate about the world without bending its representation to the expectations of a particular academic paradigm.

Paradoxically, this reliability is grounded in the openness and personalization of gesture typified by the doodle. In some ways, Töpffer's theory confirms media purity, by suggesting that a multi-channel medium is necessary in order to capture the complex features of experience that do not allow for efficient depiction in one medium alone. At the same time, his theory opposes the formalization of boundaries and rules for knowledge production, which would suggest a radical opposition to media purity and adherence to medium-specific rules. Thus, while French comics had a founder and theorist that embraced a multi-track medium, German comics did not. Therefore, it is plausible that the articulations of logocentrism, mimesis, abstraction, and purity in German philosophy and aesthetics continued to shape the reception and production of German comics to a great extent.

CONTENT

After reading Töpffer's *Faust* spoof, *Voyages et aventures du Dr. Festus*, Goethe defied a long-standing tradition of prejudice against image and graphic narrative by recognizing the intellectual and emotional potential of what would later become comics; but he still found something missing. Writing in the subjunctive mood, which in German expresses the hypothetical and counterfactual, Goethe stresses that Töpffer *would* do truly great things if he only concentrated on a more serious topic. Emboldened by Goethe, Töpffer published his work, but he did not select a more serious subject, and instead continued to publish parody and satire. While the above section focuses specifically on form, this interaction also points to the importance of content and narrative for the reception of comics in Germany, which is the focus of the current section.

For the period in which comics arose (the nineteenth and early twentieth centuries), it is especially useful to consider the way that expectations for the novel may have shaped attitudes and expectations for comics. Geörgy Lukács treats the form of the novel as a contextual and era-specific adaptation of a more general impulse in art toward the organization of incongruity as a totality. More specifically, he writes, "Every art form is defined by the metaphysical dissonance of life which it accepts and organizes as the basis of a totality complete in itself" (71). For the modern period, Lukács argues, the organization occurs through the lens of the individual, and thus takes a biographical narrative form that we know as the novel (77). This is significant for comics, because the biographical focalization of the novel is used as a criterion for the consideration of graphic narratives as both comics and literature. As Bart Beaty notes, many Americanists focus on recurring characters as one of the important criteria for consideration as a comic (31). One possible explanation for this is that recurring characters allow for the development of a longer, continuous narrative and a deeper, more complex biographical perspective. When a comic is neglected in the study of literature, it is often one with no recurring characters. Many comic strips—published as short three panel sequences and meant to produce a chuckle or two on a Sunday morning—fall into this category. By contrast, comics and graphic novels that establish a continuous biographical perspective are considered to have greater depth and interiority, which facilitates consideration by literary critics. Töpffer's work, for example, features strong, recurring characters. Another contemporary example is Art Spiegelman's *Maus*, which is commonly hailed as the first comic that successfully broke into the world of literature. *Maus* is structured as a series of interviews between the author and his father, a Holocaust survivor, and dives deep into the psychology and history of both interviewer and interviewee. Initially published as a serialized comic, the episodes and recurring characters were bound together, and are now treated as a singular whole, hence the term "graphic *novel.*" Therefore, the importance of a biographical, novel-like focalization must not be overlooked here.

In addition, attitudes toward irony and satire also offer an explanation for differences during the early period of comics creation in the nineteenth century. While a new critical space opened up for comics in America, France, and Belgium, in which frivolity, satire, and play were elevated, the German tradition exhibited a desire to retain continuity with other forms of art and literature. Parody, was thus not the first use of comics in Germany, as it had been in Switzerland with Töpffer's work. In addition to Lessing's *Laokoon*, Smolderen highlights Jakob Engel's book on gesture in theater, *Ideen zu einer Mimik* (*Ideas on a Facial Expression*), as a treatise that implicitly encouraged a system for diagramming gesture in theater (Smolderen 37). Together, these works inspired heightened interest in theater, gesture, and action and led to drastically different forms of illustrated inquiry in German- and French-speaking areas. Töpffer developed a new medium built on gesture, abstraction, and movement that he deployed most frequently for parody. German artist and playwright Joseph Franz von Goez, on the other hand, attempted to create a non-ironic illustrated drama, which made greater use of stasis and mimesis.

Along these lines, one could argue that Goez is the author of the first graphic novel, which he published in 1783, roughly fifty years before Töpffer began publishing his French-language satirical comics. As mentioned, Goez's work is much less ironic than Töpffer's and shows greater integration or conformity with prevailing expectations for both visual and narrative art. Rather than treating comics as a parodying meta-discourse about prevailing arts and media, Töpffer attempted unironically to make comics a part of those prevailing media. The inclusion or subjugation of the comics form to dominant theories of art and literature may thus offer one explanation for differentiation in German-language graphic narratives as compared to other parts of Europe. Goez based his melodrama, *Lenardo und Blandine,* on a ballad by the poet Gottfried August Bürger, and it centers on the collapse of an arranged marriage after it is discovered that the young woman has another lover. Her father kills the lover and she falls into madness and dies. *Lenardo und Blandine* was conceived and sketched simultaneously and incredibly quickly (Betzwieser 83). Goez wrote of his creative process, "one idea forced the next, one image brought the next, and so arose a monologue which within the hour flowed unceasingly from my feather" (eine Idee drängte die andere, ein Bild das andere, und so entstand ein Monolog

welcher in eben der Stunde unaufhaltsam in meiner Feder floß; Betzwieser 83). These comments reveal a creative process that resembles contemporary comics creation. The connection between images as a narrative
whole was a driving force during Goez's creation of the work. Although
the illustrations were not the final product for audience consumption,
considered on their own, the images do form a coherent narrative whole
(figure 1.1). This formal aspect of the work warrants its consideration as a
comic. The salient features of the content, however, are the presence of
literary adaptation and the aspiration to standards of greatness that have
defined world literature. This offers a telling comparison between *Lenardo und Blandine* and contemporary graphic novels. Goez's illustrated play
thus merits further investigation as part of an unexplored, integrative
stream in the production of graphic narratives and comics. Only today
has that undercurrent reemerged or converged with mainstream comics
in the form of graphic novels and other forms of high-brow comics. I
suggest with this interpretation then that *Lenardo und Blandine* shows
German comics beginning with an attempt to integrate with dominant art
forms of the time, in this case with theater. Töpffer's rejection of Goethe's
demand to work within more canonical themes thus underscores the
differences emerging during this period.

Nonetheless, it would be misleading to characterize German comics
and graphic narratives as generally "serious" and primarily motivated by
attempts to integrate with canonical literature. Beginning in the early
modern period, German graphic narratives also serve as a platform for
folktales. Many of these prominently feature foolhardy deviants, who are
critical of both the canonizing institutions and the customs of their times.
Such works present a mass-produced, illustrated, and moral critique of
their times, which are the essential features of David Kunzle's historical
definition of comics (2). One notable work is *Ein kurtzweilig lesen von Dil
Ulenspiegel* (*Entertaining Readings of Till Eulenspiegel*) from 1510. *Eulenspiegel* is exceptional with regard to its frequent and skillful use of image, as
well as in terms of its popularity. Due to the preponderance of text over
image, the work cannot strictly be considered a comic under today's
formal definitions, for example, Will Eisner's and Scott McCloud's, which
stress the importance of a sequence of images that develops and advances the narrative. Nonetheless, such formal definitions are constantly
in flux and this early modern folktale played a crucial role in the birth of
comics and continues to shape the expectations for both form and content
in many graphic narratives.

Eulenspiegel follows the eponymous merry prankster who journeys
through Europe, finding work in whatever form he can. Frequently, Eulenspiegel exposes the hypocrisy of religious, political, and cultural authorities. Oftentimes, however, he simply enjoys tricking people. As Werner Wunderlich notes, no one escapes Eulenspiegel's pranks: neither the
emperor nor the beggars (40). In one story, Eulenspiegel is employed as a

Figure 1.1.   Example of narrative continuity between images from *Lenardo und Blandine*. Goez, Joseph Franz von. *Versuch Einer Zalreichen (sic) Folge Leidens-chaftlicher Entwürfe für Empfindsame Kunst- und Schauspiel-Freunde*. Augs-burg: Akademische Handlung, 1783. 233, 235, 237, 239.

sexton and overhears a priest passing gas in the church, after which he points out to the priest the lack of respect before God that this gesture implies (*Dyl Ulenspiegel* History XII, Blat XVI). The priest is indignant and defends his right to do so, suggesting it would even be within his limits to defecate in the church. Eulenspiegel exploits the priest's hypocrisy and bets the priest a barrel of beer that he does not have the courage to defecate "in the middle of the church," upon which the priest raises his robe and follows through with the request. In a pubescent wordplay and hairsplitting execution of his occupation, Eulenspiegel demonstrates that the bowel movement is not exactly in the middle of the church, and thereby wins a barrel of beer at the priest's expense (*Dyl Ulenspiegel* History XII, Blat XVI). Wunderlich notes the importance that gesture and body have in *Till Eulenspiegel*: both subjects that define nineteenth-century German comics. Wunderlich writes: "In particular the anal area (which the name of the eponymous hero hints at) plays an important role in Eulenspiegel's body language, because the joker literally expresses his stinking and dirty contempt and retribution" (Überhaupt spielt der Anal-bereich, auf den der Name des Titelhelden hinweist, in der Körper-sprache Eulenspiegels eine wichtige Rolle, da der Schalk Verachtung und Strafe hingebungsvoll und stinkend und schmutzig buchstäblich aus-drückt; 44). *Eulenspiegel* is thus important for connecting the folktale, physical humor, and political critique in a format similar to a graphic novel. Its illustrations, although limited to one per chapter, exceed the mere depiction of the events and often encapsulate many of the themes of the chapter, or even add new information.[3] Although Eulenspiegel wins the bet in this story, the illustration adds a sour twist. As a sexton he must nonetheless clean up the mess, and he is shown somberly sweeping the church as the priest looks on: a reaffirmation of the priest's power (figure 1.2).

    Eulenspiegel provides a prototype for illustrated folktales and social criticism that remains internationally relevant in comics today, and especially in German-language comics. The physical humor and comedy of errors developed in both the text and illustration of *Till Eulenspiegel* provide the backbone of German comics in the late nineteenth century. John A. Lent also points to Munich publisher Rolf Kauka's *Fix und Foxi*, as one example of how early modern illustrated folktales still shape the features of comics in today's German-speaking countries, taking famous heroes such as Till Eulenspiegel, Baron Münchhausen, and Reineke Fuchs and reissuing them as contemporary comics figures (71).

    In the nineteenth century, Wilhelm Busch capitalized on the prototype of early modern fools and folktales and combined it with a book-length format, a "folksy narrator" (separate from the main figure), and child protagonists (Smolderen 113). The result was *Max und Moritz*, a mischievous pair of young boys known for their slapstick pranks. The preference for a stand-alone novel format, as Smolderen notes, underscores that

Figure 1.2.   Eulenspiegel cleans the priest's mess. *Dyl Ulenspiegel.* **(Straßburg: Johannes Grüninger, 1515.) History XII, Blat XV.**

German illustrators like Busch presented an exception to the tendency in nineteenth-century European comics to move away from the form of the "novel in print" (Smolderen 69). In addition, Groensteen points out that European comics in the nineteenth century were primarily for adults (30). German comics, such as Busch's *Max und Moritz*, thus stood out from other European comics of the nineteenth century both in their book-length format and in their targeting of a youth audience. It is likely a combination of the folksy content and book-length format that led *Max und Moritz* to be seen as one of few illustrated alternatives to the "Schmutz-und-Schund-Literatur" [trash or pulp literature], characterized by American Comics that flooded West Germany after World War II (Plauen 85). The foundational early American comic strip *The Katzenjam-*

mer Kids is also explicitly based on Busch's type of deviant figure (Smolderen 112), and reinforces that this type of German comic played an influential role early on in the international development of comics.

To summarize this section concerning content, in the earliest period of
production, German comics notably present a non-ironic attempt to integrate with established forms of artistic production. Goez's *Lenardo und
Blandine* typifies this goal with its preference for drama, mimesis, and
stasis as contrasted with Töpffer's ironic, moving gestures. At the same
time, many German comics also draw from a rich history of illustrated
folktales and fools. Contrary to Goez's attempts at integration, such figures have been canonized internationally in the comics community and
serve as pillars of twentieth-century comics.

PRODUCTION

During the early period of comics production around the beginning of
the nineteenth century, comics were often the product of a singular vision
and execution. Töpffer and Goez's work, for example, embodied the will
of a singular creator. This allowed comics creators to be considered
"great" artists under theories, such as Friedrich Nietzsche's, which
praised the individual authorial will over service, cooperation, and defer-
ence. The core of Nietzsche's definition of greatness is captured in section
6 of his *Jenseits von Gut und Böse* (*Beyond Good and Evil*) from 1866, in
which Nietzsche discusses greatness in relation to his perception of the
weakening of will. Here he remarks, "Today, the will is weakened and
diluted by the tastes and virtues of the times, and nothing is as timely as
weakness of will: this is why precisely strength of will and the hardness
and capacity for long-term resolutions must belong to the concept of
'greatness'" (Nietzsche 107). Nietzsche specifically frames this kind of
will in opposition to specialization, which allows for more efficient cooperation in a team environment. Instead, Nietzsche wants individuals to
be generalists and to accept total control of their philosophical and artistic endeavors. Such an individual commands when needed, but leaves as
little as possible to be determined by the will of others. Some comics,
which are conceived and executed by one individual, have greater appeal
under this notion of greatness. Many others, which have historically de-
pended on a complex network of letterers, authors, inkers, colorists, and
printers for their production, complicate a relationship between comics
production and Nietzsche's notion of greatness. On the one hand, the
top-down hierarchical organization of comics production might confirm
the importance of Nietzsche's strong-armed, lone leader as the driving
force behind great works in the comics tradition. On the other hand, the
history of cooperation required to produce comics might be seen as precisely the kind of subservient specialization that Nietzsche condemns. No

matter which is true, comics have frequently been seen to lack a strong authorial vision and are often treated as a group-think commodity or "entertainment engine," in Beaty's phrasing (96). In more extreme cases, their hierarchical production can be interpreted as a mark of state-sponsored propaganda.

During the time that nineteenth-century illustrated children's literature was developing into what would one day become twentieth-century comics, adult political cartoons were also on a trajectory that would lead them to intersect and, to an extent, merge with children's literature, most powerfully, as mentioned above, in the form of state-sponsored propaganda. This form of production and the accompanying fears of persuasiveness and loss of individual autonomy figure prominently in comics reception in Germany during the twentieth century.

The illustrated periodical *Der Stürmer* is a telling example of state endorsed propaganda in World War II Germany. Published by Julius Streicher, who was seen by the allies as the symbol of "Judenhass" or "hatred of Jews" ("Angeklagt" 1), *Der Stürmer* featured extreme right articles, comics, and readers' letters. Randall Bytwerk identifies the paper's intended goal of reaching the lowest common denominator in the German population (55). In illuminating the newspaper's methods, Bytwerk turns to Streicher's court historian, Heinz Preiss, who wrote of Streicher: "Since he wanted to capture the masses he had to write in a way that the masses could understand, in a style that was simple and easy to comprehend. . . . Writing had to adopt the style of speaking if it were to have a similar effect" (55). Noteworthy here, is that the simple conversational style is a hallmark of comics. Furthermore, as Bytwerk points out, illustrations were a natural continuation of this approach (56). Produced by Philippe Rupprecht, also known as Fips, the racist caricatures and cartoons featured in *Der Stürmer* were some of the most pointed and obscene in any periodical of that period (Bytwerk 55). The result was a news journal that retained enough textual tradition to be considered adult, but nonetheless employed many simplifying tactics that resembled strategies at work in illustrated children's literature. Whereas *Der Stürmer* was intended for adults, Rupprecht and Streicher also collaborated on an illustrated anti-Semitic children's book called *Der Giftpilz*, which centered on the poison mushroom as a metaphor for the presence of Jews in German society (Hiemer Front Cover). *Der Giftpilz* shows the completed integration of children's literature, illustration, and propaganda. It fully leaves the context of journalism and, in a cruel appropriation of Busch's use of the genre, reprograms the folktale as an instrument of the state. Accompanying this move there is also a shift away from biographical focalization toward the expression of a kind of nationalistic ethos. These targeted applications of comics and illustrated journalism during the era of National Socialism may have resulted in a conflation of group production with state sponsorship and nationalist goals.

In the postwar period, it is likely that memories of this type of war-time propaganda and concerns about market-oriented production direct-ly contributed to negative attitudes toward comics. During that time, as Bernd Dolle-Weinkauff notes, German comics were dominated by trans-lations and imitations of American and French comics, particularly West-ern, Crime, Thriller, and Romance comics (96). Such comics were de-signed according to market demand and contained an unprecedented level of violence, which for many youth was the main attraction. In 1954, after German-American psychologist Fredric Wertham testified about the correlation between comics and delinquency in the United States, Ger-mans followed the American response (Comics Code Authority) and also created a board for the censorship of comics (Dolle-Weinkauf 108). Thus, just as hierarchical comics production could be seen as synonymous with state-sponsored propaganda, it could also be seen as a stand-in for profit- and market-oriented American values.

In the context of divided Germany, comics nonetheless became a por-tal for introducing children to the polarized values and expectations of the East and West German states. As German comics theorist Ole Frahm points out, one great example of this tension is documented in the alter-native visions of the future offered by the Federal Republic of Germany's *Nick der Weltraumfahrer* (Nick the Space Explorer) and the German Demo-cratic Republic's *Digedags* in the government-endorsed magazine *Mosaik*. Nick, on the one hand, lives in an individualist science-fiction future where danger awaits at every turn. However, despite these constant dan-gers, Frahm writes, readers can find comfort in the fact that Nick always overcomes them, implying a future of limitless expansion in which capi-tal can even dominate space (223). The Digedags, on the other hand, comprise a humble and physically diminutive group that inexplicably appears in various epochs, both past and future. They must work togeth-er in order to overcome challenges. When an alien or creature appears to the Digedags, there is a real danger that humans will actually lose their central place in the universe, as well as the possibility of economic col-lapse. As Frahm highlights, this is realized in one story, as they discover a planet that is shattered and marred by the collapse of capitalism (Frahm 244). Like many comics intended for children, both *Nick* and the *Digedags* contain an obvious didactic component, which in these examples reflects the individualism or communitarianism of each society. The success of such comics also shows the importance that production had during this period. The state-endorsed *Mosaik* must have appeared to the West as a form of propaganda, while the market-oriented *Nick* likely appeared to the East as a hollow sales-driven pulp magazine. In their respective coun-tries of production, each native comic may have been preferred due to the alignment of production and message with the cultural norms of the land.

CONCLUDING THOUGHTS

After the fall of the Berlin Wall in 1989, many new and significant categories have appeared within German comics and graphic novels. Among these are travelogues, adaptations of world literature, and historical biographies. In short, the original model of Goez's *Lenardo und Blandine* is in vogue and there is a push to place comics under the same set of expectations as world literature. Greatness, depth, and interiority are in some ways becoming more important than satire, play, and frivolity. Comic artists have adapted Kafka's *Die Verwandlung* (*The Metamorphosis*), Goethe's *Faust*, and many other canonical German works. Likewise, there are now graphic biographies of Richard Wagner, Martin Luther, and other major German historical figures. Travelogues have been produced for many countries including Israel and Japan. Two notable examples are Dirk Schwieger's *Moresukine*, which chronicles the author's stay in Japan and the anthology *Cargo—Comicreportagen Israel-Deutschland*, which aims to foster a cultural dialogue between Israel and Germany. Such travelogues show that comics now engage in the processing of Germany's moral identity after World War II and the Holocaust, and in reestablishing connections to affected countries.

Monika Schmitz-Emans interprets the rise of canonical literary themes within graphic novels as evidence of the general increasing importance of comics to world literature. She writes "The great number of contemporary Literature-Comic publications makes it plausible that comics are now actively taking part in the negotiation of world literature. Therein exists the necessity of comics themselves to become world literature" (Die große Zahl der aktuellen Literatur-Comic-Publikationen macht es plausibel, dass der Comic an der Verhandlung von, Weltliteratur' inzwischen aktiv teilnimmt. Dazu gehört auch der Anspruch, selbst, Weltliteratur' zu sein; 252). Schmitz-Emans's approach highlights the increasing continuity between the aesthetic values used to evaluate literature and comics. Nonetheless, the unpretentious history of comics continues to offer authors and readers asylum from the assumptions and values of the more canonized media of text and film. As Frahm writes of comics, "Greatness appears in their little drawings as ridiculous" (Das Große erscheint in ihren kleinen Zeichnungen als lächerlich; 9). The best examples of this use of comics today come from small underground artists, who have more freedom than those releasing their work through the big publishing houses. Even so, comics as a whole (also those published by larger firms) still offer an alternative to more established media held in higher aesthetic esteem. It is perhaps for this reason that comics have attracted so many voices from the queer, feminist, and punk scenes in Austria and Germany. Some of the most exciting comics and graphic novels are being produced at the intersection of these groups and their various interests. A good example comes from Austrian comics artist Ulli Lust, whose 2009 graphic novel *Heute ist der letzte Tag vom Rest deines Lebens* (*Today is the Last Day of the Rest of Your Life*, 2013) achieved much acclaim both in Germany and abroad. The novel is a coming-of-age story that follows a group of young anarchists from Vienna who travel through Italy. The popularity of Lust's work and its acceptance by both radical and conventional artists and critics underscores the contradictions inherent in the reception of comics today.

In the postmodern era, comics, like many other media, have both forked and hybridized into multiple related forms that cater to opposing aesthetic perspectives and political commitments. It is worth noting that only after the rise of postmodern literature have comics been considered legitimate as art and literature. In an era of cultural production in which it is increasingly the case that "depth is replaced by surface, or by multiple surfaces" comics no longer stand out as particularly superficial (Jameson 62). Likewise, as Beaty notes, audiences have become more open to "marginalized cultural forms" and comics have "grown up" (13). It is in this context that German comics and graphic novels are now able to bloom into a kind of renaissance after a period dominated by adaptations and translations after World War II. While Germany remains a country devoutly committed to the value of literature and the virtues of the text-only book, it is increasingly difficult to distinguish German-language comics from literature. With the popularity of the graphic novel and the ease of individual production, text narratives and comics appear as merely two different media to explore Lukács' biographical organization of the world. Mimesis and abstraction appear simply as different brushes with which comics artists can accentuate and complicate various themes. The presence of image is no longer the main hindrance to the reception of comics as literature. Nonetheless, logocentric and medium-specific expectations carried over from literature continue to shape the reception of works produced in the medium. Thus, although many celebrate the closing of the breach between literature and comics, some note the dangers. Particularly, Frahm's view that the small panels of comics reveal the ridiculousness of all that claims to be great (9), appears to play a diminished role in the reception of newer comics, which increasingly aim to embody greatness themselves. Still, seen purely in terms of the sheer quantity and diversity of original German-language comics being produced in German and the increased scholarship on comics worldwide, the present is undoubtedly one of the most exciting and important periods for German comics.

NOTES

1. Johann Wolfgang von Goethe on early comics creator Rodolphe Töpffer (Goethe 503).

2. Klages' anti-Semitic views are well known. In this case, however, his formal work on "logocentrism" can be relevant without reference to the ideological features of his professional work and private life.

3. For more on relations of text and image, see *Understanding Comics*, in which McCloud differentiates between six different relationships.

REFERENCES

"Angeklagt Im Nürnberger Prozess: Albert Speer und Julius Streicher." *Spiegel Online* 21 April 2005. Web. 1 October 2015. http://www.spiegel.de/sptv/special/a-351341.html.

Beaty, Bart. *Comics versus Art*. Toronto: University of Toronto Press, 2012.

Betzwieser, Thomas. "Text, Bild, Musik: Die Multimediale Überlieferung des Melodrams Lenardo Und Blandine (1779). Eine Herausforderung für die Editionspraxis." *Editio* 25.1 (2011): 74–100.

Bytwerk, Randall L. *Julius Streicher: Nazi Editor of the Notorious Anti-Semitic Newspaper Der Stürmer*. 1st edition. New York: Cooper Square Press, 2001.

Corbeyran, Eric, and Richard Horne. *Die Verwandlung*. München: Knesebeck, 2010.

Derrida, Jacques. *Of Grammatology*. Trans. Gayatri Chakravorty Spivak. Corrected editon. Baltimore: Johns Hopkins University Press, 1998.

Dinter, Tim. *Cargo: Comicreportagen Israel—Deutschland*. München: Avant, 2005.

Dolle-Weinkauff, Bernd, and Klaus Doderer. *Comics: Geschichte Einer Populären Literaturform in Deutschland Seit 1945*. Weinheim: Beltz, 1990.

Dyl Ulenspiegel. Straßburg: Johannes Grüninger, 1515.

Flix. *Faust. Der Tragödie erster Teil*. Hamburg: Carlsen, 2010.

Frahm, Ole. *Die Sprache des Comics*. Hamburg: Philo Fine Arts, 2010.

Goethe, Johann Wolfgang von. *Conversations of Goethe with Eckermann and Soret*. Trans. John Oxenford. London: George Bell & Sons, 1875.

Goez, Joseph Franz von. *Versuch einer zalreichen Folge leidenschaftlicher Entwürfe für Empfindsame Kunst- und Schauspiel Freunde*. Augsburg: Akademische Handlung, 1783.

Groensteen, Thierry. "Why Are Comics Still in Search of Cultural Legitimization?" *Comics and Culture: Analytical and Theoretical Approaches to Comics*. Eds. Anne Magnussen, and Hans-Christian Christiansen. Copenhagen: Museum Tusculanum Press, 2000. 29–42.

Hiemer, Ernst. *Der Giftpilz: Ein Stürmerbuch für Jung u. Alt*. Nürnberg: Verlag Der Stürmer, 1938.

Jameson, Fredric. "Postmodernism, or the Cultural Logic of Late Capitalism." *New Left Review* I/146 July-August (1984): 53–92.

Klages, Ludwig. *Der Geist als Wiedersacher der Seele*. Bonn: Bouvier Verlag Herbert Grundmann, 1981.

Kunzle, David. *The Early Comic Strip; Narrative Strips and Picture Stories in the European Broadsheet from c. 1450 to 1825*. Berkeley: University of California Press, 1973.

Lent, John A. "The Comics Debates Internationally." *A Comics Studies Reader*. Ed. Jeet Heer and Kent Worcester. Jackson: University Press of Mississippi, 2009. 69–76.

Lessing, Gotthold Ephraim. *Laocoon*. Trans. William Ross. London: J. Ridgway & Sons, 1836.

Lukács, Geörgy, and Anna Bostock. *The Theory of the Novel*. Trans. A. Bostock. New ed. London: The Merlin Press Ltd., 1971.

Lust, Ulli. *Heute ist der letzteTag vom Rest deines Lebens*. München: avant, 2009.

———. *Today is the Last Day of the Rest of Your Life*. Seattle: Fantagraphics, 2013.

Nietzsche, Friedrich Wilhelm, Rolf-Peter Horstmann, and Judith Norman. *Beyond Good and Evil : Prelude to a Philosophy of the Future*. Cambridge ; New York: Cambridge University Press, 2002.

Plato. *Republic*. Ed. C. D. C. Reeve. Trans. G. M. A. Grube, 2nd edition. Indianapolis: Hackett Publishing Company, 1992.

Plauen, E. O., and Wilhelm-Busch-Museum. *Erich Ohser, E.O. Plauen: Politischen Karikaturen, Zeichnungen, Illustrationen und alle Bildgeschichten, Vater und Sohn*. Konstanz: Südverlag, 2000.

Schmitz-Emans, Monika, and Christian A. Bachmann. *Literatur-Comics: Adaptionen und Transformationen der Weltliteratur*. Berlin ; Boston: De Gruyter, 2012.

Schwieger, Dirk. *Moresukine: Wöchentlich aus Tokio*. Berlin: Reprodukt, 2002.

Smolderen, Thierry. *The Origins of Comics from William Hogarth to Winsor McCay*. Jackson: University Press of Mississippi, 2014.

Willems, Philippe. " 'This Strangest of Narrative Forms:'" Rodolphe Topffer's Sequential Art." *Mosaic: A Journal for the Interdisciplinary Study of Literature* 41.2 (2008): 127–47.

Winckelmann, Johann Joachim. *Johann Joachim Winckelmann on Art, Architecture, and Archaeology*. Trans. David Carter. Rochester: Camden House, 2013.

Wunderlich, Werner. "Till Eulenspiegel: Zur Karriere eines Schalksnarren in Geschichte und Gegenwart." *Monatshefte* 78.1 (1986): 38–47.

TWO

Before They Were "Art"

(West) German Proto-Comics and Comics: A Brief and Somewhat Subjective Survey

Eckhard Kuhn-Osius

The situation of contemporary comics in Germany is analogous to the status of literature after Gutenberg invented the printing press around 1440. The field shows vivid growth in all its forms, from comics versions of chapbooks for the masses to works that aspire to the status of high and rarefied art. As demonstrated in other contributions to this volume, comics scholars continue to tease out criteria to determine which is which. As part of this larger scholarly initiative, this chapter considers the time before comics aspired to be seen as "real" art and when readers regarded them, at best, as a pastime. At the time of the comics' respective publications, the German public did not, in general, grant German comics artists serious status, even if today's comics enthusiasts and scholars often argue otherwise. The examples examined in this chapter have, however, contributed to a rich and varied twentieth-century German comics tradition and have essentially taught Germans how to read and appreciate comics.

In this chapter, I identify the point between pre-art and art as that moment when comics are no longer "comic" in the humorous sense of the word, but claim to contain serious messages for adult readers. Taking comics seriously means subjecting them to a system of aesthetic evaluation similar to that applied to high literature and art. This study aims to trace a lineage of German pictorial literature, and, in the spirit of German reception theorist Hans Robert Jauss, to describe the "horizon of expectations" (*Erwartungshorizont*) that German readers of modern graphic literature hold when reading an *Autorencomic* or new graphic novel. Jauss's term encompasses factors that contribute to the reader's expectation for the work, such as genre convention, style, and form (24). Since comics have straddled cultural categories for decades, and expectations can derive from multiple categories and reading experiences, this analysis necessarily takes low and high art into account. The present examination focuses mainly on pictorial narratives created by Germans. It also includes, however, discussions of several imported comics that have found a wider readership in Germany than comics of German origin, and have also strongly influenced the horizon of expectation for German comics readers.

THE GERMAN CULTURAL CLIMATE: KITSCH AND THE STRUGGLE FOR RESPECTABILITY

The traditional aversion to "kitsch," or slickly emotional art considered to be in poor taste, among educated Germans has slowed the reception of German-language graphic narratives for decades. Traditionally, German intellectuals have distanced themselves from works that appear to play on emotions in trivial but potentially dangerous ways, one important reason being the theoretical lines drawn between kitsch and Nazism.[1] The current appreciation of graphic literature in German-speaking countries vacillates between dismissal as kitsch and avid postulation of the literariness of the graphic medium. Tellingly, recent years have seen the number of people willing to bestow the Kunst (art) label on the comics of their youth multiply in step with the prices and collectibility of comic books, while the aversion to kitsch has decreased.[2] The German folklorist Hans Naumann spoke of "sunken cultural goods" (gesunkenes Kulturgut), postulating that cultural practices or texts migrate downward in a simplified, coarsened form from the social elites to the common folk (Dow 49). The history of German-language graphic literature in the late twentieth century suggests the opposite, namely, "ascending cultural goods" (aufsteigendes Kulturgut).[3] More specifically, comics in their ascent to graphic literature are apparently gaining in respectability, while the delineations between fine art and kitsch continue to blur.

A peculiarly German organization demonstrates very well the strange straddling of cultural categories that comics can perform. The "German Organization of Non-Commercial Followers of Pure Donaldism" (Deutsche Organisation der nichtkommerziellen Anhänger des lauteren Donaldismus, or D.O.N.A.L.D.) was founded in 1977 in Hamburg and celebrated its thirty-eighth annual convention in Schwerin, Germany, in 2015. The organization's website characterizes the annual convention as follows: "As far as possible, the convention always takes place in temporal proximity to the fighting day of Donaldism on April 1, and thus also close to Carl Barks's birthday (March 27, 1901) (der Kongress [findet] nach Möglichkeit immer zeitnah zum Kampftag des Donaldismus am 1. April und somit auch in der Nähe zu Carl Barks' Geburtstag [27. März 1901] statt; www.donald.org). The organization's publication *Der Donaldist* covers, in a mock positivistic manner, topics such as "The Effect of Electric Current on the Ducks" ("Die Wirkung des elektrischen Stroms auf die Ducks"; issue 147) or "Donald Duck and the New York Main Post Office" ("Donald Duck und das New Yorker Hauptpostamt"; issue 148). The *Frankfurter Allgemeine Zeitung* journalist and comics expert Andreas Platthaus, a well-known Donaldist, assigns German Donaldism an apparent scholarly seriousness when dealing with Carl Barks's Donald Duck stories. Platthaus writes: "German Donaldism considers them as authentic reports from an otherwise inaccessible world, whose living situation we are tasked with researching" (Der deutsche Donaldismus betrachtet sie als authentische Berichte aus einer uns auf andere Weise unzugänglichen Welt, deren Lebensverhältnisse es zu erforschen gilt; Platthaus 2008, 135). The non-guilty fascination with the emotionally rich Duck family from "Entenhausen" has aptly reflected the status of comics among the German educated classes well into the 1990s.

Ironic detachment allows Donaldists to enjoy the comics of their youth without the risk of appearing to fall for kitsch. Donald Duck seems to be the only comic hero to have spawned this type of fan club in Germany while other comics fan clubs and websites, such as those for *Asterix and Obelix*, are much more matter of fact than that of the Donaldists, whose exalted passion thrives in an ironic world. In this chapter, I apply the words "irony" and "ironic" to the reading of graphic literature to indicate that words and pictures are understood by the reader to express or suggest meanings that in some dimension are the opposite of what they ostensibly express. Comics can create intertextual irony when the artist borrows from other texts or pictures to create an incongruity between words and images. As in other media, irony as a device in the graphic narrative medium can be verbal, situational, parodistic, or sarcastic. It may consist of over- or understatement; and the artist may also use elements of caricature. Graphic narratives access verbal and visual signifying systems, which may be static or suggest temporal sequences akin to drama. By virtue of providing visuals rather than descriptions, visual narrators can exert more control over descriptive elements of their stories than a prose writer, and unlike dramatists they do not have to rely on directors, stage designers, or actors. They are thus in control of their message on multiple levels and have much greater access to ironic, multifaceted communication than artists who are tied to the restricted channels of traditional art. Nonetheless, irony may also have to do with reception by readers, who may, for example, laugh about a text that the artist intends to be serious or profess reverence toward a text that does not seem to warrant it, as the phenomenon of "Donaldism" has shown.

NARRATIVES AND PICTURES

Most comics scholars would agree that the medium consists of three very basic components in various combinations: story, words, and picture. Instead of proposing an abstract definition of the comic and thereby adding to the many existing definitions,[4] this chapter will take a brief look at various narrative constellations of words and images to develop a descriptive system of terms that expands on the basic story, words, and picture, to include implicit external meta-story, internal meta-text, and illocutionary text. A central issue that arises when reading and understanding graphic literature concerns the extent to which pictures autonomously tell stories and to what extent they only illustrate pre-existing stories that must be conveyed to the viewer. In graphic narration, words and pictures cooperate to present a complex (quasi)referential story,[5] a term used here to indicate that all stories seem to refer to an outside reality and that a reader can understand and discuss a text without having to decide initially whether it actually refers to an external reality (= referential) or only purports to do so (= quasi-referential).

In this chapter, I employ the term "implicit external meta-stories" to designate existing stories illustrated by individual pictures or picture sequences. Such meta-stories are commonly used in traditional, non-modernist painting. The pictorial narratives that have developed, especially in print media since the nineteenth century, can tell previously unknown stories because they bring the story into the pictorial space, very often with the help of textual elements. The function of words in pictorial narratives will be the topic of the subsections that follow the discussion of implicit external meta-stories. Two subsets derive from this larger heading, depending on who is addressed by the story's text. In the case of internal meta-text, the narrator speaks to readers directly, similar to an auctorial narrator; but illocutionary text shows the protagonists in the story speaking to each other. By reading internal meta-text, the readers become part of the communication. By contrast, when they read illocutionary text, they take on the role of observer. While the text types will be discussed, there will be no specific discussion about the type of pictures needed in pictorial narratives, as many types of picture can be used for pictorial narrative. Some of my later discussion regarding the quality of comics will consider not only the picture-text constellations that relate to the genre, but also the many areas of experience that may enter the telling and reading of a story. The aesthetic quality of a comic may result from the artist's capability to bring multiple aspects of experience into the graphic narrative.

Traditional Illustrative Pictures: An Example of Implicit External Meta-stories

The perceived similarity of poetry and pictures was commonplace from the time of Horace's "Ut pictura poesis" until the eighteenth century, when Gotthold Ephraim Lessing drew a distinction between them in his 1766 seminal work *Laokoon, oder über die Grenzen der Malerei und Poesie* (*Laocoon: An Essay on the Limits of Painting and Poetry*):

> [B]odies, with their visible properties, are the legitimate subjects of painting. . . . Actions are . . . the legitimate subjects of poetry. All bodies, however, exist in time as well as space. . . . Painting may, therefore, represent actions, but it can only be by intimation, through means of bodies. The painter can only employ, in his composition of co-existing bodies, one single moment of the action. (151–52)

For Lessing, both literature and the visual arts present the "great stories," but the idea of storytelling through pictures lies beyond Lessing's horizon. Presumably, Lessing was familiar with painting cycles about texts, such as Fénélon's well-known novel *Télémaque*, or picture cycles about Christian themes,[6] but his demand that the artist find the "most telling moment" to illustrate a story strongly suggests that he thinks in terms of individual pictures that refer to a pre-existing story instead of sequences that could tell a story in their own right. Within the context of my proposed term "implicit external meta-stories," this means that certain culturally known stories are implicitly contained within the visual work. Without the background information, the picture's iconographic content would be elusive. That is to say that viewers who have no familiarity with the implicit external meta-story of a picture may come to some sort of understanding of what the picture shows, but a correct iconographic understanding can only be reached if the viewer knows about the specific depicted story. The famous art historian Erwin Panovsky offers the following example. A picture of *The Last Supper* seen on a pre-iconographic level—that is, by someone who knows nothing of the Christian tradition—simply shows thirteen people eating at a table.[7] The stories are external, because the viewer cannot find their complete meanings in the picture, even if the contents and contexts of *The Last Supper* seem blatantly obvious to the initiated. To adduce the correct implicit external meta-story, viewers must draw upon previous textual knowledge. To "read" the picture, one must recognize the part of the implicit external meta-story that the picture represents.[8] The explanation of traditional pictures and sequences usually connects with specific heroic names and actions, often rooted in classical antiquity, hagiography, or the Bible. In contrast to a contemporary understanding of graphic narrative art, these types of pictures or sequences refer to narratives, but they are not themselves narrative in nature.

Pictorial Narratives: Independent Story Telling

The analysis in this chapter concerns itself with picture and word sequences with enough information to establish a story line that viewers can construct on the basis of their own culturally mediated world experience without having to recall a specific external text, tradition, or (quasi-) referential person. The visual narrative's pictures and text contain everything viewers with general life experience need for a basic understanding. Although visual narratives may be adaptations of traditional stories, it is not necessary for the viewer to possess previous knowledge of the depicted story from elsewhere. Visual narratives tell any story as if it is new, and they do so by appealing to the viewer/reader's life experience, making the story accessible for readers who have no more than a general knowledge of sequences of events. The move away from the exemplary heroic narrative and toward connections to personal and private events parallels the rise of the novel during the Enlightenment in the eighteenth century. Elements of this appeal to world knowledge can be observed early on in genre paintings and in picture series that tell extended cultural story lines, such as some cycles by William Hogarth (e.g., *The Rake's Progress*), or later graphic cycles by Max Klinger or Franz Masereel (see Pommeranz-Liedtke). Some graphic narratives gained wide distribution in the pictorially rich *Bilderbogen* (picture sheets or broadsheets) of the nineteenth and twentieth centuries, which were a popular form of novelty "infotainment" for the somewhat literate masses.[9] Some of these stories could be understood without words, just as one may understand actions of people whom one observes from a distance because general world knowledge suffices to interpret what s/he sees. Most of these pictorial narratives, however, contain accompanying text, even if limited. Language in pictorial narratives can be classified into two major types, which I term, as explained briefly above, internal meta-text and illocutionary text.

Pictorial Narratives and Language: Internal Meta-Text

Internal meta-text is textual communication between the artist or author and the reader about the story narrated through pictures. Comics often show internal meta-text in text boxes rather than speech bubbles. These elements contribute to the overall work, but function somewhat like a voice-over in the cinema: they are not part of the happenings within the picture story. Internal meta-text may be so dominant that the picture story says little more than the text.[10] In contrast to the implicit external meta-story, the internal meta-text is part of the pictorial narrative and the reader has no need to recall a specific external story. The minimal internal meta-text in picture stories is a headline or subtitle that helps the reader activate schemata for understanding the story and serves as a label of sorts for the picture sequence.[11] This use of language predominates when the French-speaking forerunner of graphic literature Rodolphe Töpffer tells his stories mostly with meta-textual headlines for each drawing, as in this example: "[Mr. Oldbuck] seeks to conquer the tender passion by study. / Mr. Oldbuck finding study ineffectual, tries music. / He discovers that all his efforts are in vain. / Looking from the window, Mr. Oldbuck espies his ladye-love [sic]" (Töpffer). The internal meta-text names plot elements while the images add descriptive and expressive detail. This sounds like an application of Lessing's findings: the pictures show "bodies, with their visible properties"; the text advances the action. But in most graphic narratives, including comics, the internal meta-text is even more important for evaluative judgments, which often cannot be rendered visually.

In Töpffer's textual labels to his drawings above, evaluative expressions like "conquer the tender passion" or "ineffectual" are essential to an understanding of the story line. Internal meta-text dominates many narrative *Bilderbogen* of the nineteenth century; and the reader could theoretically read the internal meta-text in isolation. This type of non-integrated densely illustrated story is called a *Bildergeschichte* [picture story] and is frequently found in German pictorial narratives well into the 1960s. In the comics debates of the 1950s that threatened to relegate comics to the categories of pulp literature and trash, *Bildergeschichten* without speech bubbles were somehow considered to be culturally superior, presumably because the texts were more coherent.[12] But readers can find dominant internal meta-text in many perhaps unexpected, less culturally superior places. A picture from the then-scandalous *Tales from the Crypt* (Entertaining Comics, 1951) partially shows two humans, one lying on his back while the other is seen from the rear, looking on. The picture looks innocent enough and could be the drawing of someone who slipped on a banana peel. But then we read the text box with the internal meta-text: "He lay sprawled grotesquely on the cobblestones . . . white as chalk! Two punctures trickled claret on his neck! He was dead! I had drained his blood . . ."(Frahm 2010, 328). The picture alone cannot adequately deliver the decisive evaluative information, but the internal meta-text transports the horror. Drawings can also convey meta-textual information when they show things whose meaning is not accessible to the protagonists in the story, or when they just show who is uttering certain statements.

Pictorial Narratives and Language: Illocutionary Text

Illocutionary text is what the figures within the pictures say to each other, to themselves, or even to the reader within the confines of the narrative. In comics, illocutionary language, typically, but not necessarily, appears in speech bubbles. For language to be classified as *illocutionary* or as *internal meta-text*, however, the type of language matters more than its representation. *Illocutionary text* makes pictorial narratives sometimes appear like theater: between seeing pictures of the characters' actions and reading their illocutionary text, the reader can follow the story. A German-speaking forerunner of graphic narration is Joseph Franz von Goez. Superficially, the brief lines under each picture in his 1782 pictorial "enactment" of a ballad by Gottfried August Bürger look similar to Töpffer's creations a few decades later. But the images mostly show the protagonists, Lenardo and Blandine, lamenting their sad fate in dialogue and later monologue by Blandine. Goez's work turns out to be essentially the opposite of Töpffer's since the bulk of Goez's text consists of illocutionary speech.[13]

GENRE DEFINITIONS AND
OBSERVATIONS ON QUALITY

Based on these elements and their interplay, we may posit that in the most advanced comics, *internal meta-text*, image, and *illocutionary language* complement and interpenetrate each other in correlative ways, a topic about which Scott McCloud has written extensively (see 146–69). But now the issue changes from the generic question of whether something is done to how it is done. A comic that shows advanced genre characteristics is not high art by this criterion alone, but the advanced integration of image, internal meta-text, and illocutionary language makes it easier to narrate complex stories. A generically advanced comic, which intertwines word and image, is likely to contain a smaller amount of redundant information and show greater economy of expressive means and thus increases the likelihood for richer, more developed stories with deeper characters. By giving voice to the various actors in a story, well-developed illocutionary text presents a more variegated and interesting story with more complex characters than one that relies largely on internal meta-text. The evaluative quality of internal meta-text will influence the story's appeal to readers by framing it. Intertextuality with the avoidance of cliché plays an important role if one wants to evaluate a comic's aesthetic quality. Will Eisner stresses the need for the comic artist to pay attention to the "commonality of experience. This demands of the sequential artist an understanding of the reader's life experience if his message is to be understood" (7). It is especially on the level of intertextuality that the question of kitsch and high art can be determined. A comic that readers are to take seriously does not content itself with the readers' life experience because a comic that only corroborates what the reader already knows may fall into the category of kitsch. To be sure, readers can understand pictorial stories as presented, but, related to Jauss's horizon of expectations, knowledge of the tradition from which they derive enriches the reading experience and engagement.

AN HISTORICAL OVERVIEW
OF GERMAN GRAPHIC NARRATION

Having established some categories and terms to describe and classify graphic narratives, it is now time to take a look at a number of such narratives that form an unbroken German tradition beginning in the nineteenth century. I will treat these works in several subgroups, beginning with the oldest graphic narrative works that are still widely read and ending with the contemporary Gerhard Seyfried.

The Founders: Heinrich Hoffmann (1798–1874)

Any treatment of modern-day graphic narration in Germany must begin with Hoffmann's *Struwwelpeter* (1845). Although the comic's extreme portrayals of the punishment of undesirable behavior in children have raised significant concerns among parents, these stories are among the earliest samples of pictorial narration that young German readers still encounter up to the present day.[14] Some of the characters' names have proverbial status, such as "Suppenkaspar "(soup Casper [who refuses to eat]) or "Hans Guck-in-die-Luft" (Hans Skygazer). The stories usually take the form of *Bildergeschichten* with a strong dose of internal meta-language, which reduces most pictures to illustration status. One example is "Der böse Friedrich" (Evil Frederick):[15]

> Frederic, Frederic.
> He was a terrible ruffian.
> He caught the flies in the house
> and tore out their wings.
> He slew both chairs and birds.
> Cats suffered great distress.
> And just listen how bad he was:
> He even whipped his [caretaker] Gretel.

> Der Friederich, der Friederich
> Das war ein arger Wüterich
> Er fing die Fliegen in dem Haus
> Und riss ihnen die Flügel aus.
> Er schlug die Stühl und Vögel tot
> Die Katzen litten große Not.
> Und höre nur, wie bös er war.
> Er peitschte seine Gretchen gar! (Hoffmann 3–4)

While the drawings largely correspond to the internal meta-text, the images elaborate on the textual element. Drawings of a killed cat, dead birds, and Friedrich's acts of violence confirm his bad behavior. Similar visual elaborations are the pictures with the little ash heap that used to be Paulinchen (Hoffmann 7), or the soup bowl placed on Suppenkaspar's grave (Hoffmann 17). There are also non-verbalized premonitions, as in the case of Zappelphilipp (Fidgety Philipp). The text stops when the boy lies on the ground, covered by the food and the table setting he has torn down after he has tipped his chair over. The text states the parents' reactions in very simple terms: "Both are very angry, / [since] they have nothing left to eat" (Beide sind gar zornig sehr, / Haben nichts zu essen mehr; Hoffmann 20). But the decorative border separating the last picture and text provides more information. It contains two crossed pairs of "Ruten" (switches), which the reader can assume will be used to punish Philipp (20). While most of the language in *Struwwelpeter* consists of internal meta-text, the narrative weaves in some illocutionary parental admonitions and commands as well as Suppenkaspar's fatally defiant "I won't eat my soup! No, my soup I won't eat!" (Ich esse meine Suppe nicht! Nein, meine Suppe ess' ich nicht; Hoffmann 17). Although clearly situated in the *Bildergeschichte* tradition, Hoffmann's *Struwwelpeter* demonstrates a move toward the interplay of pictures, internal meta-text, and illocutionary text that more closely approximates contemporary graphic narration.

The Founders: Wilhelm Busch (1859–1884)

Wilhelm Busch has undoubtedly produced the seminal works of graphic narration in Germany. His breakthrough came in 1865 with *Max und Moritz*, still extremely popular and often sold in department stores bound together with *Struwwelpeter*. The book serves as the source of many quotable quotes, such as "Dieses war der erste Streich, doch der nächste folgt sogleich" (This was the first trick, but the next one will follow right away). While Busch's rhymed stories often have a strong internal meta-text, they display a remarkable interplay between word and image. The following brief example from 1875's *Tobias Knopp: Abenteuer eines Junggesellen* (Tobias Knopp: Adventures of a Bachelor) serves to illustrate the point. Tobias Knopp is a middle-aged man traveling to find a suitable bride. First he visits his old flame Adele who did not accept his marriage proposal in their youth. Tobias still, however, has her portrait in his possession. Tobias arrives at her house:

> Full of perspiration and anxiety
> He has arrived at her door.
> Oh, his heart, it beats so much
> And then finally he knocks, too.
> "Heaven" she cries
> "Oh what Happiness!"
> Knopp's sweat recedes.

> Transpirierend und beklommen
> Ist er an die Tür gekommen.

Ach, sein Herze klopft so sehr.
Und am Ende klopft auch er.
Himmel! ruft sie "welches Glück!"
Knopp sein Schweiß der tritt zurück. (Busch 157)

The pictures display what the text does not communicate. Adele is an old maid and no longer as pretty as she used to be. The text only hints at this fact by way of Knopp's diminishing perspiration. Words and images interact with greater complexity and subtlety than in *Struwwelpeter*. Image, internal meta-text, and illocutionary text show the situation clearly and without redundancy. The illocutionary text verbalizes Adele's enthusiasm, Knopp's emotions are suggested in the internal meta-text, and the pictures convey the reason for his change of heart. Such a strong non-redundant correlation among the three elements of the graphic story is most easily achieved when the text and picture convey disparate information because discrepancies of meanings are easily assigned to different textual levels of the graphic narration. Irony allows the pictorial and verbal elements to reflect on each other with the least redundancy. Moreover, heavily ironic texts also avoid kitsch and correspond to Busch's morose worldview.

Hoffmann and Busch begin the German graphic narrative tradition with what today would be called *Autorencomics*, comics created and controlled by the authors or artists themselves. While other comic artists have copied and parodied Hoffmann (see, for example, *Struwwelliese*, *Struwwelhitler*), Busch's bitingly ironic tone has proven hard to parody.[16] Especially when presenting boys' pranks in the *Max und Moritz* tradition, artists have often imitated but never equaled Busch. In fact, I would contend that the scope, quality, and success of Wilhelm Busch's work are important reasons for the oft-observed lag in German comic adoption until after World War II. True, Germans showed an aversion to things emanating from the enemy countries of the Great War, and Third-Reich political repression, control of the arts, and lack of foreign currency also stood in the way of the new art form. But one must also acknowledge that Busch's "brand" of storytelling had all but cornered the market on high-quality pictorial narratives appealing to various age groups, a fact which would scare away would-be successors and their publishers. Also noteworthy is that both Hoffmann and Busch affect a high moralistic, even teacherly tone, which is definitely ironic in Busch's case, and which is ironized by readers of *Struwwelpeter* as they outgrow the drastic lessons provided in the book. In practice, both authors have produced early examples of extremely black humor. It may even be that one cannot read Hoffmann seriously after having been exposed to Busch's fake moralism.

A Lone Master: E. O. Plauen (1903–1944)

E. O. Plauen's *Vater und Sohn* (Father and Son) comics, which ran between 1934 and 1937, is the only widely known German comic series between the time of Wilhelm Busch and the end of World War II in 1945. Erich Ohser from the town of Plauen published the stories under the pseudonym E. O. Plauen. Having not been allowed to publish because of his critical anti-Nazi cartoons during the time of the Weimar Republic, he had to earn money after the Nazis' rise to power. The strips were begun at the behest of *Berliner Illustrierte*, which was looking for something to lighten up its pages and create reader loyalty. The strips function almost entirely without words, although each episode is titled (internal meta-text) and occasional textual elements are integrated into some stories. One key example is the story "Der kleine Auskneifer" (The Little Run-Away; also known as "Der verlorene Sohn" [The Prodigal Son]). It shows a boy who has evidently broken a window while playing soccer inside the apartment.[17] The father is ready to punish him and the son runs away. The father sits down to read the newspaper, but becomes anxious as the hours pass and his son does not return. The father goes out and roams the streets to find his son, but without success. When he returns and approaches the door to his apartment, the soccer ball flies through the other window and hits him in the face. His son has returned and played indoor soccer again. But now the puzzled son finds himself lovingly embraced by his relieved father. Plauen's wordless strip follows a tradition of wordless picture stories in Germany since the nineteenth century. Eckart Sackmann classifies the *Vater und Sohn* series as a toned-down version of the popular *Bubenstreiche* (rogue boys' tricks) strips in the tradition of *Max und Moritz*, but wonders how Plauen's series remained popular into the 1960s with a format that was already old-fashioned when the stories first appeared (2012b, 79). A brief examination of the quality of E. O. Plauen's stories may provide a response to this query.

The attractiveness of *Vater und Sohn* rests on almost archetypical situations that Plauen draws with painstaking emotional accuracy, showing the anger, sorrow, fear, and relief felt by the father, as the example above illustrates. Instead of base slapstick, the superior specimens of Plauen's formally old-fashioned strips blend complex emotional states and everyday situations that most readers can follow without words, and that have rather far-reaching appeal. Hans Joachim Neyer interprets the domestic quality of the events as a protest against official Nazi hero worship (83). Erich Ohser's later suicide in a Gestapo prison lends this interpretation a certain degree of plausibility, but it is not compelling since much Nazi propaganda thrived on projecting a whole and wholesome world (*heile Welt*). The *Vater und Sohn* comics constitute the first widely known series of short-sequence serial comics with recurring characters in Germany. They are also *Autorencomics*, which artistically "belonged" to the artist even if the newspaper publisher bought the rights. The *Vater und Sohn* stories stand out as a singular example in the German graphic narrative tradition that carries an emotional depth rarely reached since.

Commercial Mascot Strips: Lurchi (since 1937)

Another subcategory in the history of German graphic art is the marketing comic. The "Lurchi" series of free comic booklets was started in 1937 to entertain and quiet down children while their parents shopped for shoes in the Salamander footwear chain. The salamander hero of the series belongs to the species "Lurch" or amphibian. The comic series was relaunched after World War II in 1951, and since then a total of 149 comic booklets has been produced, with occasional revisions in layout, language, and Lurchi's wardrobe. The series has been republished in book form in eight volumes. Traditionally, the stories are narrated as *Bildergeschichten*. The *internal meta-text* in uneven verse is printed in school cursive at the bottom of each page and illustrated with one, two, or four panels in the top half. The plotline of most stories is linear, problems tend to be solved through the hearty use of solid shoes, and the story ends with some version of the words "For a long time the forest reverberates with the cheer, hooray for Salamander" (Lange tönt's im Walde noch, Salamander lebe hoch). The numerous characters are flat; and the problems are suitable for young readers and reminiscent of "Kaspertheater" puppet shows.[18] Lurchi is significant to a history of German graphic narratives because of its status as one of the most successful and long-lived German marketing comics; its reference to elements of German folk culture (Lurchi's hat, forest creatures, gnomes) and impressive press runs into the millions.[19] While not an artistic masterpiece, the Lurchi series introduced many children to graphic narration, even if on the most basic level.[20]

Adventure Strips: Jimmy das Gummipferd

Strips in the tradition of *Tarzan* (original in German 1952), *Batman*, *Superman*, *The Phantom*, to name a few, did not enjoy expected popular success because of local competition from Hansrudi Wäscher and the Lehning publishing house after 1953 and 1954. The amazingly prolific cartoonist Wäscher singlehandedly created and drew comics series in the American style, namely, *Sigurd* (medieval knight, 324 booklets), *Falk* (knight, about 120 booklets), *Akim* and *Tibor* (Tarzan types, 183 booklets), *Nick der Weltraumfahrer* (space travel, 121 booklets).[21] In 1953, the major illustrated magazine *Der Stern* started a children's insert, *Sternchen*, which presented rhymed gag strips of "Reinhold das Nashorn" (Reinhold the Rhinoceros) from 1953–1970, drawn and texted by German humorist Vicco von Bülow, better known as Loriot. From 1953–1977, *Stern-*

chen also presented the *Autorencomic Jimmy das Gummipferd* (Rubber Horse Jimmy) by Roland Kohlsaat. The series follows Gaucho Julio and his rubber horse, which can be inflated and deflated, ridden upon, and sometimes filled with objects such as gold coins or Brazil nuts. Julio and his horse are the only consistent elements in the story. Julio exhibits some superhero characteristics, but he lacks a superhero's physique, a superhero's metropolis, and a superhero's enemies. Julio and his rubber horse amble through many adventurous situations on the Pampas, in the jungle, on the sea floor, underground, in space, and in other mysterious settings. But after all the more or less fantastic adventures, they usually make it home in time for Christmas. Julio is a rather static character; but the fantastic environments in which he finds himself add unexpected elements, perspectives, and depth, although they admittedly reveal stereotypes of the time periods when the stories were created. Kohlsaat's narration strikes a comic-style balance between image and illocutionary text, and the meta-textual narrative of a densely illustrated *Bildergeschichte*. Kohlsaat's rich visual detail obviates the need for excessive description. In fact, it would seem nearly impossible to describe his fantastic landscapes verbally.

A sample scene from *Jimmy das Gummipferd*fo illustrates Kohlsaat's artistic process. During a New Year's party, Julio is asked by a fan of his, "Conjure up a Moon in the sky for us" (Zaubere uns einen Mond an den Himmel). Julio complies with the request by placing a candle inside his rubber horse. "Right away, Jimmy begins to shine with a mild glow, because his rubber skin is translucent. Then Julio ties his Lasso to the saddle strap and waits until the air inside Jimmy's inside warms up from the candle flame" (Sofort beginnt Jimmy in mildem Licht zu leuchten, denn seine Gummihaut ist lichtdurchlässig. Dann befestigt Julio an Jimmys Sattelgurt sein Lasso und wartet, bis sich von der Kerze die Luft in Jimmys Bauch erwärmt).[22] The reader can detect a considerable amount of internal meta-text in this segment. The original request, however, that precedes the physical description of Jimmy and sets the action into motion is given as illocutionary text. The interplay between the unrealistic properties of Jimmy and the application of basic principles of physics, for example, when Jimmy is used as a hot-air balloon, also typifies the series. Not only the described example and the fact that his strip does not follow international models confirm Kohlsaat's originality, but also the observation that he has had few, if any, imitators.

Three Imported Giants: Petzi

Despite the strong homegrown German comics tradition, three imported comic figures (or comic families) dominated in West Germany: *Petzi, Donald Duck,* and *Asterix.* Other possible contenders, such as *Lucky Luke* and *Tim und Struppi* (Tin Tin), have not reached the same level of popularity in Germany. The Danish series *Petzi*[23] (originally Rasmus Klump), begun in 1951 for younger children, maintained decades-long success, as evidenced by a print run of over twelve million. The series is the bedrock publication of the major comic and manga publisher Carlsen, which was founded as a German outlet for *Petzi* stories. The *Petzi* stories contain panels with text blocks underneath. In spite of the layout, the text is almost exclusively illocutionary; and the reader must figure out who says what in the absence of speech bubbles. In *Petzi*'s case, the panel layout matters less than the text itself. This becomes obvious when one regards an unsuccessful attempt by Carlsen to change the text of the *Petzi* stories, perhaps with the misguided aim to make the books more accessible to readers. For example, the opening frame of *Petzi im Doggerland* originally included the caption: "Our new ship floats great, right? Unfortunately it doesn't move forward" (Unser neues Schiff schwimmt prima, was? Leider kommt es nicht vom Fleck). Readers would likely have no difficulty figuring out that the characters in the text speak this *illocutionary text*. The revised text replaces the original caption with "Petzi and Pingo were standing on board of the 'Mary' talking with each other. 'Such a trip is always the most beautiful thing there is,' said Pingo. 'It is strange that we are not moving forward'" (Petzi und Pingo standen an Bord der "Mary" und unterhielten sich. "So eine Reise ist doch immer wieder das Schönste, was es gibt," sagte Pingo. "Merkwürdig ist nur, daß wir nicht recht vom Fleck kommen"; "petzi-forschung"). The intrusive, boring, and redundant revised internal meta-text reduces the generically more advanced and diverse illocutionary texts to a rather primitive internal meta-text. This tinkering with the language led to a backlash from the fans and eventual reinstatement of the original text. Like *Jimmy das Gummipferd*, the *Petzi* books are "road comics," following the protagonists' travels, except that Petzi only encounters nice strangers. Plans are made, obstacles occur and are mastered, new characters pass by and are interacted with, and in the end, as in many a fairy tale, Petzi will go home to his mother. The long-lived commercial success of the *Petzi* series demonstrates one source by which millions of children learned how to read the interactions of pictures and illocutionary text that comprise comics.

Three Imported Giants: Disney and Carl Barks's Donald Duck

Disney comics, especially the *Donald Duck* stories by Carl Barks, were the undisputed leader of the German comic world until the 1970s. *Micky Maus* magazine has been published since 1951 by the Egmont Ehapa group, which owned the Disney rights for Europe and has benefited from excellent translators. The role of Erika Fuchs (Dr. phil.) in the translation and stylistic elevation of *Donald Duck* comics (from 1951–1988) and the changes she has brought to the German-language versions have often been acknowledged (Pannor). The role of language and parallel location in the German translation is worth noting and may explain in part why the German *Donald Duck* more decisively approaches, but in no way reaches, high art status in Germany. Fuchs translates "Duckburg," a US town with American customs and somewhat colloquial English ("Unca Donald"), into a geographically and historically detached "Entenhausen," which is clearly not set in contemporary Germany. Adding to the comic's ambivalent status between entertainment and high art, Entenhausen's language avoids colloquialism or slang and liberally uses literary allusions. One story in particular illustrates this application of language. Donald has just managed to trick his nephews into taking a shower of sorts. Going for a walk with his newly clean nephews in their Sunday best, he exults, "How gloriously nature shines for me! How cleanly all creatures radiate! Oh, it is a pleasure to be alive!" (Wie herrlich leuchtet mir die Natur! Wie sauber strahlt jedwede Kreatur! Ach, es ist eine Lust zu leben!; Barks 24). Donald begins with Johann Wolfgang von Goethe's poem "Maifest" (How gloriously nature shines for me! [How the sun laughs! How the land radiates!]), continues with an original statement, and ends with a quotation from the aristocratic humanist Ulrich von Hutten. Donald's most salient characteristic is his ability to lose at almost anything he does, but he displays a wide range of emotions and together with his family members experiences the gamut of human existence (see Platthaus 2009). Disney comics thrive on the interaction between image and illocutionary language. Fuchs's choice of standard register helps to make the stories longer-lived since the language is neither regional, nor does it become dated. Additionally, her polishing of the German text not only removes it from the humdrum of the everyday, but also emphasizes the polished irony of the best Donald Duck stories: the story line of Sunday showers does not qualify as high art, and the Goethe quotation is seriously out of place.[24]

Three Imported Giants: Asterix (since 1961)

After 1968, Egmont Ehapa began to publish *Asterix*, which soon replaced *Micky Maus* comic books as the top seller among German educated young adults: "While the first volume of *Asterix* in 1968 took its time to reach 50,000 sold copies, volume 13, *Asterix and the Copper Cauldron* appeared in 1972 in a print edition of 1.2 million copies . . ." (Brachte es der erste 'Asterix'-Band 1968 nur schleppend auf eine Verkaufsauflage von 50 000 Stück, so erschien Band 13, *Asterix und der Kupferkessel*, 1972 schon in 1,2millionen-Auflage . . . ; "Comics: Schwermetall").[25] The role of translator Gudrun Penndorf may be as important for *Asterix* comics as Erika Fuchs was for *Donald Duck*. *Asterix* started out in Germany as part of the Kauka empire (see note 24), but unhappiness with his translation led to the reassignment to the Ehapa publishing company (see Pannor; Heine; Sackmann 2006). While the first volume eliminated the obvious mistranslations and reinterpretations of the Kauka version, the wit of the French author René Goscinny's illocutionary and internal meta-text slowly began to shine forth when Penndorf delivered better translations, especially of the playful names. *Asterix*'s irreverent, but friendly fun-poking at all kinds of stereotypes from small-town habits to the conquests of Julius Caesar in a rich inter-textual web of words and images which intertwines Roman times and the present in numerous internal meta-textual boxes and visual has irrevocably shaped the German public's *Erwartungshorizont* for graphic literature.

Ironic Political Comics for Adult Readers: Nick Knatterton (1950–1959)

Germans were prepared for the advent of the popular *Asterix* comic because of their previous exposure to Manfred Schmidt's highly ironic and parodistic *Autorencomic* for adults, the detective series *Nick Knatterton*, an over-the-top spoof of Anglo-American detective novels. Schmidt found the detective genre distasteful, but was so successful that he published the strip from 1950 until 1959 (printed in *Quick*, a weekly illustrated magazine published from 1948 until 1992). Schmidt liberally employs inter-textual and self-referential comments and puns to present his characters with great ironic distance. While he narrates the action of *Knatterton* generically smoothly in pictures and with illocutionary language, he introduces a second and third level of communication through abundant internal meta-text that makes excessive reference to contemporary postwar Germany. The narrator copiously and ironically comments on and explains his pictures, the story, the characters, current politics, historical events, German rearmament, or taxes. Occasionally, he even adds comments by purported readers. The result is a work of stunning absurdity, which in many respects set a new standard for German comics art and political satire.

A closer look at a scene from one *Knatterton* adventure demonstrates the novelty of Schmidt's accomplishments in his comic. In this scene, Nick and his client and family sit in a car. The picture's caption reads: "The trip goes to the site of Murx Inc., where the wedding banquet is to take place in the private restaurant of the supervisory board." In a speech bubble, Mr. Murx says: "I am scared . . . life is the highest of all goods!," which is glossed in a little box with an arrow pointing to the bubble, "This is said by an arms manufacturer! We are outraged." His wife (mother of the bride) adds to her husband's comment, "Especially so shortly before the wedding. . . ." Nick Knatterton answers the husband "The only thing that helps against fear is emigration!," which is again glossed in a box with an arrow, "This would result in mass migration!" Two frames later, the family is told by the bride "The bouquet has disappeared!" Nick replies: "That won't do any good now anymore!" While the father of the bride (armaments manufacturer) answers: "My best customer. . . ." This is a pun on the last name of Franz Josef Strauß (Strauß also means bouquet), the controversial first West German secretary of defense. An explanatory box with arrows to both Nick's and the father's speech bubbles states: "Both of them are thinking of the defense secretary! The lost bridal bouquet will be brought an hour later." (Die Fahrt geht zur Murx A.G., wo im Aufsichtsrats-Casino das Hochzeitsessen stattfinden soll." Murx: "Ich habe Angst . . . Das Leben ist der Güter höchstes!" Text box: "Das sagt ein Waffenfabrikant! Unerhört!" Mrs. Murx: "Vor allem so kurz vor der Hochzeit. . . ." Nick Knatterton: "Gegen Angst hilft nur eins—auswandern!" Text box: "Das gäbe eine Völkerwanderung!" Bride about bouquet: "Der Strauss ist weg!" Nick: "Das nutzt jetzt auch nichts mehr!" Murx: "Mein bester Kunde. . . ." Text box: "Beide denken an den Minister! Das verlorene Brautbukett wird eine Stunde später gebracht.") The multiplicity of drawings, comments, explanations, and anticipated reader comments creates a highly sophisticated, multi-layered, ironic, and often satirical web of meanings in which pictures and words interact in remarkable ways. Schmidt does not use the internal meta-text as a means to sum up the comic heroes' actions. Instead he firmly inserts his implicit author as a commentator who prescribes to his readers' how to relate to what they read and recognize their own historical and political situation.

Schmidt's is the first German comic in which pictures, illocutionary text, and internal meta-text address the reader simultaneously with diverging messages because Schmidt insists on forcing the intertextual references upon his reader. Schmidt does not simplify and concentrate the content of his pictures to what is relevant for the progress of the story; instead he overwhelms with the presence of everything, thus pointing up the inevitable connectedness of his stories to the general social situation. *Knatterton* consistently ridicules all romantic and kitschy notions, which he copiously includes in his story to subject them to his withering commentary. *Nick Knatterton* paves the way for a scathingly ironic mode of graphic literature production, in some ways similar to the ironic readerly reception of the *Donald Duck* comics by the D.O.N.A.L.D. organization. The *Knatterton* stories could count as the great novel about postwar Germany in the 1950s. Schmidt's criticisms were shared by many young people who set out on a left-wing countercultural quest to become new and better (socialist) human beings than their parents had been. But most countercultural individuals eventually have to settle down and begin to make the compromises of everyday life, which bares their lives to the same type of ironic treatment and criticism that their generation had so liberally bestowed on their elders. After the 1960s a new generation of satirical comics poked fun at the countercultural pretensions of the aging '68ers, or protest generation. While these comics are very self-critical of the protest movement, they are not as overtly political as Schmidt's comics had been because they mostly no longer make overt references to then-current political events.

Ironic Political Comics for Adult Readers: Clodwig Poth (1975–1993) and Others

The self-ironic trend reached an early peak with Chlodwig Poth's *Mein progressiver Alltag* (My Progressive Daily Life), based on work published in the satirical magazine *Pardon* and published in book form in 1975. One scene shows an evidently post-coital naked couple in bed. In four similar pictures, the following dialogue ensues.

1. "Are you going to tell your wife that you were with me?" "In principle yes,
2. because we have firmly resolved to abolish falsehood in our marriage.
3. But on the other hand: She can't go through with it. Because if I tell her, she will go and sleep with someone else.
4. That always totally wears me down. I get deeply depressed and can't work for days."

1. "Sagst du deiner Frau, dass du bei mir warst?" "Im Prinzip schon,
2. denn wir haben uns vorgenommen, nicht mehr zu heucheln in unserer Ehe.
3. Aber andererseits: Sie kann es ja nicht durchhalten. Denn wenn ich es sage, geht sie hin und schläft mit einem anderen.
4. Das macht mich immer total fertig. Ich habe tiefe Depressionen und kann tagelang nicht arbeiten." (Poth)

The way in which illocutionary text is applied to almost identical panels takes the place of internal meta-text to suggest some temporal and emotional development. Poth uses the illocutionary talk of the characters to communicate certain information about them. He very much relies on the commonality of experience between himself and the readers who must remember the counter-culturalists' noble goals, such as being honest in their marriage, almost as if that were an implicit external meta-story. With his strips, Poth connects the speakers with social discourses outside of the narrated story. What Poth did for left-wing counterculture is echoed, for example, in Franziska Becker's work for the women's movement and in Ralph König's for the gay community.

Silly Comics: Walter Moers (1957–)

While Poth's comics, and others like them, display a high point of comics with a critical and moral impetus, the 1980s and 1990s saw the high point of what one might call *Blödel-Comic* (silly comic).[26] Walter Moers stretches the limits of this subgenre. He posits that all figures in the comic are nothing but constellations of freely malleable pop-cultural signs and then applies this to Adolf Hitler in his 1998 strip *Adolf: Äch bin wieder da!!* (I Am Back Again). Moers, who had already proven his ability to be tactless with his *Kleines Arschloch* (Little Asshole) series begun in 1990, leaves no offensive stone unturned. Hitler crawls out of the sewer where he survived the war. He receives therapy from a doctor Furunkel (carbuncle), attacks a Jewish German TV star on camera, kills a Tamagotchi, and then is prescribed sexual intercourse as a cure for his depression. In the brothel for his therapeutic visit, Hitler meets Göring, now a female prostitute after a CIA-financed gender reassignment (as payment for organizing political murders). Before intercourse, while playing Wagner music, Göring gives crack cocaine to Hitler, who later strangles him in a crack-addicted fit. Things go downhill from here. Further characters in the story include Lady Di, Mother Teresa, extraterrestrial sociology students conducting a human breeding experiment, a mad psychiatrist, and a murdered American president. With this serial violation of all social taboos, Moers opens up any area of public life for artistic and satirical treatment. which expands the choice of topics for future German comics writers.

Gerhard Seyfried (1948–)

Gerhard Seyfried became known as the pictorial chronicler of the Berlin *Hausbesetzerszene* (squatter scene) from 1976 until its end, and stands in a class by himself. His work is characterized by detailed, expressive, and inventive drawing as well as keen observation and an exceptional richness of visual and verbal puns and intertextuality. Like Manfred Schmidt, Seyfried refuses to pare down his pictures to focus on the story. But where Schmidt uses excessive commentary, Seyfried seems to visually take in everything from the world around him, passes it through his ironic filter, and produces an enriched pictorial version.[27] He offers practically no internal meta-text to his comics; instead he lets distorted reality speak for itself. The commanding officer of KGB agent Iwan Kagebejewitsch in *Das schwarze Imperium* (The Black Imperium) has many medals dangling from his chest, but among them also other small objects, such as three-pronged Mercedes stars, bottle openers, keys, and room tags. The horrified newspaper readers on the cover of *Let the Bad Times Roll* are shocked by reading the 9.99 German marks "Savings Edition" (Spar-Ausgabe) of the "Job's Post" (Hiobs-Bote) newspaper, which identifies itself as "Dependent, Partisan, Fearful, Obedient" (abhängig, parteilich, furchtsam, gehorsam). The paper's big headline is "Poverty Tax!—[Chancellor] Kohl: Poor must no longer shirk responsibility!" (Armut-Steuer!—Kohl: Arme dürfen sich nicht länger drücken!) with smaller headlines on the back of the paper announcing disasters, which in German all employ alliteration: "Terrible Atrocities!, Gigantic Meltdown!, Poisonous Guck!,

Mean Massacre!, Grotesque Violence!, Despicable Greed, and Creepy Grave Robbery!" (Grässliche Greuel [*sic*]!, Gigantischer GAU!, Giftiger Glibber!, Gemeines Gemetzel!, Groteske Gewalttat!, Garstige Gewinnsucht, Gruseliger Grabraub!; Seyfried & Riemann, 495). This type of irony is clearly located on the meta-textual level, which sets the parameters within which the actors with their illocutionary speech and their deeds must act. It seems no accident that Seyfried's protagonists often find themselves in uncontrollable situations, which intrude into their lives while the world changes around them.[28]

In his most recent graphic novel, *Kraft durch Freunde* (Strength through Friends), evidently a play on words of "Kraft durch Freude" (Strength through Joy), a state-operated leisure organization in Nazi Germany, Seyfried tries to move beyond his own tradition of comic production and develop a serious message with a positive protagonist. Events in the story cause the hero, an engineer who invented a hugely popular personal communication device, to change his mind about NSA-like espionage through consumerist temptation and manipulation. Having worked for the system, he mends his ways and successfully fights it. This is quite different from Seyfried's previous work in which his heroes cannot control their fate and the villains are mere apparatchiks. But the solution seems a little glib since Seyfried simply returns to a heroic mode. What is noticeable is that Seyfried no longer seems to be content with his role as the highly satiric and ironic reflective agent of his contemporary time period. Instead, the comic suggests that he is eager to transcend the German comics tradition.

CONCLUDING THOUGHTS

The birth of the visual narrative mode out of the still continuing illustrative mode was completed in the nineteenth century. In many respects, the *Bildergeschichten* that rely on *extensive internal meta-text* are a transitional form since the images still illustrate a story that develops outside of the pictures, but the narrative text is brought onto the page. In having the elements of visual narratives mutually enhance each other, Wilhelm Busch set a very high standard for graphic narrative, one which his successors did not often reach. Although or perhaps because they are exclusively pictorial, however, the best *Vater und Sohn* stories show a path to deep emotional complexity. For a while, Germans clung to the *Bildergeschichte*, especially as evidenced through the widely spread commercial mascot comics; but the "new" comics that rely on the interplay of pictures and illocutionary text eventually took over. Perhaps because early comic-figures were often imported, most comics took place in a world of their own. This is true for the *Petzi* and Disney universes, but also for *Jimmy das Gummipferd* and traditional adventure comics with their circumscribed topic areas, such as knights, jungle, future, and the Wild West. Since adventure comics can easily fall into the kitsch trap by simply regurgitating cultural material, their realistic drawing style may cause readers to expect the same from any realistically drawn comic. This would place an extra burden on any comics artist who wants to be taken seriously as an artist. Abundant references to contemporary life deliberately intrude into comics with *Nick Knatterton* and then *Asterix*. The subsequent ironic and silly comics have opened up the possibility for comics as a text type for any personal theme. They also play with German themes and German taboos to a point where the requisite knowledge approaches a level we know from the traditional external meta-story. Seyfried's incredible richness of vision introduces social and cultural change as part of the story and has set a new standard. All these developments contribute to the current *Erwartungshorizont* of a German comics reader, meaning that a successful serious graphic novelist would have to negotiate this vast horizon successfully to create the perhaps still elusive Great German Graphic Novel.

NOTES

1. Significantly, German discussions on kitsch often refer to important cultural theorists such as Herman Broch, Theodor W. Adorno, Walter Benjamin and draw a clear line between Kitsch and Hitler and Nazism. See Küpper & Dettmar, 2007. See also Milan Kundera's "Sixty-three words" in *The Art of the Novel*.
2. For details on bibliophilic collection of comics, see Polland 2014.
3. For a brief introduction into this concept, see El-Shany 1997.
4. For attempts at definitions, see Sackmann 2007 and Grünewald 2010.
5. Ole Frahm (2010) seems to have this relationship in mind when he ascribes a unique parodistic semiotic status to the comics genre. "It is my thesis that comics parody the notion of an original and thus of a precedent 'thing outside' of signs. They are a parody on the referentiality of signs. They parody the notion that sign and object should have anything to do with each other." (Meine These ist, dass Comics die Vorstellung eines Originals und damit eines vorgängigen Außerhalb der Zeichen parodieren. Sie sind eine Parodie auf die Referenzialität der Zeichen. Sie parodieren die Vorstellung, dass Zeichen und Gegenstand etwas miteinander zu tun haben sollen; 30). Ascribing such unique semiotic status to the comics genre seems forced. The comic may suggest more effectively than a purely written text that the described reality, in fact, does not exist, but it may also do the opposite. It will often come down to a decision by readers whether they read a comic as referential or quasi-referential.
6. There is a set of 12 paintings by Johann Heinrich Tischbein d. Ä. in the palace of Wilhelmsthal in the vicinity of Kassel, which are based on Fénélon's *Télémaque*. Unfortunately, only one picture is available online: http://www.bildindex.de/obj20042639.html. The Télémaque story was very popular at the time, so that Schiller titled his proto-comic about his friend Körner "Die Avanturen des neuen Telemachs."
7. Grünewald 2000 makes explicit reference to Panovsky, although in his desire to produce an exhaustive description of the "demands for reception of a pictorial story" (Rezeptionsanforderungen der Bildgeschichte; 36, 37–45), he neglects the pre-iconographic levels by repeatedly jumping into intriguingly complex interpretations of pictorial stories or events. This procedure makes sense if one wants to show the unity of all pictorial narration, but it makes it impossible to see the main difference between

traditional illustrations of pre-existing stories and the innovations which the development of comics brought.

8. Grünewald cites a 1789 quotation from Johann Heinrich Meyer and Goethe, which echoes Lessing. This is of interest here because it specifically refers to cycles of paintings: "The artist who takes it upon himself to treat a story as a cycle [. . .] must find a way to choose for his pictures the points that are most significant and most convenient for its representation." (Der Künstler, welcher es übernimmt, eine Geschichte als Zyklus zu behandeln, [. . .] muss zu seinen Bildern die bedeutendsten und für die Darstellung bequemsten Punkte derselben auszusuchen wissen; 2000, 41).

9. While we discuss *Bilderbogen* in the context of pictorial narration, there are many non-narrative specimens. For a more thorough examination of their history in relation to early comics, see Sackmann, 2013. The Wikipedia page for "Bilderbogen" is quite instructive, especially as it also presents non-narrative types: de.wikipedia.org/wiki/Bilderbogen. Hirte 1968 presents a good (but not scholarly) selection of *Bilderbogen*, including a number of narrative ones, e.g., 41, 53, 56, 61, 66, 72.

10. Not all comics need to be narrative, but non-narrative comics are a special case. Texts like McCloud 1993 and Eisner are comics essays. In this genre, the text is all meta-text. The implied author (or even the real author) addresses readers using the pictures as sample material to be commented on. Of course, there are many other ways to enter language into comics panels. I will not count onomatopoetics as language proper, but linguistic elements such as posters, newspapers, etc., that appear within the comic are actually meta-textual since they situate the events in a way that is beyond the illocutionary powers of the "inhabitants" of the comic world (see the discussion of Seyfried at the end of this chapter).

11. On a practical level, we may presume that the title or label was also helpful for the publishers of the *Bilderbogen* for purposes of bookkeeping and managing orders of the prints. For an example of one-word subtitles, see, for example, the Wilhelm Busch sequence of the virtuoso's performance on the piano, where the pictures serve as illustrations of musical terms. http://konkykru.com.

12. Compare, for example: Grünewald 2010 ". . . so people thought in the context of the 'trash and smut debate' in the 1950ies that they had to distinguish between the 'good,' challenging picture story in the tradition of Wilhelm Busch or e.o. plauen and comics, which were considered inferior." (". . . so meinte man im Kontext der "Schund—und—Schmutzdebatte" in den 1950er Jahren die "gute," anspruchsvolle Bildergeschichte à la Wilhelm Busch oder e. o. plauens vom als minderwertig eingestuften Comic unterscheiden zu müssen; 1).

13. Here are the texts of three consecutive pictures in Goez's work that show the preponderance of illocutionary speech [all German spelling original]: (11) "Bland[ine]. Spouse! Don't you see my eyes glisten in the dusk of the moon?" (Bland. Gatte! Siehst nicht in des Monds Dämerung meine Augen funckeln?)
(12) "Don't you feel my longing and love?" (Fülst nicht meine Sehnsucht und Liebe?)
(13) "Len[ardo]: Woe, terror befalls me!" (Len: O weh Schreken überfalt mich!)
Please see Matt Hambro's discussion of the ballad in the present anthology.

14. For parental criticism of Hoffmann, see, for example, Botica.

15. The text can be found at http://gutenberg.spiegel.de/buch/der-struwwelpeter-3070/3.

16. The two Wilhelm Busch texts mentioned can be accessed at "Projekt Gutenberg": http://gutenberg.spiegel.de/buch/max-und-moritz-4137/1; http://gutenberg.spiegel.de/buch/tobias-knopp-4169/6. Sackmann 2012a sees the rogue-boys' tricks genre, which was inspired by *Max und Moritz*, as the most likely direct forerunner of foundational American strips like the "Katzenjammer Kids" because of the significant formal differences between *Max und Moritz* and the US strip (42). Knigge 2009 sees the connection to the US strips mostly in the sadistic Schadenfreude found in Busch's pictorial narratives as well as the later strips (12).

17. The story discussed here can be found at https://de.wikipedia.org/wiki/Vater_und_Sohn; Ohser 2000, 106.

18. An excerpt from the first "Lurchi" book can be found online: http://www.e-pages.dk/nxs/50/.

19. See also the article by Sackmann "Clever Stolz" on the narrative strips of a margarine company.

20. Another extremely successful figure of the German marketing comic is the hedgehog Mecki, namesake of the German word for a crew cut, and long-time mascot of Axel Springer's (since sold) radio and TV program magazine *Hörzu*. The figure was originally developed for a 1938/39 puppet film to entertain schoolchildren, and later German troops. In the post-war chaos, the editor of the new *Hörzu* publication commandeered the figure, but later had to cede non-print rights to the original filmmakers. "Mecki" comic strips appeared in *Hörzu* beginning in 1951. They underwent various changes, including discontinuance and relaunches. Thirteen annual non-comic books with Mecki narratives appeared until 1965. Current reprints of the books and strips are prefaced with a lengthy warning about the stories' unsuitability for children because of their now unacceptable societal values. The following website has an extensive history of the various artists: http://www.hoffmann-world.de/Comics/Thema_Mecki_Historie.htm .For additional samples of Mecki images, see http://www.meckiseite.de/Mecki-Beispielbilder.html. An exhaustive listing and good examples of the merchandising with Mecki products can be found at http://www.meckifan.de/. An informative overview with sample illustrations of the various artists can be found at the site http://www.hoffmann-world.de/Comics/Thema_Mecki_Historie.htm. More information on the figure's early history can be found on the website of the first designer of Mecki, Reinhold Escher: http://www.reinhold-escher.com.

21. Often these series appeared simultaneously so that Wäscher produced several parallel stories. Lehning's pioneering of the Italian "piccolo" format in Germany aided him in telling parallel stories since pages contained only three frames side by side on each of 32 pages, thus reducing the total number of weekly frames to be developed. Like his American and Italian models and/or competitors, Wäscher could tell stories in comics form rather than as a *Bildgeschichte*. His narration is built on picture and illocutionary text more than internal meta-text and he uses speech bubbles rather than text blocks. Wäscher's stories do not transcend adventure models; they are escapist texts that invite sociological rather than literary analysis. Still, they are unpretentious and well told, and increased audience demand for well-told stories ("Comic-Pionier").

22. This episode can be found at http://www.tria-seligenstadt.de/jimmy/geschichte/jimmy-59-01.htm.

23. The two text versions with the picture frames can be found at http://www.petzi-forschung.de/index.html.

24. This concentrated attention to language and setting differentiates Disney comics from Disney's German emulator, Rolf Kauka, a.k.a. the "German Disney." Kauka's *Fix und Foxi* magazine appeared from 1953 into the 1990s with fitful attempts at revival since 1994. Like Disney, Kauka left most day-to-day work to draftsmen often from other countries. One must wonder if this added to the nagging quality problems of the stories. Kauka's use of contemporary language and slang results in language and situations that seem forced and flat. In the story "Der Taxi-Trick" (1970, no. 50, 28–30), character Lupo walks from his house, complaining, "Terrible, this footwork! Outright tiring!" (Furchtbar, diese Fußarbeit! Direkt anstrengend!) To call walking "Fußarbeit" is as strained as Lupo's comment when a car approaches, "In such a car it's easier to walk" (In so einem Auto läuft sich's leichter). Lupo wants to earn riches as a taxi driver, but is cheated by a customer. He then decides to also cheat (using the "Taxi-Trick"), but is found out because he is too stupid. While *Fix und Foxi* is said to have sold up to 400,000 booklets per week in its heyday. Stories such as "Der Taxi Trick" are too reminiscent of fabliaux and chapbooks to suggest that such numbers were sustainable.

25. A sample of an *Asterix* page may be found here: http://www.asterix.com/la-collection/first/05de.jpg.

26. An additional example is the *Werner* series. The book by Brösel (Rötger Feld-mann) had a press run of well over 500,000 and even developed a cult following. Today, the "Werner" website advertises comic albums, beer, animated films, and mer-chandise. *Werner* drops all pretenses to seriousness. Reading *Werner* is a mad-cap anthropological field trip to a boozy small-business subculture of motorcycle hot-rodders in northern Germany. Brösel's comics and films apply wild anarchic humor in order to highlight the hero's copious beer drinking, motorcycle tuning, and troubles with the police, without any pedagogical aim or pretense of enlightenment. While Poth casts a light on the internal contradictions of a generation, Werner mostly asserts his freedom by refusing to participate in public life altogether.

27. For some samples of Seyfried's approach, see his website at http://gerhard seyfried.de.

28. Seyfried is quite closely connected with the tradition of *Wimmelbilder*, a type of "busy picture" that may go back to Hieronymus Bosch and Dutch/Flemish genre painting (Hill 2010). The pictures are somewhat similar to the American *Where's Waldo*, but the idea is to let one's eyes wander across many unrelated scenes which all take place in one panoramic picture, such as a cityscape or a beach, and to discover many suggested stories and events of, for example, people shopping, playing, having car accidents, or playing tricks on each other. The genre is very popular in German-speaking countries both in home and school contexts. The modern founder of this genre is Ali Mitgutsch, who published his first *Wimmelbuch* in 1968. Rotraut Susanne Berner added a narrative element to this by having some of the same people pursuing actions from one panoramic picture to the next. For example, someone gets on the bus and is seen riding the bus in a different part of town in the next picture, meeting someone on the bus in the third, and so on. A different type of narrative develops in the "urban development comics" of Jörg Müller (1974, 1976), who shows dystopian modernizing changes in the same cityscape or landscape through "snapshots" from the same perspective over two decades. The German reader of graphic literature is likely used to patiently scrutinizing larger splash panels for significant details, which, in the case of Seyfried, add to the ironic incongruity of the world he is portraying. The serious *Wimmelbilder* shift the perspective of action in similar ways as Seyfried. The world changes around us, and we must deal with the change.

REFERENCES

Arnold, Heinz Ludwig, and Andreas C. Knigge, eds. *Comics, Mangas, Graphic Novels, Text + Kritik* Sonderband. München: Richard Boorberg, 2009.

Barks, Carl. "Die drei dreckigen Ducks," *Donald*, Entenhausen Edition, Vol. 3. Berlin: Egmont,15–25.

Becker, Franziska. *Mein feministischer Alltag 1.* Köln: Emma, 1980.

Berner, Rotraut Susanne. *Frühlingswimmelbuch.* Hildesheim: Gerstenberg, 2004.

Beyer, Gemmo. "Mecki," http://www.meckiseite.de/. Accessed November 2015.

Botica, Melania 2009. "Heinrich Hoffmann: Ein Irrenarzt sorgt für Furore." 13 June 2009. Web. 15 December 2015. http://www.focus.de/familie/kinderspiele/medien/ein-irrenarzt-sorgt-fuer-furore-heinrich-hoffmann_id_1747597.html.

Brösel [Feldmann, Rötger]. *Werner - Eiskalt.* Kiel: Semmelverlach, 1985.

Busch, Wilhelm. *Sämtliche Werke und eine Auswahl der Skizzen und Gemälde in zwei Bänden* [1959]. Ed. Rolf Hochhuth. Vol. 2: *Was beliebt, ist auch erlaubt.* München: Bertelsmann, 1982.

"Comic-Pionier Hansrudi Wäscher: 'Er hat das Tempo der Mangas vorweggenom-men'" 18 July 2011. Web. 15 December 2015. http://www.spiegel.de/kultur/literatur/comic-pionier-hansrudi-waescher-er-hat-das-tempo-der-mangas-vorweggenomme n-a-770154.html.

"Comics: Schwermetall für Erwachsene." *Der Spiegel.* 13 September 1982. Web. 15 November 2015. http://www.spiegel.de/spiegel/print/d-14352234.html.

Dolle-Weinkauff, Bernd, Sylvia Asmus, and Brita Eckert. *Comics Made in Germany: 60 Jahre Comics aus Deutschland: Eine Ausstellung der Deutschen Nationalbibliothek Frankfurt am Main und des Instituts für Jugendbuchforschung der Johann Wolfgang Goethe-Universität Frankfurt am Main*. Gesellschaft für das Buch, Band 10. Wiesbaden: Harrassowitz, 2008.

Dolle-Weinkauff, Bernd. *Comics: Geschichte einer populären Literaturform in Deutschland seit 1945*. Weinheim: Beltz, 1990.

Dow, James R. "Hans Naumann's gesunkenes Kulturgut and primitive Gemeinschaftskultur." *Journal of Folklore Research* 51.1 (2014): 49–100.

Eder, Barbara, Elisabeth Klar, and Ramón Reichert, eds. *Theorien des Comic: Ein Reader*. Bielefeld: Transcript, 2011.

Eisner, Will. *Comics and Sequential Art: Principles and Practices from the Legendary Cartoonist*. New York: Norton, 2008.

El-Shany, Hasan 1997. "Gesunkenes Kulturgut." *Folklore: An Encyclopedia of Beliefs, Customs, Tales, Music, and Art*. Volume 1, ed. Thomas A. Green. Santa Barbara, CA: ABC-CLIO, 1997. 419–22.

Foster, Harold Rudolph. *Prinz Eisenherz: Auswahlband*. Bonn: Bocola, 2013.

Frahm, Ole. *Die Sprache des Comics*. Ed. Jan Frederik Bandel. Fundus-Bücher vol. 179, Hamburg: Pilo Fine Arts, 2010.

"Gans, Grobian" 1970. *Die Ducks: Psychogramm einer Sippe* [1970]. Reinbek: Rowohlt, 1972.

Goez, Joseph Franz v. 1783. *Versuch einer zalreichen [sic] Folge leidenschaftlicher Entwürfe für empfindsame Kunst- und Schauspielfreunde: Lenardo und Blandine* (Augsburg 1783). http://daten.digitale-sammlungen.de/bsb00065526/image_1. Accessed November 2015.

Grünewald, Dietrich. "Das Prinzip Bildgeschichte." n.d. Web. 15 November 2015. http://www.comicforschung.de/tagungen/06nov/06nov_gruenewald.pdf.

Grünewald, Dietrich. *Comics. Grundlagen der Medienkommunikation*. Tübingen: Niemeyer, 2000.

Hansen, Carla, and Vilhem Hansen. *Petzi: Die gesammelten Reiseabenteuer 1951–1955*. Hamburg: Carlsen, 2013.

Heine, Matthias. "Der Kauka-Effekt." 22 March 2005. Web. 15 December 2015. http://www.welt.de/kultur/article559486/Der-Kauka-Effekt.html.

Hill, Darjan. *Die Wiederentdeckung des Wimmelbildes—von "wo ist Walter" bis Breughel*. Hochschule für Gestaltung und Kunst, Basel, 2010. Web. 15 November 2015. http://issuu.com/darjanhil/docs/hil_wimmelbilder_final.

Hirte, Werner, ed. *Die Schwiegermutter und das Krokodil: 111 bunte Bilderbogen für alle Land- und Stadtbewohner soweit der Himmel blau ist*. Berlin: Eulenspiegel, 1968.

Hoffmann, Heinrich. *Der Struwwelpeter oder lustige Geschichten und drollige Bilder für Kinder von 3 bis 6 Jahren* [1845], Frankfurter Originalausgabe. Frankfurt: Loewe, n.d.

Jauss, Hans Robert. *Literaturgeschichte als Provokation*. Frankfurt: Suhrkamp, 1970.

Knigge, Andreas C. "Zeichen—Welten: Der Kosmos der Comics." *Comics, Mangas, Graphic Novels, Text + Kritik* Sonderband. Ed. Heinz Ludwig Arnold and Andreas C. Knigge. München: Richard Boorberg, 2009. 5–34.

Kohlsaat, Roland. *Jimmy das Gummipferd: Die Abenteuer von Julio und Jimmy*. Oldenburg: Lappan, 2003.

König, Ralf. *Der bewegte Mann*. Rororo Tomate. Hamburg: Rowohlt, 1987.

Kundera, Milan. "Key Words, Problem Words, Words I Love." *New York Times*, 6 March 1988. Web. 15 November 2015. http://www.nytimes.com/1988/03/06/books/key-words-problem-words-words-i-love.html?emc=eta1&pagewanted=2.

Küpper, Thomas, and Ute Dettmar, eds. *Kitsch*. Stuttgart: Reclam, 2007.

Lessing, Gotthold Ephraim. *Laocoon*. Trans. William Ross. London: J. Ridgway & Sons, 1836.

Lurchis Abenteuer: Das lustige Salamanderbuch. Band 1–8. Mit frdl. Genehmigung der Salamander GmbH. Esslingen: Esslinger Verlag, 2009–2012.

Mahne, Nicole. *Transmediale Erzähltheorie: Eine Einführung.* Göttingen: Vandenhoeck, 2007.

McCloud, Scott. *Understanding Comics: The Invisible Art* [1993]. Harper Perennial. New York: Harper, 2011.

Mecki-Gesammelte Abenteuer Jahrgang 1958. Esslingen: Esslinger Verlag, 2009.

Mitgutsch, Ali. *Mein schönstes Wimmelbuch.* Ravensburg: Ravensburger, 2015.

Moers, Walter. *Adolf: Äch bin wieder da!!* Frankfurt: Eichborn, 1998.

Müller, Jörg. *Hier fällt ein Haus, dort steht ein Kran und ewig droht der Baggerzahn oder Die Veränderung der Stadt.* Aarau and Frankfurt: Sauerländer, 1976.

Müller, Jörg. *Alle Jahre wieder saust der Presslufthammer nieder oder Die Veränderung der Landschaft.* Aarau and Frankfurt: Sauerländer, 1973.

Neyer, Hans Joachim. "Die Bildgeschichten *Vater und Sohn.*" Erich Ohser. *Politische Kartikaturen, Zeichnungen, Illustrationen und alle Bildgeschichten von* Vater und Sohn. Konstanz: Südverlag, 2000. 83–85.

Ohser, Erich / e.o. plauen. *Politische Kartikaturen, Zeichnungen, Illustrationen und alle Bildgeschichten von Vater und Sohn.* Konstanz: Südverlag, 2000.

Pannor, Stefan. "Comic-Neuauflage: *Fix und Foxi* vollfettkrass." 26 October 2005. Web. 15 Decmeber 2015. http://www.spiegel.de/kultur/literatur/comic-neuauflage-fix-und-foxi-vollfettkrass-a-381720.html.

Petzi-Forschung. http://www.petzi-forschung.de/petzi_textversionen.html. 15 November 2015.

Platthaus, Andreas. "Entenhausener Dramaturgie: Wie uns Comics illusionieren." *Comics, Mangas, Graphic Novels. Text + Kritik.* Ed. Heinz Ludwig Arnold and Andreas C. Knigge. Edition Text + Kritik. München: Boorberg, 2009. 57–73.

Platthaus, Andreas. *Die 101 wichtigsten Fragen: Comics und Manga.* Becksche Reihe 1862. München: Beck, 2008.

Platthaus, Andreas. *Im Comic vereint: Eine Geschichte der Bildergeschichte.* Insel Taschenbuch 2724. Frankfurt: Insel, 2000.

Polland, Günther. *1. Allgemeiner Deutscher Comic Preiskatalog 2015.* Wien: Günther Polland, 2014.

Pommeranz-Liedtke, Gerhard. *Der graphische Zyklus von Max Klinger bis zur Gegenwart: Ein Beitrag zur Entwicklung der deutschen Graphik von 1880 bis 1955.* Berlin: Deutsche Akademie der Künste, 1956.

Poth, Chlodwig. *Mein progressiver Alltag.* Hamburg: Rowohlt, 1975.

Sackmann, Eckart "Bonnhalla am Rhein — Asterix als Politklamauk." *Deutsche Comicforschung,* 3 (2007), (Hildesheim: comic+, 2006): 128–39.

Sackmann, Eckart 2012 a. "Das 19. Jahrhundert — vom Bilderbogen zur Comic Section." *Deutsche Comicforschung,* 9 (2013), (Hildesheim: comic+, 2012), 23–46.

Sackmann, Eckart 2012 b. "Erich Ohsers 'Vater und Sohn' — eine Ikone aus neutraler Sicht." *Deutsche Comicforschung,* 9 (2013), (Hildesheim: comic+, 2012), 63–79.

Sackmann, Eckart 2012 c. "Clever Stolz Bildgeschichten — der Comic zum Margarinewürfel." *Deutsche Comicforschung,* 9 (2013), (Hildesheim: comic+, 2012), 93–101.

Sackmann, Eckart, Thomas Vité 2012. "Zauberer und Zeichenkünstler: Walter Sperling alias Tagrey." *Deutsche Comicforschung,* 9 (2013), (Hildesheim: comic+, 2012), 52–62.

Sackmann, Eckart. "Comic. Kommentierte Definition." *Deutsche Comicforschung,* 4 (2008), (Hildesheim: comic+, 2007), 6–9.

Schikowski, Klaus. *Der Comic: Geschichte, Stile, Künstler.* Hamburg: Carlsen, 2015.

Schmidt, Manfred. *Nick Knatterton: Aufgezeichnet von Manfred Schmidt: Alle aufregenden Abenteuer des berühmten Meisterdetektivs.* Oldenburg: Lappan, 2007. See also: http://www.pnn.de/mediathek/714295/2/www.pnn.de/digital/3/.

Schmitz-Emans, Monika, and Christian A. Bachmann. *Literatur-Comics: Adaptionen und Transformationen der Weltliteratur.* Linguae & Litterae 10. Berlin: De Gruyter, 2012.

Schnorr von Carolsfeld, Julius [1860]. *Die Bibel in Bildern. 240 Darstellungen, erfunden und auf Holz gezeichnet.* 2nd reprint of ed. by Leipzig, Wigand, 1860. Zürich: Theologischer Verlag, 1989.

Seyfried, Gerhard 2008. *Die Werke — Alle!* Frankfurt: Verlag, 2001.
Seyfried, Gerhard and Ziska Riemann. *Die Comics — Alle!* Frankfurt: Verlag, 2001.
Töpffer, Rodolphe 1839. *Les amours de Mr. Vieux Bois.* Geneva: no pub. http://archive.
    lib.msu.edu/DMC/Comic%20Art/amoursvieuxbois.pdf. 20 November 2015. Trans-
    lation: *The Adventures of Mr. Obadiah Oldbuck.* New York: Wilson & Co. 184ff. http://
    www.dartmouth.edu/~library/digital/collections/books/ocn259708589/.

II

GERMAN CULTURAL EDUCATION

THREE

"Nothing but Exclamation Points?"

Comics in the Bavarian Academic High School

Jens Kußmann

Imagine finding on your kitchen table a German textbook left by one of your children who attends *Gymnasium* (academic high school) in Munich. You, a comic enthusiast, flip through the book and wonder why it contains nothing on comics or comic theory. Pure chance? In 2013, inspired by this question of inclusion and representation of comics in German educational materials, I analyzed all the textbooks that the *Staatsministerium für Bildung und Kultus, Wissenschaft und Kunst* (State Ministry of Sciences, Research and the Arts) accredited for German classes in Bavarian high schools.[1] The findings are not surprising. Nearly all of the publishing companies either completely neglected to include graphic literature, or used it only as an object of comparison, for example, to explain cutting techniques for film production. In the rare case that a textbook treated graphic literature as a medium in its own right, it was done with insufficient depth and with a striking deficiency of comics expertise on the part of the textbook authors. This essay aggregates, critically evaluates, and contextualizes the findings of the above-mentioned textbook analysis. Additionally, it outlines current comics research by German educators, and finally speculates on reasons for the current lack of comic inclusion in German textbooks.

DIDACTIC ASSESSMENT OF COMICS:
A BRIEF HISTORICAL OVERVIEW

Similar to the general societal disdain for comics in Germany in the 1950s and 1960s, a widespread dismissal of comics also characterized pedagogical discussions at that time.[2] Among many other assertions that had circulated, three key arguments repeatedly emerged. First, reading comics inhibits the development of advanced reading skills, which could result in illiteracy; second, comic book readers lose their ability to assess reality; and third, reading comic books places children at risk for psychological damage and criminality (Lange 40). Particularly prevalent at German high schools in the 1950s and 1960s was the "Bekämpfung der Comics," or combating of comics, a stated aim of Robert Ulshöfer, whose *Methodik des Deutschunterrichts* (Methodology of German Instruction) enjoyed widespread influence for many years among German teaching professionals. Ulshöfer did indeed include comics in his instructional materials for the fifth to the seventh grades in the context of an *Introduction to the Basic Questions of Literary Assessment in Fifth to Seventh Grade* (*Einführung in elementare Fragen der literarischen Wertung im 5. bis 7. Schuljahr*). As part of Ulshöfer's curriculum, teachers did have students assess comics, but merely as a method for developing a sense of good literary taste by examining inferior texts such as comics. The point, according to Ulshöfer, was to have the students recognize the "tastelessness, inferiority, falseness of comics" (das Geschmacklose, Minderwertige, Unwahre der Comics; 31). All total there were "nearly 200 pamphlet-type comic publications of varying quality in circulation" (annähernd 200 recht ungleichwertige, zum großen Teil pamphletische Veröffentlichungen; Baumgärtner 25) at a time when critics vehemently asserted the low literary quality of comics. A generalized fear of eroding cultural values, "along with defending the social status quo and resistance against the unknown" (verbunden mit der Verteidigung des Gewohnten und dem Widerstand gegen das Unbekannte; Müller 194), typified the critical discourse of the time.

Negative attitudes toward comics gradually began to change, but estimations of when exactly that turning point occurred vary according to the professional perspectives and the criteria used by those making the assessments. In the mid-1960s, general prejudice against comics began to wane, and professionals in literary studies, if hesitantly, viewed comics as part of an expanded definition of literature, or a literary genre that could be analyzed as such. Consequently, formal German instruction could no longer totally elide this general tendency. Representatives in the field of literary study subsequently called for changes to the pejorative view of what many critics called trivial literature, and encouraged instructors at the time to embrace the type of literature that children and youth actually enjoyed reading: a category to which comics undoubtedly belong. It must be mentioned that the inclusive attitude toward comics, however, seems to have been politically motivated in order to push for a *Demokratisierung des Literaturunterrichts* (democratization of literature instruction; Burgdorf 70).

In 1973, Jutta Wermke published, *What are COMICS Good For?!* (*Wozu COMICS gut sind?!*), one of the first scholarly studies about comics in German instruction. In her study she compiles and analyzes various professional opinions on the valuation of the medium and its pedagogical application, and also develops arguments against two chief trends. For these reasons, her work led to heated debate among her contemporary educational professionals. First, her study argues against the concept of "aesthetic education," the supporters of which subscribed to a very narrow definition of art to advance the theory that comics can have detrimental effects on readers' personal character. Second, she challenges the popular ideologically critical assertion that comics, along with all other pop literature, have negative consequences for society because they can hinder free individual development. Arguing against these claims, Wermke makes the case in her study for breaking down normative theories and prejudices against comics, and calls for an expanded understanding of what constitutes literature (Frederking 2008, 19). Indeed, Wermke's study enjoyed enormous wide-ranging appeal. Her dissertation sold over 10,000 copies in four print runs, and researchers continue to cite her groundbreaking work to this day (Frederking 2008, 10). Nonetheless, a number of more conservative German instructors maintained their negative views; and even advocates of comics could not quite agree on the proper incorporation of comics into their instruction (Baumgärtner 28–29). Subsequent years and decades saw the expansion of the 1970s paradigm shift; and many additional pedagogical and scholarly works were published that treated the constructive and positive use of comics in the German classroom. Moreover, researchers further attempted to dismantle fears and prejudices with regard to comics for leisure reading and in the classroom.[3]

Today, most German instructors, as well as researchers in the field of children's and young adult literature, advocate for incorporating books that are popular with students as an effective first step in guiding them toward an objective and reflective discussion and analysis of comic works (Lange 40). Speaking to this popularity, research conducted during the time of the theoretical discussions had already demonstrated that "comics already had, despite reservations, secured a place in children's and youth literature" (der Comic [hat] sich in die Kinder- und Jugendliteratur, entgegen allen Vorbehalten, schon lange eingeschrieben; Roeder 2). Over the course of the last three decades, actively exploring the medium-specific interplay of text and image in graphic literature through practical hands-on approaches (*Handlungs- und Produktionsorientierung*) has become a pedagogical focus. A variety of methods and procedures has been discussed and field-tested, including circumscription, altering accompanying text, sketching a picture to match or correspond to speech bubble text, writing based on a visual prompt, or designing original comics, to name just a few field-tested possibilities. Lange also identifies specific groups of activities that go beyond simple "reading," such as analyzing content, assessing the form, learning about production and distribution of graphic texts in Germany, and reflecting upon the positive and negative attitudes toward comics and their origins (40). At present, it can be stated that comics, along with film, undoubtedly belong to an "inventory" of pedagogical research and practical application. Articles about graphic literature can be found in nearly all current publications that deal with German pedagogy, the topic is widely discussed at academic conferences, and graphic literature is mentioned increasingly in texts that survey German-language pedagogy, as well as introductory German-language textbooks.[4]

While preconceived notions and fears concerning comics among instructors have become less common, they continue to be propagated to some extent. Readers can still find headlines like the following in professional magazines that ironically play with these prejudices: "Harr! Harr! Comics in Children's and Young Adult Literature" (Harr! Harr! Comic in Kinder- und Jugendliteratur; Roeder 2), or "Help! My child only reads comics" (Hilfe, mein Kind liest nur Comics; Zinke 46). In response to this "negative press," the German comics scene offers the sound advice that educators must first learn and understand the rules and mechanisms of comics in order to fully recognize the potential of the graphic narrative form for classroom use (Schikowski 15). Often teachers who use comics in their instruction do so "more out of a fondness for the medium . . . , and less because they possess a deep understanding of it" (eher aus Sympathie zum Medium heraus . . . , als aus einem tiefen Verständnis desselben; Dinter). Theoretical pedagogical discussions and concrete designs for lesson plans often disregard the fact that instructors do not always have an adequate background in critically reading and teaching comics. Michael Staiger remarks much more categorically that, in spite of a fully executed expansion of the term "narrative" beyond the purely verbal, instructors still plan lessons using "visually dominant stories . . . at best as tools for media criticism" ([v]isuell dominierte Erzählungen . . . allenfalls als Gegenstände von Medienkritik; Staiger 41), as opposed to using them as building blocks.

The fact that the acknowledgement of comics as legitimate literary objects is still largely lacking in Germany begs the question to what degree comics have actually "arrived" in German academic high school classrooms. The following examination of current textbooks used in Bavarian secondary schools at the *Unterstufe* level (grades five to seven)[5] may shed some light on the type of publications that German textbook companies currently provide, and how or to what degree the authors of those books esteem graphic literature.

COMICS IN GERMAN TEXTBOOKS
FOR THE *UNTERSTUFE* (LOWER GRADES)

What follows is a summary of and commentary on the results of the examination of all six textbook series with regard to their treatment of comics. The analysis encompasses language arts, reading, as well as combined language arts and reading books approved for the lower grades by the *Bayerische Staatsministerium für Unterricht und Kultus* (Bavarian State Ministry for Education and Cultural Affairs).

"Kombi-Buch Deutsch. Neue Ausgabe" Series (C. C. Buchner Schulbuchverlag)

The books in this series for fifth graders do not address comics. The authors mention picture stories, but only as a prompt to compose a written story from a wordless comic. By contrast, a cursory glance at the cover of the series' sixth grade textbook gives the distinct and correct impression that the authors have in fact paid some attention to comics. A photograph of Uderzo and Goscinny, the creators of the *Asterix* comic series, adorns the front cover along with their characters Asterix, Obelix, and Idefix. In the subsection "Comics: How Stories Are Told with Pictures" (Comics: Wie sich mit Bildern Geschichten erzählen lassen), comics, both as narrative form and medium, become the subject of instruction in its own right (45–49). Eighteen questions and exercises based on excerpts from the comic series *Asterix, Spirou und Fantasio*, as well as an untitled Greek comic, are designed to make the world of comics accessible to students. Here is a sampling of questions related to the activities:

- What visual evidence suggests who the good guys are and who the bad guys are in the *Asterix* comic?
- At first glance, what distinguishes Asterix from Spirou?
- What clues do the comic pictures offer about their protagonists' characteristics?
- What effect does the choice of particular details in various pictures have?

In additional exercises, the students must write a fact sheet about the characters, describe a bird pictured in *Spirou* from the perspective of an ornithologist, transform the *Spirou* comic into a written narrative, and determine the artistic perspective of all the panels. The textbook provides a series of follow-up activities as a way to check and ensure the acquisition of skills (*Überprüfen und Sichern*).

- Fill in the speech bubbles of a comic from which the words have been removed.
- Consider the differences between conventional narrative and narrative located in speech bubbles.

- Identify the characteristics of a fable as displayed in the above-mentioned Greek comic.
- Clarify the artistic techniques of an anthropomorphic rendition of the wolf in the Greek comic.
- Detail the medium-specific possibilities for the visual representations of physical and mental strength and weakness.
- Provide reasons for the assertion that, despite his appearance, Asterix is immediately recognized as a "Starker" (strong guy).

A box that lists key terms mentioned in the exercises, such as perspective, picture details, and text elements, is situated between the questions, exercises, and comic panels. Unlike the sixth grade edition discussed here, the new edition of seventh grade text does not include graphic literature at all.

"Kombi-Buch Deutsch" (C. C. Buchner Schulbuchverlag)

Although new editions of textbooks are published, older editions may still remain on the list of classroom resources approved by the Bavarian State Ministry of Sciences, Research and the Arts.[6] For example, the 2009 edition of *Kombi-Buch Deutsch,* still in use, is very similar to the 2010 edition, yet with some differences. This series features comics in the materials for sixth grade only. In the subsection analogous to the one discussed above, there are seven instead of eighteen questions and exercises. Excerpts from *Asterix* are used in this edition as well. Unlike in the new edition, however, assignments in the old editions prompt students to think about the differences between picture stories and comics, and include an exercise that involves using a stopwatch to compare the time needed to read a comic with the time needed to read a conventional narrative (27–29). The glossary entry for "Comics" in the old edition is much more expansive than the new one in that word and picture are designated as juxtaposed parts that contribute equally to meaning:

> The pictures tell the story, express feelings, and direct the reader's interpretation. The texts can be narratives in frames or panels, characters speak in speech or thought bubbles. In addition, words designating sound or exclamations appear directly in the picture. In early examples of this relatively new text type, funny characters appeared in humorous stories. More recently, exciting adventures with realistic characters are also being drawn.

> Die Bilder erzählen die Geschichte, bringen Gefühle zum Ausdruck und lenken die Deutung des Lesers. Texte können Erzählertexte in Kästen sein, Figuren reden in Sprech- oder Gedankenblasen. Daneben gibt es auch noch Geräuschwörter oder Ausrufe direkt im Bild. Am Anfang dieser relativ jungen Textsorte traten nur lustige Figuren in

komischen Geschichten auf. In neuerer Zeit werden auch spannende
Abenteuer mit realistisch erscheinenden Figuren gezeichnet. (350)

In the new edition, however, the authors provide a very much truncated definition of comics in the glossary: "Comics are a text type in which pictures and words are linked" (Comics sind eine Textart, in der Bilder und Texte miteinander verbunden sind; 47).

"Das Buchner Lesebuch" (C.C. Buchner Schulbuchverlag)

In this textbook series by the same publisher, the materials for fifth grade do not treat comics extensively, but they do include four panels from E. O. Plauen's (written as e.o. Plauen in the text) wordless picture stories *Father and Son* (*Vater und Sohn*). The exercises are relatively limited, directing learners to provide captions for the pictures, to retell the pictured story in their own words, and to sketch a situation similar to one shown in the cartoon. An additional exercise urges an examination of the artist's name choice (128); and would prompt students to discover that E. O. Plauen is a pseudonym for the comic strip's author and illustrator, Erich Ohser, who was not permitted to publish during the time of the Nazi regime because of his political engagement. He later received permission to publish, but in a very limited capacity and under the condition that he would remain removed from politics.[7] This critical thinking activity demonstrates the value comics can have for more profound cultural and historical inquiry.

C. C. Buchner Press pursues comics in more depth in the materials developed for sixth grade. In connection with a two-page reprint from Hergé's *Tintin: Destination Moon* (*Tim und Struppi: Reiseziel Mond*), the textbook's authors have included a short text about the comic series, a definition of comics, and three exercises (124–26). In addition to providing a character description of a comic figure, students are asked to regard the visual methods used for representing emotion, as well as ways that word and picture cooperate in making meaning. The short definition points to the etymology of the term "comic" and the characteristics of the sequential narrative method, and also references speech balloons and onomatopoeia.

Another chapter from this textbook contains an additional comic excerpt that spans two pages, this time from Uderzos and Goscinny's *Asterix the Gaul* (*Asterix der Gallier*) followed by a short informational passage about the series and six corresponding exercises (188–90). One of the exercises takes a historical angle by asking what the Romans have to do with modern-day France? Another assignment directs the students to find out whether an edition of *Asterix* exists in their local German dialects, for example, Bavarian or Swabian, depending on the students' origins. Another prompt requires the students to take a closer look at the drawings and to examine how the comic visually represents the Romans and the Gauls. The textbook also provides some hands-on practice with comics, having students write a version of the beginning of the comic narrative based on the pictures. The two remaining exercises are standard: compare the comic with the description on page 130; and produce a short character description of one of the characters.

The seventh grade reader also contains comics, in this case an eight-panel episode from Dik Browne's *Hager the Horrible* (*Häger, der Schreckliche*). Only the first of four exercises, however, addresses comics as a medium, and prompts students to explain the joke contained in the comic. The remaining three exercises refer to Scandinavian stereotypes, personal travel stories, and famous Scandinavians (168). Aside from these exercises, the authors only mention comics in the glossary. Contrary to what one might expect, this edition does not provide the same definition found in the glossary of the sixth grade book. Instead, it contains the following notably shorter and markedly less nuanced version:

> Comics: Comics are a series of pictures combined with words. Picture and word should complement one another. Either the text is found outside the pictures, or it is contained within the comic inside speech bubbles. Accordingly, the text can only be short and succinct. This means that a comic narrative cannot contain a lot of detail. Oftentimes the text is reduced to simple interjections: *Wow! Crash! Boom!*

> Comics: Die Comics sind Bilderserien in Verbindung mit Texten. Bild und Text sollten sich gegenseitig ergänzen. Der Text steht entweder außerhalb der Bilder oder er ist in Form von Sprechblasen eingebaut. Der Text kann jeweils nur knapp und kurz sein. Dies bedeutet, dass in den Comics die Erzählung nicht auf Feinheiten eingehen kann. Oft ist der Text zu bloßen Ausrufen geschrumpft: *Wow! Crash! Bum!* (192)

"Deutschbuch. Sprach- und Lesebuch" (Cornelsen Verlag)

Starting with the fifth grade materials, Cornelsen Press addresses comics in its *Language and Reading Book* (*Sprach- und Lesebuch*), but not with the objective of studying comics as visual art. Instead, the authors address comics as part of the chapter "Telling Stories with Prompts" (Wir erzählen Geschichten nach Vorgaben). One exercise requires students to pay close attention to what is said in each speech bubble and then compose dialogue tags, which are the "he said" or "she replied" that appear in narrative, for an excerpt from a 1976 *Asterix* story (78). This exercise requires that students work with the vocabulary of comics because they have to understand both the textual and pictorial designs found in the medium in order to complete the activity. The rest of the activities have nothing to do with comics. The text for seventh grade contains some comics, but they primarily serve as foils to illustrate other topics. For example, a short comic about Robin Hood is used in order to demonstrate photographic depth of field and camera perspective (252–54). Clearly, this activity revolves around the storytelling techniques of film as opposed to comics. Materials for seventh grade do not include comics.

"Deutsch Gymnasium. Bayern" (Schroedel Verlag)

The textbook in this series for fifth grade does not mention graphic literature. Materials for the subsequent school year also do not highlight comics as a discrete subject of study, although the sixth grade book does include a few panels for use as a media comparison to film. Excerpts from *Asterix in England* (*Asterix bei den Briten*) are juxtaposed with the storyboards from the animated cartoon of the same name in order to introduce film terms such as "perspective" and "cut." In addition, students are asked to bring comics to class and compare them with their corresponding cinematic versions (178). In the new edition for seventh grade, the book's authors employ comics in order to motivate students' engagement with particular parts of speech by prompting students to answer questions about the use of adverbs or adverbial clauses in the comic series (87). As the nature of this exercise suggests, it has very little to do with comic art or comics as a discrete discipline.

REVIEW OF THE FINDINGS

The sixth grade textbook in the popular (meaning sales were high enough to warrant printing another edition) series *Kombi-Buch Deutsch Neue Ausgabe* is the only one that takes a serious approach to teaching and learning with comics. On a very positive note, students work with three different examples of graphic literature, which speaks to the pluralism and variety of the current comics market. The text also devotes eighteen tasks to working with comics; and the exercises actually cover key concepts within comics studies by focusing equally on graphic and verbal components. With a hands-on approach and production-oriented activities, these texts would seem to be on the cutting edge. Despite that apparent progress, however, the texts still largely treat the art of comic narration and the variety of comic types selectively and stereotypically. Regrettably, the books leave out more meaningful activities such as the interaction of word and picture in favor of, to a large extent, meaningless activities such as "Describe the birds from the perspective of a bird watcher." The teacher's manual appears downright amateur: it does not even include common and accepted terms used in comics studies, such as *Denkblase* (thought bubble) or panel. Instead, the authors use invented and literal terms "circle with little bubbles" (*Kreis mit Bläschen*) or "little boxes" (*Kästchen*) to refer to panels (15).

The majority of the activities designed for the 2010 edition mirror those in the earlier *Kombi-Buch Deutsch* textbook from 2009. The assignments situated under the heading "How Comics Tell Stories" (Wie Comics erzählen), however, must be reviewed separately. The instructions for a partner activity read: "Read the two comic pages and time each other with a stopwatch to see how long it takes. Share your average time with the group" (Lest euch die beiden Comicseiten durch und messt partnerweise mit einer Stoppuhr, wie lange ihr dafür benötigt. Anschließend könnt ihr in der Klasse die Durchschnittslesezeit ermitteln; 29). Another exercise directs students to "Compare the time it takes to read a comic with the time it takes to read a conventional text and explain the difference" (Vergleiche das Lesetempo im Comic mit der Zeit, die das Lesen eines Erzähltextes erfordert, und erkläre den Unterschied; 29). This pair of activities calls to mind the statements and publications from the 1950s and 1960s that contributed to an embittered crusade against trashy literature, or *Schundliteratur*. They endeavored to defend "high" literature, for which one needed particular effort and concentration, and argued against the presumably trivial and textually stunted comics.[8] The authors of these assignments ignore the fact that the time needed to read comics increases immensely when one has learned and continues to practice the art of reading graphic literature. The textbook activity makes comics seem like a kind of fast-food literature. In other words, the competitive atmosphere created by the stopwatch incites students to race through the text rather than to take their time reading the cooperative meanings of word and picture.

Buchner Lesebuch 6 succeeds at calling students' attention to visual techniques, and in particular interactions between word and picture. It limits itself, however, to an inadequate evaluation of how artists represent emotions. Moreover, the choice of excerpts from *Tim und Struppi* and *Asterix* points up an antiquated understanding of the medium and underscores a lack of awareness of the newer and the most current groundbreaking German-language graphic publications.[9] Of course, *Tim und Struppi* and *Asterix*, begun in 1929 and 1959, respectively, have become classics in Germany and would be familiar to many students. But the textbook authors have indeed missed an opportunity here to introduce students to newer German-language works and to broaden students' "comic-horizon" with as yet lesser-known but nonetheless high-quality works, which have incidentally garnered their share of serious scholarly attention. The accompanying teacher's guide for *Lesebuch 6* reveals that the textbook authors do not discuss the classic series' relevance for comics studies. For example, the manual could, but does not, mention Hergé's unique position as an important trailblazer of European comics by way of his *"ligne claire"* (clear line), referring to his distinctive style of drawing.

For the most part, the glossary entry in *Lesebuch 6* provides adequate scope and accuracy:

> Comic (picture sequences): The comic or picture story "narrates" an event with the help of visual renditions (drawings, photographs). The picture story can be without words; the observer must then come up with an appropriate text; he has to discover it through the pictures sequences. The picture story can also be accompanied by words; pictures and text supplement each other; together they reveal the entire story. The text can either appear outside the picture, as explanatory accompanying text or as a complete story, or is incorporated into the pictures by way of speech bubbles. Either the words of the characters or the plot is explained in these speech bubbles. In modern picture stories (comics), which appear as series in newspapers or as comic books, a unique "bubble language" has developed. This serves oftentimes like a soundtrack (wow! peng! crash!) for what is happening in the story. Picture stories or comics have simple plots and narrative methods. What is happening has to be immediately transparent.

> Comic (Bildergeschichte): Der Comic oder die Bildergeschichte "erzählt" ein Ereignis mithilfe bildlicher Darstellungen (Zeichnungen, Fotos). Die Bildergeschichte kann ohne Worte sein; der Beobachter muss sich dann den Text selbst dazudenken, er muss ihn aus den Bildern und ihrer Abfolge erschließen. Die Bildergeschichte kann auch von einem Text begleitet sein; Bild und Text ergänzen sich gegenseitig, sie ergeben zusammen die ganze Geschichte. Der Text steht entweder außerhalb der Bilder—als erläuternder Begleittext oder als vollständige Geschichte—oder ist durch Sprechblasen in die Bilder eingefügt. In diesen Sprechblasen können entweder wörtliche Reden der einzelnen Bildgestalten stehen oder es wird das Geschehen erläutert. In den modernen Bildergeschichten (Comics), die als Serien in Zeitungen oder als Comic-Hefte erscheinen, hat sich eine eigene "Blasensprache" entwickelt, die oft nur noch lautliche Untermalung ("Wau," "Peng," "Crash") des Geschehens ist. Bildergeschichten oder Comics haben einen einfachen Handlungs- und Erzählverlauf. Das Geschehen muss sofort "durchschauber" sein. (216)

Comics scholars and enthusiasts would agree, however, that for decades now, comics can really no longer be described as "modern picture stories that appear as series in newspapers or comic books" (modern[e] Bildergeschichten (Comics), die als Serien in Zeitungen oder als Comic-Hefte erscheinen; 216). This definition does not consider the colorful variety of numerous comics and graphic novels; and it gives the false impression that comics only appear in the form of newspaper strips or individual comic books.

The glossary entry in *Lesebuch 7* is simply exasperating:

> Comics: Comics are a series of pictures combined with words. Picture and word should complement one another. Either the text is found

outside the pictures, or it is contained within the comic inside speech bubbles. Accordingly, the text can only be short and succinct. This means that a comic narrative cannot contain a lot of detail. Oftentimes the text is reduced down to simple interjections: *Wow! Crash! Boom!* (192)

> Comics: Die Comics sind Bilderserien in Verbindung mit Texten. Bild und Text sollten sich gegenseitig ergänzen. Der Text steht entweder außerhalb der Bilder oder er ist in Form von Sprechblasen eingebaut. Der Text kann jeweils nur knapp und kurz sein. Dies bedeutet, dass in den Comics die Erzählung nicht auf Feinheiten eingehen kann. Oft ist der Text zu bloßen Ausrufen geschrumpft: *Wow! Crash! Bum!* (192)

An absolutely pejorative definition like this one, claiming that comics cannot narrate in any kind of detail and that they are reduced to simple exclamations, could more accurately be located in a textbook from the 1960s. In spite of a complete revision and updating of the rest of the book, this inadequate entry has simply been transferred to the new 2006 edition. This is regrettable because students who read this definition get the wrong impression about the current German-language comic landscape. The wording of the entry strongly implies that the authors have never read any of the numerous recent graphic novels that distinguish themselves through their extensive dialogues, high percentage of text, and subtle storytelling.[10]

One could justify the complete absence of graphic literature in the *WortArt* series because it falls into the category of a grammar textbook. A language and reading book, however, should offer a thorough treatment of comics. Instead, as has been discussed, the publishers print comics in the fifth and sixth grade books, but fail to discuss particular characteristics that make them representative of the comics medium. Disregarding completely the question of how comics work, the authors of *Deutschbuch* incorporate graphic literature as a prompt to produce a "real" written story or to explore the functionalities of other media, in this case film. One particular exercise supports this assertion: students are asked to observe mannerisms, gestures, and posture in the film version of *Asterix* as a first step in collecting appropriate adjectives. If this were an exercise that concentrated on the comics medium, it would ask students to observe and think about the creative methods of expression that the artist uses. Ancillary information on the history of comics theory is completely absent. *Deutschbuch* does not provide a negative assessment of graphic literature. Instead, it just ignores it.

In the book series *Deutsch Gymnasium Bayern*, released in 2012, the authors also fail to treat comics as a discrete topic of instruction. Only one exercise in the textbook for the sixth grade actually treats comics: "Bring comic books to class and compare them with their film versions" (Bringt Comics mit und vergleicht sie mit ihrer Verfilmung; 178). The book incorporates this exercise almost as an afterthought; and it makes little sense for two main reasons. First, the characteristics of each media type should be sufficiently discussed if students are to compare them, yet the book series does not provide such background information. Second, besides the already investigated film versions of *Asterix*, the students would be familiar with very few, if any, comics that have been made into films. The majority of the film versions of comics are usually American comics that were and are only well known in very small circles in Germany. Moreover, because sixth graders presumably have only rudimentary historical film knowledge, they would simply not be familiar with older film versions of comic series, such as *Spiderman* and *Batman*.

MAKING THE CASE FOR COMICS IN GERMAN INSTRUCTION

Despite the gradual acceptance of comics by teaching professionals, the survey of textbooks shows that publishers are not producing materials that offer instructors guidance on effectively using the medium. Thus, the following arguments in favor of using comics in the classroom target instructors, textbook authors, and textbook publishers. One argument has to do with inspiration and incentive. Young readers demonstrate a comparably high intrinsic motivation for reading comics because "comics are fun to read" (Serchay 58). This is particularly relevant for language instructors because motivated students read a larger amount of material; and an "increased volume of reading material generally results in increased levels of reading comprehension" (die Lesemenge positiv beeinflusst und eine erhöhte Lesemenge ein gesteigertes Leseverständnis bewirkt; Schiefele 121). Moreover, researchers have argued that strictly adhering to the literary canon can dampen a love of reading because canonical texts appeal to very few students (Ruch). By contrast, as evidenced by the current Kinder und Medien (KIM) Study, a longitudinal German study examining media use among 1,209 six- to thirteen-year-olds, comics are still popular, even given the stiff competition from television, video games, and other forms of entertainment.[11] Thirty-six percent of those surveyed read comics one or more times a week, and 4 percent read comics every day. In particular boys, who are often seen as hard to motivate "problem children" in the German classroom, read comics: 47 percent as opposed to the 33 percent among girls. Conventional books, which are viewed as standard texts in the German classroom, are not read much more frequently. Thirty-four percent of those surveyed read one or more times a week and 16 percent daily.[12] The results of these surveys call into question the idea that comics would be seen as an "outsider" genre. In fact, graphic literature plays a "significant role in (world) knowledge and in the aesthetic experiences of youth" (eine bedeutende Rolle im [Welt-] Wissen und in der ästhetischen Erfahrung von Jugendlichen; Jost xi). It would seem to make sense for reading instructors and textbook publishers to build upon this existing and strong interest.

Another argument concerns using the comic medium to increase knowledge of visual literacy components. Because nearly every young reader in the German-speaking world has some experience with comics—most German children have seen or read the popular *Lucky Luke*, *Mickey Mouse*, or *Asterix* series—instructors could take advantage of the background knowledge students already have about comics. At the same time, however, readers have often not yet developed an adequate knowledge base of the theories and history of graphic literature. In order to discover comics, it is important to investigate the form and content as a method for recognizing structures. This means that the set of rules governing comic art has to be studied first (Schikowski 15). The German classroom is the ideal place to convey to the students this technical knowledge, which they can use to decipher the codes of the artwork and in particular comics. As Pierre Bourdieu has argued, the readability of works of art depends "on the distance between the more or less complex and sophisticated code that the work requires and individual expertise" (von dem Abstand zwischen dem mehr oder weniger komplexen und verfeinerten Code, den das Werk erfordert, und dem individuellen Sachverständnis; 175–76). When this background knowledge of graphic literature is neglected, then students will not understand—let alone enjoy—a majority of the current graphic novels, which often feature complex verbal and visual structures and artistic designs. In the German classroom, the ability to read and review comics can be taught, and the students' literary horizon can be expanded beyond the offerings usually found at the corner kiosk (Grünewald 2012, 29).[13]

Yet another argument has to do with the suitability of comics to teach literary concepts. As Rocco Versace has argued: "In addition to making use of standard literary devices such as point of view, narrative, characterization, conflict, setting, tone and theme, they also operate with a very complex poetics that blends the visual and the textual" (64). To date numerous articles have appeared elsewhere and in the present volume that outline methods for promoting skills of literary analysis and literary competence using German-language graphic novels (see Ludewig and Krueger). Also, instructors can use graphic novels to introduce further discussions about what literature actually is, which societal forces value those decisions, how the critical discourse is structured, and which works become part of the canon. No less important, however, graphic literature also has the potential to contribute to the development of individual personality, as the students must learn to appreciate different perspectives and to reconcile competing perspectives represented in literature (Gubesch 24).

In terms of pure instructional practice, many comics, aside from graphic novels, present compact, self-contained texts that can be studied as such in class. This has the advantage that the instructor does not always have to use excerpts from longer works, or cover longer works for an extended period of instructional time. The pool of materials is extremely large and easy to acquire: instructors can use anything from *Mickey Mouse* to Waterson's *Calvin and Hobbes* to Sammy Harham's *Poor Sailor* or German graphic novelist Andreas Michalkes's *Bigbeatland* strips, to name just a few. Individual comic strips can also be effective in classes with students of varying reading abilities, as McTaggart articulates: "They *enable* the struggling reader, *motivate* the reluctant one, and *challenge* the high-level learner" (32). Martin Schüwer summarizes the answer to the still persistent "why comics" question with regard to foreign language learning, but his observations can also be applied to German classes for native German high school students. Schüwer has argued that comics motivate students because they enable students to gain access to the linguistic or verbal through the visual, they appeal to different learning styles with their combination of words and pictures, they train students in media literacy, they encourage creativity because students must create their own stories (whereby graphics can counterbalance weaknesses in verbal skills), and finally they expose students to texts with complex content yet mostly accessible narratives (4–5). Other contemporary scholarship confirms the practical experiences and field-tested approaches that instructors have developed and continue to use in their classes (see, for example, Versaci, 2001 and Mandaville, 2005).

SUGGESTIONS FOR REPOSITIONING
COMICS IN THE GERMAN *GYMNASIUM*

Although many very valuable English-language instructional resources exist, the same cannot be said for pedagogical materials published in the German-language. Thus German instructors must create materials themselves. Instructors might employ and adapt the many standard English-language texts that have been published within the last several decades, such as those by Versaci, Monnin, and Bakis. Additionally a German edition of Scott McCloud's seminal 1993 publication *Understanding Comics* (1993) appeared in 2001 as *Comics richtig lesen*. McCloud's text not only helps students but also their instructors to understand comic theory when presented in this transparent and tangible format. Just as important, students must be able to understand the mechanisms of graphic literature in a playful or practical way. For example, to begin an instructional unit, the instructor should activate and gauge the breadth of the students' prior knowledge by asking about their existing experiences with comics. At the same time, the students can slide into the role of experts as they present a selected comic, an activity for which, as reports from foreign language instruction show, students are very motivated

(Gubesch 20). In this section, I will provide a brief overview of ways that instructors can implement comics in the German classroom. The following remarks are to be taken as suggestions only, and are neither exhaustive nor authoritative.

A brief history of comics can serve as an introduction to the instructional content. An examination of the historical development of the medium helps to clarify its peculiarities and to give an idea of the parameters of the topic. Above all, knowledge about the history of comics may change how students view individual works. It is recommended to engage with this history before working with the primary texts. This also holds true for treating the grammar and vocabulary of graphic literature. Stefan Dinter rightly suggests that "teachers and students must speak the same language" (Lehrer und Schüler müssen die gleiche Sprache sprechen; 2007, 21) For this reason it is necessary "to impart the ABCs of comics" (das ABC des Comics zu vermitteln; Dinter 2007, 21). A discussion of the mechanisms of the comics would logically follow an overview of the historical development of the medium. As mentioned above, Scott McCloud's *Understanding Comics* has become the standard reference for comprehending how comics work. The structure of his book can also help instructors organize and outline their instructional units. The depth of instruction must correspond to the exact goals of the unit and to the age and background knowledge of the students. Irrespective of age, the basics of comic theory—jumping from frame to frame (*Bildsprünge*), time, movement, signs, symbols, frames, and interaction of word and picture— must all be discussed in class in order to elicit quality reflection about the comic form. A thorough introduction to essential specialized terms will enable students to participate in a discussion that incorporates both comics analysis and literary analysis. For example, the instructor can help the students understand these terms by distributing a comic strip or an excerpt from a longer story in which the text from the speech bubbles has been removed. Students will immediately notice that a "removal, without substitution, of the words leads to an abundance of gaps in meaning that make these passages unreadable as a narrative unit" (eine ersatzlose Entfernung der Schrifttexte [. . .] zu einer derartigen Menge an Leerstellen [führt], die diese Passagen als narrative Einheiten unlesbar machen; Dolle-Weinkauff 18–19). The assignment could read: "Develop a story by filling in the speech bubbles with text" (Gestaltet die Erzählung aus, indem ihr die Sprechblasen mit Text füllt). By completing the task, students become aware that pictures determine the words, but the text can also influence how they interpret the pictures. Depending on the type of class, a more in-depth or theory-based discussion can follow the activity and exchange of results.

In order to facilitate an orientation in the vast cosmos of comics, a comics horizon must be developed. As one way to move toward this goal, each student in the class could give a presentation on a certain

German comic or comic author. As the presentations progress, students
can draw parallels between works in terms of graphic styles, genre, or
individual stylistic trends, such as Hergé's *ligne Claire*, the *école marcinelle*
(often in opposition to the former, and concentrating on conveying movement), or *manga*. Criteria that determine artistic quality can also be discussed. The instructor and students can refer to previously studied topics
of the grammar and vocabulary of comics. Certain curricular standards
can also be fulfilled as the students give their presentations: for example,
becoming familiar with the school library (grade 5); practice using and
implementing media (grade 6); and developing the ability to give constructive criticism (grade 7). Comic genres should be highlighted if they
have not been adequately covered in the presentations or the discussion
of comic history. A more nuanced approach by genre lends the subject of
graphic novels a logical structure. During discussions and hands-on activities using comics, it helps a great deal to have an understanding of the
"big" genres, such as autobiography, superhero, or comics journalism, in
order to categorize new primary texts and to compare them with other
works of graphic literature. At the same time, students become aware of
the difficulties of assigning categories when they realize that many works
cannot be easily classified.

As mentioned, many resources have already been published that describe how to effectively incorporate and employ graphic texts in the
classroom. I would like to concentrate on German sources and related
skills that have particular significance in German schools. For example,
the core competency of visual literacy (*Bilderlesen*) is becoming increasingly more important in German classrooms. Studying comics—as opposed to strictly verbal narratives—can both support and challenge the
acquisition of this skill.[14] In the course of reading excerpts or complete
works, students can detect and examine a plethora of general literary
phenomena, such as:

> [t]he differences between flat (typecast) and round (nuanced) charac-
> ters, between heroes and villains, between inner monologue and narra-
> tive commentary, single and multiple layered stories, back story and
> punchline, realism and fantasy, epic and drama . . . , universally epic
> story patterns (e.g., the poetically fulfilled happy ending) as well as
> cultural motifs . . . , symbols . . . , the phenomenon of intertextuality. . . .

> [D]ie Unterschiede zwischen flachen (typisierten) und runden (diffe-
> renzierten) Charakteren, zwischen Helden und Schurken, zwischen Ei-
> genrede und Erzählkommentar, ein- und mehrsträngigem Erzählen,
> Vorgeschichte und Pointe, Realismus und Fantastik, Epik und Drama-
> tik . . . , universelle epische Handlungsmuster (z.B. das poetisch gerech-
> te *happy ending*) sowie kulturell eingespielte Motive . . . , Symbole . . . ,
> das Phänomen der Intertextualität. . . . (Frederking 2008, 131)

It is not contradictory to enjoy reading a contemporary comic and at the same time performing a close reading of the work and its literary devices and style. Graphic literature in the German classroom almost always means elaborating on the reading of pictures and reflecting on the cultural convention of pictures, or "aesthetic education" (Frederking 2008, 136). In relation to comics, it could be asked why Batman's costume is black while Robin's consists of bright colors, and what effect that has on the viewer. With analytical questioning of this type, however, instructors must proceed carefully. The mastery of specific terms and categories is necessary in order to recognize and to discuss certain phenomena. Frederking, referencing film analysis, warns that activities should not simply implement these techniques, "but rather should build upon specific goals of comprehension, not for their own sake, but instead as part of concrete goals for comprehension" (nicht systematisch zum Selbstzweck [aufgebaut], sondern situativ im Zusammenhang mit konkreten Verstehenszielen; Frederking 2008, 186). Although Frederking speaks here about film, his warning also perfectly applies to the implementation of the comics medium in instruction.

The field of media critique (Medienkritik) has been and remains one of the most important instructional aspects in the German classroom. Even though the focus should not be, as in the 1970s, on one-sided and biased readings of comics as "commercial products of the so called culture industry," (kommerzielle Produkte der sogenannten Kulturindustrie), graphic literature must nonetheless be read with mature eyes (Frederking 2008, 133). Media critique must include critical analyses, such as the representation of sexuality in Manga, the representation of violence in action comics, or the misrepresentations and distortions of fact in documentary comics. There is also some value to not limiting the primary texts to only pedagogically valuable ones, thereby allowing a realistic overview of the current comic market. Comic adaptations of "classic" literature can also be used in class as "post-texts" with which to compare the original that students will already have read. For the secondary level, many of the classic works cannot be studied, but many age-appropriate graphic texts have appeared in the last few years, such as Antoine de Saint-Exupéry's *Der kleine Prinz* (2009 adapted by Joann Sfar), Lewis Carroll's *Alice im Wunderland* (2010 adapted by David Chauvelle und Savier Colette), or Morton Rhue's *Can't get there from here* (published 2011 by Stefani Kampmann als *Asphalt Tribe*).

Instructors and students can also experiment with practical applications of graphic literature outside the classroom. For example, the selection of comic texts in the school library must be increased. Another possibility is comic readings as part of school-sponsored "reading nights." Instructors could encourage and allow reading from comics as another possibility for such an event at the lower grade levels. This would require some technical preparation on the part of the reader. Specifically, the verbal portion would be read while the corresponding panels are projected on the screen. At professional comic readings, it is customary to have a regular panel appear, then to "page through" and then have another page "appear." This presents a challenge for the reader to experiment with the sound of the language in order to create suspense, while also finding the right tempo for moving through the slides. Incorporating comic readings can also breathe new life into the traditional German recitation contests. This would have to be done, however, in individual schools or as part of regional contests where the rules could be more easily altered. As further evidence of the exclusion of comics in Germany, the current rules of the country-wide Recitation Competition of the German Trade Book Association (*Vorlesewettbewerb des Deutschen Buchhandels*), with nearly 700,000 participants annually, does not allow for comic readings.

CONCLUDING REMARKS

This analysis of school textbooks has evidenced the persistence of the extensive antithetical relationship between subject-specific pedagogical skills and those related to literary studies offered in schoolbooks. Sharply contrasting the high esteem that graphic literature has enjoyed lately in scholarship worldwide, comics are largely ignored in German textbooks, or only used as points of comparison for other media concepts. If they are the main focus of instruction—in the sixth grade texts consistently across publishers surveyed—this occurs to an unsatisfactory degree, without expertise, or with pejorative descriptions. Only in a few cases have the authors presented comics appropriately, meaning that they regard them as forms of media in their own right. Of course these findings only address the reality in Bavarian secondary schools to a limited extent. We can assume, however, that very few teachers in the federal state of Bavaria, and perhaps in others as well, focus on comics in their instruction. I summarize here observations to support this hypothesis:

- The lack of basic instructional materials available.
- No strong theoretical base for comics in Bavarian secondary school lesson plans.
- The only partially successful and often negatively formulated treatment of graphic literature in approved textbooks.
- The perpetuated reservations and fear on the part of the instructors concerning comics and their contents.

In order to remedy this situation, comics must occupy a secure place in curricula and standards. If this were the case, the publishing companies would be compelled to revise the contents of their books to recognize comics studies. The growing distribution of graphic literature in the German-speaking world and an increasing establishment of research and pedagogy of comics at universities and beyond suggests that in the coming years, further pedagogical materials and professional opportunities will exist. The importance of this step is not to be underestimated as a way for teachers who have recognized the potential of comics for instruction and who have done a lot of work to develop materials. If teachers articulate their desire for more specialized pedagogical material and professional development in this area, the textbook companies will have to respond.

An experience that the *Literaturhaus Stuttgart* and its cooperating partners had implies that perhaps a new cohort of younger teachers is needed in order to change the status quo.[15] Specifically, there were not enough registered participants to justify conducting the two-year professional development workshop "Comic and Film in German Instruction" that had been scheduled to run from October 2013 until July 2015. Younger teaching professionals may have fewer prejudices because they have not grown up with the idea that comics represent nothing more than inferior pulp fiction. Additionally, this new generation of teachers has also likely read scholarly articles about the pedagogical value of graphic literature, and may have even had experiences with comics as part of their own education.

The textbook materials that regard comics and that are available for the lower level have demonstrated that there is plenty of room for the development in Bavarian high schools of lesson plans that treat graphic literature; and that forging links between comics and instructional units is entirely possible. Moreover, scholars, experts, and instructors have advanced numerous arguments supporting the use of comics in schools. In no way are those arguments only valid for the lower levels of the Bavarian academic secondary school: they can also be applied in curricular decisions for the lower levels of other German secondary schools. Armed with concrete suggestions for a repositioning of comics in instruction, teachers must have the courage to venture into this new territory and to solve problems creatively. Especially by using hands-on and process-oriented methods in the classroom, instructors can explore the possibilities of graphic literature in the language classroom, and students can at the same time improve their reading comprehension and analytical skills.

Scientific research in the area of comics in schools is severely lacking in the German-speaking realm. Because a direct connection between the sparse treatment of comics in textbooks and their implementation in classrooms is also lacking, a larger research project would require a broadly defined empirical study in the form of a longitudinal survey aimed at teaching professionals. This would help produce solid evidence about the actual treatment of graphic literature in German classrooms. Even without such a thorough study of the topic at present, it can be expected that the public discussion will undergo a transformation in the coming years. Hopefully soon teachers will no longer have to explain why they teach with comics, but instead why they do not.

—Translated from the German by Lynn Marie Kutch

NOTES

1. Although it varies by federal state, there are typically three types of high schools in the German school system. Each school is linked to a specific certificate of completion that qualifies the student for a certain trade, or to study at the university level: the *Hauptschule*, basic-track school, *Realschule*, intermediate-track school, and the advanced-track or academic track school, the *Gymnasium* (Bartl 51). The books in this essay are used at the *Gymnasium*.

2. While picture stories, with a clear division between text and drawings were generally accepted, the expressive emotional comic provoked open rejection in German post-war society. The fascination of German youth for American comic books (German original productions were rare) could not be stopped. The distribution of comics, however, was fought vehemently by societal and political forces.

3. See, for example, Pforte, Greiner, Kerkhoff, Pantel, and Grünewald.

4. Here, I am referring to German-language sources and textbooks published by German textbook companies. See, for example, Abraham and Kepser (2009) and Frederking, Krommer, and Maiwald, 2008.

5. Translator's Note: Because students choose in fourth grade which track (*Hauptschule, Realschule, Gymnasium*, see note 1) they will pursue, their secondary school career begins with grade five. Classes are divided into *Unterstufe* (grades 5–7), *Mittelstufe* (grades 8–10) and *Oberstufe* (grades 11 and 12). In this essay, I will translate *Unterstufe* with "lower grades."

6. See the agency's official website: http://www.km.bayern.de/lehrer/unterricht-und-schulleben/lernmittel.html.

7. Please see Eckhard Kuhn-Osius's discussion of *Vater und Sohn* in chapter 2 of this anthology. Also, see Schulze for an extensive study.

8. The solution listed in the corresponding teacher's handbook states: "Faster reading speed in comics because of the limitations of the story to speech bubbles and literal speech" ([S]chnelleres Lesetempo im Comic durch die Beschränkung auf die Lektüre der Sprechblasen/wörtlichen Rede; 8).

9. See in particular Mawil's *Kinderland*, Ulli Lust's *Heute ist der letzte Tag vom Rest deines Lebens*, Reinhard Kleist's *Der Traum von Olympia*, Simon Schwartz's *Packeis*, Isabel Kreitz's *Haarmann*, Ralf König's Schwulen-Comics, Volker Reiche's *Strizz*-Strips or *Kiesgrubennacht*, Flix's *Faust* oder sein *Don Quijote*, along with other works mentioned in this anthology.

10. In addition to other comics mentioned in this chapter and the rest of the anthology, see also Joe Sacco's comic reportages, David B.'s *Auf dunklen Wegen*, Will Eisner's *The Plot*, Chris Ware's *Jimmy Corrigan* or *Building Stories*, Jacques Tardis' *Elender Krieg*, Alain Keler's, Emmanuel Guiberts und Frédéric Lemerciers *Reisen zu den Roma*.

11. Please see http://www.mpfs.de/fileadmin/KIM-pdf14/KIM14.pdf, especially p. 6.

12. By contrast, a current study of psychologists in Heidelberg and Bamberg who studied reading comprehension and vocabulary development shows different results. With almost the same number of participants (1,215), the researchers found that 21 percent of seventh graders read comics several times a week, 12.8 percent several times a week, and 6.7 percent several times a day. (Pfost 94). Because the KIM study surveyed students between the ages of 6 and 13, it could be argued that as children get older, they read less comics.

13. Some recent examples include: Danial Clowes's *David Boring*, Art Spiegelman's *In The Shadow of No Towers*, David McGuires's *Hier*, among many others.

14. In part also "visual literacy" and thus defined as the "ability . . . to accurately recognize, understand and interpret visual information and various messages" (Teilweise auch als 'visual literacy' und somit als die "Fähigkeit . . . visuelle Informationen bzw. Unterschiedliche Botschaften . . . zutreffend zu erkennen, zu verstehen und zu interpretieren; Kain 31).

15. There were not enough registered participants for the implementation of the two-year professional development workshop "Comic and Film in German Instruction" that was supposed to have run from October 2013 to July 2015. The workshop would have been part of the program "Literary Writing in Schools" that was initiated by the *Literaturhaus* Stuttgart in cooperation with the Institute for Teaching German Language and Literature at the University of Bamberg, and the Ministry for Culture, Youth and Sport of Baden-Württemberg.

REFERENCES

Abraham, Ulf, and Kepser, Matthis. *Literaturdidaktik Deutsch. Eine Einführung*. Berlin: Erich Schmidt, 2009.

Bakis, Maureen. *The Graphic Novel Classroom. Powerful Teaching and Learning with Images*. Thousand Oaks: Corwin, 2012.

Bartl, Walter, and Reinhold Sackmann. "Path Dependency, Demographic Change, and The (De)Differentiation of the German Secondary School System." *Zeitschrift für Soziologie* 43.1 (2014): 50–69.

Baumgärtner, Alfred Clemens. "Comics in der Schule. Ein Überblick über bisherige Unterrichtsversuche." *Comics im ästhetischen Unterricht*. Ed. Dietger Pforte. Frankfurt am Main: Athenäum, 1974. 22–41.

Bourdieu, Pierre. *Zur Soziologie der symbolischen Formen*. Frankfurt am Main: Suhrkamp, 1974.

Burgdorf, Paul. *Comics im Unterricht*. Weinheim: Beltz, 1976.

Dinter, Stefan. "Comics erzählen." *Comics machen Schule. Möglichkeiten der Vermittlung von Comics im Schulunterricht*. Ed. Stefan Dinter and Erwin Krottenthaler. Stuttgart: Klett, 2007. 18–53.

Dinter, Stefan. "Fünf Fragen: Stefan Dinter." *graphic-novel.info*. n.d. Web. 14 November 2013. http://www.graphic-novel.info/?p=16522.

Doetsch, Marietheres. *Comics und ihre jugendlichen Leser*. Meisenheim: Hain, 1958.

Dolle-Weinkauff, Bernd. "Schrift und Bild als Lesevorgabe im Comic." *Deutschunterricht* 55 (2002): 17–20.

Ensberg, Claus, ed. *WortArt 5. Sprachbuch für Gymnasien in Bayern*. Brauschweig: Westermann, 2003.

———. *WortArt 6. Sprachbuch für Gymnasien in Bayern*. Brauschweig: Westermann, 2004.

———. *WortArt 7. Sprachbuch für Gymnasien in Bayern*. Brauschweig: Westermann, 2005.

Epple, Thomas, et al. *Deutsch Gymnasium. Bayern 5. Kompetenzen, Themen, Training*. Braunschweig: Schroedel, 2012.

———. *Deutsch Gymnasium. Bayern 6. Kompetenzen, Themen, Training*. Braunschweig: Schroedel, 2012.

———. *Deutsch Gymnasium. Bayern 7. Kompetenzen, Themen, Training*. Braunschweig: Schroedel, 2013.

Frederking, Volker, Axel Krommer, and Klaus Maiwald. *Mediendidaktik Deutsch: Eine Einführung*. Berlin: Schmidt, 2008.

Frederking, Volker, and Petra Josting. "Laudatio auf Prof. Dr. Jutta Werkme." 26 January 2007. Web. 11 June 2015. http://www.ag-medien.de/dokumente/aktuelles/Laudatio-Homepage-Fassung.pdf.

Frey, Nancy, and Douglas Fisher. "Using Graphic Novels, Anime and the Internet in an Urban High School." *Building Literacy Connections with Graphic Novels. Page by*

Page, Panel by Panel. Ed. James Bucky Carter. Urbana: National Council of Teachers of English, 2007. 132–44.

Frey, Nancy, and Douglas Fisher. "Using Graphic Novels, Anime, and the Internet in an Urban High School." *The English Journal* 93.3 (2004): 19–25.

Gaiser, Gottlieb and Karla Müller, eds. *Kombi-Buch Deutsch 5. Lese- und Sprachbuch für Gymnasien*. Bamberg: C. C. Buchner, 2004.

———. *Kombi-Buch Deutsch 6. Lese- und Sprachbuch für Gymnasien*. Bamberg: C. C. Buchner, 2005.

———. *Kombi-Buch Deutsch 6. Lese- und Sprachbuch für Gymnasien. Lehrerhandbuch*. Bamberg: C. C. Buchner, 2004.

———. *Kombi Buch Deutsch 5. Lese- und Sprachbuch für Gymnasien. Neue Ausgabe Bayern*. Bamberg: C. C. Buchner, 2009.

———. *Kombi Buch Deutsch 6. Neue Ausgabe Bayern*. Bamberg: C. C. Buchner, 2009.

———. *Kombi Buch Deutsch 6. Neue Ausgabe Bayern. Lehrerhandbuch*. Bamberg: C. C. Buchner, 2009. 15.

———. *Kombi-Buch Deutsch 7. Lese- und Sprachbuch für Gymnasien*. Bamberg: C. C. Buchner, 2005.

———. *Kombi Buch Deutsch 7. Lese- und Sprachbuch für Gymnasien. Neue Ausgabe Bayern*. Bamberg: C. C. Buchner, 2010.

Gorman, Michele. *Getting Graphic! Using Graphic Novels to Promote Literacy with Preteens and Teens*. Worthington: Linworth, 2003.

Greiner, Rudolf, ed. *Comics für die Sekundarstufe*. Stuttgart: Reclam, 1974.

Grünewald, Dietrich. *Comics, Kitsch oder Kunst? Die Bildgeschichte in Analyse und Unterricht. Ein Handbuch zur Comic-Didaktik*. Weinheim: Beltz, 1982.

Grünewald, Dietrich. "Vom kritischen zum genießenden Blick. Bildergeschichten im Unterricht." *JuLit* 38 (2012): 27–34.

Gubesch, Swenja, and Martin Schüwer. "Calvin and Hobbes. 6. Schuljahr. Comics als authentische Texte." *Der Fremdsprachliche Unterricht Englisch* 39 (2005): 18–24.

Hotz, Karl and Hans/ Rötzer, eds. *Das Buchner Lesebuch 5*. Bamberg: C. C. Buchner, 2003.

———. *Das Buchner Lesebuch 6*. Bamberg: C. C. Buchner, 2005.

———. *Das Buchner Lesebuch 7*. Bamberg: C. C. Buchner, 2006.

———. *Deutschbuch. Sprach- und Lesebuch 5. Gymnasium Bayern*. Berlin: Cornelsen, 2010.

———. *Deutschbuch. Sprach- und Lesebuch 6. Gymnasium Bayern*. Berlin: Cornelsen, 2009.

———. *Deutschbuch. Sprach- und Lesebuch 7. Gymnasium Bayern*. Berlin: Cornelsen, 2005.

Jost, Roland, and Axel Krommer. "Vorwort." *Comics und Computerspiele im Deutschunterricht. Fachwissenschaftliche und fachdidaktische Aspekte. Baltmannsweiler*. Ed. Roland Jost and Axel Krommer. Baltmannsweiler: Schneider Hohengehren, 2011. vii–xv.

Kain, Winfried, *Die positive Kraft der Bilderbücher: Bildertagebücher in Kindertageseinrichtungen pädagogisch einsetzen*. Weinheim: Beltz, 2006.

Kerkhoff, Ingrid. *Literaturunterricht. Didaktik und Theorie am Beispiel der Comics*. Gießen: Anabas, 1975.

Kukkonen, Karin. *Studying Comics and Graphic Novels*. Chichester: Wiley-Blackwell, 2013.

Lange, Günter. "Comic." *Textarten—didaktisch. Grundlagen für das Studium und den Literaturunterricht*. Ed. Leander Petzoldt. Baltmannsweiler: Schneider Hohengehren, 2011. 37–41.

Lehrplan für das Gymnasium in Bayern. Fachprofil Deutsch. *Staatsinstitut für Schulqualität und Bildungsforschung München* . n.d. Web. 8 October 2013. http://www.isb-gym8-lehrplan.de/contentserv/3.1.neu/g8.de/index.php?StoryID=26329.

Luhmann, Niklas. "Lesen lernen." *Short Cuts*. Ed. Niklas Luhmann. Frankfurt a.M.: Zweitausendeins, 2000. 150–57.

Mandaville, Alison. "Why I Teach Comics Literature." *The Comics Journal* 272 (2005): 168–78.

McCloud, Scott. *Comics richtig lesen. Die unsichtbare Kunst.* Hamburg: Carlsen, 2001.

———. *Understanding Comics: The Invisible Art.* Northampton, MA: Tundra Publishing, 1993.

McTaggart, Jaquelyn. "Graphic Novels. The Good, the Bad, and the Ugly. Teaching Visual Literacy. *Using Comic Books, Graphic Novels, Anime, Cartoons, and More to Develop Comprehension and Thinking Skills.*" Ed. Douglas Fisher and Nancy Frey. Thousand Oaks: Corwin, 2008. 27–46.

Medienpädagogischer Forschungsverbund Südwest. *KIM-Studie 2014. Kinder + Medien, Computer + Internet. Basisuntersuchung zum Medienumgang 6– bis 13–Jähriger in Deutschland.* February 2015. Web. 11 June 2015. http://www.mpfs.de/fileadmin/KIM-pdf14/KIM14.pdf.

Mitchel, Adrielle Anna. "Exposition and Disquisition. Nonfiction Graphic Narratives and Comics Theory in the Literature Classroom." *Teaching Comics and Graphic Narratives. Essays on Theory, Strategy and Practice.* Ed. Lan Dong. Jefferson: McFarland, 2012. 198–209.

Monnin, Katie. *Teaching Graphic Novels. Practical Strategies for the Secondary ELA Classroom.* Gainesville: Maupin House, 2010.

Müller, Sonja: "Verderbliche Bilderflut." Die Bekämpfung der Comics seitens der Literaturpädagogik der 1950er und 1960er Jahre." *Vom Wettstreit der Künste zum Kampf der Medien? Medialitätsdiskurse im Wandel der Zeiten. Beiträge des 2. Gießener Studierendenkolloquiums vom 27. bis 29.10.2006.* Ed. Mario Baumann and Yvonne Nowak. Marburg: Tectum, 2008. 177–99.

Pantel, Volker: *Comics. Ein Arbeitsheft für den Deutsch- und Kunstunterricht ab dem 5. Schuljahr.* München: List, 1980.

Pforte, Dietger. "Plädoyer für die Behandlung von Comics im ästhetischen Unterricht." *Comics im ästhetischen Unterricht.* Ed. Dietger Pforte. Vol. 5. Frankfurt am Main: Fischer Athenäum Taschenbuch Verlag, 1974. 9–13.

Pfost, Maximilian, Tobias Dörfler, and Cordula Artelt. "Students' Extracurricular Reading Behavior and the Development of Vocabulary and Reading Comprehension." *Learning and Individual Differences. Journal of Psychology and Education* 26 (2013): 89–102.

Platthaus, Andreas. *Die 101 wichtigsten Fragen. Comics und Manga.* München: C. H. Beck, 2008.

Roeder, Caroline. "Harr! Harr! Comic in Kinder- und Jugendliteratur" *kjl&m* 61 (2003): 2.

Ruch, Hermann, and Martin Sachse. "Leseförderung nach PISA." June 2005. Web. 20 December 2015. http://www.leseforum.bayern.de/download.asp?DownloadFileID=2717424b069c7d59f1b6db9a5eb0df08.

Schiefele, Ulrich, Cordula Artelt, Wolfgang Schneider, and Petra Stanat, eds. *Struktur, Entwicklung und Förderung von Lesekompetenz: Vertiefende Analysen im Rahmen von PISA 2000.* Wiesbaden: VS Verlag für Sozialwissenschaften, 2004.

Schikowski, Klaus. "Die Bilder lesen lernen. Comics machen Schule." *Möglichkeiten der Vermittlung von Comics im Schulunterricht.* Ed. Stefan Dinter and Erwin Krottenthaler. Stuttgart: Klett, 2007. 14–15.

Schulze, Elke. *Erich Ohser alias e.o. plauen: Ein deutsches Künstlerschicksal.* Konstanz: Südverlag, 2014.

Schüwer, Martin. "Teaching Comics. Die unentdeckten Potenziale der grafischen Literatur." *Der Fremdsprachliche Unterricht. Englisch* 39 (2005): 2–8.

Serchay, David S. *The Librarian's Guide to Graphic Novels for Children and Tweens.* New York: Neal Schuman, 2008.

Staiger, Michael. "Bilder erzählen. Zum Umgang mit visueller Narrativität im Deutschunterricht." *Bilder—in Medien, Kunst, Literatur, Sprache, Didaktik.* Ed. Ingelore Oomen-Welke and Michael Staiger. Freiburg: Fillibach, 2012. 41–51.

Ulshöfer, Robert. "Bekämpfung der Comics. Einführung in elementare Fragen der literarischen Wertung im 5.-7. Schuljahr." *Der Deutschunterricht* 6 (1961): 31–41.

Versaci, Rocco. "How Comic Books Can Change the Way Our Students See Literature: One Teacher's Perspective." *English Journal* 91.2 (2001): 61–67.

———. "'Literary Literacy' and the Role of the Comic Book. Or, "You Teach a Class on What?" *Teaching Visual Literacy. Using Comic Books, Graphic Novels, Anime, Cartoons, and More to Develop Comprehension and Thinking Skills*. Ed. Douglas Fisher and Nancy Frey. Thousand Oaks: Corwin, 2008. 91–111.

Wermke, Jutta. *Wozu COMICs gut sind?! Unterschiedliche Meinungen zur Beurteilung des Mediums und seiner Verwendung im Deutschunterricht*. Berlin: Scriptor, 1979.

Zinke, Brigitte. "Hilfe, mein Kind liest nur Comics." *Praxis Schule 5–10*. 19.1 (2008): 46–47.

FOUR

The Book of Revelation as Graphic Novel

Reimagining the Bible in Present-Day Europe

Jan Alexander van Nahl

> They seeing see not; and hearing they hear not, neither do they understand.
>
> (Mt 13:11–13)[1]

This chapter builds upon the premise that the subgenre of German-language graphic novels[2] based on biblical narratives, along with their scholarship, is still in its early stages. More than is the case with other types of literature, adapting biblical books raises questions about whether a graphic artist can possibly do justice to religious ideas, which not only have laid the foundations of the Western mind-set, but also influence current sociopolitical treatments of phenomena such as interculturality. These ancient texts maintain current relevance in various cultural contexts. For example, German politicians tend to frame their arguments with biblical references, and scholars as well as ecclesiastical organizations endeavor to make German laypeople aware of the Bible's impact on Western culture. Understanding contemporary contexts inspires the question as to how graphic novel adaptations compare to classical readings of biblical texts and whether they serve similar or different didactic purposes. I have divided my contribution to these topical questions into four parts. The first part outlines the wider sociocultural aspects of the study at hand, with a particular focus on Germany in early 2015. The second part centers on the formal appearance and intended readership of Matt Dorff's and Chris Koelle's graphic novel *The Book of Revelation* (2012,

German version 2013, which notably uses Luther's translation of the Bible). The third and most extensive part provides a close reading of a selection of crucial passages from the graphic novel focusing on the question of how aesthetics[3] and didactic demands work in synergy. *The Book of Revelation*'s possible impact on readership, especially with regard to its emotive character, is addressed in the concluding section, which also offers ideas for further debate and scholarship.

SOCIOCULTURAL ASPECTS

2017 marks the 500th anniversary of the Protestant Reformation in Germany. Half a millennium ago, Martin Luther's translation of the Bible into German not only shaped the German language but also extended the possibility for education to a large part of the population that had had no access to it before that time. In 2008, the Luther Decade, a ten-year-long celebration focusing on the Reformation, Christianity, and the Bible, was opened in Wittenberg, Germany. During the same time period (between 2007 and 2012), Pope (em.) Benedict XVI offered a three-volume study about the depiction of Jesus in the Gospels. The publication synthesized a theological assessment of the written texts with a historical-critical examination of the sociocultural conditions at the time of their composition and inspired a high number of subsequent publications by other theologians. The work's main purpose, however, was not to introduce a scholarly reading of the Gospels, but rather to make the New Testament accessible to a wider audience by bridging the widening gap between an understanding of the Christ of Church and the historic Jesus of Nazareth.[4] At a plenary meeting of the German Bible Society (*Deutsche Bibelgesellschaft*) in 2014, chairman Manfred Rekowski likewise drew attention to the fact that today's challenge was no longer about physical access to the Bible, but about ensuring widespread understanding of the biblical narratives.[5]

On the one hand, the apparent frequency of these concentrated efforts to reintroduce the Bible to a wider audience, and to make people aware of its fundamental impact on Western thought, suggests that in the early twenty-first century the Bible's wealth of complex narratives has faded into obscurity. On the other hand, these efforts evidence the perhaps renewed belief that biblical narratives still have the capability to contribute to laypeople's education in the broadest sense. Not only have events such as the *Charlie Hebdo* shooting in Paris in early 2015 renewed the Western world's awareness of the fact that people have always committed infamous deeds in the name of one or another religion, but the fusion of subsequent discussions and pseudo-political movements such as the increasingly radicalized German *PEGIDA*, or Patriotic Europeans against the Islamization of the Occident (*Patriotische Europäer gegen die Islamisie-*

rung des Abendlandes), have also underscored that people must understand their *own* cultural roots first in order to understand religious beliefs beyond cultural borders. This insight might not sound like anything groundbreaking; and yet it must be taken seriously in light of a "Europe in Movement."[6] It may come as no surprise that Navid Kermani, German author and specialist in Middle Eastern Studies, was awarded the Peace Prize of the German Book Trade in 2015.[7] In his haunting speech, he states:

> Only three hours' flight from Frankfurt, entire ethnic groups are being exterminated or expelled, girls are being enslaved, many of humanity's most important cultural monuments are being blown up by barbarians, cultures are disappearing and with them an ancient ethnic, religious and linguistic diversity that, unlike in Europe, had still persisted to a certain extent into the twenty-first century—but we only assemble and stand up when one of the bombs of this war strikes us, as it did on 7 and 8 January in Paris, or when the people fleeing from this war come knocking at our gates.[8]

In this context, the Reformation's significance might appear rather irrelevant to an interculturally broader audience. Indeed, events such as the third *Berliner Religionsgespräche* in October 2015, which brought together renowned humanist scholars such as Jan Assmann and Volker Leppin, focused on the relations of religious reformation and society within Muslim, Jewish, and Christian communities, aiming at a deeper understanding of such complex interrelations.[9]

The present chapter takes a slightly different approach to the debate by considering the popular, yet by scholars widely disregarded, field of graphic adaptations of biblical narratives; and considers the question whether the graphic format enhances accessibility and comprehensibility of the outlined debate to different populations. At first glance, the New Testament, with its focus on the struggle of early Christianity to compete with other religious systems, allows for different interpretations. A closer examination such as this one that seeks to evaluate both the narrative structures and possible sociocultural contexts calls into question, however, pseudopolitical attempts at reading "the good news" as a call for adamant religious confrontation. Because of political conditions brought about by religious conflict, people in the Western world ought to re-familiarize themselves with the complexity of the biblical narratives, with the result ideally being an increased awareness of how and why people have consistently exploited religious beliefs for propaganda's sake in order to strengthen and maintain their own positions within a specific society.

In analyzing the Bible's highly enigmatic Book of Revelation, heavily oscillating between violence and salvation,[10] scholars have "pessimistically observed that there are almost as many proposed outlines for the book as there are commentators" (Stephens 164). Some 250 years ago, Johann Gottfried Herder vividly depicted Revelation's intellectual demand on any modern reader when he declared that anyone in fear of "his mental health" (die Gesundheit seines Kopfes) should read neither Revelation nor Herder's commentary (9). According to Richard Bauckham, the challenge of interpreting Revelation's messages has not changed considerably since that time:

> Revelation is a book of profound theology, intense prophetic insight and dazzling literary accomplishment. But most modern readers find it baffling and impenetrable. They do not know how to read it. Nothing in the rest of the New Testament—or in modern writing—prepares them for the kind of literature it is (1287).[11]

Despite a gap of roughly 2,000 years since Revelation's composition, however, this plethora of readings makes the Bible's final book a frequently cited source up to the present day, also in political-ethical terms, and especially regarding the moral judgment of political action.[12] Focusing on Germany, we might cite the recent debate on euthanasia in the Federal Parliament, with Vice President Peter Hintze drawing upon Revelation in favor of palliative medicine—a citation which yielded a lot of public comments on Revelation's current repute:

> Looking at the Bible, the Bible's final book, the ultimate biblical hope, the ultimate Christian hope is that, one day, there will be life without suffering. The Book of Revelation says: no sorrow, no crying, no more pain. That is the Bible's vision. No sorrow, no crying, no pain. The whole Western system of values is grounded on the quest to allow people a self-determined, good life. Hence, we want to strengthen palliative care.[13]

> Wenn wir in die Bibel schauen, in das letzte Buch der Bibel, dann ist die große biblische Hoffnung, die große christliche Hoffnung, dass es einmal ein Leben ohne Leiden gibt. So heißt es in der Offenbarung des Johannes: Kein Leid, kein Geschrei, kein Schmerz wird mehr sein. Das ist die biblische Vision. Kein Leid, kein Geschrei, kein Schmerz. Die ganze Werteordnung der westlichen Welt ist vom Bestreben getragen, Menschen ein selbstbestimmtes, gutes Leben zu ermöglichen. Deswegen wollen wir die Palliativmedizin ausbauen.

Yet, despite such insistent words, John's visions allow for less peaceful and sanguine readings. The German publisher *Deutscher Taschenbuchverlag* recently introduced a new book on Revelation by drawing upon the biblical apocalypse's flexibility in political applicability:

> In the beginning, the "bad guys" were the followers of Paul the Apostle, but they could also be the Jews, Romans, heretics or heathens. War, persecution, and catastrophes become meaningful through the apoca-

lypse. Particularly that makes Revelation the Bible's most dangerous book to this day.

Die "Bösen" waren ursprünglich die Anhänger des Apostel Paulus, konnten aber auch die Juden, Römer, Häretiker oder Heiden sein. Krieg, Verfolgung und Katastrophen erhalten durch die Apokalypse einen Sinn. Gerade das macht sie bis heute zum gefährlichsten Buch der Bibel.[14]

The task of interpreting John's visions seems to have become all the more urgent because of a "boom in end-of-the-world books since Sept. 11" (Ostling). As Rebecca Skaggs and Thomas Doyle state: "Although the Apocalypse has always fascinated laypeople and scholars alike, current interest has escalated. . . . More intensely than ever, the question is being asked and considered: is violence ever acceptable, even when it is used to bring about a just cause?" (221). To put it somewhat pointedly, in the early twenty-first century, Revelation's political dimension seems to have come to the fore of broad public interest. Following on-going debates surrounding, for instance, the "Islamization of the West," the frequent popular citation of passages from Revelation thus hardly comes as a sur-prise. However, a brief survey indicates that a significant number of pub-lic commentators admit to their own inadequate understanding of the biblical book. Yet, perhaps, those commentators who have obviously not bothered to read it, but nonetheless attest to a personal understanding of the Bible's apocalyptic message to Christians, are all the more alarming.

Within this complex political and intellectual atmosphere, the 2015 Luther Decade topic, "Image and Bible," intriguingly advances the ques-tion of how biblical messages are communicated through visual media today. Indisputably, the claim that "the Reformation was also a media revolution," creating a "new semantic and visual language,"[15] has partic-ular relevance for current debates. In the late twentieth and early twenty-first centuries, the traditional dictum "seeing is believing" has gained new importance due to the increasing quantity and quality of visual im-ages in almost every aspect of life (Lobinger 55–62). As they gain in popularity, graphic novels, and especially those that adapt biblical mate-rial, earn a critical look regarding visual media's didactic qualities.

Upon initial examination, most adaptations hardly seem to strive for theological teaching or advancement of a religious dialogue beyond cul-tural boundaries. Instead they exploit the material of the Bible for the sake of its powerful imagery.[16] Some years ago, however, in the *Theologi-cal Librarianship*, Sarah Stanley advocated for the "limitless" potential of graphic novels to serve "as a tool to study theology," because of their great success "at stimulating interest in books among even the most re-luctant of readers" (97). In 2015, German pastor Gereon Vogel-Sedlmayr likewise stated that graphic novels on religious topics, although often created by agnostics, were worth a theological debate. The underlying idea of a boundary-crossing approach to the allegedly distinct spheres of popular (low) and academic/intellectual (high) culture is worth noting, as I discuss in more detail below. Yet, only 10 percent of the graphic novels Vogel-Sedlmayr took into account for his evaluation were of German origin. This strange discrepancy between increasing endeavors to stimulate German laymen's reengagement with the Bible, and the apparent lack of both German graphic novels based on biblical texts and related scholarship solicits an intensified discussion.

FORMAL ASPECTS

Particularly relevant for this essay, scholars have repeatedly compared the Bible's final book to an "inspired picture-book" (Brownrigg 158), and one that has fascinated mankind as no other book has ever done, according to the German publisher.[17] Dorff and Koelle have a professional background in the film business, and they explicitly refer to the power of "the language of cinema" for their adaptation (Dorff and Koelle 185). This statement echoes Stanley's claim that graphic novels' "incorporation of images to tell a story provides readers with the opportunity to consider them in ways similar to the study of art and film" (97).[18] It is not a new insight that graphic "storytelling cannot be separated from its inherent materiality; the form is critical" (Baetens/Frey 2015, 163–64), "involving the co-presence and interaction of various codes" (Hatfield 132). Studies have repeatedly drawn attention to the written text in its *material* qualities, particularly the relationship of text and lettering to circumfluent graphics (see, for example, Strätling/Witte, Assmann, and Baetens/Frey). The reader's task would be to *see* a text, so to speak, and thereby recognize the textual and the visual layers as a meaningful unit: "good language and good drawing are never enough; it is the interplay between words and images that has to work" (Baetens/Frey 149).[19] In addition, the simultaneous perception of a single page's different panels might stimulate a rereading of allegedly well-known texts.[20]

The concept of such an advanced intertwining of text and visual images ought to be all the more promising in the case of Revelation because the narrative constantly refers to John's visual observations. Thus, it is significant that the adaptation at hand does *not* interweave written text and graphics. Although the panels are clearly image-dominant, the adaptation uses neither speech bubbles nor thought bubbles: plain, small lines of text advance the story. The common grid-shaped layout shows a slight tendency to break down borders due to blurring colors, and the artists do not adhere to a strict pattern concerning panel size. On various occasions, a biblical verse is split up into sections across several panels, but there are also examples of several verses contained in one single panel.[21] Despite the complexity of the graphic novel's source text, the overall layout of the graphic adaptation is rather simple.

In an attempt at explaining the artists' apparent reluctance to intertwine written text and visual images in a more sophisticated manner, it is necessary to consider the subgenre at hand. The depiction of biblical narratives in a graphic novel is something of a tightrope walk, although rendering a graphic novel based on an *entire* biblical book is not totally new. When assessing Revelation from a scholarly point of view, however, "all the accumulated details seem to correspond to a theological intention more than to a concern for rendering the representation plausible, or for describing any existent phenomena" (Prigent 306). Without a doubt, the theological dimension presents a major challenge for any attempt at visualization. As illustrator Chris Koelle has indicated, the main task was to "respect the text and respect its readers" (Challies). A brief investigation into other visual adaptations of the Bible, whether films or comics that target a wider audience, indicates that these versions reduce the plot by focusing on fewer aspects. Given this insight, it seems necessary to note that the graphic adaptation of Revelation, on the contrary, quotes every line of the biblical text, with, as far as I can see, no additions and only one accidental omission.[22] Reverend Mark Arey—who contributed to the new translation of Revelation used for the graphic adaptation—states that it was "the text, and nothing but the text" (Miller/Arey). Arey's assertion concerning fidelity to the biblical text in fact appears to be a tentative safeguard against criticism. His claim to provide the readership with nothing but the text—"we are not trying to imagine or re-imagine Scripture" (Miller/Arey)—, however, is problematic, as it belittles the potential of the multimodal medium to have a considerable impact on both narration and reception. Quite in contrast to these statements, Arey also claims that this graphic novel is indeed a "page-turner" (Lewis), intended "to reengage the reader, or maybe capture a reader for the first time"—"the visuals are there to carry the reader like water upholds a boat" (Miller/Arey). This metaphor seems to suggest a rather superficial approach to the graphic novel, and raises the question as to whether the reader is really supposed to simply flip (or float) through the panels, without any attempt at grasping the narrative's structure and possible deeper meaning.

Significantly, the publishers market the graphic novel's German version differently than the US-American version, which invites audiences to "take a thrilling ride through ancient prophecy. Discover anew the story of the ultimate fulfillment of John's faith as the final battle is fought between God and Satan."[23] By contrast, the German publisher addresses an audience interested in Revelation's influence on modern culture:

> *The Book of Revelation* is the unique depiction of mankind's most famous and terrifying prophecy. An astonishing work that also informs us

about the origin of many motives, figures, and symbols which still have
an impact on our language and mind-set.

Das Buch der Offenbarung ist die einzigartige Umsetzung der berüh-
mtesten und erschreckendsten Prophezeiung, die die Menschheit
kennt—ein erstaunliches Werk, das auch über die Herkunft zahlreicher
Motive, Figuren und Symbole Auskunft gibt, die heute unsere Sprache
und Vorstellungswelt prägen.[24]

While the English version sounds like an advertisement for a video game,
the German introduction seems to strive for higher aspiration, promising
deeper understanding of both the Bible and Western culture. These distinctions have particular significance not only because of the reference to
Luther's contributions to the German language, but also within the context of the distinction discussed throughout the present volume between
low and high culture in German-speaking countries. The differences in
marketing language can be interpreted in relation to this concern, with
the German version of the graphic novel at hand apparently counting as
a specimen of high culture. The German publisher indirectly refers to
high culture in the sense of sophisticated art that makes an audience
reflect upon cultural ideologies and mentalities. At the same time, this
explicit confidence in the didactic qualities of the graphic adaptation of a
biblical book can also be tied to the efforts described above to reintroduce
the Bible to a wider audience in Germany. In this sense, readers and
scholars might acknowledge this graphic novel's ability to transcend
boundaries, and we may thus conclude that the main challenge concerning a German audience is to create a graphic adaptation that appeals both
to readers well-versed in the Bible who strive for deeper understanding,
and readers who primarily expect thrilling entertainment.

As we move to a closer reading of the graphic novel, we also recall the
question posed above regarding the ability of a graphic artist to do justice
to religious ideas, conveyed by way of written texts, which have funda-
mentally contributed to the Western mind-set. More than with any profane narrative, the graphic adaptation of biblical books causes scholars to
ponder the relation of aesthetics and didactic purposes. In what follows, I
will consider the extent to which these layers work in synergy, promoting
the reengagement of a reluctant readership through a modified method
of narration, as well as the possibly added benefits of graphic adaptations
compared to classical readings of biblical texts.[25]

SCRIPTURAL EVIDENCE AND GRAPHIC ADAPTATION

The scope of the source material means that any analysis must be highly
selective, not only in the choice of textual passages but also in the choice
of cited academic references (see Boxall). The first chapter of Revelation

provides a general narrative frame, focusing on John's assignment to write down everything he encounters as a way to testify to the word of God. The book's last chapter refers to this initial situation. Revelation is essentially John's report of what he witnessed *in spiritu*, in a divine encounter. Right at the beginning (Rev 1:10–12), John reports that he hears a great voice behind him and tries to catch a glimpse of its source. This striving for visual acknowledgment is interesting to observe: John does not believe his ears, so to speak, but relies only on his eyes. Having seen a mighty angelic being (like a Son of Man), he falls to the ground as if dead. One is reminded of Moses's request: "Shew me thy glory" (Ex 33:18), and the Lord's answer: "Thou canst not see my face: for there shall no man see me, and live" (Ex 33:20). It is the human ability to *hear*—namely, the word of God—which became an essential idea for the Western religions: "Blessed is the one who reads and all who listen to the words of this prophecy" (Rev 1:3). The Christian revelation is not only about the visual, but about the aural as well, with both layers working in synergy (Aune 1,185).

Breaking down the "deeply symbolic, highly incoherent and thus always cryptic" grand narrative into visually understandable units appears as both a challenge and an opportunity for the graphic adaptation (Witte). Upon initial examination, the biblical text only makes rather formulaic references to the human senses, and an average audience reading Revelation for the first time easily puts aside John's role as an observer. Yet this specific kind of framing adds structure to the narrative and makes the reader aware of a fundamental precondition: the capacity of human senses determines how John will be able to pass down his encounter—"John, like biblical writers in general, has to strive to convey, in an adequate human language, what limited human minds cannot comprehend in the first place" (Harrington 26). Providing several (extreme) close-ups of John's awestruck eyes right from the beginning (figure 4.1), the graphic novel makes the reader aware of the act of hearing, too, either depicting John covering his ears from the mighty words he attends, or with his hands behind his ears to catch every single word.

The artists' leading concept of a juxtaposition of the witnessed events and the observer himself is auspicious: the panels are constantly shifting between a third-person-view of John and frames shown from his own point of view. These transitions take place on a single page. It thus takes on a dynamic look, in the sense of rapidly changing visual links, which the artists explain in part with the language of cinema:

> The twenty-seventh book of the New Testament has presented a great challenge to artists throughout the ages. [. . .] What had not been invented at the time these artists created their visionary masterpieces was the language of cinema. None of the pre-twentieth century classic art based on the book of Revelation included reaction shots of John. That simple juxtaposition of an image depicting an event and an image de-

Figure 4.1.   Scene from *The Book of Revelation* by Matt Dorff and Chris Koelle. Dorff, Matt, and Chris Koelle. *The Book of Revelation*. Grand Rapids, MI: Zondervan, 2012. 30.

> picting an observer observing the event is the visual key to this version
> of Revelation. (Dorff and Koelle 185)

On the one hand, this frequent juxtaposition of panels focusing on John and panels depicting his observations can serve as a powerful tool to guide the reading and to urge the reader to fill in the gaps with his own interpretations. On the other hand, as becomes apparent at this early stage of analysis, the third-person framings—we observe the observing protagonist from an external point of view—not only intensify readers' awareness to the human dimension of the biblical revelation, but they also allow the artists to cleverly bypass difficulties in interpretation. In the latter case, most or even all of John's (or other spectators) surroundings are suppressed, and the reader views only a black backdrop. We might cite the statement that from the Son of Man's mouth came forth "a razor swift dazzling double-edged sword" (Rev 2:12). If we consider this metaphorical reference in Revelation (Rev 2:12, 16; 19:15, 21) as well as in other biblical texts, the sharp sword is the spoken word, stressing the importance to listen to God and to obey him: "For the word of God is quick, and powerful, and sharper than any two-edged sword, piercing even to the dividing asunder of soul and spirit, and of the joints and marrow, and is a discerner of the thoughts and intents of the heart" (Heb 4:2). However, the artists refrain from any attempt at implying such a clarification: they render the sword/word metaphor as glowing lines only. The references in Rev 2:12 ("the One Who possesses the razor swift, dazzling, double-edged sword"), and 2:16 ("I will return swiftly and strike them with the sword in My mouth"), then, are displayed only through the fearful eyes of those who are threatened by the lethal divine encounter.

Chapter 4 leads to a new stage in Revelation, namely, John's spiritual ascension to Heaven, and provides another significant example of such third-person framing. The depiction of the first verses constantly shifts between an external perspective on John and shots depicting his reaction with close-ups of his eyes. The center of these repeated illustrations of John is He who is seated on the throne: "The One Who sat on the throne was like an epiphany of jasper and sardius . . . and from all around His throne shone an emerald rainbow" (Rev 4:3). Jasper and sardine stone are illustrated by reddish colors (similar to chapter 15), creating an indistinct anthropomorphic shape. By contrast, the reference in Rev 20:11 – "I beheld an enormous, gleaming white throne and the One Enthroned upon it" – refocuses on John's face again, with nothing but a slight reddish reflection of Him in his eyes. In the adaptation of this chapter, John's face, filling a whole page, is split into two sections, shining bright on the left side, symbolizing the brilliance of the white throne, and dark on the right side, probably referring to the terrifying impact of God's face from which "heaven and earth fled" (Rev 20). On the other hand, the greenish glint of the emerald in Rev 4, like a rainbow, is hardly depicted at all. Nothing but a slight reflection in John's awestruck eyes reminds us of its presence (figure 4.1). There is a reference to the rainbow in Rev 10:1: "I saw another mighty angel descending from heaven with a rainbow about his head"; but the artists do not illustrate the descent at all. Instead they render it as plain text only. From a theological point of view, this neglect of the rainbow on two occasions goes hand in hand with the omission of a crucial reference to the Old Testament: the rainbow is a prominent symbol for God's merciful promise to mankind (Rütersworden), as found in Genesis: "And God said, This is the token of the covenant which I make between me and you and every living creature that is with you, for perpetual generations: I do set my bow in the cloud, and it shall be for a token of a covenant between me and the earth" (Gen 9:12–13).

At first, the graphics in these chapters seem to provide only a loose guideline for how to read the biblical narrative, causing one to wonder why the artists largely leave attempts at a deeper understanding to the audience. From a slightly different perspective, however, this reluctance on the artist's part to provide complete clarity can be regarded as a strong point of this graphic adaptation. Instead of presenting the reader with clear explanations and explications of specific passages, it draws the reader *emotionally* into the narrative. Revelation provides manifold accounts both of God's unlimited power and disastrous events caused by this power; and these catastrophes have always acted as a major stimulus to artists. It is no wonder that the graphic novel stresses the discrepancy between human and God, sitting on His throne in the midst of lightning, thunder, and heavenly beings. This represents a clever way of bypassing the depiction of God, which, nevertheless, makes the reader aware of His dual merciful and destructive presence, and the magnificent yet frightening moment of an encounter far beyond the normal capability of human senses. John's hesitant approach of the throne stresses this extraordinary status all the more through a number of panels that switch between long shots and close-ups on John's wide eyes. The design of the panels suggests that he takes his time, trying to realize what is going on around him. The visual treatment of the text's allegorical meaning and possible references both to other chapters of Revelation and the Bible in general is subordinated to the purpose of creating a constant state of thrill and insecurity.

Having reached the inner circle, John is ready to face one of the most vital events in Revelation: the entrance of "a Lamb, standing upright, bearing the wounds of His own sacrifice. He had seven horns and seven eyes" (Rev 5:6).[26] The work of many theologians over the centuries leaves little doubt about the allegorical meaning: Jesus Christ, crucified for mankind, is standing up, and is worthy of taking the scroll from God's hand and of opening it—the Lamb is the key to understanding history as salvific history (Strobel 185). By the sixth century AD, a lamb had become a well-established symbol of Christ within the visual arts, mostly depicted in its natural form (Nielsen). However, ultimately, the scene in Rev 5

> is impossible to visualize, for we have not only a lamb in the place of the expected lion, but the morphology of the animal is quite unusual and the situation rather strange. One would be mistaken in taking great pains to render all this coherent or even merely imaginable; such was absolutely not the author's concern, for in accumulating these bizarre details he obviously had only one goal, which was theological. (Prigent 251)

Nevertheless, Dorff and Koelle painstakingly attempt a visualization, proposing a fusion of terio- and anthropomorphic characteristics which might appear odd to an audience having knowledge of the traditional depictions. Besides a large number of more or less stereotypical images of the Lamb throughout history, however, some rather grotesque examples are to be found as well. Albrecht Dürer's famous woodcuts *apocalypsis cum figuris* from the late fifteenth century come to mind, depicting the Lamb literally with seven eyes and seven horns—probably a somewhat bewildering portrayal for Dürer's contemporaries, who were used to a different tradition. From this point of view, the graphic novel's choice can hardly be called a much stranger solution, and even less so because the depiction of the Lamb can be considered a good example for the artists' claim to adhere to the language of twenth-first-century cinema.

Evidently they strive to appeal to a wider audience by offering a very concrete, yet alien depiction of a central figure of the Bible—"see the Lamb . . . as never before," as the English publisher states.[27] Interestingly enough, a close-up of the Lamb's face fills in the whole cover of the German version, while the English version's cover shows several panels with different scenes. Comparing both covers, the latter inevitably draws attention to the form, a comic book, whereas the former might be interpreted as teasing an audience to find out more about the *meaning* of this unfamiliar face, thus even staying true to the intended marketing angle for each individual culture. From this point of view, it is even worth mentioning that the German publisher does not draw upon a thrilling new depiction of the Lamb, but, again, hints at deeper understanding: "[John] witnesses the appearance of Christ as a lamb, taking his seat next to God's throne" ([Johannes] sieht, wie Christus selbst in Gestalt eines Lamms erscheint und neben dem Thron Gottes seinen Platz einnimmt).[28]

As indicated in Rev 5, however, the third-person focus on John not only allows for the creation of a haunting atmosphere, but also for an emphasis on John's emotional reaction of disappointment and frustration, which he demonstrates by tearing out his hair and burying his face in his hands. Having awaited the revelation of imminent crucial events, the universal search for a being worthy of opening the scroll ultimately seems to amount to nothing: "All the achievements of all the priests and prophets of the world do not adequately qualify them for opening this sealed book. Using this dramatic device, the author [of Revelation] emphasizes the uniqueness of the conquest of Christ" (Aune 348). Given this singularity, the reader might have expected a number of panels depicting the desperate search in Heaven, on Earth, and beneath it, which would imply the great length of time. In fact, we are only provided with one single small panel showing the seals of the scroll bearing a bewildering diversity of symbols. The artists choose to focus on the narrative *framing*, once again: "One of the Presbyters said to me"—the panel displays one of the elders, resting his hand on the shoulder of a distressed John (Rev 5:5). Whereas the reader thus recalls John's frustration once again, the depiction misses the striking contrast between the announcement of the arrival of "the Lion of the tribe of Judah" and the actual appearance of a wounded Lamb (Rev 5:6). It is not a victorious Messiah who is worthy of breaking the seals, but a seemingly weak lamb (Harrington 25).

In assessing the graphic adaptation's emotive character, we might further instance the visualization of chapter 10, with the panels constantly shifting between an angelic being and John, respectively depicting them side by side. This mode of rendering stresses the discrepancy between the mighty angel, visualized as a bright larger-than-life figure, with flaming eyes, and lightning streaking around his body, and John, the small human, rendered in brownish colors with little contrast. The setting of a desolate seaside gives the impression that nothing can disturb this powerful picture. The little book in the angel's hand has led to discussion regarding its symbolic meaning (see Prigent 327–36). John's task to eat the book is particularly important: "It was as he said, sweet as honey in my mouth and bitter in my stomach" (Rev 10:10). As Pierre Prigent argues, this conflict of sweetness and bitterness "reveals to [John] the two aspects of his ministry: he will experience first of all for himself the sweetness and the bitterness that are connected to being God's spokesman in the world" (335). The panel simply shows a close-up of John's mouth, eliding his "frightening sense of the reality of good and evil, a reality whose bitterness burned, but whose sweetness was inexpressible" (Brownrigg 133). Only the chapter's last panel in which John stands beside the mighty angel in the middle of nowhere, looking at dark clouds gathering at the horizon, implies the burdensome nature of his task: "You must prophecy yet again for peoples, nations, tongues, and many kings" (Rev 10:11). However, once again, this last picture leaves the reader with the anxious feeling that something "big" is going to happen soon, all the more illustrated by the juxtaposition of this last panel and a pitch-black page bridging the two chapters.

Considering the emotional dimension of Revelation discussed at length here as part of an aesthetic experience, the graphic adaptation regularly provides examples of the deliberate synthesis between aesthetics and didactical purposes, particularly in terms of a historicized reading. There is consensus among scholars that the sociocultural conditions during the Roman reign had a considerable impact on Revelation's conception—although there has been some harsh criticism that "commentators on Revelation have been too eager to explain John's text by constructing a single social setting" (Friesen 352). The graphic novel's regular emphasis on the narrative's historical context not only reminds us of its human dimension again, but also of the German version's proclamation to contribute to a rational understanding of the biblical book. Following Scripture, the destruction of Earth results from God's will. In the present adaptation, however, the visualization of this destruction draws upon spectacular natural phenomena such as lightning, rain colored by reddish Sahara sand, a solar eclipse, a meteor, or a volcanic eruption. At the same time, the depiction of these events evidences again the graphic adaptation's striving for an unsettling and therefore thrilling technique of visualization. The artists provide a script sample of one of these passages (Rev 11:18) in the appendix: "Thunderbolts zigzag down from the sky nailing a squad of elite Roman soldiers marching down the road to Jerusalem. Instant death meted out supernatural assassination style, a single bolt for each pagan persecutor, no escape, instant death" (Dorff and Koelle 186).

Chapter 13, another example of the blend of appealing visuals and rational interpretation, tells us about a beast—the fusion of a leopard, a bear and a lion—crawling up out of the sea (Rev 13:1). Prigent contextualizes this creature:

we should attempt less than ever to imagine here the concrete appearance of such a strange beast. The author simply intends to convey that it sums up and includes all of the beasts announced in Dan 7: the first three in that passage resembles a lion, a bear and a leopard; they symbolized the Babylonian, Median, and Persian empires. . . . The interpretation of the animal symbolism used here belongs to the sphere of a commentary of Daniel. (405)

The graphic adaptation of that already rich imagery, once again, introduces an alien creature. In fact, the new English translation uses the word "monster," whereas Luther simply translated it as *Tier* (animal). The subsequent panel privileges the historical context again, and depicts a mighty Roman palace, hinting at the interpretation of the beast as the "demonic" Roman Empire: a young Caesar, most likely Nero, is introduced as its human personification (the famous number 666 is depicted as a tattoo on his neck in Greek letters). Consequently, "the Beast who was mortally wounded with an assassin's dagger" (Rev 13:14) is displayed as the Roman emperor with a bloody dagger stuck in his chest (as is well known, Nero committed suicide) (Aune 739). This transition from a tremendous alien creature, appealing to an audience accustomed to modern fantasy, to a historical scene, which has the potential to provide a rational interpretation, once again establishes a tie between entertainment and educational purpose.

The famous harlot Babylon serves as another example of this combination of entertainment and edification—not least because John himself is quite bewildered upon first seeing the city: "He had been invited to witness God's judgment on Babylon, yet no ruined city met his gaze. Instead, he had seen a bejeweled woman on a scarlet beast. He needs an interpreter" (Harrington 174). Most scholars agree on the identification of Babylon with Rome in this context (see Aune 829 and Harrington 151). At first, the graphic adaptation adheres to a very literal depiction of the biblical text, for example, displaying drunk people as visualization of the statement: "She [i.e., Babylon] made all Nations drunk with the wine of her ferocious debauchery!" (Rev 14:8). Then, following the description of Babylon as "a woman seated on a scarlet monster" (Rev 17:3–4), the panels show the seductive woman who bewilders John. Revelation's repeated mention of the colors scarlet and purple symbolizes both luxury and prestige and mankind's refusal to obey God. Yet, strangely enough, the graphic adaptation makes very little use of these colors. Not until the very last panel of this chapter—and after the angel's words: "Now here is wisdom, if you have spiritual understanding" (Rev 17:9)—is the woman Babylon clearly identified with a majestic city through a vivid cross-fading of the two earlier pictures. This conflation strikes the audience as the final step in the adaptation's process of merging aesthetical experience and historical-critical interpretation.

Probably the most impressive example of this visual cross-fading is the juxtaposition of two panels in both Rev 19:11–13 and 14–16, depicting the descent of the Word of God and the heavenly armies for the final battle:

> Then I saw Heaven opening before me, and behold! A shining white horse! He who rides upon it is called "Faithful" and "True," and in righteousness He judges and rides into battle. . . . His eyes flashed like fiery flames, and the crown of His head is a thick cluster of diadems, inscribed with names. And there is a Name inscribed that no one knows except Him. And He is robed in a garment steeped in and dripping with His own Blood . . . and His Name is called The Logos — The Word of God! (Rev 19:11-13)

The scene reminds us of the announcement of a mighty lion and the unexpected appearance of a slaughtered lamb in Rev 5, although the graphic novel makes no use of this striking contrast. In chapter 19, however, an impressive series of powerful pictures confronts the reader. Two panels, sharing a single page, one below the other, depict a superior warrior in brightest colors, being "the final and perfect expression of the will of God" (Prigent 545), and Jesus in brownish colors, with the crown of thorns on his head and the heavy wooden cross on his back (figures 4.2 and 4.3). The same juxtaposition, though somewhat smaller, is recapped on the next page, rendering the arrival of other divine warriors side by side to the crucified Jesus. In both cases, the reader simultaneously observes these two images in striking contrast, which creates a powerful overall impression. The graphic adaptation stresses this twofold interpretation of the Word of God even more by providing a corresponding cross-fading in the last chapter again, accompanied by the mighty words: "I! the Alpha and Ωmega, the First and the Last, the Beginning and the End" (Rev 22:13 f.).

This dominant double picture frames both the final events in the old world and the renewal of creation (Rev 21). Once again, the visualization aims at an emotive presentation. Only *after* the defeat of evil do the colors of the graphics become suddenly more brilliant, bluish, greenish, immediately illustrating a kind of paradise. John is no longer depicted as a distant observer, although Rev 21:10 would suggest such a reading: "And he took me in the spirit to a soaring, steep mountain and showed me the Holy City, Jerusalem." Instead he *enters* the great city. Doing so, with the panel's focus on his feet passing over an imaginary border, he becomes transformed from an old man into a young man, personally taking part in the overall process of re-creation.

While this abrupt visual shift allows for an emphasis on the greatness of this new world, the focus on John in natural surroundings, on the other hand, does not attempt any allegorical interpretation of the city. From a scholarly point of view, we might ask how we are to interpret the visual

Figure 4.2.   Scene from *The Book of Revelation* by Matt Dorff and Chris Koelle. Dorff, Matt, and Chris Koelle. *The Book of Revelation*. Grand Rapids, MI: Zondervan, 2012. 153.

rendering of Rev 22:2 that shows John lying under a fruit tree, eating an apple: "The Tree of Life overhangs either side of the river, bringing forth twelve different fruits, yielding its fruit every month. And the leaves of the Tree are for the healing of the Nations." Certainly, the graphics depict John as enjoying the new world order. The author of Revelation, however, hardly thought of this kind of profane joy in the face of "the proclamation of a new way of life, a new world." Instead, as Prigent argues, "the image, far from being opposed to reality, functions as a metalanguage" (Prigent 592). The streaming of the nations into the city, bringing into it "splendor and wealth" (Harrington 220), as well as the promise that "nothing profane will enter into the City, neither anyone who lies or commits loathsome, hateful acts" (Rev 21:27) are crucial conditions for the New Jerusalem. Yet the graphic novel version sums them up in one single panel that simply depicts a lily pond.

Having been confronted with a great number of detailed depictions of destructive events, one might have expected a similar collection of sanguine pictures in the end, emphasizing the Christian message to believe in God's mercy on Judgment Day. Attempting to assess the aesthetical experience, however, the shiny surface of New Jerusalem is stunning;

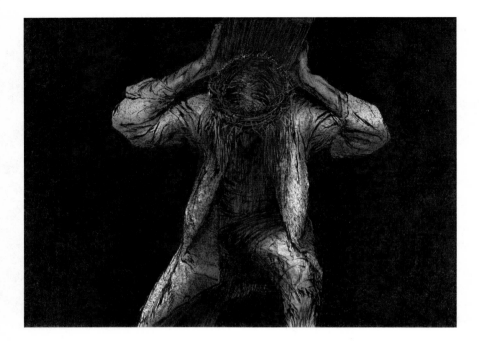

Figure 4.3.   Scene from *The Book of Revelation* by Matt Dorff and Chris Koelle. Dorff, Matt, and Chris Koelle. *The Book of Revelation*. Grand Rapids, MI: Zondervan, 2012. 153.

and the colorful images are capable of serving as a kind of emotional release. Primarily due to these bright colors, bringing about a sharp contrast to the preceding pages, the reader may instantly participate in a feeling of joy and peace. Again, we may assume that an average audience is touched by this feeling more than any theological interpretation of the benefits of the new, multinational world could have delivered. Yet, approaching a conclusion and bearing in mind the publisher's initial claim to a heightened understanding of an ancient text that has laid the foundations for Western thought, the emotional engagement could also serve as the starting point of further involvement with Revelation's multi-layered narrative.

CONCLUDING THOUGHTS

The present chapter has aimed to situate the subgenre of graphic novels based on biblical narratives within current scholarly and sociopolitical debates. In particular, it attempted to contribute not only to the ongoing and healthy methodological discussions of ways to assess this genre, but also to the Luther Decade's ongoing debate concerning how to convey the human dimension of the Bible in the early twenty-first century. This chapter's exploration of *The Book of Revelation* allows for several concluding remarks. As news reports from Germany attest, Revelation has become a source of material in explosive political debates, in the context of which the current relevance and significance of the biblical book for German culture is repeatedly discussed. Thus, one could view Revelation as an outright reflection of the complex current social mood. People do not hesitate to invoke the Bible as a kind of handbook for cultural conflicts as a way of allegedly legitimating diametrical positions. The superficial use of its arguably most dangerous chapter, however, evidences the necessity of deeper involvement to move beyond misleading conclusions or assumptions.

Considering the potential contribution of graphic novels to larger cultural debates, it is interesting to note that both the general usage and invocation of religious imagery and subject matter and the visual rendering of entire biblical books have become popular through the last decades. Yet, although aesthetic and didactical qualities of graphic novels have become a subject of international scholarly interest, as contributors in the present volume attest, relatively little has been written on graphic adaptations of the Bible, particularly in Germany, maybe due to the as yet small number of genuine German-language contributions to the subgenre. In the context of current efforts in Germany to reengage readers with the cultural significance of the Bible through visual media, it would seem that graphic novels could contribute to ongoing discussions more deliberately, not least for the self-serving purpose of a more pronounced profile of the subgenre as Vogel-Sedlmayr points out:

> Generally speaking, one has to notice that, despite some rather sophisticated publications [. . .] , genuine religious subjects are rare among graphic novels. Yet, both history of religion and religious literature ought to be discovered for the graphic novel.

> Aber generell muss man feststellen, trotz einiger niveauvollerer Arbeiten [. . .] , dass genuin religiöse Stoffe unter den Graphic Novels wenig präsent sind. Das Thema der Religionsgeschichte und der religiösen Literatur ist aber durchaus für die Graphic Novel zu entdecken.

Thus, in order to conclude this chapter, and to stimulate further debate on the topic, I will turn the focus to what I consider the most significant quality of the graphic adaptation at hand: its emphasis on the emotional dimension of Revelation.

Jan Baetens and Hugo Frey have pointed out that the graphic novel in general has "a difficult job in communicating thoughts and feelings" (174); but an emotive approach seems to be a tightrope walk for yet another reason. More than is the case with any profane bestseller or even canonized work, the reading of the Bible is often a very private experience, motivating people to transplant their own hopes and concerns into the text. These readings are thus based on strong presuppositions and expectations, which inevitably lay the foundation for the assessment of any secondary adaptation as well. The close involvement of Reverend Mark Arey in the project at hand evidences the concern for creating an adaptation in accordance with the Christian credo. Koelle's claim to "be true to the text and maintain a point of view from John's own understanding of his world" (Challies) bears witness to this concern.

Koelle's comment also draws our attention to John's role as an emotionally involved observer, and the graphic novel at hand evidences the importance of this role throughout. I have described the panel layout as relatively simple, and the vivid visual images seem to draw the readers' attention to the superficial pictorial world rather than any deeper interpretation. However, we might consider this rather common way of structuring comic pages as evidence for the human dimension of the narrative.[29] We are not facing a divine encounter ourselves, but John's stirred attempt at conveying *his* encounter to his successors: "And I, John, am the one who saw and heard these things for myself" (Rev 22:8). The artists' firm usage of juxtaposition in the rendering of this encounter thus speaks to a two-fold strength of graphic novels in general. First, this mode of visualization allows for a powerful depiction of the mighty events that John witnessed: he is, as the Bible stresses, our eyes (and ears). Second, the regular shift to a third-person-view, with close-ups of John's face, makes us aware of the encounters' impact on the human senses: John's awestruck eyes, his gaping mouth, his attempt to shield his ears from the mighty voices. Given this importance of the observer's point of view and his emotional condition, the artists' background in the film business is particularly interesting. As indicated, the novel at hand shares some aspects of modern film technique. The constant shift between different angles, as well as the preference of passages which allow for haunting depictions of monstrosities and disasters, undoubtedly appeal to an audience used to twenty-first-century cinema. The visuals continuously create a condition of tension, gripping the reader from the first page on, and the rapid transition between different perspectives keeps the reader from relinquishing this tension.

I have elaborated on this thesis throughout the examination, and the concept "emotion" thus demands a final statement. As far as the reception of a graphic novel is concerned, I would state that emotions are part of the aesthetic experience. This does not mean that the work expresses an emotion that the authors felt during the graphic novel's creation. Instead, each reader may experience a different emotion. The strong visual emphasis on John's reactions, however, suggests that Dorff and Koelle intended to make the readership aware of the spectrum of *John's* emotional condition during the state of being *in spiritu*. Compared to a classic reading of biblical texts, with John's role being rather formulaic, this illustration immediately stimulates the reader to regard and analyze his or her own feelings while experiencing the text. Although accumulated aesthetic experiences do not necessarily contribute to deeper understanding of the possible (modern) meanings of Revelation per se, the display of emotions may thus serve as a kind of guideline for the audience's own emotions; and it stirs awareness of the fundamental role of humanity in all these encounters oscillating between violence and salvation: "Human beings make the difference—not only during the Reformation, but today and tomorrow."[30] This is an awareness that in fact could allow laymen to gain new access to the Bible: "Emotion in human beings is that process in which events are related to purposes and hence to meanings" (Oatley 132). Particularly in the case of a graphic novel, we might even adopt Oatley's wording of "the flow of viewers' emotion" (109). Dorff's enthusiastic statement that the imagery expressed "the contents of John's heart as well as his soul" (Dorff and Koelle 185) can be understood this way. Repeatedly, the portrayals draw our attention to the formidability of the Bible's final book, and might give an impression of Revelation's possible impact on the Christians imagination throughout time. We might even regard the detailed striving for an emotional adaptation as the reason for omitting any additional commentary that could have dampened the feeling.

From this point of view, the graphic adaptation at hand contributes astoundingly well to a first reading of Revelation as recommended by the *International Bible Commentary*: "It is best to adopt the attitude of one who visits an art museum: simply observe and let the pictures 'hit' you" (Kuckerlkorn 1847). Considering the present adaptation of Revelation analog to the visit of an art museum—in the sense of a first step toward deeper personal involvement with the medium and its possible subtext— the frequently evoked distinction between high and low culture in scholarly debate falls short. Not only might the closer examination of the affective impact of visual images on the readership, therefore, be a worthwhile undertaking in the future study of graphic novels, but it may also increase the general awareness of the emotional, thus human, dimension of biblical narratives. Perhaps eventually it will also stir closer engagement with the Bible's possible meanings in the context of early twenty-first-century history and politics.

NOTES

1. For citation of biblical books other than Revelation, I use the King James Bible. For citation of Revelation, I use Mark Arey's and Philemon Sevastiades' new translation used in the graphic novel at hand.

2. Possible distinctions between graphic novels and comics have been debated for decades. Despite the criticism that the term "graphic novel" has repeatedly served marketing purposes only (Grünewald 19), scholars have not agreed on a clear defini-

tion so far. The current chapter follows the basal definition of "graphic novel" as a book-length work in the medium of comics (Hoover 175).

3. Remarkably, while most scholars agree on "aesthetic qualities" of graphic novels, there seems to be hardly any theoretical discussion of the actual meaning(s) of "aesthetics" within the field of comic studies. In this chapter, I tend to follow Robert Stecker's "minimal view" by describing aesthetics as "the experience derived from attending in a discriminating manner to forms, qualities or meaningful features of things, attending to these for their own sake or the sake of a payoff intrinsic to this very experience" (52–53). As Stecker states, "one is not forced to this view" (53). Yet, despite the problem of how to define "form," "quality," and "meaning," this description may serve as a working hypothesis for the examination at hand; I am aware that it is satisfactory only to a certain degree. On the possible relation of aesthetic experiences and didactics, cf. also the last part of this chapter.

4. "Der Riss zwischen dem 'historischen Jesus' und dem 'Christus des Glaubens' wurde immer tiefer, beides brach zusehends auseinander. [. . .] Dieser Eindruck ist inzwischen weit ins allgemeine Bewusstsein der Christenheit vorgedrungen. Eine solche Situation ist dramatisch für den Glauben, weil sein eigentlicher Bezugspunkt unsicher wird" (Ratzinger 2:10 f.).

5. See https://www.dbg.de/navi/veroeffentlichungen/pressebereich/detailansicht/ article/weiter-die-aktualitaet-der-bibel-vermitteln-1.html [30 Oct. 2015].

6. On the concepts of "Europe in Movement" and "Europe as Movement," and their relation to literary culture, cf. Ette 2009.

7. See http://www.friedenspreis-des-deutschen-buchhandels.de/445941/?mid=103 8399 [30 Oct. 2015].

8. See http://www.friedenspreis-des-deutschen-buchhandels.de/1038404/ [30 Oct. 2015].

9. See http://www.bbaw.de/veranstaltungen/2015/oktober/religionsgespraeche [30 Oct. 2015].

10. Most probably, the Book of Revelation was composed during the first century AD by a person called John. Despite all efforts, it has proved impossible to identify him as the evangelist (Schreiber 566 ff.; Holtz/Niebuhr 7 ff.). We might suppose that people in early Christian times were more familiar with the Apocalypse's pictorial world, and "understood its central message without undue difficulty" (Mounce 24). In this chapter, I use the capitalized word "Revelation" to label the biblical book.

11. See further Gurtner/Bauckham.

12. On political ethics, see Thompson 2013.

13. The speech can be found at: https://www.youtube.com/watch?v=VXRnmvMu2 E0 [15 Jul. 2015]. Cf. http://www.welt.de/politik/deutschland/article134315312/Peter-Hintze-zitiert-aus-der-Offenbarung-des-Johannes.html [30 Oct. 2015].

14. See http://www.dtv.de/buecher/apokalypse_34842.html [30 Oct. 2015].

15. See http://www.luther-in-thueringen.com/en/the-luther-decade.html [30 Oct. 2015].

16. One might think of Doug Mauss' and Sergio Cariello's *Action Bible* from 2010, for instance, depicting key scenes from both the Old and the New Testament on some 700 pages. Recent films such as Darren Aronofsky's *Noah* or Ridley Scott's *Exodus* (both 2014) evidence a renewed fascination with epic biblical stories in the international film industry as well.

17. See http://www.atrium-verlag.com/index.php?id=178&tx_fsvsgbooks_pi1[titel] =Das%20Buch%20der%20Offenbarung&tx_fsvsgbooks_pi1[isbn]=3-85535-072-8&tx_ fsvsgbooks_pi1[link]=detail&cHash=154efdd70b [30 Oct. 2015].

18. See further Rosell.

19. See Kartalopoulos for a brief but vivid reflection upon "multitasking and multimodal information processing" while reading comics.

20. The question of graphic novels' *literary* qualities, in the sense of "high literature" is still a source of controversy (Hansen): "A case for comics is still fighting against a popular and academic perception that comics are for children and comics are a weak

cousin to both literature and visual art. One avenue to exploring and better appreciating the strengths of comics/graphic novels is to examine graphic adaptations of traditional texts" (Thomas 192). Attitudes seem to change—we might instance the granting of the renowned Heinz Maier-Leibnitz Prize to comic theorist Stephan Packard (http://www.pr.uni-freiburg.de/pm/2015/pm.2015-04-02.52 [30 Oct. 2015]) or the research group "Digital and cognitive approaches to graphic literature" at the University of Paderborn, funded by the German Federal Ministry of Education and Research (BMBF) with 1.9 million euro (https://idw-online.de/de/news631871 [30 Oct. 2015])—but there are "some myths about the discipline which scholars are working hard to dispel. [. . .] We do not yet take advantage of the power of comics to educate, inspire and challenge students. The ever-increasing number of comics scholars worldwide aim to change that" (Murray). However, scholars from the field of comic studies are apparently still rather uncertain as to how these theoretical insights ought to shape the tools (and terminology) used in examination.

21. Due to Revelation's regular shift in space and time, panel transition includes, following Scott McCloud, action-to-action, or "featuring a single subject" (70), as well as subject-to-subject, or "staying within a scene or idea" (71), and scene-to-scene, or "transitions, which transport us across significant distances of time and space" (71).

22. Rev 3:7 is only fragmentary in the German edition. Moreover, the artists note that they made minor changes in Luther's German translation.

23. See http://www.zondervan.com/the-book-of-revelation-1 [30 Oct. 2015].

24. See http://www.atrium-verlag.com/index.php?id=178&tx_fsvsgbooks_pi1[titel]=Das%20Buch%20der%20Offenbarung&tx_fsvsgbooks_pi1[isbn]=3-85535-072-8&tx_fsvsgbooks_pi1[link]=detail&cHash=154efdd70b [30 Oct. 2015].

25. The didactical qualities of comic books became subject to debate already shortly after their general breakthrough in the first decades of the twentieth century. In a 1949 survey for the *Journal of Educational Sociology*, Katharine Hutchinson concluded "many teachers discovered comic strips to be particularly useful in special classes and for slow learning pupils in regular classes" (240). On the other hand, she observed a certain degree of negative criticism among educational personnel (244). Interestingly enough, in the face of growing skepticism against comics in the 1950s, graphic adaptations of *biblical* narratives were introduced as an option to improve comics' reputation among an adult audience (Jolly 334).

26. Whereas the King James Bible and the English Standard Bible describe the Lamb as "having been slain," the new translation directly interprets this wording as the stigmata ("the wounds of His own sacrifice," Rev 5). The visualization follows this interpretation by providing close-ups of these wounds.

27. See http://www.zondervan.com/the-book-of-revelation-1 [30 Oct. 2015].

28. See http://www.atrium-verlag.com/index.php?id=neuerscheinungen&tx_fsvsgbooks_pi1[titel]=Das%20Buch%20der%20Offenbarung&tx_fsvsgbooks_pi1[isbn]=3-85535-072-8&tx_fsvsgbooks_pi1[link]=detail&cHash=154efdd70b [30 Oct. 2015].

29. A similar interpretation was put forth by Don Jolly (337) regarding Robert Crumb's *Genesis*.

30. See http://www.luther2017.de/en/2017/reformationsjubilaeum/standpunkte/stephan-dorgerloh [30 Oct. 2015].

REFERENCES

Assmann, Aleida. "Wie Buchstaben zu Bildern werden." *Die Sichtbarkeit der Schrift*. Ed. Susanne Strätling and Georg Witte. München: Fink, 2006. 191–202.

Aune, David. *Revelation*. 3 vols. Nashville: Nelson, 1997–1998.

Baetens, Jan, and Hugo Frey. *The Graphic Novel. An Introduction*. Cambridge: Cambridge University Press, 2015.

Bauckham, Richard. "Revelation." *The Oxford Bible Commentary*. Ed. John Barton and John Muddiman. Oxford: Oxford University Press, 2001. 1287–306.

Boxall, Ian. "The Apocalypse Unveiled. Reflections on the Reception History of Revelation." *The Expository Times* 125.6 (2014): 261–71.

Brownrigg, Ronald. *Who's Who in the New Testament*. London: Routledge, 2002.

Challies, Tim, and Chris Koelle. "The (Graphic Novel) Book of Revelation." *Challies*. 7 Sept. 2011. Web. 30 Oct. 2015. http://www.challies.com/interviews/the-graphic-novel-book-of-revelation.

Dorff, Matt, and Chris Koelle. *The Book of Revelation*. Grand Rapids, MI: Zondervan, 2012.

Dorff, Matt, and Chris Koelle. *Das Buch der Offenbarung*. Zürich: Atrium, 2013.

Ette, Ottmar. "European Literature(s) in the Global Context." *Literature for Europe?* Ed. Theo D'haen and Iannis Goerlandt. Amsterdam; New York: Rodopi, 2009. 123–60.

Friesen, Steven J. "Satan's Throne, Imperial Cults and the Social Settings of Revelation." *Journal for the Study of the New Testament* 27.3 (2005): 351–73.

Grünewald, Dietrich. "Die Kraft der narrativen Bilder." *Bild ist Text ist Bild. Narration und Ästhetik in der Graphic Novel*. Eds. Susanne Hochreiter, and Ursula Klingenböck. Bielefeld: Transcript, 2014. 17–51.

Gurtner, Daniel M., and Richard Bauckham. "Revelation." *The Bible Knowledge Background Commentary: John's Gospel, Hebrews-Revelation*. Ed. Craig A. Evans. Colorado Springs, CO: Cook, 2005. 341–400.

Hansen, Kathryn S. "In Defense of Graphic Novels." *English Journal* 102.2 (2012): 57–63.

Harrington, Wilfrid J. *Revelation*. Rev. ed. Collegeville: MN: Glazier Books, 2008.

Hatfield, Charles. "An Art of Tensions." *A Comics Studies Reader*. Ed. Jeet Heer and Kent Worcester. Jackson: MS: University Press of Mississippi, 2009. 132–48.

Herder, Johann Gottfried von. *Johannes Offenbarung*. Stuttgart, Tübingen: Cotta'sche Verlagsbuchhandlung, 1829 [1779].

Holtz, Traugott, and Karl-Wilhelm Niebuhr, eds. *Die Offenbarung des Johannes*. Göttingen: Vandenhoeck & Ruprecht, 2008.

Hoover, Steven. "The Case for Graphic Novels." *Communications in Information Literacy* 5.2 (2012): 174–86.

Hutchinson, Katharine H. "An Experiment in the Use of Comics as Instructional Material." *Journal of Educational Sociology* 23.4 (1949): 236–45.

Jolly, Don. "Interpretive Treatments of Genesis in Comics. R. Crumb & Dave Sim." *The Journal of Religion and Popular Culture* 25.3 (2013): 333–43.

Kartalopoulos, Bill. "Why Comics Are More Important Than Ever." *Huffingtonpost*. 29 October 2014. Web. 30 Oct. 2015. http://www.huffingtonpost.com/bill-kartalopoulos/why-comics-matter_b_6056736.html.

Kuckerlkorn, Eduardo A., Manuel D. Mateos, and Tomás Kraft. "Revelation." *The International Bible Commentary*. Ed. W. R. Farmer. Collegeville, MN: Liturgical Press, 1998. 1843–879.

Lewis, A. Davis. "Revelation Graphic Novel. A New Media Approach to John's Visions." *Publishers Weekly* 17 Apr. 2013. Web. 30 Oct. 2015. http://www.publishersweekly.com/pw/by-topic/industry-news/religion/article/56861-revelation-graphic-novel-a-new-media-approach-to-john-s-visions.html.

Lobinger, Katharina. *Visuelle Kommunikationsforschung. Medienbilder als Herausforderung für die Kommunikations- und Medienwissenschaft*. Wiesbaden: Springer, 2012.

McCloud, Scott. *Understanding Comics: the Invisible Art*. Northampton, MA: Tundra Publishing, 1993.

Miller, Joel J., and Mark Arey. "A New Way to See the Book of Revelation." *Patheos* 20 June 2013. Web. 30 Oct. 2015. http://www.patheos.com/blogs/joeljmiller/2013/06/a-new-way-to-see-the-book-of-revelation/.

Mounce, Robert H. *The Book of Revelation*. Rev. ed. Grand Rapids: Eerdmans Publishing, 1998.

Murray, Christopher. "Comics Studies Has Been Undervalued For Too Long." *The Guardian* 18 Feb. 2015. Web. 30 Oct. 2015. http://www.theguardian.com/higher-education-network/2015/feb/18/comics-studies-has-been-undervalued-for-too-long-were-fighting-to-change-this.

Nielsen, Jesper T. "Lamm, Lamm Gottes." *Bibelwissenschaft.* n.d. Web. 30 Oct. 2015. https://www.bibelwissenschaft.de/wibilex/das-bibellexikon/lexikon/sachwort/anze igen/details/lamm-lamm-gottes/ch/28d310b45a980d04c19c83b38fcd7cff/.

Oatley, Keith. *Such Stuff as Dreams. The Psychology of Fiction.* Chichester: Wiley-Black-well, 2011.

Ostling, Richard N. "Scholar Tries to Untangle Revelation's Images in Commentary." *Lubbock Avalanche-Journal.* 12 Jan. 2002. Web. 30 Oct. 2015. http://lubbockonline. com/stories/011202/rel_0112020113.shtml#.VphYB0vN9NY.

Prigent, Pierre. *Commentary on the Apocalypse of St. John.* Tübingen: Mohr Siebeck, 2004.

Ratzinger, Joseph (Benedikt XVI.). *Jesus von Nazareth.* 3 vols. Freiburg i.Br.: Herder, 2007–2012.

Rosell, Sergio. "John's Apocalypse. Dynamic Word-Images for a New World." *HTS Teologiese Studies/Theological Studies* 67.1 (2011). Web. 30 October 2015.

Schreiber, Stefan. "Die Offenbarung des Johannes." *Einleitung in das Neue Testament.* Ed. M. Ebner, and Stefan Schreiber. Stuttgart: Kohlhammer, 2008. 559–85.

Skaggs, Rebecca, and Thomas Doyle. "Violence in the Apocalypse of John." *Currents in Biblical Research* 5.2 (2007): 220–34.

Stanley, Sarah. "Drawing on God. Theology in Graphic Novels." *Theological Librarian-ship* 2.1 (2009): 83–88.

Stecker, Robert. *Aesthetics and the Philosophy of Art. An Introduction.* Lanham, MD: Rowman & Littlefield, 2010.

Stephens, Mark B. *Annihilation or Renewal? The Meaning and Function of New Creation in the Book of Revelation.* Tübingen: Mohr Siebeck, 2011.

Strätling, Susanne, and Georg Witte, eds. *Die Sichtbarkeit der Schrift.* München: Fink, 2006.

Strobel, August. "Apokalypse des Johannes." *Theologische Realezyklopädie* 3 (1978): 174–89.

Thomas, P. L. "Adventures in Genre! Rethinking Genre through Comics/Graphic Nov-els." *Journal of Graphic Novels and Comics* 2.2 (2011): 187–201.

Thompson, Dennis F. "Political Ethics." *The International Encyclopedia of Ethics.* 1 Feb. 2013. Web. 30 Oct. 2015. http://onlinelibrary.wiley.com/doi/10.1002/9781444367072. wbiee633/abstract.

Vogel-Sedlmayr, Gereon. "Theologie in Graphic Novels I & II. Gott im Comic." *Deut-sches Pfarrerblatt* 4/2015 & 5/2015. Web. 30 Oct. 2015. http://www.pfarrerverband.de/ pfarrerblatt.

Witte, Tobias. "Apokalyptische Bildfolgen." *texte und bilder.* 7 Jul 2013. Web. 30 Oct. 2015. http://www.texteundbilder.com/offenbarung/.

III

GRAPHIC NOVELS: HANDS-ON

FIVE

Using Graphic Novels for Content Learning in the German-Studies Classroom

The Basel City Reportage Operation Läckerli

Julia Ludewig

While comics and graphic novels[1] have reached elementary and secondary language arts classrooms, instructors of adult language learners have been more hesitant to fully embrace the graphic medium as a vehicle for second language acquisition. In her article "Bridging the Gap: A Literacy-Oriented Approach to Teaching the Graphic Novel *Der erste Frühling*" (*The First Spring*) Elizabeth Bridges writes that there is "surprisingly little scholarship that deals with graphic novels in L2 settings" (154). Bridges wrote her article in 2009; and little has changed since that time. Even though some material exists on foreign-language learning with the aid of comics and graphic novels,[2] these studies focus mainly on the elementary or high school classroom, with relatively few publications targeting adult learners. Although it is still relatively rare and new to teach an integrated language and content class with the help of graphic narratives, they have great potential for improving results in the foreign language classroom. The existing modest body of research indicates that, by and large, students enjoy reading and analyzing graphic novels and comics. Beyond a general boost in motivation, graphic novels can also introduce and strengthen language acquisition and language arts skills.[3] Understandably, the theme of language acquisition skills dominates articles written by foreign-language instructors, but graphic novels are also promising sources for content learning, or the attainment of knowledge and skills beyond the foreign language proper. This would include information about the cultural history of a certain geographic area or, as I emphasize here, the capacity to understand, contextualize, and critically engage visual materials. In addition to teaching aspects of history and the socio-cultural specifics of a region (roughly captured by the German term *Landeskunde*),[4] graphic novels offer instructors ways to develop students' transcultural competence. This is a central tenet of foreign-language education in the United States, which the MLA Ad Hoc Committee has defined as "the ability to comprehend and analyze the cultural narratives that appear in every kind of expressive form" (MLA Ad Hoc). Additionally, this notion of transcultural competence ties in with the "Culture" as well as the "Comparison" facets of the American Council on the Teaching of Foreign Language's (ACTFL) five C framework ("Standards for Language Learning").[5]

Inspired by current literature in the field, I have developed specific content-and-culture-oriented classroom activities using two stories from *Operation Läckerli* (Operation Gingerbread Treat), a collection of short graphic vignettes published in 2004 by the Berlin-based Monogatari collective. *Operation Läckerli* falls into the subgenre of comics journalism, more specifically that of *Stadtreportage* (city reportage). In many of the existing phenomenological observations of big-city life that are typical of *Stadtreportage*, the reader frequently views city streets in major German cities such as Munich, Hamburg, and Berlin.[6] The artists' renderings both introduce readers to the cities and invite them to view these places in a new light. In comic reportage, journalistic observations blend with often stylized representations of scenes and people, and thus also blend two sets of ethics: the ethics of reporting "truthfully" and that of creative license which allows the artist to play with and "distort" representation. *Operation Läckerli* zooms in on Basel, Switzerland, and thereby brings into focus a city and a national culture often neglected in German Studies. The book gathers six "snapshots" of Basel, which together create a kaleidoscopic impression of the city. As *Operation Läckerli* was created for a native German-speaking audience, the German instructor must carefully prepare materials that will appropriately guide the foreign-language students' reading process. Some stories are easier to decode than others, both visually and linguistically. Hence pedagogical selectiveness and preparatory framing are all the more important. In this essay, I will discuss Jens Harder's "Schnell, Schuss" (Quick, Kick) and Ulli Lust's "Ein Platz in Mitteleuropa" (A Square in Central Europe), henceforth "Ein Platz."[7]

Students at beginning levels of language proficiency would be able to read some stories in *Operation Läckerli*, one example being Lust's "Ein Platz." Most of the stories, however, require at least an intermediate level of language proficiency as described by the ACTFL Proficiency Guidelines (16–18); an advanced high level is even preferable for some stories. Regardless of level, the strength of *Operation Läckerli* lies in the diversity of its entries. For the purpose of this essay, my focus is on visual, historical, transcultural, and literary aspects of the book, although I also make suggestions for exercises that train linguistic skills. In the following sections, I emphasize the possibility of integrating language, content, and multi-literacy through the use of graphic literature, which provides language instructors and learners with a powerful tool to become critical users of and commentators on linguistic and literary subjects. Perhaps most importantly, students learn to read and critique multimodal codes that operate in combination to create a single message. A book like *Operation Läckerli* allows students to hone these skills while also enjoying the reward of engaging with a timely work of art designed for native speakers.

VISUAL AND MULTIMODAL SKILLS

Since most students will likely have little prior knowledge of reading and learning with graphic novels, it is advisable for the instructor to familiarize them with the idea that these books are not a different type of text or genre, but instead a different medium, just as prose texts, film, or photographs would be considered different media. In order to develop an understanding of this notion, the class can regard a story that has been adapted for different media, for example, Uwe Timm's *Die Entdeckung der Currywurst* (*The Invention of the Curried Sausage*, 1993). Illustrator Isabel Kreitz turned Timm's original novella into a graphic novel in 2005, and three years later a movie based on the same story opened in German theaters. Comparing these three renderings of the "same" story students will find significant differences in the expressive possibilities of each medium. For instance, movies dictate the speed at which the viewer takes in the events while prose and graphic narratives allow for a self-paced reception. Yet, as opposed to exclusively verbal literature, movies and graphic novels add visual-verbal modalities to convey these events.

With the goal of gradually moving students toward the graphic novel medium after a survey of other media types, the instructor can assign students to compile the characteristics that set this medium apart from other media. Before analyzing *Operation Läckerli*, learners at various language levels will benefit from composing a list of typical elements of the graphic novel, such as images appearing in a sequence and combining with text in speech and thought bubbles. Basic prompts such as "How do we read graphic novels?" or "Which elements are important?" can elicit initial thoughts from the students about comic art. It would also benefit students to compile their responses on posters or a class wiki. This activity would give them the opportunity to practice their language skills and at the same time supply their classmates with concepts that they can reuse and reference later in the course.

INTRODUCING "SCHNELL, SCHUSS"

"Schnell, Schuss" is Jens Harder's graphic musing about rampant soccer fever and Switzerland's most successful club, the *Fußball Club Basel* or FCB for short. "Schnell, Schuss" uses more classical graphic-novel elements than "Ein Platz" and may thus work well as an introductory piece and a foil of comparison if the instructor plans on reading "Ein Platz" as well as "Schnell, Schuss." In order to guide students toward discovering these classic elements, the instructor might ask: "Which typical graphic-novel elements do you see here?" Drawing upon the information they had previously gathered as a group about graphic texts, a brainstorming session may yield elements like speech and thought bubbles set apart by different shapes, iconographical conventions such as motion lines, and onomatopoetic expressions like the yawning sound "UUA-HAA!" (n.pag.). This preliminary exercise can also be used as a vocabulary builder, allowing students to become familiar with the respective German terminology used to describe graphic texts.[8]

Remarkably, Harder employs varying degrees of realistic depiction when rendering people's faces. For example, while the faces of most of the fans at the soccer matches are reduced to a cartoonish minimum, interviewees on the streets and individual soccer players have fully sketched, recognizable physiognomies. Students can speculate on the reasons behind Harder's stylistic decisions, led by questions like: "Why does Harder use different styles of drawing for different individuals?" or "What kind of effect does that have on you as a reader?" These questions are particularly fruitful when students have previously talked about the goals and tools of comics journalism, because this discussion can lead to an association between visual realism and the journalistic ethos of showing authentic people. The visual abstraction, in turn, belongs to the rhetoric of comics and cartoons in which people function as placeholders and foils for identifying with the reader, rather than as individuals. With his abstracted figures, Harder invites readers to put themselves into the shoes of the depicted characters, an effect Scott McCloud calls "masking" (43). In this way, the reader can become part of the collective body of fans, a representation that visually captures the leveling and anonymizing effect of fandom.

INTRODUCING "EIN PLATZ"

Lust's "Ein Platz" is a nearly textless collage of impressions and encounters that occur in Basel's Barfüsser Square, a transportation hub and popular meeting place in the Swiss city. "Ein Platz" has some traditional graphic-novel elements as well, such as motion lines and dialogue, yet it challenges the basic tenets of classic iconography more than most graphic narratives and certainly more than mainstream comics. "Ein Platz" is inventive in many ways: it often omits panel borders, uses merely two colors, lacks a continuous narrative and uses captions and dialogue sparingly. Also peculiar to "Ein Platz" is that it features non-realistic and potentially alienating techniques such as "transparent" people through whom the reader can see the contours of other people and objects that would normally be hidden from view (figure 5.1). Directing students to describe what effects these artistic decisions have on their reading experience serves at least two pedagogical purposes. First, students can practice writing or speaking competencies, and second they can become aware of the way they interpret and appreciate visuals. Expected reactions may focus on how the graphic narrative challenges or discourages them as readers, or, alternately, how the techniques keep them intrigued and curious precisely *because* they slow down the meaning-making process: their eyes and minds "stumble" over unusual elements.

In order to grasp particular techniques of storytelling in graphic novels, students can focus on panel transitions in "Ein Platz." First, students would learn about different types of transitions using, for example, the classification suggested by McCloud in *Understanding Comics* (70–72). Based on McCloud's matrix, students then find examples for the different degrees of temporal and spatial relation maintained—or sometimes not maintained—between panels. Lust's story contains examples of action-

Figure 5.1.   Panel from "Ein Platz in Mitteleuropa." Ulli Lust. "Ein Platz." *Operation Läckerli: Comicreportagen aus Basel.* **Berlin: Monogatari, 2004, n.pag.**

to-action transitions in which the reader observes a single subject performing distinct actions; a man waits at the tram station in one panel and
then searches through a trash bin in the next (n.pag.). The most common
transition, however, is the aspect-to-aspect shift in which the reader turns
into what McCloud would call a "wandering eye" that roams around
Barfüsser Square, capturing snapshots of places, ideas, or moods without
following any one person or event in particular (McCloud 72). This is a
tool that is well suited to the aims of *Stadtreportage* since it delivers a
dense chain of impressions that only the city's character holds together.
Differentiating between types of transitions sharpens students' abilities
to produce detailed observations about visual sequential components
and their possible relations.

HISTORY AND *LANDESKUNDE*

Operation Läckerli can be used to introduce students to aspects of Switzerland's geography, history, political organization, and culture. Although
the city of Basel is the central focus, the instructor could connect Basel to
other areas of Switzerland and Europe. Before delving into *Operation
Läckerli*, instructors might activate students' existing knowledge and pre-
conceptions of Switzerland and Basel by using brainstorming questions
such as: "Which famous people, products, and landscapes do you associate with Switzerland?" "Which cities and rivers can you name?"
"Where are they located?" or "What would you like to know about Switzerland and Basel?" Locating cities and rivers on a blank map of Switzerland offers a good starting point for geographical orientation. Students
learn that Basel is Switzerland's third most populous city after Zurich
and Geneva, that it lies in the dominantly German-speaking part of Switzerland, and that its "home river," the Rhine, flows through nine European countries including six in which German is an officially recognized
language.[9] Having pooled their prior knowledge, students work in
groups or by themselves to add new information using German-language
web resources such as Basel's official web page, general Internet information sites, or pages geared toward special interest areas, such as Basel
University, international companies like Roche, or sports celebrities like
Roger Federer.

    After this introductory phase, the class can utilize specific stories in
Operation Läckerli for exploring Switzerland and Basel's culture. Begin-
ners and intermediate learners may wish to focus on the notion of "Mitte-
leuropa" which appears in Lust's story "Ein Platz in Mitteleuropa."
Lust's portrayal of Barfüsser Square specifically invites considerations
about the cultural and geographic coordinates of Basel within Europe.
Lust quotes medieval Swiss scholar Jeremias Gotthelf: "One stands at a
European artery here; because everything and everybody who travels

comes together here like in a knot and then parts again to many different countries" (Man steht an einer Pulsader Europas, denn hier laufe zusammen wie in einem Knoten und dann wieder auseinander in vieler Herren Länder, was reiset und laufet; n.pag.). Using this vivid quote, the class can debate exactly who or what comes together in Basel, the city at Europe's "artery," or convergence point. This quotation alone enables students to visualize the city; and it is worth pointing out that it owes its vividness precisely to the power of verbally mediated visual imagery (the simile "like in a knot") and of motion, two vital elements for graphic narratives. Located in the so-called *Dreiländereck* (three-country triangle) between France, Germany, and Switzerland, Basel lies in the center of Europe and, much like Barfüsser Square itself, is a place where travelers come together and part ways again.

The religious past of Basel and its Barfüsser Square is another pedagogically valuable aspect in Lust's story. With the help of the instructor and additional sources, students can discover that Barfüsser Square is named after the nearby Barfüsser Church, which in turn refers to the religious order of Franciscans, also called "Barfüsser" (the bare-footed ones). Lust opens "Ein Platz" with a reference to this fraternity by juxtaposing a Bible verse with a picture of a monk walking barefoot through Birsig Creek. Lust shows the monks as misty-eyed men, smiling and gesturing in a paradisiac landscape—the connection to would-be Barfüsser Square being Birsig Creek—and taking a lesson from the "birds of the air" (Vögel in den Lüften) and the "lilies of the field" (Lilien auf dem Felde) who do not work, but are still nourished by the Lord ("und unser Herr im Himmel ernährt sie doch" n.pag.). This image can serve as an entry point into a discussion of the legacy of religious orders in Europe and Switzerland, the importance of cloisters for preserving and disseminating culture, as well as religious fault lines which fractured central Europe along Protestant and Catholic lines. Lust's Barfüsser Square is ripe with religious signs such as statues showing Samson and Delilah as well as St. George the dragon-slayer. Yet the square is also a decidedly secular sphere and thus embodies the situation in many German-speaking countries. Upon closer examination of the drawings, students will discover that the former Barfüsser Church has been secularized and now serves as the *Historisches Museum Basel* (Historical Museum of Basel). As Lust writes at the beginning of her story with reference to the former bare-footed friars: "Devoutly walking barefoot is long out of style. Instead, one wears love handles and a belly button for all to see" (Das demütige Barfuss-Gehen ist längst aus der Mode. Man trägt stattdessen Hüftspeck und einen öffentlichen Bauchnabel; n.pag.). Here, Lust connects Basel's medieval past to its modern present, with lightheartedness in both her language and her brush.

Harder's "Schnell, Schuss" supports an instructional unit on soccer culture in German-speaking countries and in Basel specifically. By examining the people whom Harder depicts, students can discover the different attitudes people have toward their local sports teams. Students become acquainted with disapproving inhabitants such as a nun who snaps that "God doesn't play soccer" (Gott spielt kein Fußball; n.pag.), and whose indignation Harder conveys by showing her in half profile, grim-faced, and avoiding eye contact. But of course, students also find those enthusiasts who demonstrate their devotion with arms up in the air, bright smiles, and chants like "Stand up if you are from Basel" (Steh auf, wenn du ein Basler bist; n.pag.). The immediacy and details of these visuals allows the reader to observe these people, their facial features, and mannerisms closely, thus developing with them a feeling of intimacy.

Continuing with the theme of the true soccer fan, the class can consider what it takes to be a true fan of a sports club. Buying the FCB refrigerator priced at 4,000 Swiss francs (roughly $4,000 US dollars), which Harder displays on a page full of fan merchandise (n.pag.)? Reconnecting this theme with visual literacy, students may also inquire how branding works by means of showing and decoding the social meaning of certain shapes, colors, and objects found on flags or clothing. This type of branding marks fan articles as devotional objects, and thus functions much like signs of religious or socio-cultural communities. In other words, branding and other forms of cultural symbolism, including religious symbolism, share the semiotic function of marking a space, object, or person as belonging to a certain group. By using repeated and easily recognizable shapes, colors, and melodies, groups can establish links between objects and their institution such that when a viewer or listener connects an element of the branded repertoire with the brand or social group, s/he unconsciously associates a much larger set of values, memories, and ultimately worldviews with it.

Students may further explore the FCB's home stadium, St. Jakob Park, both in Harder's rendering and on the team's website, which offers a rich resource for practicing skills of visual analysis as they pertain to web pages. Additionally, students can identify parallels between how the page's design influences viewing and clicking habits and, in analogous terms, how comic layout influences ways of reading. In terms of content, students could learn about ticket prices, the issue of fan-related hooliganism, as well as the stadium's alternative uses, such as a staging of Verdi's *Aida*. In one panel, Harder shows the iconic, solemn procession of priests in *Aida* drawn in a minimalist style. This contrasts with previous panels that show the same as the venue for a soccer match. While the sports event appears in dynamic images which include details of the audience's reaction, the opera scene is abstract, static, and stage-oriented. Thus, one can argue that Harder plays with a popular cliché according to which cultural events are bloodless and boring while sport matches promise real entertainment. An alternative interpretation could be that Harder presents the soccer industry as equally stage-oriented as opera. These differences in possible interpretations anticipate the possible range of student interpretations.

Finally, an advanced class can describe and evaluate modern architecture in detail, as Harder does himself. With a tone that straddles awe and irreverence, Harder describes the stadium as "spacy" (spacig; n.pag.) and as a "gem" (Schmuckstück) that has a "futuristic plastic shell square" (futuristische[s] Plastikschalengeviert). He combines this with a drawing that stresses the modern and futuristic quality of the stadium. Floodlit in a Basel night and surrounded by hundreds of waiting soccer fans, it takes on the look of a spaceship, half attractive, half off-putting. In tune with his ironic tone, Herder allows himself a visual joke and smuggles a MONOGATARI sign on top of the otherwise ostensibly sober representation of the stadium. Following the artist's model, students can come up with their own descriptions of the building, either mocking or serious, and then discuss their aesthetic reactions as a group. Approaching the influence of visual representation from the opposite direction, the class can also search for different images of FC Basel's home stadium and then reflect on how diverging aspects such as light, angle, or captions inform the beholder's reaction toward the stadium as beautiful, modern, or cold.

TRANSCULTURAL COMPETENCE

Operation Läckerli offers ample opportunities to enhance students' transcultural competence, and instructors can use the collection to unveil cultural narratives that Switzerland develops about itself and about the cultural "other." The visual narratives in *Operation Läckerli* not only touch upon Switzerland's status as one of the most popular immigration destinations and as a global-economic powerhouse, but they also thematize Switzerland's homegrown multilingualism and multiculturalism. The indigenous multiculturalism differs from the immigration-based multiculturalism in that the former dates back centuries and is limited to European, Christian, and, more marginally, Jewish traditions. New immigration, by contrast, adds non-European cultures to the picture and thus gives urgency to debates about cultural proximity and otherness. Those are precisely cultural *narratives*, or ideologies of purism or multiculturalism, which students can learn to understand in their political bias: no narrative is ever ideologically neutral.

Prior to discussing *Operation Läckerli's* individual stories, students can explore the autochthonous language diversity in Switzerland in which French, Swiss-German, Italian, and Rhaeto-Romance dialects are spoken in different areas and with different degrees of official recognition. The instructor may wish to guide students in thinking about what it means to live in a country that recognizes four national languages. What does that

imply for a national identity or for schooling? Do people perceive themselves primarily as Swiss or as Swiss French, Swiss Italian, Swiss German,
and so on? Students can also critically question the reality of Switzerland's multilingualism. Separating societal and individual multilingualism, students will discover that Switzerland may indeed have four official languages, yet most inhabitants only speak one language as their
mother tongue, while mastering other languages with various levels of
proficiency (Franceschini 118). Another interesting task is to compare
multilingual societies worldwide, including Canada and many African
countries. In which countries does a majority of the population actually
speak several languages fluently? What kinds of ethnic and political tensions can arise from multilingualism? Here, too, a class can integrate
visual cues to answer these questions, such as political cartoons about or
from Francophone Canada, goods or banknotes labeled in Swahili,
French, and/or English in Rwanda, or news that report about the tensions
between Kurds and Turks as it appears in broadcasts from both sides.

Apart from this indigenous multiculturalism and multilingualism, immigration has of course become a major contributor to an ethnically and
linguistically diverse Switzerland. The instructor can educate students
with additional materials such as newspaper articles or lexicon entries
that talk about the major countries of origin for Swiss immigrants as well
as about the existing immigration laws. In order to practice visual literacy
further, instructors and students can use visual sources of the desired
information, such as maps, graphs, or cartoons. How, for instance, are
European immigrants portrayed in political campaigns? In 2014, the
Swiss people voted down by a slight margin a referendum that would
ease the naturalization of immigrants' children (Birrer 2014). In preparation for the referendum, the pro-immigration committee "ID SWISS"
commissioned a poster on which we see four seated naked babies from
behind, two with darker skin color under the English heading "Made in
Switzerland." Here a positive label which used to denote "Swissness" is
humorously applied to human beings and extended to include new pros-
pective citizens (Selezione n.pag.).

Students might be surprised to learn that Switzerland is the leading
country of immigration admissions per capita and that despite prevalent
assumptions, the majority of immigrants come from EU countries ("Gefragtes Land" n.pag.). While Switzerland is one of the most coveted immigration destinations, a considerable part of the population is less toler-
ant of immigration and immigrants, supplying a spectrum of reactions
from skepticism to xenophobia. Here, again, visual sources abound that
the instructor can use to build students' literacy, among them infograph-
ics, symbolically charged photographs, or even protesters' posters. Moreover, with the aid of statistical and visual data, the class can find out
about the importance of direct democracy in Switzerland and the extraordinary influence Swiss citizens can wield through plebiscites; most re-

cently with a 2014 referendum against *Masseneinwanderung* (mass immigration). Students can, for example, analyze visual political propaganda for and against immigration. In a remarkable image, the anti-immigration campaign by the SVP (*Schweizerische Volkspartei* or Swiss People's Party), depicts a map of Switzerland crushed by the roots of an apple tree, a tree which arguably represents the wealth immigrants reap from Switzerland, together with the slogan "end mass immigration" (Masseneineinwanderung stoppen) ("Plakatkampagne" n.pag.). The fact that a portion of the Swiss populace positively regards other nations also becomes visible in the protest banner reading "vigil for Palestine" (Mahnwache für Palästina; n.pag.), which Lust depicts in one panel.

Even though no concrete political posters for or against immigration appear in *Operation Läckerli*, the very people who populate the streets allow students to speculate about the multicultural composition of Basel. A reflection question could prompt students to identify and describe instances in which Lust shows people who appear to have immigrated to Switzerland from non-European countries. Among these people are a little braided black girl playing with a balloon, a lady with a turban or cap who seems to be of African or Middle Eastern descent, two black men shown from behind, as well as a woman wearing a headscarf and long-sleeved tunic. The artist often shows these people facing the viewer or placed prominently on the page. Students may interpret these signs as an indication of their acceptance in the cityscape.

Yet Lust does not shy away from exposing the more gruesome realities of immigrant life. The longest textual passage in Lust's otherwise text-light story is uttered by a Kurd. He tells a woman on a bench the painful story of his past and escape to Switzerland where he found asylum. As he reports, despite his efforts he cannot find a job or apartment and remains poor. Lust heightens the impact of his story by positioning it underneath a neutral depiction of Barfüsser Square where people drink, chat, or catch a streetcar. When the Kurd narrates his story, the peaceful, everyday images clash with the disheartening content of the text and thus create a tension between word and image. It is precisely after the Kurd's story that the reader sees the above-mentioned little black girl who appears as a single prominent figure without verbal complement in the middle of the square holding a balloon. Because Lust also shows other immigrants, however, one could therefore argue that she plays with a double tension. She shows both the balancing act between positive and negative experiences that immigrants have in Basel and develops a formal tension between images and text to represent the opposition. Lust's perspective on multicultural Basel provides a mixed yet arguably authentic picture of the conditions in which immigrants find themselves in many European cities. The story thus has the potential to shatter negative or positive stereotypes students might hold about Europe's immigration policies. A subsequent task could direct students to conduct further research into these specific matters.

"Schnell, Schuss" is a text that plays with and ironizes national stereotypes, a humorous stance implicit in the title which can also be read as a pun on *Schnellschuss*, meaning an overly hasty action or judgment. With his amusing and amused tone, Harder names and depicts allegedly typical behavior in Swiss people as well as in the international fans who accompany their soccer teams to the *Alpencup* 2003. Thus, he characterizes Basel and Switzerland's inhabitants as "civilized, distinguished friendly people" (wohlerzogene, distinguiert freundliche Menschen), "deeply rooted in traditional cultural consciousness" (tief verwurzelt in tradiertem Kulturbewußtsein) who live in a "lovely swath of land" (lieblicher Landstrich; n.pag.). Students can discuss what exactly these clichés about Swiss people and landscapes mean and if they correspond to their own ideas regarding "the Swiss." Thinking about questions like: "Which stereotypes do you associate with Switzerland and its people?" students can come up with lists of positive and negative assumptions. It is noteworthy that Harder does *not* affirm these stereotypes and instead depicts a population whose dominant characteristics are its diversity and ordinariness.

Leaving behind assumptions about Switzerland and the Swiss, "Schnell, Schuss" also provides opportunities to identify and question stereotypes about people from other countries. In the *Alpencup*, FC Basel competed against the Turkish club Beşiktaş, Croatia's Dinamo Zagreb, and Germany's Hannover 96. In a voice that is as professional as it is mocking, Harder comments on what he perceives as a soccer "virus" and its expression in different nationalities: "The symptoms are as diverse as the nations" (Vielfältig wie die Nationen sind die Symptome; n.pag.). He continues to describe each fan block with gleeful truisms. There is the stereotype of the loud, musical Turk whose female companion wears a headscarf to the game ("Hearty drumming and turbulent waves of scarves in the Turkish block" [Tüchtiges Trommeln und Tücherturbulenzen im Türkenblock; n.pag.]) while the Croatian fan body appears as cheeky and violent as it "prefers to blast effects with sound and smoke" (vertraut . . . lieber auf Knalleffekte und produziert ordentlich Schall & Rauch; n.pag.) with fireworks at the stands and on the soccer field. German fans are shown performing a half-charming, half-ridiculous conga line, drinking beer, and sporting beer bellies. They also strip down and rub each other with sunscreen, which alludes to the nudity-loving German *Freikörperkultur*—a nudism movement—as well an ostensible German fondness for outdoor activities ("Derweil erfreut sich Hannover 96 am schönen Wetter"/Meanwhile Hannover 96 enjoys the beautiful weather, n.pag.).

The routine national stereotypes of the fans stand in ironic contrast to the international makeup of the teams themselves. Thus, the three young

FCB fans Harder sketches in a follow-up panel are all wearing jerseys that bear the names of foreign-born or multi-ethnic players, here Argentinians Christian Giménez and Julio Rossi, as well as Swiss-Turkish Murat Yakin. Once students have spotted these stereotypes, they can then step back for meta-analysis led by questions like: "Why do we have prejudices? Which social functions do they serve? Why are they dangerous?" The class thus ponders stereotypes as a social phenomenon, searching for the people and institutions that disseminate them and benefit from them, as well as for the socio-psychological boons and banes of such clichés.

LITERARY ANALYTICAL SKILLS

Comics and graphic novels are special types of texts that challenge notions of literature as purely verbal artifacts. Instead of bypassing this discussion, the instructor can have the class debate the literary nature and quality of the comics medium, posing the question: "What, exactly, is literature?" The class could read excerpts from classics such as Jean-Paul Sartre's *What Is Literature?* (1949) or Terry Eagleton's introduction to his book *Literary Theory* (1983) which both muse about the same question. The instructor may divide the class into groups who brainstorm individual aspects of literature, aspects such as medium, language, fiction, the act of reading, market/society, and critics/canon. Students will likely generate a prototypical image of literature as a monomodal text that employs sophisticated language, has a complicated and/or powerful fictional narrative, reflects issues in society, and is valued by professional critics. After that, the class explores the fringes of literature such as pulp fiction guided by the provocative questions "Is this still literature, why or why not?" Such reflections will lead students to embrace the relativity of literariness, which is contingent on historical, cultural, and personal values. Graphic novels similarly contest high-brow definitions of literature. It is an oft-repeated concern—and an extension of charges already made about comics—that graphic novels rely too much on pictures to tell their stories and thus take away from the reader's pleasure to visually imagine story elements. Another point of contention is that some comics and graphic novels feature personae like superheroes or mythical creatures, and, even worse, contain sexual and violent themes. In these cases, graphic novels are prone to draw upon themselves the age-old charge of escapism and of moral deprecation.[10] As has been shown with cultural themes, instructors can also use *Operation Läckerli* to tap into the literary and aesthetic debates surrounding "true" literature and graphic novels. One approach is to have advanced classes read literary criticism. Reviews of *Operation Läckerli* have appeared, for instance, in the newspaper *Berliner Morgenpost* ("Operation Läckerli"), the Swiss *Programmzeitung* (Brunner 2004), and the German online service *Informationsdienst Wissenschaft*

(Fleischmann 2004). Students can seek out critics' observations and see if they noticed similar aspects of the work, particularly with respect to the book's graphic dimension. While the reviewer of the *Berliner Morgenpost* does not make any detailed comments at all, Fleischmann and Brunner both appreciate the stylization that comic journalists bring to their subject and which sets the comic reportage apart from traditional photo journalism. Both note the "formal unity" (formale Einheit), which text and image constitute in a comic reportage. It is noteworthy, however, that none of the reviewers discusses the *specific* ways in which texts and images actually achieve unity or the *different* ways in which the Monogatari artists arrive at this unity in *Operation Läckerli*. The lack of criticism could serve as a productive prompt for an advanced writing exercise.

Another literary pedagogical idea is to compare the graphic novel with a genre of German-language poetry called *Großstadtlyrik* (big-city poetry). This genre flourished predominantly in the early twentieth century and conceptualized the city as the embodiment of modern life with all its advantages and disadvantages. The class can read naturalistic *Großstadtlyrik* as gathered in a 1903 anthology by the same title and then contrast that with the expressionist poems from Kurt Pinthus' 1920 collection *Menschheitsdämmerung* (Dawn of Humankind) or *Um uns die Stadt* (Around us the City, 1931; Seitz and Zucker). A representative stanza from *Großstadtlyrik* can be found in Hedwig Lachmann's "Unterwegs" (On the Way) in which melancholy observations of nature fuse with the anonymity of city life:

> I wander in the large city. A dull
> Veil of autumn fog flutters around the roofs,
> The daily work whirs and roars past my senses,
> And a thousand people walk past me.

> Ich wandre in der
> großen Stadt. Ein trüber
> Herbstnebelschleier flattert um die Zinnen,
> Das Tagwerk schwirrt und braust vor meinen Sinnen,
> Und tausend Menschen gehn an mir vorüber. (Möller 20)

Many later poems contain darker imagery and emphasize the mechanized, accelerated, and de-individualized character of urban life. One can compare big city poems across cities and historical periods since the notion of the metropolis is an entrenched trope in twentieth-century cultural production across Europe, and arguably elsewhere. How, then, do different views of a city compare to the perspective of the Monogatari artists? What is at stake in the Basel vignettes; naturalism or psychologization, nostalgia or urban *tristesse*? Which tropes and elements reappear in the selected poems and the comic reportage? Do both oeuvres have features such as heavy traffic, anonymity in the metropolis, uniformity of living and dressing, and pleasure-oriented lifestyles? Those questions are all valuable primers for analyzing the literary dimension of individual stories in *Operation Läckerli*.

Students can furthermore work out the variations that the different media create in the big-city portrayals when they appear as poems versus graphic narratives. For example, while poems can highlight meanings with the help of rhythm and rhyme, graphic narratives use other techniques to shape their narratives, techniques such as contrasting colors or of different placements on the page. An interesting task could be to compare how poems and graphic narratives represent central aspects of big-city life, for example, movement and sound. While the poems use dynamic verbs such as "wander," "flutter," and "whir," graphic representations indicate movement with conventions such as "quivering" contours. Sound is another key concept that cannot be reproduced in either medium, but still plays a vital role. Poetry uses the semantics of words such as "roar," and "shouting," and can moreover play with the musicality of language per se, that is, the sounds of words and lines in general (e.g., staccato accentuation in accumulations of nouns such as "Geschrei. Geklingel" [screaming, ringing]). A graphic artist invents other means to make his or her images "sound," ranging from the tellingly labeled "loud colors," to bold-printed or capitalized letters, or entrenched symbolic representations such as when Harder's referee blows his whistle and out comes a musical note (n.pag.).

Lust's "Ein Platz" provides a good basis for discussing the notion of literary genres, particularly comic reportage. An introduction to the concept of genre might begin with sampling students' knowledge about different genres ("What are genres? Which genres do you know?"), and then asking what distinguishes genres from one another, elements like "topics," "characters," "places," "moods," and so on. A literary-theoretical excursion could also lead students to explore how different instances of city reportage speak to each other and thus to the concept of intertextuality.[11] As previously noted, the comic reportage lies at the crossroad between a journalistic report and fictional impressions. The tension between these two forms of expression and the different ethos a journalist and a graphic-novelist bring to a city is at the very heart of the format. Students can ponder the questions: "What do I expect from a good reportage, what from a fictional narrative?" They will quickly arrive at different criteria that would determine quality in the two genres. Hence the journalistic ethos aims at being objective, true, and current, while the literary goal is often to produce something that is personal, interesting, and timeless.

Having defined the criteria of the two spheres that come together in comic reportage — journalistic reportage and fictional narrative — the class can collect examples of how these spheres manifest themselves in *Operation Läckerli*, a task that may be assigned to two groups. The journalism group will find in Lust's text many panoramic images of the square that resemble wide shots in photojournalism. The detailed close-ups of people in their respective environments are typical tools of photojournalism. Lust also eavesdrops on a seemingly authentic conversation between a woman and a man, the above-mentioned Kurd, and reports minute details of this meeting. As pointed out above, the student group working on the fictional aspects of "Ein Platz" will find non-realistic elements such as multi-perspective drawings of streetcars which seem to topple out of the picture, people drawn with transparent outlines, or the above-mentioned statue of St. George who appears inexplicably "adorned" with a red nose, a bra, and a sock.[12]

This search for the contribution of different spheres or domains in the comic reportage can be extended throughout the whole book. There are many, often ironic, gestures toward journalistic rigor, for example, in the blurb that bemoans the group's "compulsive urge to observe" (zwanghafter Beobachtungstrieb; n.pag.), the introduction in which Monogatari writes about "get the pens" (Stifte [. . .] zücken) and about "get closer to the little town" (dem Städtchen näher [. . .] rücken; n.pag.). And of course, the book's very title, *Operation Läckerli*, mocks the grave tone of a journalistic or even military mission by juxtaposing the term "Operation" with such a mundane code name as "Läckerli," a type of gingerbread. Similarly, Harder's text highlights the author's "brave close reporting" (mutigen Naheinsatz; n.pag.) and announces that Basel was "scrutinized" (unter die Lupe genommen; n.pag.), in the course of which Harder found out how the soccer fever affects its victims. He also interviews many people, some of whom refuse to comment in a manner typical of spontaneous street interaction: "I don't have time right now, but do ask the man over there . . ." (Hab grad keine Zeit, aber fragen Sie doch den Mann da drüben . . . ; n.pag.). In summary, "Ein Platz" and the other stories in this collection use the tools of both journalism and fiction, of authenticity and artificiality, but also intermix and question the boundaries between them.

"Schnell, Schuss" is more text-heavy, that is to say that the text accounts for a bigger portion of the meaning-making than in "Ein Platz." To put this observation into a more general framework, students can think about and gather examples of different text-image relations in *Operation Läckerli* and elsewhere. Students can ask themselves how much they base interpretations on verbal information and how much on pictorial. What do they decipher first and how do artists manipulate our reading habits, by placing elements in certain spots or deliberately creating complicated reading paths?

Using Harder's piece, the instructor can combine classical literary with visual analysis. The literary analytical part comes into play because the narrator employs a stylized, humorous tone with many poetic devices. Consider the opening reflection, parts of which I already cited above, and which are contained in a syntactically complex, rhetorical question: "How is it possible that civilized people from a lovely swath of land, deeply rooted in traditional cultural consciousness all of a sudden turn into a thousand-armed animal—screaming, cursing, and reeking of sulfur?" (Wie kommt es nur, daß wohlerzogene Menschen aus einem lieblichen Landstrich, tief verwurzelt in ihrem tradierten Kultur-bewußtsein, sich plötzlich in ein tausendarmiges Tier verwandeln—schreiend, fluchend und nach Schwefel stinkend?) Here we find, for instance, deliberately old-fashioned expressions (*lovely* swath of land), accumulations of participle constructions (screaming, cursing), hyperboles (thousand-armed), and metaphors (turn into a[n] . . . animal). The humorous contrast between the allegedly friendly to phlegmatic Swiss people and the sudden outburst of tumultuous action finds its visual counterpart in the preceding opening page. There, Harder shows four panels, three of which contain stereotypical scenes of unhurried Basel and Swiss life: a panorama of Basel along the calmly flowing Rhine, an irenic outdoor scene within the city with cafés, pedestrians, and a streetcar, as well as the pinnacle of Swiss folklore: people in traditional costumes holding alpenhorns. Harder has colored all three scenes in subdued blue hues. Yet, amid these postcard-like impressions of serenity and tradition, Harder includes one panel that shows an almost indistinguishable mass of fans in a stadium's grandstand, ecstatically waving hands and shawls, many with open mouths, shouting. This panel is drawn in an earthy red and therefore contrasts in color as well as in mood with the other three panels. Putting together literary and visual analysis, the class can work out the parallels that exist between the two adjacent pages, parallels such as "thousand-armed animal" into which the ecstatic fan body transmogrifies in both image and text.

Other literary devices that Harder uses heavily are sickness metaphors. Hence, in the above-mentioned opening panel he reports that "there is a rampant fever" (ein Fieber grassiert; n.pag.), contemplates its "incubation period" (Inkubationszeit; n.pag.), how "highly contagious" (extrem ansteckend; n.pag.) it is, and how affected victims can be "cured" (geheilt; n.pag.). Not only do these rhetorical devices produce vivid and funny reading experiences, they also help students understand the mechanism of metaphors. Specifically prepared exercises could require them to work out the two parts that contribute to each example of metaphorical imagery—sports passion and sickness—as well as the ways in which ways these two semantic spaces overlap.

Having understood the way Harder uses rhetorical means to enrich the verbal plane of his narrative, students can then search for parallel structures on the visual plane. A striking visual metaphor can be found when two soccer players are shown with soccer balls in place of their heads while they kick around a real head (figure 5.2). This panel provides a solid basis for demonstrating how visual metaphors work: two elements share a characteristic (here, the shape and size of both the ball and a human head) and therefore can be substituted in the drawing. Of course the artist not only likens two similarly-shaped objects, but also makes a statement about the psychological implications of the soccer fever: the players are so passionate about their sport that their entire heads are occupied by the game. Hence, Harder captures a quasi-magical equivalence with his visual metaphor.

CONCLUDING THOUGHTS

In this chapter, I have outlined ways that German instructors can use graphic novels as tools for content learning in the German language classroom.[13] On the basis of even one collection such as *Operation Läckerli*, instructors of German can teach their students to analyze visual images and literary texts, improve skills of transcultural competence, as well as gather insights about the history and culture of Switzerland. Performing all these tasks in the target language undoubtedly promotes linguistic competencies as well. Most importantly, perhaps, *Operation Läckerli* encourages both instructors and students to look beyond Germany as the

Figure 5.2.   Panel from "Schnell, Schuss." Jens Harder. "Schnell, Schuss." *Operation Läckerli: Comicreportagen aus Basel.* **Berlin: Monogatari, 2004, n.pag.**

sole representative of German-speaking countries and to embrace a plurality of cultures.

At first, *Operation Läckerli* may seem an unusual choice for a graphic novel–based content class. Instead of offering a continuous narrative, it assembles different artists' perceptions and often tests the formal boundaries of traditional comics iconography. Moreover, comic reportage is a lesser-known subgenre of the graphic-novel medium and might be seen as secondary behind classics such as Art Spiegelman's *Maus*. However, it is precisely the diversity of the story collection that makes *Operation Läckerli* a compelling educational tool that offers the instructor many choices as to how easy or challenging the readings should be, both on a linguistic and a visual level. Monogatari's book can accommodate different learner levels and styles, because there are text-light and text-heavy passages as well as visually more traditional and more innovative contributions. Moreover, by definition the comic reportage connects to a tangible cultural reality that many students will appreciate because they literally see the people, buildings, and events that exist in the "outside" world.

With this essay, I have tried to spark interest in using *Operation Läckerli* or other similar works of comic reportage in the German-studies classroom. *Operation Läckerli,* much like other representatives of the genre, is as whimsical as it is challenging. Ultimately, this kind of work does much more than showcase the many faces of a city. It is also a pedagogical resource that draws students closer to an understanding of a city's and a country's history, to literary and visual effects in storytelling, and, hopefully, to a medium they may find fascinating and entertaining enough to continue reading even after the semester has ended.

I would like to thank Lynn Marie Kutch and Joshua Kavalovski for their insightful comments on earlier versions of this chapter.

For a longer version of this essay and accompanying worksheets please visit https://jludewig.wordpress.com/german-and-l2-teaching/.

NOTES

1. For the purpose of this essay I treat the terms "comics" and "graphic novels" as equal.
2. Works that provide a first impression about the literature in this field include, for example, those by Rossetto and Chiera-Macchia, Chun, Davis, Derrick, Hallet, Jüngst, Templer, and Vanderbeke.
3. The scope of possible learning goals ranges from vocabulary building that capitalizes on pictures acting as "mnemonic devices" (Kutch 60), to grammatical knowledge such as the imperative forms and the *du-Sie* distinction (Bridges 157), to becoming familiar with colloquial and archaic varieties of a language (David-West). Pragmatic aspects of language use are another area of linguistic competence that we can

practice with the help of comics and graphic novels. Hence, David Broersma has taught conversational implicatures, among others, and Neil Williams discusses elliptical sentences.

4. Rainer Veeck and Ludwig Linsmayer define *Landeskunde* as "Gesamtheit aller Informationen und Deutungstheoreme, die dazu dienen, das Interaktionswissen . . . eines jeweiligen Sprachenlerners zu optimieren, sein Verständnis der Zielkultur und ihrer historischen und gesellschaftlichen Bedingungen zu verbessern . . . (the totality of information and interpretative schemes which allow the learner to improve his interactional skills as well as his understanding of the target culture together with its historical and social conditions; 1160).

5. The other components are "communication," "communities," and "connections." Many language programs in the United States use ACTFL guidelines to develop their foreign-language curriculums as well as their assessments.

6. Munich is the location in Uli Oesterle's *Frass* (Muck, 2002), Hamburg in Kati Rickenbach's *Jetzt kommt später* (Now comes later, 2011), and Berlin in Monogatari's *Alltagsspionage* and *Fashionvictims, Trendverächter* (Everyday espionage, Fashion victims, Dispraisers of trends).

7. All translations from *Operation Läckerli* and other German-language sources are mine.

8. Some English-language resources are Scott McCloud's *Understanding Comics* (1993), Maureen Bakis' *The Graphic Novel Classroom* (2011), Danny Fingeroth's *The Rough Guide to Graphic Novels* (2008), Katie Monnin's *Teaching Graphic Novels* (2009), and Douglas Wolk's *Reading Comics* (2007). Shorter articles about comics terminology can be found in Jane Griffin's "Brief Glossary" as well as on Andrei Molotiu's website "Comics Forum." Among the literature in German are Martin Schüwer's *Wie Comics erzählen* (2008). Inspired by an initial list by Pascal Lafèvre, comic researchers from various countries have assembled a list with comics terms in various European languages, among them German. This "Wörterbuch" can be found at http://comicforschung.de (Lafèvre).

9. Those six countries are Germany, Austria, Liechtenstein, the Netherlands, Belgium (with its vicinity to the Rhine basin), and, of course, Switzerland (plus the Italian region South Tyrol in which German is recognized as a regional language as well).

10. For a historical discussion of the "comics scare" in the United States, see Hajdu as well as Nyberg.

11. By "intertextuality" I mean the idea that texts point to other texts and meaning-making always happens with reference to elements that lie "outside." Intertextuality operates on several levels: it links elements in individual texts with other elements outside, for example, when Lust inserts a Bible quote into her story. Intertextuality also functions on a genre level. This means that readers who encounter instances of a genre automatically compare these instances to one another. Hence, Harder's story is one depiction of a city next to five others in this collection, and his take on Basel is both similar to and different from his colleagues' perspectives. Drawing on an even larger scope, this collection is in intertextual relation with other collections, for example, Monogatari's own Berlin reportage *Alltagsspionage* or cities as far away as the Middle East *Tel Aviv Berlin* (2010) by Rutu Modan and colleagues.

12. A humorous twist on real-life objects can also be found in Tim Dinter's contribution "Basler Museumsquartett," the last story in *Operation Läckerli*. Dinter plays visual puns when he, for example, lets a person in Renaissance clothing (who looks much like the reformer Zwingli) go past the museum for contemporary art or shows the museum for ancient art in just that moment when somebody throws an unidentifiable, but definitely valuable artifact out the window (n.pag.).

13. I highlighted two of the six stories in *Operation Läckerli*, yet the remaining contributions are just as conducive to language and content learning.

"GGG & DDT" by Kai Pfeiffer is an eclectic assemblage of disparate images of everyday objects and places, but also includes historic landmarks which the author juxtaposes with bits of texts such as street signs, names of businesses, and advertisement slogans. Following Pfeiffer's artifact-oriented way of getting to know a city, students can become hunter-gatherers who piece together a picture of Basel's people, their work hours, and occupations. They can then move along to Basel's bars and businesses, churches and commercial slogans. Step-by-step, students thus make sense of a seemingly disorganized linguistic and pictorial mosaic of Basel.

Tim Dinter's "Museumsquartett" (Happy Families of Museums) contains little text and therefore would be another good tool for beginner-intermediate classes. In "Museumsquartett," students get an overview of the museum landscape in Basel—the "Antikenmuseum" (Museum of Ancient Art), "Museum für Gegenwartskunst" (Museum of Contemporary Art), "Puppenmuseum" (Doll Museum), "Karikatur & Cartoonmuseum" to name but a few—and could extend their learning by researching the real museums, doing virtual tours, or starting a more general discussion about who visits museums and why.

Mawil's "Basel Beach" as well as Tim Dinter and Kai Pfeiffer's "Der Flaneur" (The Flaneur) are better suited for advanced learners due to the amount and sophistication of the texts they contain. "Basel Beach" offers the most traditional type of comic narrative in *Operation Läckerli* with an engaging story that is relatable and funny at the same time. For a German class, Mawil's experiences as a tourist in Basel, his hapless flirtations, and his offhand conversations with his travel companion, are a treasure of colloquial German with a Berlin touch ("Welches [Bier] nehmwan?," "Wattne Hitze!"/ Which [beer] do we take?, What a heat!).

"Der Flaneur" is the opposite of Mawil's cheeky charm. It features stylized language which allows advanced students to segment and analyze what makes language literary and humorous. For example, Dinter and Pfeiffer describe Basel as an "A place of cleanliness. Here, nobody eats from the ground just because nobody would tolerate such a soiling" (Ort der Reinheit. Hier wird nur deshalb nicht vom Boden gegessen, da niemand eine solch frevelhafte Verschmutzung desselben wagen würde). This sentence contains sophisticated constructions and words such as the genitive ("der Reinheit"), the passive voice ("wird . . . gegessen"), or the use of "da" instead of "weil" all of which account for the tone of highbrow sarcasm. Other aspects in "Der Flaneur" touch upon how the cities of Berlin and Basel are different—here: in their cleanliness— or what art is, reviewing the debate about how "rubbish" can be considered art in modern times.

REFERENCES

"ACTFL Proficiency Guidelines 2012." *American Council on the Teaching of Foreign Languages.* 2012. Web. 6 June 2015. http://www.actfl.org/sites/default/files/pdfs/public/ ACTFLProficiencyGuidelines2012_FINAL.pdf.

Althoff, Gerlinde, and Christoph Heuer. *Der erste Frühling.* Hamburg: Carlsen Verlag, 2007.

Bakis, Maureen. *The Graphic Novel Classroom: Powerful Learning and Teaching with Images.* Thousand Oaks: Corwin Press, 2011.

Birrer, Raphaela. "Volk sagt Ja zur SVP-Initiative — Entsetzen in Berlin." *Tagesanzeiger.* 9 Feb. 2014. Web. 26 June 2015. http://www.tagesanzeiger.ch/schweiz/standard/ Volk-sagt-Ja-zur-SVPInitiative--Entsetzen-in-Berlin/story/29489952.

Bridges, Elizabeth. "Bridging the Gap: A Literacy-Oriented Approach to Teaching the Graphic Novel *Der erste Frühling.*" *Die Unterrichtspraxis/Teaching German* 42.2 (2009): 151–62.

Broersma, David. "Do Chicken Have Lips? Conversational Implicature in the ESL Classroom." Annual Meeting of the International Conference on Pragmatics and Language Learning. Urbana, IL. February, 1994. Presentation.

Brunner, Dagmar. "Mit dem Zeichenstift unterwegs." *Programmzeitung,* December 2003. 14.

Chun, Christian. "Critical Literacies and Graphic Novels for English-Language Learn-
ers: Teaching *Maus.*" Journal of Adolescent & Adult Literacy 53.2 (2009): 144–53.
David-West, Alzo. "Comics, Contractions, and Classics: *At the Sign of the Lion* in the
University EFL Classroom." *The Journal of the Faculty of Foreign Studies.* Aichi Prefec-
tural University. *Language and Literature* 44 (2012): 103–14.
Davis, Randall. "Comics: A Multi-dimensional Teaching Aid in Integrated-Skills
Classes." *ESL-lab.* Web. 6 Jul. 2014. http://www.esl-lab.com/research/comics.htm.
Derrick, Justine. "Using Comics with ESL/EFL Students." *The Internet TESL Journal*
11.7 (2008): n.pag. Web. 19 Jun. 2014. http://iteslj.org/Techniques/Derrick-Using
Comics.html.
Eagleton, Terry. *Literary Theory: An Introduction.* Oxford: Basil Blackwell, 1983.
Fingeroth, Danny. *The Rough Guide to Graphic Novels.* London: Penguin, 2008.
Fleischmann, Birgit: "Baseler 'Läckerli' zum Blättern — Berliner Künstlergruppe
'monogatari' mit neuer Comicreportage." *Informationsdienst Wissenschaft,* Informa-
tionsdienst Wissenschaft, 25 May 2004. Web. 14 May 2015. https://idw-online.de/en/
news80622.
Franceschini, Rita. "Stimmt das Stereotyp der mehrsprachigen Schweiz?" *Sprache und
Identität in frankophonen Kulturen/Langues, identité et francophonie.* Ed. Manfred
Schmeling and Sandra Duhem. Wiesbaden: Springer, 2003. 101–24.
"Gefragtes Land für Einwanderer: Schweiz führt globales Ranking an." *Schweizer
Radio und Fernsehen,* 1 Dec. 2014. Web. 17 May 2015. http://www.srf.ch/news/
schweiz/gefragtes-land-fuer-einwanderer-schweiz-fuehrt-globales-ranking-an.
Griffen, Jane. "A Brief Glossary of Comic Book Terminology." *Series Review* 24.1 (1998):
71–77.
Hajdu, David. *The Ten-Cent Plague: The Great Comic-Book Scare and How it Changed
America.* New York: Farrar, Straus and Giroux, 2008.
Hallet, Wolfgang. "Graphic Novels. Literarisches und multiliterales Lernen mit Com-
ic-Romanen." *Der Fremdsprachliche Unterricht Englisch* 117 (2012): 2–9.
Jüngst, Heike. "Textsortenrealisierung im Comic-Format. Comics zum Fremdspra-
chenlernen." *Lebende Sprachen* 47 (2002): 1–6.
Kreitz, Isabel. *Die Entdeckung der Currywurst. Nach einem Roman von Uwe Timm.* Ham-
burg: Carlsen, 2005.
Kutch, Lynn. "From Visual Literacy to Literary Proficiency: An Instructional and Assessment Model for the Graphic Novel Version of Kafka's *Die Verwandlung.*" *Die
Unterrichtspraxis/Teaching German* 47.1 (2014): 56–68.
Lafèvre, Pascal, Frank Madsen, Domingos Isabelinho, Sergio Garcia, Thierry Groen-
steen, Gert Meesters, Eckart Sackmann, and Gianfranco Goria. "Wörterbuch." *Co-
micforschung.de.* 2009. Web. 17 June 2015. http://www.comicforschung.de/woerter
buch.html.
Lust, Ulli, and Kai Pfeffer. *Fashionvictims, Trendverächter: Bildkolumnen und Minirepor-
tagen aus Berlin.* Berlin: Avant-Verlag, 2008.
McCloud, Scott. *Understanding Comics: The Invisible Art.* Northampton: Kitchen Sink
Press, 1993.
MLA Ad Hoc Committee on Foreign Languages. "Foreign Languages and Higher
Education: New Structures for a Changed World." *Modern Language Association,*
2007. Web. 10 June 2015. https://www.mla.org/Resources/Research/Surveys-Repo
rts-and-Other-Documents/Teaching-Enrollments-and-Programs/Foreign-Language
s-and-Higher-Education-New-Structures-for-a-Changed-World.
Modan, Rutu, et al. *Tel Aviv Berlin: Ein Reisebuch.* Berlin: Avant-Verlag, 2010.
Möller, Heinz, ed. *Großstadtlyrik.* Leipzig: Voigtländer, 1903.
Molotiu, Andrei. "List of Terms for Comics Studies." *Comics Forum.* 26 July 2013. Web.
17 June 2015. http://comicsforum.org/2013/07/26/list-of-terms-for-comics-studies-
by-andrei-molotiu/.
Monnin, Katie. *Teaching Graphic Novels. Practical Strategies for the Secondary ELA Class-
room.* Gainsville: Maupin House, 2009.
Monogatari. *Alltagsspionage: Comicreportagen aus Berlin.* Berlin: Monogatari, 2001.

Monogatari. *Operation Läckerli: Comicreportagen aus Basel.* Berlin: Monogatari, 2004.

Nyberg, Amy Kiste. *Seal of Approval: History of the Comics Code.* Jackson: University Press of Mississippi, 1998.

Oesterle, Uli. *Frass.* Wuppertal: Edition 52, 2002.

"Operation Läcerli — Comicreportagen aus Basel." *Berliner Morgenpost* 4 Sept. 2004. Web.

"Plakatkampagne: Masslosigkeit schadet — Masseneinwanderung stoppen." 10 Dec. 2013. *SVP.* Web. 26 June 2015. https://www.svp.ch/aktuell/medienmitteilungen/plakatkampagne-masslosigkeit-schadet-masseneinwanderung-stoppen/.

Rickenbach, Kati. *Jetzt kommt später.* Zurich: Edition Moderne, 2011.

Rossetto, Marietta, and Antonella Chiera-Macchia. "'Visual Learning is the Best Learning—It Lets You Be Creative while Learning': Exploring Ways to Begin Guided Writing in Second Language Learning Through the Use of Comics." *Babel* 45.2–3 (2011): 35–39.

Sartre, Jean Paul. *What Is Literature?* New York: Philosophical Library, 1949.

Schüwer, Martin. *Wie Comics erzählen: Grundriss einer intermedialen Erzähltheorie der grafischen Literatur.* Trier: Wissenschaftlicher Verlag Trier, 2008.

Seitz, Robert and Heinz Zucker, eds. *Um uns die Stadt.* Braunschweig: Viehweg, 1931.

Selezione, "Made in Switzerland." *Fear of communists—fear of foreigners.* n.d. Web 26 June 2015. http://www.swissinfo.ch/eng/political-posters-_fear-of-communists---fear-of-foreigners/35888800.

Spiegelman, Art. *Maus: A Survivor's Tale.* New York: Pantheon Books, 1986–1991.

"Standards for Language Learning: Preparing for the 21st Century." *American Council on the Teaching of Foreign Languages,* n.d. Web. 6 June 2015. http://www.actfl.org/sites/default/files/pdfs/public/StandardsforFLLexecsumm_rev.pdf.

Templer, Bill. "Graphic Novels in the ESL Classroom." *Humanising Language Teaching* 11.3 (2009): n.pag. Web. 3 Sept. 2014. http://www.hltmag.co.uk/jun09/mart03.htm.

Timm, Uwe. *Die Entdeckung der Currywurst.* Köln: Kiepenheuer & Witsch, 1993.

Vanderbeke, Dirk. "Comics and Graphic Novels in the Classroom." *Cultural Studies in the EFL Classroom.* Ed. Werner Delanoy and Laurenz Volkmann. Heidelberg: Winter, 2002. 365–79.

Veeck, Rainer, and Ludwig Linsmayer. "Geschichte und Konzepte der Landeskunde." *Deutsch als Fremdsprache: Ein Internationales Handbuch* (=HSK 19.2). Ed. Gerhard Helbig. Berlin: de Gruyter, 2001. 1160–167.

Williams, Neil. "The Comic Book as Course Book: Why and How." 29th Annual Meeting of the Teachers of English to Speakers of Other Languages, March 1995, Long Beach, U.S.A. Unpublished conference paper. 1995. Education Resources Information Center. Web. 22 September 2014. http://files.eric.ed.gov/fulltext/ED390277.pdf.

Wolk, Douglas. *Reading Comics: How Graphic Novels Work and What They Mean.* Cambridge: Da Capo Press, 2007.

SIX

"Show and Tell"

Using Graphic Novels for Teaching East German History in the Novice and Intermediate Foreign-Language German Classroom

Antje Krueger

For many of the current undergraduates, most born in the mid- to late 1990s, the time of the German Democratic Republic (GDR), which existed from 1948 to 1990, seems like a far-away and foreign era. Most beginning German textbooks published in the United States (US) (as defined by the ACTFL Proficiency Guidelines)[1] offer no more than a cursory overview of GDR history. For instance, the commonly used textbooks *Deutsch: Na Klar* (6th edition), *Vorsprung* (3rd edition), and *Treffpunkt Deutsch* (6th edition) include brief chronologies of German history in English or German that outline the basic facts but do not provide a deeper understanding of life and politics in the GDR during the Cold War. Reasons for the superficial treatment and omissions could be attributed to limited space in these textbooks, learners' restricted linguistic abilities, or even a lack of scholarly interest in the topic among the textbook authors.

The GDR has been called a "footnote" in German history, a phrase that German author Stefan Heym coined in 1989 during a demonstration on the Alexanderplatz in Berlin. Heym's quotation was subsequently used apodictically in public and scholarly debates in Germany and within the field of German Studies to denounce any future impact of the GDR as a state.[2] Nevertheless, the history and legacy of both German states have shaped present-day life in today's reunified Germany, where research on the GDR has been flourishing since reunification in 1990

(Großmann 1). A wealth of scholarship on the GDR since that time examines in detail various aspects of GDR politics, culture, and everyday life. Before 2009 more than 16,000 books, articles, and essays in anthologies had been published about the GDR, with a focus on state persecution and GDR history from the perspective of victims of the regime (Jessen). More recently, however, social and cultural histories have integrated aspects of everyday life (*Alltagsgeschichte*) to paint a broader, more nuanced picture of life in the GDR. All of these studies show that understanding the GDR as a "footnote in history" is a rather simplified concept that too quickly dismisses the history of the GDR as a subject worthy of study. It also ignores the fact that the historical legacy of the GDR shaped the biographies of many of today's German citizens.

With this surge of recent attention to the former GDR, it comes as no surprise that GDR history has become a standard part of the curriculum in the German secondary school system. If instructors of German in the US wish to adopt and develop the same aspects of German history for their own teaching, however, they often face the challenge of finding suitable texts in the target language. There are certainly many recent books, films, and materials that give excellent insights into GDR history, but they often prove to be very challenging and too difficult to use with novice and intermediate students of German.

A GRAPHIC NOVEL CHRONOLOGY

During my search for materials and texts, I was surprised to discover that several German authors have addressed the topic through a specific format that is somewhat underrepresented in German Studies: the graphic novel. Since the German graphic novel as a medium was mostly shaped by developments in the US, I will first discuss two exemplary works: Art Spiegelman's *Maus: A Survivor's Tale* (1980) and Alison Bechdel's *Fun Home* (2006). They both present personal stories within larger historical contexts, albeit employing vastly different methods.

With *Maus*, Spiegelman presents and interprets a Holocaust survivor's story using a method considered highly unusual at the time. Spiegelman shows his father's account of life in pre-war Poland and his parents' struggle to survive Nazi persecution. By including himself in the story as listener, narrator, and creator of the graphic novel, Art Spiegelman finds a way to connect the present and the past. In addition, he draws the characters as anthropomorphized animals, a decision that led to new discussions about how and if Holocaust experiences could be represented (see Witek and Hirsch). Spiegelman's *Maus* was not only the first comic to win a Pulitzer Prize (1992) in the Special Awards and Citations category, but it also showcased new possibilities for comics to engage with history. Spiegelman's work led to a wealth of new scholarship on graphic novels and inspired the continued growth of the comic as a respected literary medium across the globe.

Alison Bechdel also combines her personal story with the biography of her father in *Fun Home*. She uses the medium for coming to terms with her father's closeted homosexuality, its impact on their family life, and her own sexual identity as a lesbian. Similar to Spiegelman, she includes herself in the story, yet she tells a coming-of-age story. Both graphic novels could be understood as "family sagas" or "family novels," a term adapted from the German concept of *Familienroman* or *Generationenroman*, which refers to a genre in which the author explores a multi-generational family story in a broader socio-historical context while also reflecting on the process of accessing and re-narrating memories.[3] Spiegelman and Bechdel base their stories on facts, but also add a strong storytelling component that conveys their subjectivity, emotions, and imagination. These works oscillate between fact and fiction, and could fall into the classification of "creative nonfiction graphic novels" (Monnin 67).

Comics scholars have argued that this particular way of autobio-graphical storytelling in the medium of a comic book can be linked to the American underground comix scene of the 1960s and 1970s. Josef Witek emphasizes in his groundbreaking study, *Comic Books as History*, in which authors such as Harvey Pekar, Jack Jackson, and even Art Spiegelman dedicated themselves to telling the stories of marginalized figures and events in US history, and claims that these stories needed an alternative narrative medium: "the culturally marginalized form of comic books" (92). Adding to Witek's work, Charles Hatfield points to the fact that the autobiographical impetus of many of today's graphic novels was in-spired by Harvey Pekar's autobiographical serial *American Splendor*. In his work, Pekar displays everyday life, characters, and events with a form of realism based on observations of the world around him. Accord-ing to Hatfield, Pekar's documentary style influenced a "new school of autobiographical comics" that "tended to stress the abject, the seedy, the anti-heroic, and the just plain nasty" (111).

The term "graphic novel," however, was not used commonly until the early 1980s. In *The Graphic Novel: An Introduction*, Jan Baetens and Hugo Frey describe how individual comic artists in the 1970s had pushed the aforementioned comix material in new directions that led to changes in the formats and content. Likewise the publishers of these works agreed that the titles were not comix but something different, precisely because they were lengthier, more serious, reflexive, and sophisticated. This breach between comix and different, implicitly more serious works is how the need for a label such as "graphic novel" essentially developed (Baetens 73).

In the 1980s, in addition to *Maus*, *The Dark Knight Returns* (1986) and *Watchmen* (1987) appeared, which are commonly viewed as standard models for today's notion of the graphic novel (Baetens 74). Since their publication, the market for these comic books has grown remarkably. In particular, the 1990s and 2000s have seen a boom in comic book sales. According to *The Comics Chronicles* (June 30, 2015) comics and graphic novel sales in the US hit a new twenty-year high in 2014, and half of those sales were from graphic novels.[4]

Correspondingly, the field of comics studies has also expanded, which has led to renewed debate over the term "graphic novel." Some scholars see it as a "tag" for a "vague new class of cultural artifacts" (El Refaie 6), and instead prefer terms like "comics," "adult comics," "alternative comics," or "post-underground" (Baetens 3). For the present study, I find Witek's emphasis that graphic novels offer an alternative medium for presenting marginalized figures useful for the discussion on graphic novels that treat GDR history. Additionally, Hatfield's insightful study of graphic novels as a mode of autobiographical storytelling highlights particular features of the format and narrative structure. Baetens and Frey's definition of the graphic novel synthesizes the tendencies that the other theorists identify. They state that the graphic novel reflects the comic book form and has some "propensity for autobiography, reportage, and historical narrative" (19), and is a so-called one-shot, longer narrative (20). These descriptions aptly correspond to the subject matter I discuss here.

Similar to developments on the US market, German graphic novels have seen new stylistic developments, international success, and an increase in sales and publication numbers over the last twenty years. In 2010, German journalist and comics scholar Andreas Platthaus wrote enthusiastically "German Comics are Back!" in an article accompanying a touring exhibition called "Comics, Manga & Co" sponsored by the Goethe Institut. In particular, Platthaus points to the influence of an East Berlin collective of artists called "PGH Glowing Future" (*PGH Glühende Zukunft*), a group that included Anke Feuchtenberger, Holger Fickelscherer, Henning Wagenbreth, and Detlef Beck, and that was established after the fall of the Berlin Wall in 1989. While works by the members of the *PGH Glowing Future* and other comics artists have been influential for a new wave of and interest in German graphic novels in the first two decades after unification, only a small number of artists displayed interest in GDR history, which contrasts more current trends, defined by a marked uptick in graphic novelists interested in that historical time period. Having appeared after the twentieth anniversary of the fall of the Berlin Wall, the majority of works have been produced by a new generation of artists (Nijdam 149). Specifically, those who grew up in East Germany belong to the so-called Third Generation East, a term that loosely refers to a specific "generation" of children born in the GDR between 1970 and 1985, and that was coined by a group of people who founded the Initiative Third Generation East Germany (*Dritte Generation Ostdeutschland*) in 2010.[5]

A CHRONOLOGY OF GRAPHIC
NOVELS ABOUT THE GDR

In 2009, three influential works about experiences with a divided Germany were published by Third Generation East members: *drüben!* by Simon Schwartz, *Grenzgebiete: Eine Kindheit zwischen Ost und West* by Claire Lenkova, and *Da war mal was* by Flix. Since then, many graphic novels have followed that engage with GDR history. Some examples of well-received graphic novels are Susanne Buddenberg and Thomas Henseler's three graphic novels *Grenzfall* (2011), *Berlin—Geteilte Stadt: Zeitgeschichten* (2012), and *Tunnel 57: Eine Fluchtgeschichte als Comic* (2013), in addition to *Kinderland* (2014) by Mawil and *17. Juni: Die Geschichte von Armin und Eva* (2013) by Alexander Lahl, Tim Köhler, Max Mönch, and comic artist Kitty Kahane.

Whether intentional or not, most of these texts incorporate and display the criteria and characteristics of the graphic novels mentioned in the above chronology. Very often, they are based on personal accounts and integrate social and political contexts: in this case, those of divided Germany. Nijdam underscores the uniqueness of these texts, which "communicate the East German experience visually as well as textually," and provide "a point of reference for an entire generation now trying to understand their heritage" (149). They are "written at the intersection between formal history and individual memories" (149). While not all of these texts are autobiographical, they can be categorized as creative nonfiction graphic novels, which are texts that focus on "factually accurate events, people, places and/or times AND [sic] the author's use of creative license" (Monnin, 67). In addition, they capture the above-mentioned *Alltagsgeschichte*. These texts give a voice to stories and people who were marginalized for a long time as part of the histories of both German states.

When telling their stories, many authors could draw on what the graphic novel does best, according to Hatfield, which is showing "unpleasant facts" (114). None of these authors shies away from telling and showing their readers how the GDR state oppressed, persecuted, and terrorized ordinary people. The flexibility of the medium allows graphic novelists to tell remarkable heroic stories, such as tales of escape and dissidents' biographies or to portray the quotidian effects of life in a dictatorship. By showing and telling these different stories, they contribute to a nuanced picture of living in the GDR.

USING GRAPHIC NOVELS AS
TOOLS FOR TEACHING GDR HISTORY

Commenting on his incorporation of historical topics in English as a Second Language (ESL) instruction, Christian Chun points out that teaching history is often "a boring exercise in the classroom primarily due to many standardized and sanitized textbooks" (147). Yet creative nonfiction graphic novels like the ones mentioned above offer a potentially compelling way for students to engage with personal and public GDR histories. In contrast to standard textbooks, these graphic novels tell stories that offer insights into "the dramas and contradictions that constitute our histories" (Loewen xvi). The storytelling allows students to empathize with another person's biography and experiences while at the same time gaining insight into historical conditions. In addition, the multiple modalities of these texts, the visual and textual presentation of the graphic novels, foster reading engagement. For instance, Eva Burwitz-Melzer points out that research on the use of graphic novels in the second-language classroom has shown that these texts have a "beneficial effect on reluctant readers and also enhance the reading of good learners" (72). Colleen MacDonell maintains that many students select graphic novels for pleasure reading, which is critical for language acquisition. Instructors can employ graphic novels about GDR history to achieve reading goals and also increase cultural competence. This chapter considers the particularly engaging stories *Tunnel 57, Grenzfall, and drüben!,* whose linguistic levels are also well suited for the novice and/or intermediate German-language students. All three offer very different approaches and insights into GDR history while telling authentic, personal stories.

TUNNEL 57

Buddenberg and Henseler's *Tunnel 57* documents the true story of the successful construction of a tunnel between West and East Berlin in 1964. Supported by a team of about thirty people and generous funds from the city of West Berlin, five young men dug the 145 meter (roughly 478 feet) tunnel. They had planned to help about 120 people, mostly family and friends, escape from the GDR, and had scheduled the crossing from East to West Berlin for October 3rd and 4th, 1964. However, one of the refugees turned out to be an informant and relayed information about the tunnel and details of the escape to the East German *Staatssicherheit* or *Stasi* (secret service). Two GDR border guards tried to stop the group on the second night of the escape, but the armed tunnel diggers exchanged fire with the guards and were able to save themselves and the people who accompanied them. Altogether, fifty-seven people escaped through the tunnel. While the young men were honored in West Berlin, they were vilified in the GDR. East German news reported that one of the West Berliners had killed a border guard during the escape. However, *Stasi* documents discovered after the fall of the GDR revealed that the guard had in fact been killed by his fellow border guard who had fired a machine gun salve in the direction of the tunnel diggers.[6]

Tunnel 57 is divided into two parts. The first twenty-eight pages are devoted to the story itself while the second section consists of an interview with the authors, excerpts of interviews with eyewitnesses, an article about the history of the Berlin Wall, and discussion questions and assignments for students. This second section also tells the history of the story itself. It was first presented as an exhibition in the subway station Bernauer Straße. For novice learners, the story facilitates access to the language. Students need only a short introduction to the history of the Berlin Wall in order to understand the motivation of the tunnel diggers. Furthermore, a straightforward story line and the visual representation of the scenes clearly convey the plot to novice students.

While students might not understand all of the verbal descriptions at first, the text and image combination should help increase vocabulary acquisition. Graphic novels also aid students' internalization of grammatical concepts. Long before the recent interest in graphic novel pedagogy, Stephen Krashen pointed out in 1989 that the visual narrative offers clues for unfamiliar words and grammatical structures (402). Eva Burwitz-Melzer asserts that studies in the US from the last twenty-five years, "have shown the 'mixing' of words and images is a proven way to foster comprehension and memory skills" (72). This research has formed the pedagogical basis for the teaching unit I briefly describe here in which students use the graphic novel to acquire vocabulary, and deepen their understanding of basic grammatical structures. The particular teaching outcomes for this unit are based on skill sets suggested by the National Council of State Supervisors for Languages (NCSSFL) and the American Council on the Teaching of Foreign Languages (ACTFL) in their published Standards for the Novice Low to High NCSSFL-ACTFL Can-Do Statements.[7]

The following lessons deal with the first four pages of *Tunnel 57* (6–9). The students receive copies of the pages with the text obscured. Before they start working with these pages, the instructor introduces new vocabulary that is used in the text: a combination of nouns, verbs, and adjectives that describe the protagonists' biographies, the setup of the tunnel, and daily activities related to digging the tunnel. The instructor distributes these words, printed on paper snippets or on self-adhesive notes to the students, and projects a scanned version of the same pages onto a screen or white board. He or she presents these four pages as a storyteller would, pointing to specific images to convey their content. During the presentation, students label their own text and images with the vocabulary words. The presentation is followed by a review of the presented information and the new vocabulary. For example, the instructor could ask students to label the images on the screen and/or let them summarize or retell what they have heard about the characters or about the construction of the tunnel and the Berlin Wall.

This short lesson serves the following outcomes: students are exposed to interpretive listening and acquire new vocabulary in that process. Beniko Mason and Krashen have demonstrated that storytelling supplemented by form-focused activities, or tasks that "focus students specifically on learning the new words in the story," results in effective vocabulary acquisition (28). With this activity, students will work on "recognizing and sometimes understanding words and phrases that they have learned for specific purposes."[8] In addition, students can demonstrate knowledge about cultural facts related to the Berlin Wall. By engaging with *Tunnel 57*, students learn about a specific product of the target culture that reflects its history, a desired skill articulated in the ACTFL standards.[9]

For assessing content and new vocabulary comprehension, students are asked to choose one of the characters. As homework they write down simple sentences about one of the figure's biographies. Depending on the students' language levels, they can also use the notes to take on the role of one of the tunnel diggers in a subsequent class period. They can present their characters and ask each other questions about the character they are impersonating. This way they can work on "presenting information about others using phrases and simple sentences."[10]

Creative writing and drawing assignments are another way to engage with the graphic novel, as the medium lends itself to interpretation and personal reaction. Students can think about the reactions of those refugees who successfully crossed into West Berlin, but also about those who had to stay behind. Students could be given research tasks that shed light on what life was like in East and West Germany and then write or draw additional scenes in which they describe what could have happened to different people in different scenarios. Students can research historical information by consulting resources listed in the back of the book or the *Berlin Wall Memorial*.[11] Its web page offers access to supplementary material about other escape stories and the history of the Berlin Wall, information that students can use to compose or draw their stories.

In summary, this unit allows students on the Novice Low to Novice High levels to work on developing a variety of language skills by introducing them to a specific product of the target culture that reflects an important epoch in Germany's history.

GRENZFALL

Grenzfall was Buddenberg and Hensel's first graphic novel based on documentary material. They have stated that they became increasingly intrigued with historical subjects and personal stories while researching material about GDR history (57). *Grenzfall* recounts the story of a young man named Peter Grimm who was denied higher education in the GDR and subsequently became involved in the opposition movement. The book begins with Grimm's plan to attend the funeral of the well-known GDR dissident Robert Havemann on April 9, 1982. *Stasi* officers try to stop people from attending the funeral by changing the schedule of a bus line, blocking streets, and checking people on their way to the funeral ceremony. Grimm is able to attend the funeral, yet he becomes one of the persons the *Stasi* registered that day. The graphic novel recounts how Grimm became involved in the opposition movement by getting to know Havemann's friends and family following the funeral. Shortly thereafter, the reader sees a *Stasi* officer ask Grimm to work as an unofficial collaborator (*inoffizieller Mitarbeiter* or *IM*). Even though the *Stasi* officer implies that Grimm could get expelled from his high school if he does not agree, he refuses to work for them and affirms his commitment to the opposition movement. Following that encounter, the graphic novel describes how Grimm had to leave his school due to his "immoral character and attitude" ([*falsche*] *moralisch-charakterlich*[*e*] Grundhaltung; 40) just nine days before taking the *Abitur* (university-entrance examination). His father, a director of a sawmill, calls party officials and complains about his son's expulsion, an exercise that only confirms his powerlessness. The reader then finds out that Grimm's father has died of a heart attack, just a few days after this incident.

The graphic novel narrates how Peter Grimm became more and more involved in the opposition and peace movement in the GDR. He attended so-called peace circles or *Friedenskreise*, which were informal groups affiliated with the Protestant Church that devoted their time to human rights issues in the GDR. In 1985, he became a member of the Initiative for Peace and Human Rights (*Initiative Frieden und Menschenrechte* or *IFM*), which along with other groups, campaigned for the right to education, access to information, the right of free assembly, free speech, and unrestricted travel (55). Grimm became a speaker for the group, one of the most influential dissident initiatives, along with prominent GDR citizens Wolfgang Templin, Ralf Hirsch, Bärbel Bohley, to name a few.

In June 1986, Grimm began publishing an opposition magazine called *Grenzfall* along with Peter Rölle, Ralf Hirsch, and Rainer Dietrich. The magazine documented the work of the *IFM* and offered a platform for views that opposed those of the GDR government. The possession of a printing device was illegal, so Grimm and other contributors to *Grenzfall* had to constantly move and hide their scripts and printing materials. It turned out that a member of the group was a *Stasi* informant and in October 1987, he alerted his fellow officers to an upcoming printing meeting. At the last minute, Grimm cancelled that meeting, and although the *Stasi* had no evidence of illegal activity, everybody was arrested during that night's raid. All of the group members were released, but the raid contributed immensely to the popularization of the peace and opposition movement in the GDR because of extensive West German media coverage of the incident.

As this series of events implies, *Grenzfall* retells a highly engaging, personal story. While following Grimm's struggles with the *Stasi*, the reader becomes acquainted with the secret service's methods of controlling everyday life in the GDR. In addition, *Grenzfall* highlights the emergence of the peace groups in the GDR. The graphic novel mentions some of their members, describes their goals and actions, and visually depicts their meeting places. In contrast to *Tunnel 57*, this story demands much more in-depth linguistic and cultural knowledge. In addition, the story does not convey all of the background information, and the reader needs to be familiar with specific terms, events, and people. In contrast to other graphic novels mentioned, it is a longer text with dense dialogues more suited for intermediate or advanced students. *Grenzfall* is an insightful read for students who have achieved a higher language level or visited Germany already, but it would be difficult to teach in a beginners' classroom.

In her article "From Visual Literacy to Literary Proficiency: An Instructional and Assessment Model for the Graphic Novel Version of Kafka's *Die Verwandlung*," Lynn Marie Kutch describes in detail how a graphic novel can be used at the intermediate level to train students in core literary analytical proficiencies. She stresses the importance of aiding students in developing this proficiency step-by-step; and describes with a detailed curriculum ways that students can use graphic novels to develop various levels of language proficiency with a trajectory for skill-building she calls "visual to verbal." This entails that students work with describing images and scenes first, and then add the next step with regard to comprehension questions, evaluating text and images, or analyzing specific scenes. Thus, Kutch aims "to activate vocabulary and cultural knowledge so as to strengthen students' aptitude in performing advanced analytical tasks with increasing adeptness" (60). Kutch gives a very detailed description of her approach; however, I will only outline how her ideas can be adapted for other graphic novels, in particular *Grenzfall*.

For this unit, students work specifically with the pages that show Grimm's father complaining about his son's expulsion from his high school (figure 6.1), and his son's reaction to his death (figure 6.2). The teaching outcome relates to the NCSSFL-ACTFL Can-Do Statements for the Intermediate High level. First, students describe the scenes in detail.

Kutch explains in her article that students should move from more descriptive tasks to interpretive and analytical reading. I suggest a similar approach as it guides students smoothly to a more adept understanding of a scene in a graphic novel. To start, students could work with tasks and questions such as: "Describe the images in which we see the father," "What do the backgrounds of the pictures convey about his position in the factory?" "What is his job?" "How do the first three pictures differ from the fourth one?" "What do you see in the fifth and sixth pictures?" The responses to these questions should be short summaries that demonstrate the students' understanding of the scene. As a next step, students comment on the form and style of image and text. Questions such as the following guide the students: "How is the image composed?" "Describe the style of language." "Do the pictures contain information that the verbal portion does not contain?" As Kutch argues, introductory questions like these allow students to discuss plot elements and to comment on their verbal and visual representation (61) before the instructor would guide them into capstone activities that require analysis and higher level thinking.

In this capstone phase, instructors ask students to examine the function of particular images, the composition of the panel, and the particular relation between text and images. More specific examples include: "Which images have a symbolic meaning?" "How does the absence of text in the fifth and sixth panels impact your perception of the images?" "How are the panels arranged?" "How do you interpret the change in perspective and composition in the sixth panel?" The selected scenes offer insight into the function of the imagery and page layouts. While the text conveys the plot in an informative style, the images carry emotions and symbolic meanings, such as the feeling of inevitable loss, powerlessness in the GDR, or confinement. Instead of directly expressing these meanings, however, the images evoke certain meanings or invite inference. For instance, the wordless pictures (figures 6.1 and 6.2) require the students to infer and describe, and thus "fill in" content, emotional reactions, and symbolic meaning. In addition, the change in perspective and the transition from a standard page layout (figure 6.1) to a splash (full-page) panel (figure 6.2) lead to a discussion about the function of layouts. The described exercises require the student to perform a very close reading of the visual and verbal cues on both pages in order to understand the pivotal change in the plot structures.

By engaging with these guiding questions, students acquire skills that are tailored to the Intermediate High level according to the NCSSFL-ACTFL Can-Do Statements. This means they will "understand the main idea of texts related to everyday life, personal interests, and studies" and they will be able to "follow stories and descriptions about events and experiences in various time frames."[12] In addition, this approach introduces students to basic skills needed for an analytical reading of a scene

Mein Vater als Direktor eines Sägewerks hat noch versucht, seinen Einfluss geltend zu machen und mir zu helfen.

Er bombardierte die Leute mit Eingaben, hat mit Parteileuten, mit staatlichen und kirchlichen Stellen gesprochen.

Aber selbst er konnte da nichts mehr machen.

Wenige Tage später ist er an einem Herzinfarkt gestorben.

Figure 6.1. Scene from *Grenzfall* by Susanne Buddenberg and Thomas Henseler. Susanne Buddenberg and Thomas Henseler. *Grenzfall*. Berlin: avant-verlag, 2011, 41©Zoom & Tinte/avant-verlag, 2011.

Figure 6.2.   Scene from *Grenzfall* by Susanne Buddenberg and Thomas Henseler. Susanne Buddenberg and Thomas Henseler. *Grenzfall*. Berlin: avant-verlag,
2011, 42©Zoom & Tinte/avant-verlag, 2011.

in a graphic novel. Furthermore, students can apply these skills to a more global discussion of the structure and the themes of the book. Students could use the above-mentioned techniques to analyze key scenes in the book—such as the funeral, the expulsion from high school and the death of his father, his work for the IMF, and finally the *Stasi*'s unsuccessful raid—and could identify the authors' voice, their writing style, and particular artistic devices with regard to text and image.

Grenzfall is a good example of a "biographic creative nonfiction graphic novel," according to Katie Monnin's definition (67). Indeed *Grenzfall*'s authors make certain creative choices to tell Grimm's stories. For instance, Henseler and Buddenberg employ a very detail-oriented, realistic drawing style, which students may discuss as a method of portraying facts in a specific manner. Likewise, the authors use a realistic narrative voice, opting for a non-diegetic narrator whose voice cannot be attributed to a specific person inside or outside of the story. This narrative voice masks any subjectivity and suggests that it just recounts the facts.

Discussing these artistic choices and text elements leads students to reflect on the makeup of the biographical graphic novel *Grenzfall*. By way of assessment, students might consider the ways in which they would structure and narrate a biographical graphic novel. Instructors can assign the task of working with a particular biography and outlining scenes and creating a storyboard. For instance, Ilko-Sascha Kowalczuk's *Für ein freies Land mit freien Menschen: Opposition und Widerstand in Biographien und Fotos* (For a Free Land with Free People: Opposition and Resistance in Biography and Photographs; 2006) offers exemplary biographies. Students could create drawings, or, as an alternative, they could write summaries of scenes and present these along with photographs as a final project.

DRÜBEN!

The last section of this chapter also discusses ways that an instructor can introduce students to analyzing and discussing particular structural elements of graphic novels on the Intermediate High level. The third graphic novel, *drüben!*, by Simon Schwartz, does not tell an extraordinary story in the sense of a sensational escape or a remarkable case of resistance against the East German regime. Yet Schwartz's creative and insightful composition, plot, and thematic content offer manifold ways for students to engage with the country's history.

Published in 2009,[13] *drüben!* portrays scenes from Simon Schwartz's (b. 1982) autobiography, but focuses mostly on his parents' biographies. His parents left the GDR in 1984 after submitting an application to permanently leave the GDR (*Antrag zur ständigen Ausreise aus der DDR*).[14] Since Schwartz spent only the first two years of his life in the GDR, his graphic novel illustrates the perspective of a generation that did not experience living in the GDR for a very long time, yet whose lives were entangled with and shaped by GDR history. The figures and his style emphasize the above-mentioned "third generation" perspective: he inserts himself as a child, and he sometimes uses the child's perspective (e.g., a worm's-eye view) and a child's narrative voice to tell the story. Schwartz introduces his graphic novel with an aphorism that points to the difficulties of accessing the past: "Anyone who tries to penetrate the past with the knife of the present will always act in vain. The past is invulnerable. Such attempts can only cause the present or the future to bleed" (Schwartz 2015, 4). Here, the author suggests that although the past might be "invulnerable" in the sense of inaccessible, it will nevertheless have a powerful, or even hurtful, impact on the present and the future if we choose to confront it with poignant questions. Schwartz juxtaposes the quotation with a drawing of the Berlin Wall and its fortifications on the subsequent page. The iconic image triggers collective memories of the border and its lasting impacts. The choice to open his story with this quotation and this type of image represents Schwartz's approach to history: he combines his personal history with collective memories of the GDR past and the time of the Cold War.

Schwartz uses the drawing of the Berlin Wall as a starting point for the story set in West Berlin in 1987, three years after the Schwartz family left the GDR. Through flashbacks that are sometimes interrupted with scenes from the year 1987, the reader learns about the Schwartz family's arrival in West Berlin, and his paternal grandparents' discontent with their decision to leave. His paternal grandparents were loyal to the SED (*Sozialistische Einheitspartei*, the official party in East Germany). They refused to have any contact with their son after their departure. Following these introductory scenes, Schwartz gives insights into the social and historical context of his parents' childhood. He focuses in particular on his father's story, who represents those who grew up in families that internalized and idealized socialist ideas and the GDR as a state. In his childhood, Schwartz's father shared the views expressed by the SED, but personal experiences with the *Stasi* and various political events motivated him to slowly distance himself from official GDR ideology.

For instance, Schwartz narrated how his father and some of his friends and fellow students became "more and more aware of the contradictions between propaganda and the real world" (2015, 42). He explains that the official state youth movement in the GDR, the Free German Youth (*Freie deutsche Jugend* or *FDJ*), encouraged students to think critically about improvements to socialism. Yet his father and his peers witnessed a fellow student's expulsion from the university precisely because he suggested improvements for society. Schwartz vividly portrays their outrage at the hypocritical party policies by intensifying gestures and facial expressions in his drawing of the characters. He adds one more scene in which a

friend comments on East German singer and poet Wolf Biermann's expa-
triation and the fact that many intellectuals left the GDR as a consequence
of that incident (2015, 43). [15] By providing these images and commentary,
Schwartz combines personal experience and the historical fact to illustrate and explain his parents' view of GDR politics and their motivation
to leave.

After the completion of their university studies, Schwartz's parents
become more and more appalled with the ways that the state treats its
citizens. His father starts working as a teacher; and at the school, he finds
out the principal has asked a student to report on him. At that moment,
his father realizes how far-reaching and intricate the *Stasi* network of
surveillance system is. He cannot even trust his students or fellow teachers. As some of their friends start to leave the GDR after having submitted an application, Schwartz's parents begin to consider that option.
However, first Schwartz's father gets the position he had hoped for: he
becomes an art instructor on the university level. Yet when his superior at
this university asks him to talk about the invasion of Afghanistan by
Soviet troops in 1979, he is not allowed to speak about his own opinion
on the political situation but has to present a ready-made speech justify-
ing the invasion. This experience makes it increasingly difficult to remain
in the GDR, and the parents finally submit their application.

In addition to presenting experiences like this that challenge his parents' patience, Schwartz documents how the party and in particular *Stasi*
officers discriminated against his parents and persecuted them after they
had submitted their application to leave the country. His father's SED
party membership is revoked, they are not allowed to continue working
in their jobs, and they become more and more isolated, as many of their
friends have already left the GDR. Readers learn that Schwartz's parents
have to wait three years before they are allowed to leave. During that
time, his parents are constantly spied on by *Stasi* officers, and are ran-
domly interrogated about incidents they did not commit (88–95).
Schwartz also depicts a scene in which his mother is sexually harassed by
a *Stasi* officer (94). By way of explicit visual presentation, the graphic
novel offers students greater insight into the ways in which ordinary
people were humiliated, persecuted, and physically harmed in the GDR.

Contrasting the realistic style of *Grenzfall*, Schwartz does not strive for
a documentary approach. Instead he clearly presents an aesthetically
formed view of the past through his own interpretation of past events
and drawings that take on a simplified, cartoonish style marked by crisp
bold lines. He also often disrupts the chronology, works with different
perspectives, or mixes regular and irregular page layouts. These artistic
choices remind the reader that "comic art calls attention to its fictionality
by displaying its narrative seams" (Fletcher 381). While *Grenzfall* often
tries to mask that effect, *drüben!* emphasizes it. In an interview included
in the German-language version of the book, Schwartz states:

I believe that is was strange for my parents to see themselves in a comic book. Especially for the scenes they told me about. Of course, I tried to present the narrated events as exactly as possible, however it will never be the same. It is an artistic interpretation of reality. But they like the book very much and they are very proud of it.

Zunächst war es für meine Eltern, denke ich, etwas seltsam, sich so in einem Comic zu sehen. Speziell in den Szenen, die sie mir nur erzählt haben. Natürlich habe ich versucht, das Erzählte so exakt wie möglich umzusetzen, aber es wird nie so sein, wie es war. Es ist ja eine künstlerische Übertragung der Realität. Aber sie mögen das Buch sehr und sind sehr stolz darauf (*drüben!*, 113).

Schwartz's comment conveys that he does not aim for an exact representation of the past events but instead provides his own artistic interpretation. In *drüben!*, readers encounter a powerful biographical story that offers many methods for engaging with the multimodal text. Students may start working with the text by analyzing key scenes, in a similar fashion as described above for *Grenzfall*. In particular, *drüben!* invites a reflection on Schwartz's presentation that combines personal story with collective memory. By analyzing different scenes, students can learn how censorship and oppression shaped East German life in the late 1970s and early 1980s. The graphic novel shows how teenagers and young adults were restricted in their choice of profession (40), and gives insights into banned popular music, literature, and art (42–47). It also illustrates daily life in the GDR, such as shortage of fresh fruit, the reading of restricted Western magazines, East German vacation attractions, and the restrictions and surveillance that accompanied daily life.[16]

As I have done with the other graphic novels that deal with aspects of East German culture, I will briefly describe a lesson that demonstrates how students could investigate Schwartz's technique of combining personal and collective memory. For this activity, students work on the scene in which his father discovers that a student has reported on him (figures 6.3 and 6.4). The basis for this scene is to provide a more detailed background on how the *Stasi* operated. This most likely requires that students first research the *Stasi* in order to supplement their base knowledge. One possibility is watching the short documentary *Zentrale des Terrors: Das Stasi-Gefängnis in Hohenschönhausen* (Terror Headquarters: The East German Secret Service Prison in Hohenschönhausen), a film that documents and illustrates how the *Stasi* functioned and recruited informants.

When examining the graphic novel, students begin by describing and analyzing the body language and facial expressions of the characters shown in this scene. For instance, the student in the scene is in a crouched body position that expresses his anxiety, and he cannot look directly at Schwartz's father. In addition, Schwartz zooms in on his father's dis-

Figure 6.3.   Scene from *drüben!* **by Simon Schwartz. Schwartz, Simon.** *drüben!*
Berlin: avant-verlag, 2009, 53.

**Figure 6.4.   Scene from *drüben!* by Simon Schwartz. Schwartz, Simon. *drüben!*
Berlin: avant-verlag, 2009, 54.**

tressed facial expression (figure 6.3, lower left panel). In this scene, there is no text to describe what Schwartz's father or the student is thinking or feeling. In the subsequent scenes, however, the reader sees how Schwartz's father gets angry and interrogates the student further. The student reveals that the principal forced him to share information.

This and the upper right panel on page 54 (figure 6.4) calls for a discussion of composition: Schwartz shows only a part of the student's head next to a huge portrait of Erich Honecker, the chairman of the GDR at that time. The instructor can use Schwartz's drawing of a Honecker portrait as a springboard to discuss the author's use of cultural artifacts and visual references. For example, the picture clearly illustrates the chairman of the GDR, and comments on his oppressive politics, and, by extension, the crimes committed by the *Stasi*. Students may also notice how Honecker's eyes, and by metaphorical extension, his thoughts, are occluded behind his eyeglasses. The scene ends with a panel showing Schwartz's father in his classroom, yet he is drawn proportionately rather small. He is obviously disturbed by the outcome of their conversation, and the use of space in the illustration expresses confinement. Overall, the drawn images convey feelings of powerlessness and distress in light of the omnipresent and oppressive surveillance techniques.

As demonstrated, the scene invites students to reflect on the use of visual clues, panel composition, page layout, and Schwartz's placement of cultural artifacts and references. A discussion of these elements underscores the importance of *how* a graphic novel is able to convey a story, in addition to telling the actual plotline. As a follow-up, students could think about more global questions such as the presentation of the historical content. Students could compare *drüben!* with other ways of telling a biographical story. For instance, they could compare Schwartz's graphic novel with *Grenzfall*. When comparing the two texts, students could be asked to discuss the relationship between fact and fiction. As mentioned above, *drüben!* emphasizes its fictionality, while *Grenzfall* stresses its documentary quality. *drüben!* allows for an empathetic reading as Schwartz vividly depicts the emotional reactions of the characters. Schwartz occasionally inserts into the narration depictions of himself as a child, while, by contrast, Buddenberg and Henseler use a non-diegetic narrator. These observations offer talking points for a class discussion, and help students to reflect on the verbal and visual composition of these biographical stories.

The autobiographical impetus of Schwartz's work could also inspire students to explore their own personal narratives and family histories through writing. Schwartz ends the story by mentioning his very first memory, the night when his parents celebrated their arrival in West Berlin. Instructors can ask students to reflect on early memories of family members or friends and write pieces that describe lives of people close to them. For the assignment, students would have to be aware, like

Schwartz, of embedding the stories in the time and place in which their subjects lived and deciding which events best represented important life decisions. Furthermore, the assignment could lead to reflection on the use of visual representations. For example, students could present their stories orally and include props, they could write short scenes and present them by a montage of texts and photographs, or they could create a storyboard that portrays important scenes.

CONCLUDING THOUGHTS

The German-language graphic novels *Tunnel 57, Grenzfall*, and *drüben!* offer fascinating opportunities for students to connect with GDR history. Although the GDR has been described as a "footnote in history," it nevertheless has had a lasting psychological impact on many of today's German citizens, as these graphic novels show and tell in great detail. Many history textbooks offer only a general introduction and standardized view of the GDR, but teaching about this epoch of German history through biographical graphic novels allows students to better relate to the time period through characters and their stories.

Students can read about extraordinary stories and remarkable people (*Tunnel 57, Grenzfall*), but they also glean insights into everyday life in the GDR (*drüben!*). In each case, the authors convey views that do not avoid presenting "unpleasant facts" about the GDR government, and give voice to untold stories and unsung heroes. In addition to providing visual contexts, the graphic novel engages students in a reading process that speaks to their verbal understanding of German. The illustrations help students directly relate to and more easily understand the content, and create space for innovative teaching activities that integrate creative writing and the arts. Incorporating *Tunnel 57, Grenzfall*, and *drüben!* into Novice and Intermediate language learning levels will make GDR history more comprehensible and accessible, and increase students' linguistic, literary, and cultural competency.

NOTES

1. See: http://www.actfl.org/publications/guidelines-and-manuals/actfl-proficiency-guidelines-2012/german.
2. In particular, Hans-Ulrich Wehler has implemented the term in his influential study "Deutsche Gesellschaftsgeschichte," 361.
3. The genre "Familienroman" refers to meta-historical texts in which family history is investigated or reconstructed laboriously. Scholars like Friederike Eigler used the terms "Familienroman" and "Generationenroman" for these novels. Early examples of this "exploratory family novel" are according to Eigler Christa Wolf's *Kindheitsmuster* (1976), or Uwe Johnson's (1979–1984). Characteristics of these texts are that they renarrate the familiy stories, and they also address on a meta-level how memory constructs past events.

4. See: http://www.comichron.com for the most up-to-date statistics.

5. The initiative is still active. Their members support a social network, meetings, research, and projects that revolve around the concept *Third Generation East Germany* (see: http://netzwerk.dritte-generation-ost.de).

6. *Tunnel 57*, 61ff.

7. "The NCSSFL-ACTFL Can-Do Statements are self-assessment checklists used by language learners to assess what they "can do" with language in the Interpersonal, Interpretive, and Presentational modes of communication. These modes of communication are defined in the National Standards for 21st Century Language Learning and organized in the checklist into the following categories: Interpersonal (Person-to-Person) Communication, Presentational Speaking (Spoken Production), Presentational Writing (Written Production), Interpretive Listening, and Interpretive Reading" (see: http://www.actfl.org/global_statements).

8. *Skill: Interpretive Listening, Novice Mid*, NCSSFl-ACTFL *Can-Do Statements.*

9. See also: ACTFL standard 2.2. *Products of Culture.*

10. *Skill: Presentational Speaking, Novice High*, NCSSFl-ACTFL *Can-Do Statements.*

11. See: http://www.berliner-mauer-gedenkstaette.de/en/index.html.

12. *Skill: Interpretive Reading, Intermediate High*, NCSSFl-ACTFL *Can-Do Statements.*

13. An English translation was published in 2015 (see: Schwartz, Simon. *The Other Side of the Wall.* Minneapolis, MN: Graphic Universe, 2015). The translation gives a language instructor new options with regard to discussing content and form on the novice and intermediate level. In this article I am concentrating on the German edition of the graphic novel. In my commentary on *drüben!*, I use the translation *The Other Side of the Wall.*

14. At the CSCE conference in Helsinki in 1975, the East German leadership agreed in principle to the right of peoples to move freely and the freedom to travel. Afterward, East German citizens started submitting applications to immigrate permanently to West Germany. The applications were not treated officially and applicants never received a written note about the status of their applications. The wait time could be months or several years. In most cases, applicants experienced repressions: they lost their jobs, were forced to sell their property, were imprisoned, and students were expelled from their high schools (see Kowalczuk, Ilko-Sascha. *Nicht mehr mitmachen — Ausreise als Ausweg*).

15. In 1965, the GDR government prohibited Wolf Biermann, a critical communist poet and singer-songwriter, to perform, publish, or travel outside of East Germany. However, that ban turned him into a symbol of non-conformity, and he gained immense popularity in East and West Germany in the following years. Even though he only performed privately, some of his albums were smuggled over to the West and released there. In 1976, the GDR government allowed him to perform again publicly, and even provided an exit visa for a concert in Cologne. Biermann accepted the offer, yet after the concert he was not permitted to return to East Germany. That measure sparked public protests in West and East Germany.

16. See pages 40, 52–53, 56–59, 69–71, and 88–96 for further examples.

REFERENCES

Baetens, Jan, and Hugo Frey. *The Graphic Novel: An Introduction.* New York: Cambridge University Press, 2015.

Bechdel, Alison. *Fun Home: A Family Tragicomic.* Boston: Houghton Mifflin Harcourt, 2006.

Buddenberg, Susanne, and Thomas Henseler. *Grenzfall.* Berlin: avant-verlag, 2011.

———. *Tunnel 57: Eine Fluchtgeschichte als Comic.* Berlin: Links Verlag, 2013.

Burwitz-Melzer, Eva. "Approaching Literary and Language Competence: Picturebooks and Graphic Novels in the EFL Classroom." *Children's Literature in Second*

Language Education. Ed. Janice Bland and Christiane Lütge. London: Bloomsbury, 2013. 53–85.

Chun, Christan W. "Critical Literacies and Graphic Novels for English-Language Learners: Teaching Maus." *Journal of Adolescent & Adult Literacy* 53.2 (2009): 144–53.

DiDonato, Robert, Monica Clyde, et al. *Deutsch: Na Klar! An Introductory German Course, Sixth Edition*. New York: McGraw-Hill, 2011.

Eigler, Friederike. *Gedächtnis und Geschichte in Generationenromanen seit der Wende*. Berlin: Erich Schmidt Verlag, 2005.

El, Refaie E. *Autobiographical Comics: Life Writing in Pictures*. Jackson: University Press of Mississippi, 2012.

Fletcher, Robert P. "Visual Thinking and the Picture Story in *The History of Henry Esmond*." *PMLA* 113.3 (1998): 379–94.

Frauendorfer, Helmuth, and Hubertus Knabe. *Zentrale des Terrors. Das Stasi-Gefängnis in Berlin-Hohenschönhausen*. Mitteldeutscher Rundfunk, 2004. Film.

Fulbrook, Mary. *Ein ganz normales Leben. Alltag und Gesellschaft in der DDR*. Primus: Darmstadt, 2008.

Gonglewski, Margaret T., et al. *Treffpunkt Deutsch, Sixth Edition*. Upper Saddle River, NJ: Prentice Hall, 2012.

Großmann, Thomas. Review of *DDR-Geschichte in Forschung und Lehre. Bilanz und Perspektiven*. H-Soz-u-Kult, H-Net Reviews. November 2010: 1–5. http://www.h-net. org/reviews/showpdf.php?id=31759.

Hatfield, Charles. *Alternative Comics: An Emerging Literature*. Jackson: University Press of Mississippi, 2006.

Hirsch, Marianne. "Family Pictures: Maus, Mourning and Post-Memory." *Discourse: Journal for Theoretical Sudies in Media and Culture* 15.2 (1992–1993): 3–29.

Hoffmann, Jeanette, and Diane Lang. "Graphic Novels im Deutschunterricht. *drüben*! von Simon Schwartz." *BilderBücher, Vol. 2*. Ed. Julia Knopf and Ulf Abraham. Baltmannsweiler: Schneider-Verlag Hohengehren, 2014. 63–74.

Jessen, Ralph. "Alles schon erforscht? Beobachtungen zur zeithistorischen DDR-Forschung der letzten 20 Jahre." *Deutschland-Archiv* 43.6 (2010): 1052–64.

Kowalczuk, Ilko-Sascha, Tom Sello, and Gudrun Weber. *Für ein freies Land mit freien Menschen: Opposition und Widerstand in Biographien und Fotos*. Berlin: Robert-Havemann-Gesellschaft, 2006.

———. "Nicht mehr mitmachen — Ausreise als Ausweg." 30 Sept. 2005. *Dossier Kontraste—Auf den Spuren einer Diktatur*. Bundeszentrale für politische Bildung. Web. Accessed 11 June 2015. http://www.bpb.de/geschichte/deutsche-geschichte/kont raste/42440/ausreise-als-ausweg.

Krashen, Stephen. "Language Teaching Technology: A Low-Tech View." *Georgetown University Round Table on Languages and Linguistics*. Ed. J. E. Alatis. Washington, DC: Georgetown University Press. 1989. 393–407.

Kumschlies, Kirsten. "Literarisches und Historisches Lernen mit der Graphic Novel *drüben*!" *Praxis Deutsch* 42 (2015): 33–35.

Kutch, Lynn Marie. "From Visual Literacy to Literary Proficiency: An Instructional and Assessment Model for the Graphic Novel Version of Kafka's *Die Verwandlung*." *Die Unterrichtspraxis/Teaching German* 47.1 (2014): 56–68.

Loewen, James W. *Lies My Teacher Told Me: Everything Your American History Textbook Got Wrong*. New York: Simon & Schuster, 1995.

Lovik, Thomas, J. D. Guy, and Monika Chavez. *Vorsprung: A Communicative Introduction to German Language and Culture, Third Edition*. Heinle Cengage Learning, 2014.

MacDonell, Colleen. "Making the Case for Pleasure Reading." *Teacher Librarian* 31.4 (2004): 30–32.

Mason, Beniko, and Krashen, Stephen. "Is Form-focused Vocabulary Instruction Worthwhile?" *Children's Literature in Second Language Education*. Ed. Janice Bland and Christiane Lütge. London: Bloomsbury, 2013. 28.

Miller, Frank. *The Dark Knight Returns*. Burbank: DC Comics, 1986.

Monnin, Katie. *Teaching Graphic Novels: Practical Strategies for the Secondary ELA Classroom*. Gainesville, FL: Maupin House Pub., 2010.

Moore, Alan, and Dave Gibbons. *Watchmen*. Burbank: DC Comics, 1987.

NCSSFL-ACTFL Can-Do Statements: Performance Indicators for Language Learners. Web. Accessed 4 January 2016. http://www.actfl.org/publications/guidelines-and-manuals/ncssfl-actfl-can-do-statements.

Nijdam, Elizabeth. "Coming to Terms with the Past: Teaching German History with the Graphic Novel." *Class, Please Open your Comics. Essays on Teaching with Graphic Narratives*. Ed. Matthew L. Miller. Jefferson, NC: McFarland & Company, 2015. 143–54.

Platthaus, Andreas. "German Comics Are Back." *Comics, Manga & Co.: Die Neue Deutsche Comic-Kultur*. München: Goethe-Institut München, 2010.

Schwartz, Simon. *drüben!* Berlin: avant-verlag, 2009.

Schwartz, Simon. *The Other Side of the Wall*. Trans. Laura Watkinson. Minneapolis, MN: Graphic Universe, 2015.

Spiegelman, Art. *Maus*. New York: Pantheon Books, 1980.

Spiegelman, Art. *Maus II: A Survivor's Tale: And Here My Troubles Began*. New York: Pantheon, 1992.

Thomas, Volker. "20 Jahre Deutsche Einheit—die DDR nur noch eine "Fußnote der Geschichte?" Web. Accessed 26 December 2015. http://www.goethe.de/ins/cn/de/tai/ges/pok/6596548.html.

Wehler, Hans-Ulrich. "Deutsche Gesellschaftsgeschichte." *Bundesrepublik und DDR 1949–1990*, Vol. 5. München: C. H. Beck, 2008.

Witek, Josef. *Comic Books as History: The Narrative Art of Jack Jackson, Art Spiegelman, and Harvey Pekar*. Jackson: University Press of Mississippi, 1989.

IV

GENERATIONS OF GERMAN HISTORY

SEVEN

Tension Acrobatics in Comic Art

Line Hoven's Liebe schaut weg

Bernadette Raedler

Although contemporary German novels have become increasingly trans-national and globalized in terms of theme and content, German history continues to be a favored subject. Graphic novels are particularly suited to represent both transcultural and historical themes by way of their inherent mutual dialogue of text and image, which can in turn complement or contradict one another. In Line Hoven's[1] *Liebe schaut weg*[2] (*Love Looks Away*),[3] the comic artist tells her family's story, a transatlantic alliance between her North American mother and her German father. The narrative encompasses four generations of the Hoven-Lorey family, with a specific focus on the narrator's parents and grandparents (figure 7.1). Both sets of grandparents married during the 1940s; and their personal life stories relate closely to the historical events of the Second World War. Significantly, Irmgard and Erich get to know each other as members of the Hitler Youth, to which at least Erich has a conflicted affiliation. Harold's patriotic attitude initially threatens both his courtship of Caroline and his wish to enlist in the United States Army "to beat those Germans," an attitude that contravenes Caroline's desire for peace (Hoven 32).[4] Charlotte, the American daughter of Harold and Caroline, meets Reinhard, the son of Irmgard and Erich, during a study visit in Bonn. The couple marries in 1970 and initially lives in the United States, but later moves to Germany because Reinhard does not feel linguistically qualified to practice medicine in an English-speaking country. The comic ends with the disorientation of Charlotte and Reinhard's first child, who had been born in the United States and later relocated to Germany. As a result of this move, the child is unable to associate the word *home* with his new residence. The artist uses visual means to convey this sense of confusion by combining the child's questions with images of the new residence from the outside. Upon arriving at their apartment building's front door, the child asks "When are we going back home, Mommy?" to which Charlotte answers "We are at home, honey" (94). During this short dialogue the two approach the house, but do not go inside. This final conversation takes place in front of the closed entrance door, and the last panel features a view of the building from the outside. The episode characterizes the novel's complex system of tensions, the analysis of which comprises this chapter's critical focus.

TENSION ART

Liebe schaut weg displays the salient structural feature of a system of multi-polar tensions, which encompass the black-and-white presentation of the scraperboard medium, German versus American language and culture, utopia versus reality, closeness versus distance, and autobiographical versus historical content. The larger scheme to which these tensions contribute creates a reflective meta-level on which the author presents these factors in opposition. The reader can visualize these tensions, understood as alternately antagonistic, parallel or hybrid forces, in the form of a trapezoid structure with an unstable equilibrium on the verge of transforming into a different shape. This chapter examines three different tensions that constitute the comic, and considers their purpose

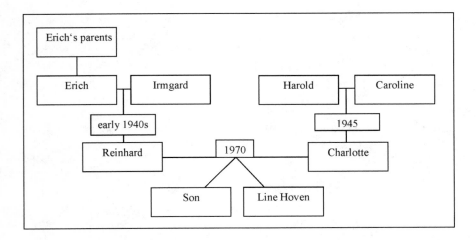

Figure 7.1.   The Family Tree.

for the overall text. Part of this analysis involves determining whether the artist employs tensions only to dissolve them, or in order to underline the conflicts between two cultures as well as between individuals and societies that lie at the heart of the comic. The title itself indicates a first tension: "Liebe" (love), normally a form of care, turns away. *Liebe* suggests a protagonist's presence that the verb *schaut weg* (looks away) cancels out or turns into an absence. The personification of an emotion likewise poses the riddle of how something that is felt also has the ability to act autonomously. Beginning on the first page, the reader must assume the role of a detective in order to understand this and the text's other various tensions.

BLACK-AND-WHITE PRESENTATION

As is often the case with graphic art, the artist's technique contributes to a text's proposed meaning and the reader's subsequent interpretation. Hoven, for example, uses scraperboard for her comic, a material that draws upon the natural opposition between black and white. The production technique is similar to linocut or wood cut because something is revealed through scratching or scraping. Scraperboard, however, is a piece of flexible paper, a much softer material. The medium consists of multi-layered cardboard with an additional layer of white clay covered by black ink. The artist begins her work in front of a completely black medium out of which something is being excavated and exposed, which then appears as white. Extending here the ancient notion of the *tabula rasa*, which conceived of the soul figuratively as a straightened wax board before it receives impressions from the external world, the scraperboard medium becomes an epistemological tool in the artist's hands. A black-and-white medium for which even the process of excavating remains ambiguous if, as on the first pages of the book, that which is to become visible only represents a new layer of disguise. On these first pages, blankets appear most prominently in white; and they disguise the underlying content, which appears to be furniture, underneath, so that the action is brought to a stop. For example, the reader does not know if someone is moving in or out, or if the furniture is covered because no one lives there anymore (4–5). Instead, the images and the technique direct the reader's focus to the inanimate objects and to that certain captured moment (figure 7.2).

The scraperboard technique can also involve the addition of colors, but in *Liebe schaut weg*, the artist uses color sparingly. The graphic novel starts with a slightly colored page, followed then by subsequent black-and-white pages before it finally concludes again with a colored page. Although the physical material used to create the comic is new, the technique is not. Hillary Chute informs that the first modern graphic narra-

Figure 7.2.   Preface. Line Hoven. *Liebe schaut weg*. Berlin: Reprodukt, 2008. 4–5.

tives, at that time called "wordless novels," were fabricated with a similar technique in the late 1930s (455). They are not very well known because they developed around the same time as the *Superman* comics, which, due to ease of production as well as consumption, eclipsed them to some degree. Hillary Chute defines these "wordless novels" as:

> beautifully rendered woodcut works—in some cases marketed as conventional novels—that almost entirely served a socialist agenda and that incorporated experimental practices widely associated with literary modernism. Although called wordless novels, these works often did incorporate text, but not as captions or as speech balloons. (455)

As the following analysis will demonstrate, each narrative feature in *Liebe schaut weg* carries essential information. Because no detail in Hoven's comic is accidental, her technique and its effects on the reader align with its established conventions, and represent a counter-narrative in respect to the hero icon that dominates the *Superman* comics, in particular its speed, its color, its supernatural powers. Allusions in Hoven's novel to the type of fascist or American liberator heroism prevalent on the temporal axis of the parent generation by means of black-and-white representation do not simply illustrate events. Instead, they represent them by reducing color to only absolutely necessary degrees, a choice that in turn emphasizes tension.

Hoven's final published result is a print of the scraperboard cut, which includes scraped paper documents inserted throughout the comic. The print looks so realistic that a differentiation between original ice rink or airline tickets, bills, or Hitler Youth identification cards (figure 7.3) and the scraperboard cuts becomes difficult (7). Readers have to study the reprint closely to recognize that they are not looking at realia or real documents, but rather at scraperboard cut prints. This deliberate ambiguity in the production process and final appearance speaks to the complexity and intricacies of the graphic novel's content despite its outwardly simple aesthetic appearance. The complex layering of tangible evidence and documentation raises questions about established standards of authenticity, such as those of legal documents. The only "originals" included in the comic, however, are the artist's scraperboard images, or more specifically prints of them. In the case of the Hitler Youth identification card, matters become even more complex. The card, complete with the signatures of Erich and his group leader and the HJ (*Hitlerjugend* or Hitler Youth) seal, looks like the real document, but the drawing of Erich inserted in place of his photo appears as a scraperboard image and not a real photograph. While the text on the identification card is the official Nazi regime wording, which ironically warns of fraudulent use, Erich's scraperboard depiction is a very subtle reminder that the artist provides the viewer with a subjective representation by fusing image and text, official and individual representation. This technique demands that the reader critically reflects on content, artistic modes of representation, and personal processes of perception. Hoven thus subtly disillusions readers by pointing them toward what Nancy Pedri has described as "the particular details of the mental processing of hard facts" (147). This processing underlines the disagreement of visual and verbal representation, a discrepancy that necessitates meditation and active questioning on the reader's part. The disillusionment is a particular strength of the comic medium because it provides both modalities (image to text and vice versa) that are needed to make visible the deviation from reality.

AUTOBIOGRAPHY AND HISTORY

Another tension in the comic appears through the juxtaposition of autobiographical content, or individual narrative, and history, or collective narrative. Readers take in the history of an individual family against the backdrop of historic twentieth- and twenty-first-century events. The bridge between these two spheres and the amalgamation of individual and society are marked in multiple ways in the comic, for example, by specific headings and by utopic content.

Headings

Reproductions of realia mark content sections as chapter headings, which are visual yet not completely wordless. The Hitler Youth membership card (7), ice skating tickets (23), a boarding pass (65), family photos

Figure 7.3.   Hitler Youth Identity Card. Line Hoven. *Liebe schaut weg.* **Berlin: Reprodukt, 2008. 7.**

(62, 63), a bill (45), handwritten annotations (42, 43), and subtitles (66), suggest the presence of autobiographic writing and create the intimacy of a photo album or diary. The autobiographical content is revoked or at least called into question, however, through Hoven's application of what Scott McCloud terms a masking effect, or the combination of minimally detailed characters with detailed backgrounds. This process allows readers to mask themselves in a character, and more importantly to identify more easily with characters than if a particular, recognizable person were depicted (McCloud 43). By way of the montage of a scraperboard print in lieu of a photograph on the identification card, the artist achieves a simplifying, neutralizing, archetypical representation of Erich Hoven. The obscured white face in the scraperboard print does not reveal individual features and can be complemented with different individuals or expressions. It does not unambiguously represent Erich Hoven anymore. This blank space in the picture technique raises, according to McCloud, the identification potential for the reader. It allows the reader to accompany the character into the imaginary world, opened through "iconic abstraction" toward representation (McCloud 50). Closure concerning the detailed definition of content, such as who is depicted, is simultaneously delayed. The stylized face prevents readers' instant assumption that they are looking at a particular individual, and challenges readers to fill in the facial features themselves. Thus, the author's autobiography is revoked, at least temporarily, in favor of the reader's biography and personal interpretation. Official documents cross-reference both the societal character—agreed upon rules, historic background, or dates and facts that apply to a group—and the autobiographic content in the comic by the artist's use of such montages. Individual and collective experience and memory become intrinsically tied to one another. Hoven's use of the masking effect illustrates that, aside from there being no unequivocal truth, individual representations are always also remediating pre-existing historical conditions.

In addition to the document-remediating headings, verbal subheadings also designate different sections of the comic and attribute interpretative weight to words. The subheading *"Come closer,"* offering no indication of who is speaking, heads the airport page that depicts Charlotte's departure to Germany, and again conveys the intimacy of a journal entry because the words are handwritten (66). The visual content of the panel, however, cannot be clearly linked to reducing physical or mental distance that would correspond to the subheading *Come closer.* Before an airplane is able to land, it has to depart; and that departure can lead in very different directions. The deserted airport panel signals internal order and security. From the tower, the situation is controlled, observed, directed, presumably by humans, who are incidentally not visible in this picture. This gives the impression that parking lots, fences, and runways, regulate machines and humans. Below the airport panel and on the following page, smaller panels feature farewell and transition scenes, which correspond to the command *Come closer* and function as a zooming-in technique. The visual cues indicate that the scope of action for the individual character is thus anchored in societal structures such as the airport, its parking lot, its runways and departure hall.

The handwritten heading *Come closer* may signal a sense of desire in Charlotte, especially because she uses those same words later in the comic when she addresses Reinhard as they dance (71). The reader could simultaneously interpret the *Come closer* chapter heading as the author's invitation for the reader to pay closer attention to the cooperative meaning of word and image in the comic as well as the correlation between verbal and visual information. If readers were to respond to this invitation, they would realize agreements as well as discrepancies between heading and panel content: responding to the command actually results in an increase in distance. As with her scraperboard technique, Hoven utilizes text and image to indicate an inability to distinguish between reality and desire, between the lifelessness of infrastructure and the liveliness of human beings. This non-identity underlines a partial compatibility that is unlikely to ever become completely congruent, as actions and thoughts remain open for interpretation, and animate and inanimate objects do not and cannot fall into identical categories.

Utopic Dimension

Another method by which Hoven initiates a discussion of the boundaries between autobiographic and historic content, and which also marks narrative progression in the comic, is through the introduction of the utopic dimension. The transition from telling Charlotte's story to telling Reinhard's story, which immediately precedes their first encounter in Germany, is carried out while Charlotte gazes out of the airplane window thinking or saying "I hope so" (68, the words are printed in a speech bubble, but Charlotte's mouth is closed). The adjacent panel then features Reinhard who finishes studying, looks at his watch, and in his mind anticipates his later plans for the day. The possibility for their mutual encounter is thus established in a yet-to-be defined space that is associated with hope in Charlotte's case and with careful planning in Reinhard's case. The imaginary component becomes more obvious in the panel following the marriage proposal. The answer to the question where the young couple is going to live, vaguely indicated by the speech balloon "over there" (87), is floating in the air beyond precisely defined locations. In this full-page panel, the rooftops of Bonn and the illuminated night-sky above them construct a setting with no tight boundaries of celestial space. Black gutter, night sky, and illuminated sky merge; the black speech balloon corresponds to the dark undefined space. The indissoluble relationship between individual and society mentioned above is not cancelled out by the imaginary. Instead, how it will evolve is undetermined: its scope is visually and verbally marked by unscraped space.

Similar to the way that Charlotte's hopes and desires motivate her actions (for example, to study in Germany, marry, and move to Germany) Reinhard's love of reading is initiated by Science Fiction booklets, a utopian or fantasy genre. While interplanetary aviation is still utopic at the time that Reinhard starts reading Science Fiction literature, it later becomes reality as proven by the television broadcast of the first Sputnik launch in 1957, and the first manned space flight in 1961. The reader already knows, while reading Irmgard's comment on Science Fiction booklets, that the manned moon landings have taken place. The historic occurrence proves that what was previously Science Fiction has now become reality, and that fiction publications on such utopian topics are no longer "Schund" as Irmgard puts it. "Schund," which closely translates to "trash" and carries a negative connotation,[5] corresponds much more closely to her confrontational personality than the more neutral *nonsense* found in the English translation of the graphic novel (51). This example shows how Hoven interlaces further subtensions into the tension between autobiography and history, such as those between closeness and distance, utopia and reality, confrontation and fusion, openness and secrecy. A multipolar tension and narrative structure evolves that complicates unambiguous interpretation, drawing attention to the complex conflicts that the artist presents through manipulation of narrative tools belonging to the graphic novel medium.

GERMAN-AMERICAN RELATIONS

In this final section, the analytical focus turns to another tension, namely, that between German and American culture and language. Hoven presents German-American relations in the comic as subject to a slow evolution that spans the time of several generations. At first glance, the bicultural relationship seems typified by polarizations in the parent generation (Caroline-Harold, Irmgard-Erich), and more specifically by an opposition of both countries and cultures. A more thorough reading reveals that such a dichotomization is not justified because the comic includes characteristics of dichotomies as well as parallelisms as regard the behaviors of the individual characters. Dichotomies refer to strong, antagonistic tensions, but parallelisms denote smaller tensions or relationships between subjects or objects that are based on less difference. This final level of analysis will lead to possible conclusions as to whether the comic dissolves the tensions between oppositions and parallelisms, or if it aims to dissolve them at all, instead treating the tensions as constitutive for the comic.

Dichotomies

The characters of Harold and Irmgard, who both belong to the parent generation, create their identities through a polarization strategy that seeks to define the self by delineating and differentiating from the other rather than by emphasizing commonalities. Harold captures Catherine's heart in the course of a competition on ice (26–27); he wants to enlist with the military because he hopes "we'll beat those Germans" (33); he takes a firm stand when he admits "Hmm, well, I'm a patriot"(34) or negatively judges his daughter's relationship to Reinhard "God, damn it!"(76). After the war he is not able to unlearn this established pattern and adheres rigidly to an obsolescent model, not suited to respond to a postwar reality, in which former enemies become allies. To Reinhard's marriage proposal to his daughter, Harold answers with "No, Catherine, not as long as I've got something to say" (81). He refuses Reinhard's offer to carry his suitcase with "No, thank you. I've already got some professional help" (79). And his remark before meeting Reinhard's parents—"Hopefully they are not as stiff as him . . . pff . . . typical German" (81)—demonstrates a behavioral pattern marked by obstinacy, that categorically, and perhaps stereotypically, differentiates between being German versus American.

Irmgard's rejection and degradation of American culture, her defense of the familiar culture, as well as her lack of communication skills are reinforced by her blindness toward her own past. In particular, the missing photo, which visually documents her Hitler Youth membership, demonstrates this impairment. As mentioned above, American Science Fiction booklets, which stand for the strong influence of the occupier culture after the war and contain highly imaginary content, are in her opinion "Schund." The verbal degradation is visually enhanced by her almost demonic appearance when she detects Reinhard's secret reading of the booklets at night (51). Her depiction in an enhanced, harsh contrast of black and white and with an extremely stiff and inflexible gaze corresponds most closely to the title of the comic *Liebe schaut weg* because she does not at all exhibit the loving care associated with a mother-son relationship in this panel. The intensified contrast of black and white underscores her extremely strong convictions. In her perception, American future-oriented attitudes transform into a child's naughtiness, a primarily annoying behavior, over which she has no control: "Wherever will they go next?"—"To the moon . . . those Americans . . ." (Wo wollen die noch überall hin?" "Zum Mond . . . diese Amerikaner . . . ; 60). By the same token, American playful inventiveness contests Irmgard's asserted seriousness and purported superiority.

The comic's polarization strategy emphasizes opposites such as good and evil, and climaxes in the depiction of the joint marriage-proposal dinner (82), for which the panel division runs through the middle of the table. In this situation, Irmgard never addresses Charlotte's family directly, but instead she mediates her speech through Reinhard. "Reinhard, ask them if they know what Black Forest gateau is. I imagine they've never had it before" (Reinhard, frag doch mal, ob sie Schwarzwälder Kirschtorte kennen. So was kennen die doch bestimmt nicht; 82). The German version contains an additional degradation that the English translation lacks: the pronoun *die* (them, those ones) carries the semantic marks "known" and "prominent" (Weinrich 380). The choice of the high-definition reference pronoun instead of the less conspicuous pronoun *sie* (they) further intensifies the conflict that is already expressed by pronominal reference instead of direct address in the receiver role (Weinrich 385–86). This not only undermines conventions of politeness but also drafts German identity in Irmgard's perception in opposition to American identity. Furthermore the polarization strategy leads, in Harold's and Irmgard's case, to the introduction of a valuation system, in which differences are not just mapped on a quantitative scale, but on a qualitative scale of legally and morally right and wrong. On this scale the familiar culture and the personal opinion are always correct. Hoven's way of representing, however, questions exactly that through the juxtaposition of mutually exclusive plural arguments.

Parallelisms

In addition to narrative strategies based on binary oppositions, *Liebe schaut weg* also features a subsystem comprised of parallelisms. For example, Harold's clandestine attempt to enlist with the United States military, contrary to official specifications as gas company workers are not allowed to enlist, reminds of Erich's attempt to listen to banned radio stations in Nazi Germany. While Harold is able to do this in joint knowledge with a friend, and the attempt also fails, Erich internally distances himself through the forbidden wiretapping of a radio station from the Hitler Youth and his friends. After the successful wiretapping of a Mendelssohn broadcast, Erich is depicted in a separate panel (18) moving in the opposite direction of the Hitler Youth gang. The lie, which Harold risks by misleading public authorities, becomes a lie among friends for Erich. Likewise and as subsequently demonstrated, both Charlotte and Reinhard struggle with language proficiencies, albeit on different levels, doctor and patient perceptions are softened to suggest parallelisms, and Caroline as well as Erich exhibits understanding attitudes toward their children.

Guidelines for Narrative Interpretation

German-American relations are represented, as I have shown, by binary oppositions as well as parallelisms and variations of these two representational concepts. Another interpretative plane is revealed through the development of the family members across several generations. This will be demonstrated using the example of language as a substantial cultural marker. Charlotte and Reinhard are the first family members in the chronology who learn and use both the German and the English languages, and who also try to practice the culturally connecting aspect of foreign language learning through their Atlantic crossings. When Charlotte's parents travel to Germany, they are dependent on their daughter's translation skills to help them communicate. Charlotte, who is learning German and wants to study German literature abroad with the native speakers, possesses the highest degree of bilingualism in the comic at first glance. She repeatedly addresses Reinhard in German, but grammar mistakes signal that she is a non-native speaker. In the sentence "Wann haben sich deine Eltern kennenlernen?" (When did your parents meet?; 75), she uses the infinitive (*kennenlernen* or to get to know/to meet) instead of the participle (*kennen gelernt* or got to know/met). Her textbook word choices consistently disrupt the natural speech flow (when she asks "Sind diese deine?" instead of the more commonly used *Sind das deine?*, "Are these yours?"; 72), and she employs verbal hybrids: "Oh, ich möchte gern eine English teacher werden," (Oh, I'd like to become an English teacher; 73). Charlotte's speech is highly understandable but contains hybrid forms of German words and English inflection as well as German and English words. Her speech clearly focuses strictly on the communicative components of language in contrast to Reinhard's.

Reinhard encounters other difficulties applying his foreign language, English. His speech is stilted ("Hello . . . Hi . . . ehmm . . . You are Charlotte?" 70, or "Ähh . . . Mr Lorey, may I . . ." 84), and he has difficulties understanding, especially while practicing medicine as a physician in the States. ("Can you repeat that, please?"—"Excuse me, I did not understand" 90). Compared to Charlotte, his problems arise from having to use much more elaborate linguistic contexts. For example, initially approaching a potential lover, proposing marriage, or a physician-patient-discourse have very different implications and a much higher risk of disaster should the communication fail than, for example, greeting a neighbor. Reinhard's grammatically correct use of the foreign language in a more difficult context or register further suggests that his communication difficulties must stem from extra-linguistic factors, such as intimidation in culturally unfamiliar and psychologically challenging situations or an approach driven by, if not completely restricted to, intellect rather than emotion. He is unable to communicate, although he speaks grammatically correctly and understands the literal meaning of the words spoken. In contrast to Charlotte, his speech is focused strictly on the cognitive aspects of language.

Charlotte and Reinhard's difficulties to communicate climax as part of their bicultural love affair when Charlotte says, "I don't understand what the problem is . . . ," to which Reinhard responds, "The problem is that I don't understand!"(91). This chiastic opposition that only differs in the response to "what" with "that," introduces a bivalent tautology concept. Two different truth values are introduced (Charlotte is questioning, Reinhard is explaining) that cannot be reconciled under one common logic and thus reveal the need for negotiation and accommodation if the communication is to be successful. Reinhard's perspective of thought is framed in opposition to Charlotte's perspective, which is in accord with the use of chiasmus since antiquity: they serve to emphasize antitheses. Hoven, however, employs Epanodos (Schweikle 193), a special case of chiasmus, which uses the exact same terms "I don't understand," "problem," "is," and thus demonstrates that a one-sided interpretation of the speech act as antithetic meets a threshold. The reader diagnoses an antithesis, as Charlotte does not understand something (*what*), whereas Reinhard understands something very well, namely, *that* he does not understand well enough. However both encounter a different problem of non-comprehension. Epanodos consists of an antithesis, or reversal of structures which puts them in opposition, enlaced with two parallelisms: the grammatical clauses display inverted parallelism, but the words are the same. By employing Epanodos, Hoven uses a hybrid form of both stylistic devices that drafts an integrative frame in which seemingly mutually exclusive arguments are in fact related to each other. This suggests that if arguments are never completely mutually exclusive, nor ever completely congruent, their frame of reference is likely different.

The conversation continues with a discussion of the significance of language for mutual understanding. In the subsequent panel Reinhard explains to Charlotte: "You know, it's . . . the responsibility is just too great. My English is never going to be good enough" (Weißt du, es ist . . . Die Verantwortung ist zu groß. Mein Englisch wird einfach nie ausreichen; 91). Charlotte answers him as follows: "But you're learning more every day. It's just a different language" (Aber du lernst doch mehr jede Tag [*sic*]. Es ist nur eine Sprache; 91). While Reinhard responds with "no" the reader sees him sideways from the back. In a mirror image, the reader also sees him sideways from the front; and he is just about to take off his hospital identification tag. The visual clue of the mirror image, in which Reinhard literally sees, or recognizes himself (the self), combined with the clear verbal answer "Nein" conveys a philosophical moment of recognition, which is only made possible in a private setting (removal of the hospital tag) and in a communicative situation (conversation with Charlotte).[6] Charlotte, his wife or the other, facilitates Reinhard's moment of self-recognition, although she herself does not share his way of recognizing. Nevertheless, the graphic novel suggests that the evolution of the individual is not able to progress without the other, just as the narrative in the comic advances with the succession of panels. The progression of the individual within the individual-versus-collective narrative is subtly indicated by comparison with the only two other mirror reflections in the comic that show both the subject in front of the mirror and its reflection: Reinhard's father Erich is depicted twice while getting ready for the Hitler Youth meeting. A moment of recognition that Hitler Youth membership may be a highly questionable affiliation lies between those reflection panels, not accompanied by verbal speech acts, legible only in the changing facial expressions and facilitated by the forbidden Mendelssohn music.

For Reinhard, who is depicted a generation later and also older, language becomes an essential and formative tool that shapes his identity and always supplements the mediated thoughts and emotions, yet has its limits in communicating the existential orientation of the inner self. Catherine's (Charlotte's mother) interpretation of his name points to a different understanding of abstract language concepts such as words, sounds, and associated meanings. She calls her son-in-law "Rainheart," while Reinhard recognizes himself more in the literal German meaning of "pure" for *"rein"* and "fixed" for *"hart."* Thus Hoven plants a narrative trajectory comprised of content and image that emphasizes differences and introduces a multiplicity of understandings and concepts. By visually and verbally spelling out the underlying structures, namely, different interpretations of abstract concepts, she transforms the comic into a reflective medium that makes the conflict transparent, but she takes no sides concerning the outcome. Along this narrative trajectory Charlotte points to the idea that language always consists of construction and interpretation on the part of the language users. Reinhard illustrates that one man can only speak with one tongue, and that speaking always remains inadequate. Possibilities and limits of monolingualism and multilingualism are thus inextricably tied together as in a trapeze, and are questioned and scanned for their potential through the corresponding complexity of verbal and visual representation in the graphic novel. The distinction between speaking and understanding is part of that trapeze experiment. While Charlotte is referring to the speaking function of language in her statement "But you're learning more every day. It's just a different language" (Aber du lernst doch mehr jede Tag [sic]. Es ist nur eine Sprache; 91), Reinhard is occupied with the listening comprehension function of language. This points to another chiastic entanglement as Charlotte, who seems convinced that the problem has only to do with the capability of expression, is not able to produce grammatically correct sentences, while Reinhard who speaks grammatically correctly, maintains that he is not able to understand adequately.

Visual representations in the graphic novel support this interpretation. When Reinhard conducts a doctor-patient consultation at the hospital, he is not visible. Instead the reader sees a speech bubble coming out of one of the hospital windows that reads "Sorry, what did you say?" (90). In the subsequent panel we only see a speech bubble behind a metal-grilled loop that visually leads into a corridor, and a closed door that says "Can you repeat that, please?" (90). The reader thus witnesses a doctor-patient discourse in which neither the physician nor the patient is visible. In the following panels the viewer only sees the doctor's white coat with an unidentifiable name tag and the patient's outline under the blanket. Though the speech balloon's arrows point to the doctor, the distinction between doctor and patient is weakened because the characters' heads are missing. A pathological component is thus ascribed to Reinhard's misunderstanding although it remains indeterminate if the misapprehension is pathological or illness-inducing, suggesting that either could be the case. Characteristics of speaking and understanding, mono- and bilingualism, potentiality, hybrid forms, and limits of foreign language learning are thus negotiated through this multi-layered technique. Charlotte's remark (which incidentally combines a German and an English phrase) "Wir können darüber reden noch einmal. . . . Just give us a little more time; 92) while embracing her pregnant body and continuing the conversation with Reinhard about where to live, refers to the time frame of another generation. The comic thus narrates a process of approximation and bridging to the other that spans generations and does not offer a solution, neither for the characters within the text nor for the reader. Therefore, the comic's main objective cannot be identified as an attempt at having two cultures and languages converge. The comic artist, by way of the meta-level of making visible, uses correspondingly complex narrative techniques to present complex problems for the readers' reflection.

CONCLUSION

Following the Woody Allen quotation preceding the comic, "I wondered if a memory is something you have or something you've lost . . ." (4–5), readers of *Liebe schaut weg* could ask whether the illustrated tensions in the comic call for resolution, or whether they are simply indispensable structural components of the narrative. While it may seem that one of these categories does not have to exclude the other, Hoven suggests that a search for better solutions will only occur if the tension relationships remain. Hoven initiates and demonstrates a creative potential for transformation by way of multi-layered and complex perspectives that mutually inform and transform each other. By withdrawing specific autobiographical components, she opens up various gaps that are subtly hinted at through missing photographs, a black gutter, and several black pages, out of which nothing has been scraped yet. Essential information hides in those gaps: the violence of the Third Reich and the Holocaust are only very indirectly hinted at by way of the Yellow Star (19), which may go unnoticed by many a reader, and through Mendelssohn's music (15–16), which could only be listened to illegally. The English broadcast in Nazi Germany (16–17) and Erich's secret manipulation of the radio, which he denies even to friends (17, 18–19), demonstrate the illegality. The excitement and happiness in Erich's face, when the wiretapping is successful, shown in half-page panels (16), and in opposition to his serious expression in a Hitler Youth uniform afterward, (17) tell another story: that of his inner distancing from the Hitler Youth. The artist visually hints at that personal turning point in a mirror reflection that depicts Erich looking at himself in his uniform (17). The double image that the mirror reflection produces also suggests two incongruent parts of the self.

Shades between sepia and yellow on the title page (figure 7.4), which remind of faded family portraits or their negatives, suggest a view from the outside into a stranger's window, which provides the viewer with a certain perspective as well.

The author's autobiography thus rises up to meet the reader's autobiography, who may fill in the gaps with his or her own experience. On

Figure 7.4.   Title Page. Line Hoven. *Liebe schaut weg.* **Berlin: Reprodukt, 2008.**
Title page.

the front cover, the curtain on the window, for example, is half drawn, revealing the contents of the room's interior with different degrees of clarity. The armchair is empty, inviting the reader to contemplate its owner or to fill this position. Readers are thus afforded "quasi-diegetic status,"[7] meaning that their position becomes a determining factor in the sequential representation of space, possibly even adopting main character status, thoughts, and actions in the story line. This invitation to participate in the plot as well as the representation of the characters and their utterances in oppositional structures advocates for a structuralist approach in *Liebe schaut weg* that narrates the development of the characters dependent on societal structures. The outline of the titular *Liebe* can be positioned within the tenets of analytical philosophy: Is love present or absent? Does it insist on a radical adaptability of distinct or abstract elements, on two different empirical values, or is it possible for the utterly different to meet in a joint entity? It is symptomatic of these art forms that they not so much require a definition of social relations, but rather encourage an analysis of the conditions that facilitate the meaning (Dierks 61). The addressing of the reader is less action-oriented than reflection-oriented. He is not prompted to come up with a solution to the puzzle but rather to try to understand the presented conflict. The comic thus is a slow medium—slow in its laborious production, slow in the reader's reception—which may be called a freeze update or strobe effect in analogy to film. This effect is achieved by dark phases between the projected images, or black pages in the comic before each chapter. Instead of a continuous motion, readers observe static life situations that enable them to reflect upon these situations, rather than getting immersed in the ongoing action.

On the one hand, Line Hoven develops the comic into a very slow visual medium, but on the other hand, she equips it with the dramaturgy of the stage including exposition, main body, and conclusion. Not only does this represent a fusion of visual techniques such as photography, film, and stage, but also of different genres such as drama, autobiographical tale, and historic non-fiction. In this sense *Liebe schaut weg* is an example of transmedial, meaning non-specific to an individual medium (Ryan 31–32), and genre-transgressing storytelling that is defined and limited by its particular combinations of image and text and of different genres. Hoven's idiosyncrasy, however, is to be found in her scraperboard cut print presentation that remediates, as Jay Bolter and Richard Grusin have defined it, "prior media forms" (273) such as wood or lino-cut technique, reviving these methods on the world's cultural map.[8]

As a real-life descendant of her invented comic figures, Hoven is fluent in both German and English, and the depicted events all belong to the past, the past of her ancestors and the past of German-American relations. Hoven interweaves the different pasts into a multifocal web of tensions that encloses the present by including the reader or viewer in the interpretation process, turning the comic into plural art. Because the comic denies a one-sided interpretation, it stimulates the reader to reflect on the conflict. An integral part of that negotiation is the interdependency of the individual and the autobiographic component with the societal and the historic component. As with the example of a marriage contract, social contracts are renegotiated and supplemented by the contemporary discussion about transnational extensions to those agreements, such as multiple citizenship or transnational legal recognition. Line Hoven's comic offers a reworking of those historical legacies that used to confine otherness into a hierarchical complementarity of identity and alterity.

Hoven challenges these antagonisms and introduces the question to which degree narratives of self-identification constitute identity as opposed to collective narratives. By complicating and subverting binaries, and creating hybrids, Hoven develops her comic into one that invites reflection and clarification by denying unequivocal signification. Furthermore "tension acrobatics" becomes a coping strategy for the reader whose task is not to answer an ambivalent stimulus with a reductionist, unambiguous reaction.

NOTES

1. Line Hoven was born in Bonn, Germany, in 1977. She studied visual communication in Kassel and illustration in Hamburg. *Love Looks Away* was her diploma thesis. Line Hoven's scratched-out scraperboard comics have appeared in the magazines *Orang* and *Strapazin*. She regularly creates illustrations for the *Frankfurter Allgemeine Zeitung* newspaper. Hoven has since illustrated two more books in cooperation with the author Jochen Schmidt: Hoven, Line, illus. *Dudenbrooks—Geschichten aus dem Wörterbuch*. By Jochen Schmidt. Berlin: Jacoby & Stuart, 2011. Hoven, Line, illus. *Schmythologie: Wer kein Griechisch kann, kann gar nichts*. By Jochen Schmidt. München: C. H. Beck, 2013.

2. In this essay, I discuss the original German edition of *Liebe schaut weg*, which is really a bilingual edition as text is quoted in the language in which it is spoken or written. The English edition contains no German in the dialogues and represents speech differences with two typefaces, handwriting for German speech, block letters for English text.

3. *Liebe schaut weg* was first published in 2007 by Reprodukt publishers, won the Independent Comic Prize in 2008 and has been translated into several languages. The English version is titled *Love Looks Away*.

4. The pages in the comic book are not numbered. I numbered them for ease of reference, starting with the title page following the cover.

5. In German, the term *Schundliteratur* ("trash literature") has frequently been used to describe comics. The English equivalent is *pulp fiction*. *Schundliteratur* was partly banned during the Weimar Republic era as literature with distinctly sensual content. During National Socialism the restrictions were replaced by *Reichsschrifttumskammer* decrees, governmental regulations that controlled publications.

6. This visual and verbal presentation reflects theories of the self from Plato to Foucault which state "the care of the self is actually something that always has to go through the relationship to someone else who is the master" (Foucault 58).

7. Translation of a term introduced by Martin Schüwer, "Erzählen in Comics." Nünning Vera, Nünning Ansgar. *Erzähltheorie transgenerisch, intermedial, interdisziplinär*. Trier: WVT, 2002. 200.

8. Furthermore, it could be suggested that Hoven's hybrid forms meet Derrida's term *différance* (Derrida 76–113), which embraces the chronological displacement as well as the non-identity as the double meaning of the verb *différer*. One possible reading of *Liebe schaut weg* can be seen in the image-text-implementation of the *différance* term as it narrates difference in recurrent processes, and narrates it just as subtly as the artificial term *différance*.

REFERENCES

Bolter, Jay, and Richard Grusin. *Remediation: Understanding New Media*. Cambridge: MIT Press, 2000.

Chute, Hillary. *Graphic Women. Life Narrative & Contemporary Comics*. New York: Columbia University Press, 2010.

Derrida, Jacques. "Die Différance." *Postmoderne und Dekonstruktion. Texte französischer Philosophen der Gegenwart*. Ed. Peter Engelmann. Ditzingen: Reclam, 2004. 76–113.

Dierks, Christiane. *Spielarten sozialer Kunst. Jochen Gerz—Pino Poggi*. Oldenburg: BIS-Verlag Carl von Ossietzky Universität Oldenburg, 2006.

Foucault, Michel. *The Hermeneutics of the Subject. Lectures at the Collège de France 1981–1982*. New York: Picador, 2005.

Hoeppner, Stefan. "Hybrid Narratives, Hybrid Identities: Line Hoven's Graphic Memoir *Liebe schaut weg*." Presentation at the MLA Convention, Los Angeles, Jan. 7, 2011.

Hoven, Line. *Liebe schaut weg*. Berlin: Reprodukt, 2008.

———. *Love Looks Away*. London: Blank Slate Books, 2013.

Marth, Nina. "Bester Independent Comic: *Liebe schaut weg* von Line Hoven. Ein Interview." Comic!-Jahrbuch 2009. Stuttgart: Interessenverband Comic e.V. ICOM, 2008. 168–73.

McCloud, Scott. *Understanding Comics. The Invisible Art*. New York: Harper Collins Publishers, 1993.

Nünning Vera, and Nünning Ansgar, eds. *Erzähltheorie transgenerisch, intermedial, interdisziplinär*. Trier: WVT, 2002.

Pedri, Nancy. "Graphic Memoir: Neither Fact Nor Fiction." *From Comic Strips to Graphic Novels. Contributions to the Theory and History of Graphic Narrative*. Ed. Daniel Stein and Jan-Noël Thon. Berlin, Boston: Walter de Gruyter, 2013. 127–54.

Platthaus, Andreas. "Anstelle einer Einleitung. Ein Motiv aus Line Hovens *Liebe schaut weg*." *Reddition* 49/50 (2009): 5–7.

Ryan, Marie-Laure. "Introduction." *Narrative across Media: The Languages of Storytelling*. Ed. Marie-Laure Ryan. Lincoln: University of Nebraska, 2004. 1–40.

Schüwer, Martin. "Erzählen in Comics: Bausteine einer plurimedialen Erzähltheorie." *Erzähltheorie transgenerisch, intermedial, interdisziplinär*. Ed. Vera Nünning and Ansgar Nünning. Trier: WVT, 2002. 185–216.

Schweikle, Günther. "Epanodos." *Metzler Lexikon Literatur*. Ed. Dieter Burdorf, Christoph Fasbender, and Burkhard Moenninghoff. Stuttgart: Metzler, 2007. 193.

Stein, Daniel, and Jan-Noël Thon, eds. *From Comic Strips to Graphic Novels. Contributions to the Theory and History of Graphic Narrative*. Berlin, Boston: Walter de Gruyter, 2013.

Weinrich, Harald. *Textgrammatik der deutschen Sprache*. Mannheim, Leipzig, Wien, Zürich: Duden, 1993.

EIGHT

Perspectivity in Graphic Novels about War

Germany's Bundeswehr *Operation in Afghanistan*

Joshua Kavaloski

The active military involvement of Germany's *Bundeswehr* (federal defense force) in Afghanistan begun in 2002 marks one of the most contentious and politically transformative events since the country's reunification in 1990.[1] When it was first established in 1955, the *Bundeswehr* was originally conceptualized as a domestic military force intended exclusively for the defense of the Federal Republic of Germany.[2] This policy was relaxed slightly when Germany began participating in international missions a few years later, but only under the condition that the United Nations (UN) or the North Atlantic Treaty Organization (NATO) declare an urgent humanitarian crisis. Since 1960, Germany's *Bundeswehr* has participated in over 130 international operations, the vast majority of which can be characterized as humanitarian since they provide relief for victims of natural disasters or protection for minority ethnic groups under threat.[3] The glaring exception to this humanitarian role is Germany's involvement in the NATO-led mission in Afghanistan officially known as the International Security Assistance Force (ISAF). In January 2002, the *Bundeswehr* deployed to Afghanistan under the auspices of ISAF, which officially ended in December of 2014.[4] While the *Bundeswehr* initially intended to help rebuild Afghanistan by digging wells and building schools for girls, it soon became engaged in a bitter armed conflict with the Taliban, as acknowledged by former German Defense Minister Karl-Theodor zu Guttenberg, who caused an uproar when he publically called it a war in 2010.[5]

The deployment of the *Bundeswehr* to Afghanistan is the subject of two German-language graphic novels, both published in 2012: *Kriegszeiten* (Times of War) by David Schraven and Vincent Burmeister, and *Wave and Smile* by Arne Jysch. These two works can be broadly described as journalistic since they depict the military, political, and social circumstances surrounding Germany's involvement both in ISAF and in the larger, less-clearly defined War in Afghanistan. But these two graphic novels do more than just capture real events. Read side-by-side, they also offer an opportunity to examine how the narrative agency of graphic novels negotiates between fact and fiction, and objectivity and subjectivity. While *Kriegszeiten* advances a unitary point of view that is highly critical of the War in Afghanistan, *Wave and Smile* offers multiple perspectives that allow readers to form their own opinions. Applying the ideas of narrative theory in general and of Russian literary critic Mikhail Bakhtin in particular, this essay argues that these two graphic novels utilize sharply contrasting approaches to journalism and history in order to present and comment on the military conflict.

Literary theory is applicable in the analysis of sequential art because it also has the capability of offering critical insights for this medium. While Mikhail Bakhtin was expressly interested in narrative prose literature, his ideas are also relevant for graphic novels, as literary historian Karin Kukkonen writes:

> The Russian critic Mikhail Bakhtin (1981) calls the phenomenon of multivoiced narrative "heteroglossia" and states that this is a key feature of the modern novel. It is also crucial to many comics and graphic novels which exploit the comics' medium's inherent juxtaposition of images and words. (24)

The term "heteroglossia" is central to Bakhtin's later theory in which he champions the literary form of the novel as a whole.[6] In his earlier writings, however, he distinguishes between different types of narrative agency in novels. In *Problems of Dostoevsky's Poetics* from 1929, Bakhtin argues that a literary work can be described as polyphonic when conflicting voices are allowed to develop autonomously, without being dominated by a single ideology or moral system. In a polyphonic novel, each character takes on a life of her or his own, representing a worldview that cannot be cleanly reconciled with the beliefs of the other characters. For Bakhtin, there is one polyphonic author *par excellence*—Fyodor Dostoevsky. With regard to the consciousness of Dostoevsky's characters, Bakhtin writes: "Such thought is not impelled toward a well-rounded, finalized, systematically monologic whole" (1984, 32). When used to describe a literary work, the adjective "monologic" signifies that a single overarching perspective controls all elements of the story. It typically carries a negative connotation and suggests a lack of openness to diverse voices.

SCHRAVEN AND BURMEISTER'S *KRIEGSZEITEN*

These notions of voice and perspectivity are central to an understanding of *Kriegszeiten* (2012), which was conceived and written by David Schraven and illustrated by Vincent Burmeister. While Burmeister is an experienced illustrator of comic books and graphic novels, Schraven is a regional reporter in the German state of North Rhine–Westphalia. Schraven's professional identity as a journalist plays a significant role in the work, whose subtitle indicates its journalistic aspirations: *Eine grafische Reportage über Soldaten, Politiker und Opfer in Afghanistan* (A Graphic Reportage about Soldiers, Politicians, and Victims in Afghanistan). For Nina Berning, "reportage" involves a form of journalism that combines factual reporting with features of fictional literature: "reportage can be defined according to its function which is not only to inform but also to entertain" (42). Despite sharing some commonalities with fictional literature, reportage emphasizes the actuality of real events and typically features an identifiable storyteller who integrates news into a narrative.

The subtitle of *Kriegszeiten* is not the only part of the work that asserts its identity as journalistic reportage. The unnamed first-person character-narrator, whose status and connection to Schraven will be further examined below, also makes a point of emphasizing the extensive journalistic research that he conducted. He states, "In the past months, I've read thousands of pages" (In den vergangenen Monaten habe ich tausende Seiten gelesen; 42).[7] Precisely this research has been highlighted by reviewers such as Reiner Metzger, who asserts that "[a]s a research-comic, it is pioneering work" ([A]ls Recherche-Comic ist das Pionierarbeit). Metzger continues, "Schraven spoke with witnesses, interviewed soldiers, and evaluated thousands of pages of confidential reports prepared by the *Bundeswehr* for the German parliament" (Schraven hat Zeugen gesprochen, Soldaten interviewt, Tausende Seiten vertrauliche Berichte der Bundeswehr an das Parlament ausgewertet). Despite this level of research, however, Schraven is by no means a pioneer of comics reportage or comics journalism, which combines written text with visual images, in order to critically investigate real-world events.

Comics journalism, in its broadest sense, has a relatively long history that can be traced back to the early twentieth or even the mid-nineteenth century.[8] And in a narrower sense, graphic novels with a journalistic dimension already have an acknowledged advocate and exemplar: the Maltese-American graphic novelist Joe Sacco. Over the past two decades, Sacco has published numerous graphic novels, focusing mainly on international conflicts like those in the former Yugoslavia and between Israelis and Palestinians.[9] Indeed, Sacco is well known for his journalistic technique of speaking with witnesses, interviewing combatants, and examining written reports; and he tends to foreground the stories of those who suffer and who are marginalized by mainstream media. Benjamin Woo describes the approach: "Sacco uses comics to report on the experiences of the victims of conflict and war with a rare depth, sensitivity, and sense of context" (166). A brief examination of the narrative agency of Sacco's work will help contextualize and situate the strategy used in *Kriegszeiten*.

All of Sacco's graphic novels feature a first-person character-narrator who is intended to evoke the writer and artist Sacco himself. This figure is present on virtually every page of Sacco's graphic novels such as *Palestine* (2001), *The Fixer: A Story from Sarajevo* (2003), and *Footnotes in Gaza* (2009). As a narrative strategy, this overt reference to the author and his role as a journalist causes the reader to reflect critically on the status of objectivity in reporting. Kristian Williams writes that "comics open possibilities for journalists that are less available in other media . . . , comics drop the pretense of detachment and emphasize perspective" (55). By conspicuously including a character who looks like himself, Sacco draws attention to the challenges and contingencies of newsgathering. This strategy also foregrounds ways that a journalist's presence can influence journalistic reporting. Williams continues:

> As the reporter comes into focus, we see that he is not a neutral conduit for news and information, but a person like ourselves—a fallible human being, vulnerable to bias and ignorance and error. By acknowledging his own humanity, the writer can encourage the reader to think critically about what he or she reads. (55)

The comic journalist's firsthand participation in the story not only raises questions about the role of the observer, but it can also unsettle the very notion of objectivity.

While Sacco draws his subjects realistically, he consistently draws himself in a comical manner with large lips and oversized glasses. One scholar points out that "Sacco appears frequently as a little ridiculous; he misunderstands situations and occasionally does not get a joke that others share, and the cartoonish image stresses this aspect" (Vanderbeke 79). By satirizing his own authority as a journalist, he effectively empowers a plurality of other voices. As a result, incommensurable opinions and perspectives are included in Sacco's graphic novels; and it is the task of the reader to negotiate between them. In *Safe Area Gorazde*, for example, Sacco's character-narrator asks, "Can you live with the Serbs again?" (160–61). In the panels that follow, eleven Bosnians provide very different answers to that question, and no one answer is explicitly privileged over the others.

At first glance, the narrative agency in Schraven und Burmeister's *Kriegszeiten* seems similar to that in Sacco's work. After all, *Kriegszeiten* also features a first-person character-narrator, which in narrative theory is sometimes referred to as a homodiegetic narrator "since he tells his own story," as Gerard Genette explains (84). Although this narrator is unnamed, he looks virtually identical to the work's author, an association that is reinforced when a drawing of the narrator in the text proper is compared with a photograph of Schraven at the end of the graphic novel (15, 125). As in Sacco's graphic novels, the character-narrator of *Kriegszeiten* is also a reporter who is investigating an international conflict, here Germany's military involvement in Afghanistan. Despite this initial similarity between Sacco and Schraven, the two writers otherwise employ contrasting narrative strategies with significant consequences. While Sacco includes himself everywhere as a comical figure, Schraven's character-narrator is largely absent. When he does appear, Burmeister, the artist, depicts him in a realistic and serious manner. And while Sacco destabilizes the notion of objectivity, as discussed above, Schraven seems committed to the notion that there is a single "true" explanation for the War in Afghanistan. For instance, Schraven writes in the afterword to *Kriegszeiten* that "[t]his comic should help to see the truth" ([d]ieser Comic soll dabei helfen, die Wahrheit zu sehen; 123). Indeed, this afterword repeatedly uses words like "Wahrheit" (truth) three times, "Realität" (reality) two times, and "Wirklichkeit" (actuality) two times. Schraven clearly believes that his mission is to uncover the real facts of the military involvement of the *Bundeswehr* in Afghanistan. For him, the truth means that Germany is involved in an active war, even though politicians do not want to admit it: "No one said clearly and distinctly that German soldiers in Afghanistan have to fight, as soldiers simply have to do in a war (Niemand sagte klar und deutlich, dass deutsche Soldaten in Afghanistan kämpfen müssen, wie Soldaten eben im Krieg zu kämpfen haben; 121). Schraven's ardent insistence on a single truth could not contrast more plainly with Sacco's non-judgmental inclusion of disparate points of view. As Kristian Williams points out: "Comics journalism entails a startling variety of approaches and styles" (52). Nevertheless, it is insufficient to simply register differences in approaches and styles. Instead, the ideological implications of those differences should be explored, as they are here.

The first-person perspective of *Kriegszeiten* is established with the first word of the main text: "ich" (I; 9). Here, the narrator declares that he was in New York City during the attack on the World Trade Center on September 11, 2001. From his vantage point on the Williamsburg Bridge, he watches the collapse of the Twin Towers and provides a verbal description of the visual drawing of the flood of people fleeing by foot across the bridge from Manhattan to Brooklyn. As one might expect from a journalist trying to achieve objectivity, the narrator himself does not convey any personal reaction to the catastrophe. Feelings, such as fear and anger, are only expressed by others, for example, by the Irish policeman trying to stop any thrill seekers from crossing the bridge from Brooklyn back to Manhattan. Depicted with a distorted, sweat-covered face, he bellows and swings his baton angrily. The narrator first shares his emotional state two days after the attacks when he sees the headline of a newspaper: "I sensed the fear in me. I trembled. The New York Post had a new headline: WAR" (Ich spürte die Angst in mir. Ich zitterte. Die New York Post hatte eine neue Schlagzeile: WAR; 16–17). It is striking that the narrator is dispassionate when he experiences firsthand the attack on the World Trade Center. Yet at the same time, the thought of a future armed conflict elsewhere in the world causes a fearful reaction. A clue to this seeming inconsistency can be found in the narrator's only other overt expression of emotion in the entire graphic novel.

When the narrator describes joining German soldiers in Afghanistan as an embedded journalist, he writes, "[t]he next morning, I was afraid to get into the dingo ([a]m nächsten Morgen hatte ich Angst, in den Dingo zu steigen; 73). The prospect of climbing into an armored military infantry vehicle and going on patrol understandably evokes palatable anxiety here. This affective state is arguably not merely caused by the immediate danger to his person. Rather, the fear arises when the narrator visits northern Afghanistan in 2010 because he recognizes that he is no longer an impartial witness to the conflict. As a journalist embedded with German troops, he understands that the Taliban will now view him as an enemy. He can no longer claim to be an objective reporter. On the Williamsburg Bridge in 2001, by contrast, the narrator can still afford to be a dispassionate observer because he knows that he is not the target of the attacks. After all, he is German, and modern Germany had, at the time of the attacks on the World Trade Center, carefully avoided involving any ground troops in what could be considered a war of aggression. As mentioned above, however, the ISAF mission of the *Bundeswehr* quickly shifted from humanitarian assistance to armed conflict. Schraven notes in the afterword: "We realize that a real war is taking place in Afghanistan (Wir begreifen, dass in Afghanistan echter Krieg herrscht; 122). Afghanistan represents a turning point in German history since it was the country's first real combat mission since World War II.

At first glance, the small number of drawings depicting Schraven's alter-ego would suggest that he plays a relatively minor role in *Kriegszeiten*. Yet Schraven's character-narrator dominates the graphic novel's narrative, which is organized such that it presents a singular perspective on the war. There are no speech bubbles for first-person statements by other characters, and the graphic novel's written text is comprised entirely of narration, which appears in rectangular boxes within the frames. In this narration, only the character-narrator has a direct voice, while the voices of former soldiers and witnesses are doubly marked by quotation marks and italicized text. Every single word of the graphic novel is therefore filtered through Schraven's character-narrator. His authority is established in the way that he evaluates and explains the story. When the character-narrator first meets the soldiers in Germany, he initiates the contact and asks them questions. And when the character-narrator retells their stories in flashbacks, he decides what to include and how to frame it. Because the character-narrator exerts such control over the information, the graphic novel can be considered monologic, which for Bakhtin describes a single overarching consciousness that directs and orders all utterances.[10]

This issue of perspective is further visible in the quotations that Schraven uses in *Kriegszeiten*. Prior to the graphic novel's story, the author inserts public statements by four former German politicians: Gerhard Schröder (Chancellor 1998–2005), Joschka Fischer (Foreign Minister 1998–2005), Guido Westerwelle (Foreign Minister 2009–2013), and Dirk Niebel (Minister of Economic Cooperation and Development 2009–2013). These politicians are all quoted as offering support for the War in Afghanistan.[11] And at the beginning of each of the graphic novel's three chapters, there are additional quotations in support of the German ISAF mission to Afghanistan by Angela Merkel (Chancellor 2005–present) and Peter Struck (Defense Minister 2002–2005). Yet Schraven does not leave these political quotations unchallenged; he counters them with two poignant statements placed like bookends at the beginning and end of the story. The first appears before the title page, where Protestant minister Margot Käßmann is quoted as saying: "Nothing is good in Afghanistan" (Nichts ist gut in Afghanistan; 3). The graphic novel's narrative is plainly aligned here with Käßmann, whose simple and direct assessment of the military situation may strike the reader as refreshingly honest. The second statement is included immediately after the end of the main story, where Johannes Rau (Federal President 1999–2004) is quoted as saying: "Hate should not mislead us to hate. Hate blinds us (Hass darf uns nicht zum Hass verführen. Hass blendet; 119). The German federal president traditionally remains above party politics and provides a moral compass for the country.[12] Rau's humanistic idealism is befitting this role and supports the ideological subtext of the graphic novel's narrative. In contrast to the apparent sincerity of Käßmann and Rau, elected German politicians come across as partisan and deceitful.

The visual images in *Kriegszeiten* sustain the divide in the text between sincere assessment, on the one hand, and subterfuge, on the other. It is worth noting that not a single one of the numerous quotations by elected politicians is accompanied by a drawing of the politician in question. Even though that might not be unusual in and of itself, it is curious that while the graphic novel's main text features grotesque drawings of many of these same politicians, not a single one of these visual renderings is accompanied by a quotation. This means that Schraven's character-narrator describes, in his own words, the actions of the politicians regarding Afghanistan, but he withholds any direct voice from these public figures.

The narrator states, for example: "The respective leadership applauds its own deeds. Chancellor Angela Merkel and her changing defense ministers say that everything is supposedly good in Afghanistan" (Die jeweilige Führung bejubelt die eigenen Taten. Kanzlerin Angela Merkel und ihre wechselnden Verteidigungsminister sagen, alles sei gut in Afghanistan; 63). This commentary is emblematic of the graphic novel's narrative, but it is problematic for several reasons. First, the character-narrator effectively employs the logical fallacy of a straw man by incorrectly representing what he perceives to be his opponent's argument. Merkel and her defense ministers never stated that everything is good in Afghanistan. Instead, Schraven's character-narrator sets them up in contradistinction to Käßmann, as discussed above. Second, the narrator here employs the subjunctive voice (*Konjunktiv I*), which in German is a linguistic mode used for rendering indirect speech. The subjunctive tends to signal that the speaker is questioning the credibility of the person whose words are being restated. To summarize: there are select quotations by politicians without images outside the main text, and images of politicians without voice inside the main text. This disconnect between word and image raises further questions about perspectivity and vocalization in the graphic novel. By separating verbal articulation from visual image, the narrator of *Kriegszeiten* exerts control and excludes politicians from competing with his own version of the truth.

This caesura between the words and images of the politicians stands in contrast to the graphic novel's depiction of German soldiers. The novel features eight different soldiers altogether, and every time that Schraven's narrator first includes the soldier's direct voice, Burmeister provides a portrait of the soldier. This technique of connecting verbal articulation with image underscores the graphic novel's journalistic aspiration since it conspicuously depicts the narrator interviewing the soldiers, and these interviews presumably offer the reader access to genuine experiences in Afghanistan. When the soldiers first appear in the graphic novel, they are often depicted in some sort of domestic space, presumably in Germany, where they are meeting with the narrator. The interview with Master Sergeant Gerd Thomas, for example, takes place at what appears to be a café, with coffee, cake, and a tape recorder sitting on the table (figure 8.1). This quotidian setting is important because it emphasizes the firsthand collection of information from a witness. By foregrounding the mechanics of the interview, these images help establish the authenticity of the soldiers' testimony. And when the soldiers begin to tell the narrator their stories, the graphic novel then flashes back to Afghanistan. In these flashbacks, or moments of analepsis as they are referred to in narrative theory, the soldiers' words appear in quotation marks in a narrative box above drawings that visually illustrate what is being told.

When describing his journalistic research for the graphic novel, Schraven writes that he only uncovered "the material to draw a damn bleak

Figure 8.1. An interview with Master Sergeant Gerd Thomas from the first-person perspective of the character-narrator. David Schraven: *Kriegszeiten. Eine grafische Reportage über Soldaten, Politiker und Opfer in Afghanistan mit Illustrationen von Vincent Burmeister* © Carlsen Verlag GmbH, Hamburg 2012.

image" (das Material, um ein verdammt trostloses Bild zu zeichnen; 42) of the War in Afghanistan. Burmeister's bleak drawings reinforce Schraven's bleak findings. The first thing that a reader might notice about the artwork is the unusual color scheme, since in addition to black, Burmeister also employs brownish-red and ochre-yellow. These colors are not arbitrary. In an interview, Burmeister provides an explanation for this selection: "The yellow stands for the wasteland and boredom when the soldiers don't have anything to do and wait in the camp. And the blood-red stands for when things suddenly happen. And together with the black, there is black, red, gold (Das Gelb steht für die Ödnis und Langeweile, wenn die Soldaten nichts zu tun haben und im Lager warten. Und das Blutrot steht dafür, wenn es plötzlich losgeht. Und mit dem Schwarz zusammen hat man ja auch Schwarz, Rot, Gold; *Die Blaue Seite*). The presence of these same three colors in Germany's national flag suggests that *Kriegszeiten* interrogates German national identity. Burmeister's particular choice of color tone here clearly does not seek to evoke warm feelings of patriotism since the brownish-red and ochre-yellow of the graphic novel are intended to disfigure the vibrant red and gold colors of the German national flag.

Kriegszeiten contains a few drawings by Burmeister that can be broadly described as realistic; he draws individual buildings, vehicles, and weapons in a relatively mimetic manner. The image of the World Trade Center on the first page, for example, is rendered clearly and will be immediately recognized, despite the surreal ochre-yellow sky. Notwithstanding these exceptions, most of Burmeister's illustrations are relatively coarse and unembellished. His depictions of people, for example, are often so deformed that they are barely recognizable. Indeed, Burmeister's drawings recall the disharmony and exaggerated emotion seen in German Expressionism in the way that he deploys vivid lines and jarring colors to evoke anxiety and discomfort.[13] As such, his art further complements Schraven's narrative, which seeks to unsettle what he perceives as subterfuge of politicians. It is worth noting that Burmeister's use of expressionistic-like drawings to capture the War in Afghanistan is not so dissimilar from German Expressionism, which was inspired in part by the chaos and destructiveness of World War I.

Because Burmeister's artistic renderings in *Kriegszeiten* are often extremely distorted, they can arguably be described as grotesque, an established trope in art history. One art historian writes, "Images gathered under the grotesque rubric include those that combine unlike things in order to challenge established realities or construct new ones; those that deform or decompose things; and those that are metaphoric" (Connelly 2). Burmeister's drawings arguably evince all three of the features of the grotesque mentioned in the above description: combining unlike things, deformation of objects, and metaphor. First, Burmeister combines unlike things when he juxtaposes the high media attention given to relatively banal domestic topics with the low-key coverage of Germany's ISAF operation. In one drawing, he draws the symbol for the Federal Agency for Work (*Bundesagentur für Arbeit*) hovering above a battlefield littered with dead bodies (figure 8.2). Here, Burmeister suggests that the political debate about employment distracts from the real news about the German soldiers who were dying in Afghanistan at the time. Second, he deforms human images, as is evident with his portraits of politicians, for example. The grotesque portraits stand in contrast to the carefully cultivated public images of politicians in the mainstream media. And Burmeister's drawings of soldiers often evoke their inner agony. Third, he often resorts to metaphors. When Burmeister draws a flatbed truck carrying portable toilets, for instance, he employs a metaphor that visually demonstrates that ISAF's 2010 offensive had no useful purpose (114). Ultimately, the expressive drawings in *Kriegszeiten* reinforce the written text's monologic narrative strategy, as Bakhtin would describe it, since the text seeks to uncover a single "truth" about the War in Afghanistan.

JYSCH'S *WAVE AND SMILE*

Wave and Smile is the debut graphic novel of its writer and illustrator, Arne Jysch, whose prior professional experience is largely as a scriptwriter and storyboard artist in the film industry. Although the main body of the work is in German, its English-language title introduces an ironic tone by referring to signs that allegedly hung in the camps of militaries participating in ISAF; these signs sought to encourage Western soldiers to be friendly in their daily interactions with Afghans in order to win their hearts and minds. Unlike *Kriegszeiten*, which as discussed above is a form of reportage, *Wave and Smile* can be best categorized as literary journalism. John C. Hartsock writes that "Literary journalism . . . attempts to engage in an 'exchange of subjectivities,' or at least tries to narrow the distance between subject and object in an empathetic engagement" (36). According to Hartsock, literary journalism de-emphasizes the didactic and instead involves the reader emotionally, for example, through classic literary techniques such as identification and catharsis. Reportage, on the other hand, largely seeks to instruct and thus less likely engages in any kind of open, discursive process with the reader.

In contrast to *Kriegszeiten*, which centers on a first-person character-narrator evocative of author David Schraven, *Wave and Smile* features a fictional third-person character named Chris Menger, a captain (Hauptmann) in the German *Bundeswehr*. As noted by one reviewer, Menger is "the stereotype of an experienced soldier who is slowly becoming resigned and whose social connection to home is slowly falling apart (der Sterotyp eines erfahrenen, langsam resignierenden Soldaten mit bröckelndem sozialem Halt in der Heimat; Lachwitz). The story is quick-

Figure 8.2.   This drawing by Burmeister juxtaposes the War in Afghanistan with domestic political issues in Germany. David Schraven: *Kriegszeiten. Eine grafische Reportage über Soldaten, Politiker und Opfer in Afghanistan mit Illustrationen von Vincent Burmeister* **© Carlsen Verlag GmbH, Hamburg 2012.**

ly summarized. After a deadly attack by insurgents on Menger's unit, a civilian photographer named Anni arrives and joins the unit as an embedded journalist. One day, Menger's team flies to a remote Afghan village by helicopter so that Anni can take pictures. On the way back to the German base, one of the two helicopters takes fire from the Taliban and crash-lands in a remote location in the mountains. Anni, Menger, and the other soldiers who survived the crash are effectively abandoned for several hours while a German ground unit slowly works its way through difficult terrain to their location. After taking refuge in a friendly village nearby, they are attacked by Taliban and one of Menger's close comrades

named Marco becomes separated from the unit and subsequently captured by the Taliban. The rest of the unit is subsequently rescued by the
German ground troops. Later, Menger returns to Germany, but he is
plagued by guilt and returns to Afghanistan in order to search for his
abandoned comrade Marco, whom he eventually discovers in an
American interrogation facility. At the end of the story, they are released,
leave Afghanistan, and return together to Germany.

One of the work's dominant themes is the tension between the troops
in the field, on the one hand, and high-ranking officers, on the other.
Shortly after three soldiers in Menger's unit are killed, he is summoned
by his commanding officer, who suggests that he and his surviving soldiers return to the site of the deadly attack in order to determine if the
mounted machine gun was correctly removed from the destroyed military vehicle, as required by official procedure. Outraged at the request,
Menger states that he is responsible for his men and will not risk their
lives by sending them back into danger needlessly. When the commanding officer then asks what will happen if he gives an order, Menger replies, "Then I am going to disobey it and you are going to have a pile of
paperwork" (Dann werde ich ihn verweigern und Sie haben eine Menge
Papierkram; 25). By standing up to his superior officer's unreasonable
request, Menger is depicted as a morally superior character whose field
experience allows him to better evaluate the risk to the soldiers. There are
also several other scenes that thematize the conflict between field troops
and higher-ranking desk officers. When the helicopter crash-lands, for
instance, the commanding officers at the base deny permission for the
second helicopter to land and pick up the downed German soldiers, even
though there is no enemy activity in the area. The callousness of this
order is underscored when one soldier injured in the crash ends up dying
because there are no military medics who can treat him. A further example for this theme is evident when Marco becomes separated from the
unit, since a commanding officer back at base tells Menger that Marco
will have to be abandoned. There is clearly a negative depiction of high-
ranking officers in the graphic novel, in which Jysch sympathizes with
the plight of ground troops and criticizes the nearsightedness and incom-
petence of those who are responsible for strategy.

The artwork in *Wave and Smile* is less innovative than that in *Kriegszeit-
en*, meaning that Jysch's drawings initially recall the unoriginal artistic
style of popular comic books. It is unclear if the visual aesthetics of the
drawings is intentional or simply due to Jysch's lack of experience with
graphic novels. Nevertheless, his drawings offer something unique and
striking, in particular their depiction of multiple visual perspectives. The
photographer Anni verbally anticipates this feature when she states,
"Propaganda is also not my job! I try to represent all sides and to remain
as neutral as possible" (Propaganda ist auch nicht mein Job! Ich versuche,
alle Seiten darzustellen und möglichst neutral zu bleiben; 46). Her at-

tempt to represent all sides is visible in the way that the graphic novel's visual images incorporate extremely different points of view. Although many of Jysch's drawings utilize a third-person perspective, some are visually affiliated with a particular character's perspective, so that we as readers sometimes view circumstances through a character's eyes. Late in the story, for example, Menger is captured by American troops who mistakenly think that he is a German-born insurgent. When they place a bag over Menger's head, the image shows what he sees—darkness (figure 8.3). Another example can be seen with the photographer Anni. When she takes pictures of local Afghans, the reader is given access to what she sees through her camera lens—a mother with her children, a German soldier offering candy to a child, and two young men with their arms around each other (43). These images demonstrate Anni's attempt to capture different facets of what she perceives as authentic Afghan life.

Since the graphic novel's primary target audience is German, it is not a surprise that the readership's sympathetic identification with the two German characters Menger and Anni is facilitated by the inclusion of drawings that share their visual perspective. What is unusual is that other drawings adopt an Afghan perspective. When Anni first visits a local village, numerous images show the armored troop transporter where she is embedded as it must have appeared from the point of view of local villagers (40). The viewer in these images is unidentified and likely belongs to neither friend nor foe—these drawings simply show how the German patrol appears to neutral Afghans. More significant for the present study is when the graphic novel includes the perspective of the Taliban. After all, the Taliban are ostensibly the enemy of the ISAF operation, and showing their point of view expands the narrative scope of the graphic novel. When Menger's unit departs a village with two helicop-

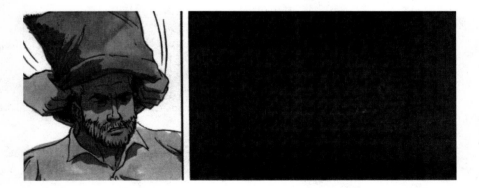

Figure 8.3. The graphic novel briefly adopts the visual perspective of the third-person character Menger when he is captured by American troops. Arne Jysch: *Wave and Smile*, © Carlsen Verlag GmbH, Hamburg 2012.

ters, one image clearly shows the point of view of an insurgent as he looks through the viewfinder of his shoulder-fired rocket-launcher (67). One particular page emblematizes the graphic novel's strategy of multi-perspectivity (figure 8.4). As Menger is secretly meeting with a group of Taliban warlords in Pakistan, we first see the site from the perspective of the American troops who have learned about the meeting and who are about to launch a devastating rocket attack. At the bottom of that same page, we see a photograph of Marco through the eyes of one of the Taliban. Here, conflicting perspectives are portrayed alongside one another, and this placement stands in contrast to *Kriegszeiten*, which consistently relies on a single point of view.

This inclusion of visual perspectives from a range of ideologically diverse individuals is reflected in the narrative of *Wave and Smile*, which does not declare any side in the conflict right or wrong. The graphic novel generally portrays the Americans neutrally, except in their interrogation of Menger, when they come across as being insensitive and somewhat incompetent. Although the bulk of the graphic novel concentrates on the experience of the German troops, it even depicts them critically on several occasions. One German soldier named Rocker, for example, expresses crude racism when he refers to the Afghans as "damn goat fuckers" (Scheißziegenficker; 78). This outburst is surely not intended to encourage readers' sympathy with the character. And even Menger is portrayed in a negative light despite the fact that his story is being told. When Menger returns home to Berlin, he loses control in a café and physically attacks a civilian who expresses disapproval of Germany's operation in Afghanistan. The graphic novel's criticism, however, is not limited to individual Germans. The mission of the entire *Bundeswehr* is even called into question when Khan, an Afghan warlord allied with them, says in English: "For the Germans, the most important thing is to come home alive . . . do you know what the British and Americans call it? They call it the 'German attitude' . . . you go to war, but you don't dare to kill . . . or get killed" (99). Yet the graphic novel is perhaps most original when it sympathetically depicts the ostensible enemy. During Menger's secret meeting in Pakistan, one Taliban warlord tells him, "We assure you, in case the Americans attack, we will defend you with our lives" (Wir versichern dir, falls die Amerikaner angreifen, werden wir euch mit unserem Leben verteidigen; 164). This warlord is fiercely protective toward his guests, even if Menger is German and by extension his enemy. Such scenes depict the insurgents as noble defenders of their country. The typography of the speech in this scene further demonstrates the graphic novel's attempt to include other perspectives. For example, the Afghan warlord speaks Arabic, which here is rendered in italicized German to show that it has been translated.

Because it expresses a range of different perspectives, both in the drawings and in the plot, Jysch's graphic novel demonstrates discursive

Figure 8.4. This page presents first-person perspectives both of the Americans attacking the village (top frame) as well as of a Taliban fighter (second-to-last frame). Arne Jysch: *Wave and Smile*, © Carlsen Verlag GmbH, Hamburg 2012.

plurality or polyphony, as Bakhtin calls it. This observation can be seen as a corrective to criticism of the work as pro-war propaganda for Germany's ISAF mission. One reviewer writes that "Arne Jysch's ISAF-war comic *Wave and Smile*, which presents itself as objectively researched docudrama, practices no-holds-barred propaganda" (Arne Jyschs ISAF-Kriegscomic Wave and Smile, der sich als objektiv recherchiertes Dokudrama ausgibt, betreibt nun knallharte Propaganda; Frisch). This critic continues by accusing Jysch's graphic novel of seeking to glorify war and to revive Germany's militaristic past. This criticism is arguably misled because the graphic novel's decentralized story has no overt narrator and presents a wide range of disparate voices without exposition or clear political stance vis-à-vis the War in Afghanistan. *Wave and Smile* has no single, dominant narrative voice; instead, it strives to include multiple voices. *Wave and Smile* displays plural meaning in contrast to *Kriegszeiten*, whose singular monologic narrative perspective promotes a certain interpretation of Germany's military involvement in Afghanistan.

CONCLUSION

For Mikhail Bakhtin, polyphonic and monologic are not merely abstract descriptors; they are ideological stances exemplified by two particular Russian writers, Dostoevsky and Tolstoy, respectively. What distinguishes Dostoevsky is that he creates an open and pluralistic world within the boundaries of the novel. In contradistinction to Dostoevsky is Tolstoy, whose novelistic style, according to Bakhtin, is emblematic of a monologic strategy that imposes a single, inflexible version of the truth onto all levels of a text. Tolstoy's morality and epistemology permeate all his novels, which are essentially fictional monologues that end with the resolution of the plot. A third-person narrative agency controls all voices and determines the ultimate meaning. If types of vocalization were mapped along a single spectrum, Dostoevsky and Tolstoy would be on opposite ends.

Although this type of narratological analysis may be well established in literary theory built on prose texts, it has been largely absent in critical examinations of graphic novels.[14] Yet it can be relevant, since Bakhtin's theoretical distinction between Dostoevsky and Tolstoy helps to highlight the contrast between Jysch and Schraven. It might be objected that this parallel is an oversimplification since Jysch's multiple perspectives do not have the depth of Dostoevsky's, and Schraven's singular point of view cannot really be compared with Tolstoy's. Nevertheless, the analogy still demonstrates the way that these two graphic novels deploy distinctly different approaches toward voice and perspectivity. While *Wave and Smile* evinces what can be described as a polyphonic plurality, *Kriegszeiten* utilizes a kind of monologic homogeneity. These respective narrative strategies have far-reaching consequences for the way that political events are depicted. Hartsock writes, "it is in the nature of literary journalism to engage in what critic Mikhail Bakhtin described as a novel of the 'inconclusive present' that resists coming to critical—including political or explicitly ideological—closure" (1984, 38). This inconclusive present is connected to the issue of perspectivity; that is, a work's narrative point of view frames its understanding of the world. What distinguishes *Wave and Smile* from *Kriegszeiten* is the way that each of the two graphic novels constructs a particular narrative agency. Because Jysch's work promotes interpretive openness, it arguably qualifies as literary journalism. It is precisely his inconclusiveness that creates possibilities for invention, interpretation, and intervention. Schraven, on the other hand, utilizes a didactic tone and seeks epistemological closure, so that his work can be best categorized as reportage. When Jysch includes extremely different perspectives, it is the task of the reader to negotiate between them. By contrast, Schraven's narrator dominates and directs the presentation of events in order to make a particular point.

Despite major differences, the two graphic novels both arrive at a common conclusion: that the conflict in Afghanistan cannot be won. When the Americans finally cease their interrogation and release Menger at the end of *Wave and Smile*, he exclaims, "Your war . . . you can lose it without me" (Ihren Krieg . . . den dürfen Sie ohne mich verlieren; 191). *Kriegszeiten* echoes the doubt about the success of ISAF expressed in *Wave and Smile*, as the narrator states in a matter-of-fact voice: "The West has already lost the war. Germany has lost" (Der Westen hat den Krieg schon lange verloren. Deutschland hat verloren; 115). These two quotations exhibit deep pessimism about the continuing military intervention of Germany and its allies in Afghanistan, a verbal sentiment that each work's final image underscores. The last drawing in *Wave and Smile* shows a military aircraft departing for Germany, with Afghanistan's gigantic mountains unchanged and unyielding in the background. For its part, *Kriegszeiten* ends with an image of military helicopters on yet another pointless mission, flying by night toward some unknown target. Both works thus suggest that Germany's participation in ISAF has not improved the situation on the ground in Afghanistan. If there is one conviction that these two methodologically diverse graphic novels ultimately share, it is that the conflict in Afghanistan has been tragic for everyone involved.

NOTES

1. For Cora Stephan, "To call what is happening in Afghanistan 'war,' as the then Defense Minister zu Guttenberg did, was equal to a revolution" (Was in Afghanistan passiert, "'Krieg" zu nennen, wie es der damalige Verteidigungsminster zu Guttenberg tat, kam einer Revolution gleich; 29). Daniel M. Rother writes, "When the soldiers

of the German ISAF advance command first touched Afghan ground on January 2, 2002, there was already talk of the Bundeswehr in general as an 'army on a mission,' yet this mission, which is still taking place today, represents a fully new dimension of Germany's military engagement" (Als am 2. Januar 2002 die ersten Soldaten des deutschen ISAF-Vorauskommandos afghanischen Boden betraten, wurde zwar schon von der Bundeswehr im Allgemeinen als eine "Armee im Einsatz" gesprochen, dennoch stellt dieser bis heute andauernde Einsatz eine völlig neu Dimension bundesdeutschen militärischen Engagements dar; 11).

2. The purview of the *Bundeswehr* is articulated in Germany's *Grundgesetz* (Basic Law or Constitution). Referring to the *Grundgesetz*, Martina Kolanoski states, "The original core task of the *Bundeswehr* is the defense of the country in the sense of protection of territorial integrity" (Die ursprüngliche Kernaufgabe der Bundeswehr ist damit die Landesverteidigung im Sinne des Schutzes der territorialen Integrität; 23).

3. Wilfried von Bredow writes, "Since 1960, the Bundeswehr has undertaken over 130 such assistance campaigns in more than 50 countries of the world" (Seit 1960 hat die Bundeswehr über 130 solcher Hilfsaktionen in mehr als 50 Ländern der Welt durchgeführt; 232).

4. The United Nations Security Council established ISAF in December of 2001, and the mission officially started one month later in January of 2002. It ended on December 28, 2014. As of summer 2015, however, several hundred *Bundeswehr* troops are still in Afghanistan since ISAF was followed by a NATO-led non-combat mission entitled Operation Resolute Support, which is designed to assist the government of Afghanistan. See Constable for further details.

5. Guttenberg stated, "Even if it doesn't please everyone to hear it, we can colloquially speak of war in light of what is happening in parts of Afghanistan (Auch wenn es nicht jedem gefällt, so kann man angesichts dessen, was sich in Teilen Afghanistans abspielt, umgangssprachlich von Krieg reden." Quoted in: "Soldaten nehmen Abschied von ihren Kameraden."

6. The concept of heteroglossia was introduced by Bakhtin in his essay "Discourse in the Novel" (1934), where he used it to describe the way that novels contain multiple perspectives.

7. Since *Kriegszeiten* lacks pagination, I have taken the liberty of assigning page numbers in order to make quotes used in the essay easier to find in the original text. I've assigned page one to the page with the four quotations by politicians.

8. Alla Gadassik and Sarah Henstra write that there is "a history to 'comics journalism' that reaches back to reportage in the pre-photography era" (245). These scholars continue by considering various claims for the origin of comics journalism, which can be traced as far back as the American Civil War.

9. It is difficult to identify the exact number of graphic novels by Sacco. His first full-length graphic novel, for instance, was *Palestine: A Nation Occupied* (1993), which was a collection of individual comic books. It was later published, along with his second graphic novel *Palestine: In the Gaza Strip* (1996), under the title *Palestine* (2007).

10. Phyllis Margaret Paryas writes, "Some genres, claims Mikhail Bakhtin, like epic and lyric poetry, exemplify monologism because the author retains the power to convey his vision of truth directly" (596).

11. Gerhard Schröder, for instance, is quoted as stating "I have assured the American President of Germany's unqualified solidarity" (Ich habe dem amerikanischen Präsidenten die uneingeschränkte Solidarität Deutschlands zugesichert; German Bundestag 1).

12. Hesse and Ellwein write that the federal president in Germany is the "Hüter der Politik" (guardian of the political sphere) (300).

13. Distortion and exaggeration are key features of early twentieth-century German expressionism, which resists aesthetic harmony or formal balance in order to arouse an emotional reaction in the viewer. Thomson writes that "In expressionism, conventional ideas of beauty, harmony, and euphony were rejected in favor of distortion and even unsightliness" (372).

14. Although narrative theory can be easily adjusted to examine the textual and visual perspectivity of graphic novels, very few scholars have applied it so far. One exception is Kavaloski (2012).

REFERENCES

Bakhtin, Mikhail. "Discourse in the Novel." The Dialogic Imagination: Four Essays. Trans. Caryl Emerson and Michael Holquist. Ed. Michael Holquist. Austin: University of Texas Press, 1981.
Bakhtin, Mikhail. *Problems of Dostoevsky's Poetics*. Trans. Caryl Emerson. Minneapolis: University of Minnesota Press, 1984.
Berning, Nina. *Narrative Means to Journalistic Ends: A Narratalogical Analysis of Selected Journalistic Reportages*. Wiesbaden: Verlag für Sozialwissenschaften, 2011.
Bredow, Wilfried von. *Sicherheit, Sicherheitspolitik und Militär. Deutschland seit der Vereinigung*. Wiesbaden: Springer, 2015.
Connelly, Frances S. "Introduction." *Modern Art and the Grotesque*. Ed. Frances S. Connelly. Cambridge: Cambridge University Press, 2003. 1–19.
Constable, Pamela. "NATO flag lowered in Afghanistan as combat mission ends." *Washington Post*. 28 December 2014. Web. 17 January 2015. https://www.was hingtonpost.com/world/nato-flag-lowered-in-afghanistan-as-combat-mission-ends/ 2014/12/28/5a3ad640-8e44-11e4-ace9-47de1af4c3eb_story.html.
Die Blaue Seite. "Interview with Vincent Burmeister." 4 December 2014. Web. 15 September 2015. http://www.die-blaue-seite.de/2014/12/04/interview-mit-vincent-burm eister/.
Frisch, Marc-Oliver. "Anatomie eines Propagandacomics: Militarismus und Kämpferkult in Arne Jyschs *Wave and Smile*." 21 August 2012. Web. 17 January 2015. http:/ /archiv.comicgate.de/Artikel/anatomie-eines-propagandacomics-militarismus-und-kaempferkult-in-arne-jyschs-wave-and-smile.html.
Gadassik, Alla, and Sarah Henstra. "Comics (as) Journalism: Teaching Joe Sacco's *Palestine* to Media Students." *Teaching Comics and Graphic Narratives: Essays on Theory, Strategy and Practice*. Ed. Lan Dong. Jefferson: McFarland and Company, 2012. 243–60.
Genette, Gerard. *Narrative Discourse Revisited*. Ithaca: Cornell University Press, 1988.
German Bundestag. *Plenarprotokoll*, 14/186. 12 September 2001. 18293–294.
Hartsock, John C. "Literary Reportage: The 'Other' Literary Journalism." *Literary Journalism Across the Globe. Journalistic Traditions and Transnational Influences*. Ed. John S. Bak and Bill Reynolds. Amherst: University of Massachusetts Press, 2011. 23–46.
Hesse, Joachim Jens, and Thomas Ellwein. *Das Regierungssystem der Bundesrepublik*. Volume I. Berlin: De Gruyter Rechtswissenschaften Verlag, 2004.
Jysch, Arne. *Wave and Smile*. Hamburg: Carlsen Verlag, 2012.
Kavaloski, Joshua. "The Weimar Republic Redux: Multiperspectival History in Jason Lutes's *Berlin City of Stones*." *Teaching Comics and Graphic Narratives: Essays on Theory, Strategy and Practice*. Ed. Lan Dong. Jefferson, NC: McFarland and Company, 2012. 145–60.
Kolanoski, Martina. *Die Entsendung der Bundeswehr ins Ausland: zur Funktion des Parlamentsvorbehalts im Kontext bündnispolitischer Verpflichtungen*. Potsdam: Universitätsverlag Potsdam, 2010.
Kukkonen, Karin. *Studying Comics and Graphic Novels*. Malden: Wiley Blackwell, 2013.
Lachwitz, Alexander. "Winken und Lächeln: Über Arne Jyschs Graphic Novel Debüt *Wave and Smile*." 30 August 2012. Web. 17 January 2015. http://comic-report.de/ index.php/rezensionen/40-rezcarlsen/425-wave-and-smile-arne-jysch-afghanistan.
Metzger, Reiner. "Recherche-Comic *Kriegszeiten*." *TAZ - die Tageszeitung*. 29 December 2012. Web. 15 January 2016. http://www.taz.de/!5076525/.

Paryas, Phyllis Margaret. "Monologism." *Encyclopedia of Contemporary Literary Theory: Approaches, Scholars, Terms.* Ed. Irene Rima Makaryk. Toronto: University of Toronto Press, 1993. 596.

Rother, Daniel M. *Die Bundeswehr in Afghanistan: Eine Zivilmacht in der Multilatalismusfalle?* Norderstedt: GRIN Verlag, 2008.

Sacco, Joe. *The Fixer: A Story from Sarajevo.* Montreal: Drawn and Quarterly, 2003.

———. *Footnotes in Gaza: A Graphic Novel.* New York: Henry Holt and Company, 2009.

———. *Palestine.* Seattle: Fantagraphics, 2001.

———. *Safe Area Gorazde: The War in Eastern Bosnia 1992–1995.* Seattle: Fantagraphics, 2000.

Schraven, David, and Vincent Burmeister. *Kriegszeiten. Eine grafische Reportage über Soldaten, Politiker und Opfer in Afghanistan.* Hamburg: Carlesen Verlag, 2012.

"Soldaten nehmen Abschied von ihren Kameraden." *Die Zeit.* 4 April 2010. Web. 17 January 2015. http://www.zeit.de/politik/ausland/2010-04/afghanistan-bundeswehr-gefechte.

Stephan, Cora. "Militärische Tradition als gesellschaftliche Frage." *Tradition für die Bundeswehr. Neue Aspekte einer alten Debatte.* Ed. Eberhard Birk, Winfried Heinemann, and Sven Lange. Norderstedt: Miles Verlag, 2012. 29–50.

Thomson, G. R. *Reading the American Novel: 1865–1914.* Malden: Wiley-Blackwell, 2012.

Vanderbeke, Dirk. "In the Art of the Beholder: Comics as Political Journalism." *Comics as a Nexus of Cultures. Essays on the Interplay of Media, Disciplines and International Perspectives.* Ed. Mark Berninger, Jochen Ecke, and Gideon Haberkorn. Jefferson: McFarland, 2010. 70–81.

von Bredow, Wilfried. *Militar und Demokratie in Deutschland. Eine Einführung.* Wiesbaden: Verlag für Sozialwissenschaften, 2008.

Williams, Kristian. "The Case for Comics Journalism." *Columbia Journalism Review* 43.6 (2005): 51–55.

Woo, Benjamin. "Reconsidering Comics Journalism: Information and Experience in Joe Sacco's *Palestine*." *The Rise and Reason of Comics and Graphic Literature: Critical Essays on the Form.* Ed. Joyce Goggin and Dan Hassler-Forest. Jefferson: McFarland, 2010. 166–77.

V

AUSTRIAN VOICES

NINE

Cultural Legitimacy and Nicolas Mahler's Autobiographical Comics

Vance Byrd

At the 2013 *Internationales Literaturfestival* in Berlin, a coalition of cartoonists, book illustrators, graphic artists, fiction writers, translators, editors, publishers, and booksellers issued *Das Comic-Manifest* (the *Comic-Manifesto*). In their view, German comics, created by cartoonists trained mostly in the fine arts, count as avant-garde publications that treat serious social issues. An intergenerational readership, an active lecture and exhibition circuit, praise in feuilleton articles, and international awards further validate the medium. According to the *Comic-Manifesto*, comic books and graphic novels had also found a place in higher-education curricula and were the focus of academic research at German universities. Despite these signs of cultural legitimacy, the signatories observed that the German comic book artists did not receive the same governmental subventions that financially support artists working in the areas of film, television, theater, music, and opera. In response to their central question of why the German state neglects to fund the academic training and livelihood of cartoonists, the signatories concluded that the German government should establish a professorship in Comics Studies in order to provide backing for German cartoonists. This form of state-sanctioned legitimacy, they reasoned, would be a crucial first step in ensuring the competitiveness of these new respectable German comics on the European market.

The creation of the *Comic-Manifesto* demonstrates that hierarchies of cultural legitimacy and respectability continue to inform debates on German comics and graphic novels. The points of reference that the signatories draw upon, namely, the fine arts, cultural criticism, opera, and higher education, lend credence to Pierre Bourdieu's critique that the push to legitimize popular art forms like comics often reinforce and reproduce established hierarchies (569). Here, Bourdieu underscores that social value, as manifested by distinctions in cultural practices and consumption, contributes to continuous struggles over power, influence, and capital. In this regard, the *Comic-Manifesto* argues that comics today have been rehabilitated from the gutter of popular culture by meeting highbrow criteria and taking their rightful place in institutions and networks of cultural consumption. By seeking to elevate and institutionalize comics, the *Comic-Manifesto* likewise recalls how the popular medium continues to be part of a debate on respectability, which had notably reached its height in the 1950s with the Comics Code Authority in the United States and the Federal Review Board for Publications Harmful to Young Persons (*Bundesprüfstelle für jugendgefährende Schriften*) in West Germany. Taken in general terms, then, much of the controversy surrounding comics has centered then and now on the appropriateness of content for adult readers and whether comics cannot be taken seriously because they align too closely with childlike entertainments (Groensteen 5). The signatories convey a rather straightforward message: comics have grown up.

The Viennese cartoonist Nicolas Mahler has been instrumental in the medium's coming of age. Renowned for graphic novel adaptations of literature by Austrian authors Thomas Bernhard (1931–1989)[1] and Robert Musil (1880–1942),[2] Mahler had already been wrestling with the issue of legitimacy a decade earlier in his autobiographical comics. Like the pioneering work of R. Crumb and Justin Green, who depicted their autobiographical selves in American underground comix as "troubled, self-doubting outsider[s]" (Mikics 18),[3] Mahler's practitioner autobiographies—*Kunsttheorie versus Frau Goldgruber* (*Art Theory versus Mrs. Goldgruber*, 2003), *Zumutungen der Moderne* (*Impositions of Modernity*, 2007), *Pornografie und Selbstmord* (*Pornography and Suicide*, 2010), and *Kafkas non-stop Lachmaschine* (*Kafka's Non-Stop Laugh Machine*, 2014)—craft stories in which the protagonist is an outsider to the Austrian bureaucracy and the art establishment.

Kunsttheorie versus Frau Goldgruber, the main concern of the present chapter, can be read as a double narrative that addresses the question of artistic and cultural legitimacy. The first narrative tells the story of the author's endeavors to gain acceptance as a cartoonist. The second one relates the story of the creation, dissemination, and consumption of comic books. Questions of cultural, governmental, and market-based legitimacy—the very issues raised in the 2013 *Comic-Manifesto*—constitute the stations found in *Kunsttheorie versus Frau Goldgruber*. In Mahler's comic, a series of episodes relates the comics artist's struggle for societal permission to call his craft legitimate art as his autobiographical avatar gradually gains recognition as an independent comics artist. In the protagonist's account, barriers such as taxation, insurance, customs and border control, fellow Viennese artists, exhibition culture, and publishers hinder cartoonists from securing a successful livelihood and prevent the books they publish from reaching broad audiences.

The opening pages of the practitioner autobiography foreground the novel's theoretical dimension. The main character, Niki Mahler, recounts how an autograph session with a famous tennis player during his youth was unexpectedly instrumental in the discovery of his passion for cartooning. This episode serves as a lens through which the entire work can be read, namely, as a commentary on aesthetic production. By making cartooning into an observable process, aesthetic production emerges as an alternative way of thinking about the value of comics that de-emphasizes arguments based on institutional support, academic study, or market considerations.

READING THE ENTIRE BOOK: AUTOBIOGRAPHICAL COMICS AND PARATEXTUAL ANALYSIS

The proliferation of autobiographical comics for educated middle-class readers has played a considerable role in legitimacy claims for comics.[4] In the United States, the mainstreaming of autobiographical comics grew out of the underground comix movement in the 1970s and intensified with the acclaim of Art Spiegelman's Holocaust graphic novel *Maus* (1980). Readers' interest in the authenticity of serious personal narratives played out in the German market as well. Dirk Rehm, who founded the German independent comics publisher Reprodukt, which publishes some of Mahler's work, noted that a shift occurred in the German-language comics market after the 1980s from collectors' comic books to largely autobiographical graphic novels for a segment of consumers "with educated middle-class reading habits" (mit bildungsbürgerlichem Leseverhalten; Rehm). German-language newspapers and traditional book publishers have been influential in the transition in readership to more broadly educated audiences. Special editions of comics published by newspapers such as *Bild, Frankfurter Allgemeine Zeitung*, and the *Süddeutsche Zeitung*, as well as the publishers of German books, S. Fischer, Kiepenheuer & Witsch, Aufbau, and Suhrkamp, have joined comics publishers such as Edition Moderne, Carlsen, and Reprodukt in issuing autobiographical comics as book-format compilations (Ditschke 267, 270).

While a more far-reaching market for sophisticated autobiographical comics is reflected in the kinds of comics published, one can hardly argue that reading comics has become as sophisticated as the medium itself. Despite signs of the broader acceptance of the medium, many critics and readers lack expertise in evaluating comics.[5] Mahler himself raises the concern that art, literature, and comics critics still do not understand the interdependence of word and image or the humor derived from "the narration, rhythm, voids, legibility and, as the case may be, unreadability" (die Erzählung, der Rhythmus, die Leerstellen, die Lesbarkeit bzw. Unlesbarkeit; Mahler 2014, 52). Building upon these concerns, I would like to advance a reading of one particular comic, *Kunsttheorie versus Frau Goldgruber*, that accounts for the interdependence of graphic narration, genre, and publication format. Such an approach to Mahler's practitioner autobiographies consider verbal and visual relations while taking into account Hillary Chute and Patrick Jagoda's observation that comics "direct attention to the physical object of the book" (6). This is not to say that I am prescribing how autobiographical comics should be read. Instead, I am using the entirety of Mahler's practitioner autobiography as a heuristic approach to show how this work stages creative production to frame a debate on cultural legitimacy.

In order to put this approach into practice, we must examine all of the components of *Kunsttheorie versus Frau Goldgruber* as a physical book, which in this case consists of an autobiographical graphic narrative that is enclosed by an illustrated cover, an apparatus of front and back matter, theoretical texts, and publication notes. Taken together, these heterogeneous paratextual elements lend autobiographical narratives coherence and provide space for reflection on the author as well as the purpose and value of comics (Lejeune 11–15; Genette 1–2). This self-referential quality underscores the inherent reflexivity of practitioner autobiographies that, as the name suggests, necessarily describe both the production process and the producer of that narrative. More precisely, *Kunsttheorie versus Frau Goldgruber* is simultaneously a book about the production of comics *and* a book about Mahler's development as a cartoonist.

An examination of the front cover, flaps, as well as front and back matter will move us closer to understanding how Mahler addresses legitimacy in this comic. As suggested above, the title and the cover art announce the practitioner autobiography's self-reflexive content (figure 9.1). As autobiography, the composition of the front cover—last name of the author, the title, a modified illustration from the first chapter, and publisher information—connects the verbal and visual narrative in *Kunsttheorie versus Frau Goldgruber* to that of a real person who stands outside of the text and produces its discourse (Lejeune 11). At the top of the cover, the author's last name (Mahler), not like the fictitious ones used, for example, by his German colleagues Mawil (Markus Witzel) or Flix (Felix Görmann), connects the story's visual and verbal narrative to that of a real person and author Nicolas Mahler. Nicolas Mahler and the main character Niki Mahler are hardly one and the same, but knowledge about the author's oeuvre, the hand-lettered appearance of the title, and the minimalist style of the illustration recall the stylistic conventions that he had established in his earlier lighthearted comics. The title's words and image, however, are at odds with such expectations and install in the work a sense of irony from the start. Our attention is focused on art theory rather than, to take the example of a comic published before *Gold-gruber*, the absurdities of love affairs, bank robbery, and drunken conversations at Bar Juanjo that Mahler had depicted in *Lone Racer* (1999). Having culled an audience for his lighthearted comics, Mahler redeploys humor to make a loftier claim in *Kunstgeschichte versus Frau Goldgruber* about the stakes of comics.

The title of the comic itself sets a certain theory of art (*Kunsttheorie*) into dialogue with a female character named Frau Goldgruber, an Austrian bureaucrat. Upon first reflection, the point of contention likely involves the artistic status of comics. It is notable, however, that Mahler has not drawn his character, which predominates the body narrative of the comic, on the cover. Rather than establishing additional connections between himself and the subject matter, the cover illustration depicts a stack of twelve books and loose papers below the title and to the left. Four books in this tower of publications have single-word English titles on each of their spines; and reinforce the notion that this particular comic book is part of an ongoing debate about art and appreciation: "I THINK IT'S ART." Who might have hesitantly asserted this claim? If Mahler is setting theoretical stakes with this comic book, his interlocutors might include fans, academics, cultural critics, other cartoonists, and the publishing industry. The cover illustration reinforces the dialogue mentioned above: the visual suggests that the stack of books is in dialogue with a female character to the bottom right holding a book-like volume. The reader might ask at this point: "Is the book under the woman's arm her contribution to a debate on the status of comics?" Once we read a few pages inside the comic and learn that the woman is an Austrian tax official named Frau Goldgruber and that she is the book's primary critic, we might return to the cover and ask if an established canon of art history and appreciation is being juxtaposed with bureaucratic regulation. And if we take the quantity of pages found under her arm, we might conclude that the Austrian tax authorities have a rather narrow definition of art.

Additional signs of autobiographical character and legitimacy emerge as the book cover folds to produce the front and back book flaps. These flaps list eight other publications by Mahler from the German-language independent comics publishers Reprodukt, Edition Moderne, Carlsen, and Luftschacht, a form of acknowledgment at odds with the main illustrated autobiographical narrative about a cartoonist struggling for acceptance. This information heightens the retrospective nature of Mahler's story: he is no longer the person whose story is told in the main illustrated autobiographical narrative. The titles on the front book flap suggest that Mahler is a successful cartoonist whose work has been accepted by the comics establishment and its readers. Even with this form of legitimacy, the flap prompts a renegotiation of the initial reading of the cover. Did Mahler create the titles being examined by Frau Goldgruber? Is the art

Figure 9.1. Cover illustration for Nicolas Mahler's *Kunsttheorie versus Frau Goldgruber*. Mahler, Nicolas. *Kunsttheorie versus Frau Goldgruber*. 2nd ed. Berlin: Reprodukt, 2007.

status of *his* oeuvre under consideration? If we flip to the end of the book and examine the back flap, the biographical sketch ties Mahler to Vienna and other original publication venues, such as newspapers and magazines. The mention of his Max und Moritz Prize in 2006 for *Das Unbehagen* (uneasiness, awkwardness) (2005) in the second edition of *Kunsttheorie versus Frau Goldgruber* further underscores the peer-based acceptance of Mahler's work.

The front and back matter likewise stand in close relation to the book's main text. A relation between the verso of the title page to the 2007 Reprodukt edition and the comic's diegetic world underscore how distinct parts of the printed book codetermine its autobiographical and theoretical character. The verso reveals that the book is a reproduction of an exhibition catalog published in June 2003 by edition selene for the City Gallery Wels (*Galerie der Stadt Wels*) in Upper Austria. This page indicates that permissions were secured from this gallery and that the theoretician Günter Mayer, who makes an appearance inside the comic's story, worked in this gallery. In the third chapter of the body narrative referenced on the front book flap, Mahler would like to recall childhood experiences, but his editor, Theoretiker Mayer asks Mahler's autobiographical avatar to address theory more explicitly. Mahler's character responds with exasperation:

> Comics narratives on their own are obviously not good enough for '*this country*' . . . A publication is only possible here when the *cloak of theory* is chic, the *discursive foundation* is established and the humor slippers have been taken off.

> Comicgeschichten allein sind "*diesem Land*" ja nicht gut genug . . . Eine Publikation ist hier erst dann möglich, wenn der *Theoriemantel* schick sitzt, das *Diskursbrett* gemacht ist und die Humorschlapferln ausgezogen sind. (2007, 26)[6]

This passage suggests that an Austrian autobiographical comic book must be underpinned with significant theoretical weight in order to be taken seriously. Seriousness, the character reasons, demands that we shed away humor. When compared to the information gleaned from the entire published book, both Mayer's objections and Mahler's broader life story appear ironic. The remediation of the exhibition catalog and second comic book edition are signs that audiences extending from the world of art exhibition to independent comic book readers accept graphic narratives. As will be shown in the next sections, the remark represents a form of deceit on Mahler's part since his theory of comics production will be so inextricably connected to the entire autobiographical narrative. His autobiographical story of media production occupies a middle ground in which comics can be both serious and funny.

We see how bridging the serious and the humorous can function as a strategy toward legitimization in an essay by one of Mahler's own readers and commentators that appears in the back matter after the main comics narrative. Christian Gasser's piece, "A Man, His Humor, and His Laments" (Ein Mann, sein Humor und seine Klagen) focuses on Mahler's life and the history of comics and pays particular attention to his expressive style and status as an artist in Austria. First, Gasser recounts his first face-to-face encounter with Mahler—"Tall and thin, black hair and clothes, also a black pair of glasses, a striking profile, carelessly shaven and an ill-tempered attitude" (Lang und dünn, die Haare und Kleider schwarz, schwarz auch die Brille, das Profil auffällig, nachlässig die Rasur und griesgrämig die Miene; 95)—and his chance purchase of *Lone Racer* and *Du Falott, Baby* in 1998. Aside from his less than flattering description of the cartoonist, Gasser expresses a great deal of admiration for Mahler's work and recognizes in it a historical parallel to the influence of Francophone publishers on German comics since World War II.

Broadly speaking, Franco-Belgian publishers provided new venues for generic experimentation and reader consumption. In the 1990s in particular the French publishing house L'Association and its cartoonists Lewis Trondheim (Laurent Chabosy), David B. (Pierre-François Beauchard), and Joann Sfar led a "French Revolution in Comics" (französische Comic-Revolution) that extended beyond the borders of France and Belgium (Gasser 96). In Gasser's account, these publishers helped independent autobiographical comics flourish throughout Europe: "From the outset, the Association authors opposed conventional genres (adventure, fantasy, superheroes, comics about historical events, crime, thrillers, etc.) with personal and often autobiographically tinged stories" (Von Anfang an setzten die Association-Autoren den herkömmlichen Genres [Abenteuer, Fantasy, Superhelden, Historiencomic, Krimi etc.] persönliche, nicht selten autobiografisch gefärbte Geschichten entgegen; 96). Most recently, an approach to publishing that promoted visual rather than verbal expression, as typified by "Pantomine Cartooning" (Pantominencomics) or "Comics without Words" (Comics ohne Worte), made financial sense for L'Association since translation and lettering costs are reduced while the international market for independent comics could further expand (Gasser 102). As a marketing strategy, these publishers draw upon a rather lofty, and perhaps unrealistic, notion of a "universal" language of visual narration devoid of verbal expression to legitimate comics.

Mahler's expressive style, an emphasis on precise visual narration in his comics *Désir*, *Flaschko*, and *Kratochvil*, aligned perfectly with the frameworks L'Association and Franco-Canadian publisher La Pastèque wanted to support. By publishing cartoonists like Mahler, the example of L'Association suggests that transnational media networks have been key to the success of German-language cartoonists and comics then and now. By foregrounding the production and circulation of books outside of the national frameworks, the inclusion of Gasser's essay heightens the absurdity of the bureaucratic situation Mahler's autobiographical avatar encounters while underscoring that national acceptance remains important for the real cartoonist.

Despite Mahler's success with Francophone publishers, he, in fact, did not experience a corresponding national breakthrough in Austria. Instead, Mahler's Austrian colleagues reject the sophisticated techniques of visual narration that Gasser praises:

> Nicolas Mahler is caught between two camps. Humor is synonymous with mainstream comics, especially where German is widely spoken. Mahler's drawing style puts him in the independent comics scene. For underground cartoonists, however, he is too conventional. For friends of conventional comics fare, Mahler is, again, too off-key. For the avantgarde, his line is, if anything, too simple and "inartistic." For conventional cartoonists, his interest in experimentation is a bit fishy. Etc., etc. A vicious circle.

> Nicolas Mahler sitzt zwischen den Stühlen. Humor wird — gerade im deutschen Sprachraum — mit Mainstreamcomic gleichgesetzt. Mahlers Zeichenstil rückt ihn aber in die unabhängige Comic-Szene. Den Undergroundisten ist er jedoch zu klassisch. Den Freunden klassischer Comic-Kost ist Mahler wiederum zu schräg. Den Avantgardisten ist sein Strich womöglich zu simpel und "unkünstlerisch." Den Traditionalisten ist seine Lust am Experiment nicht geheuer. Etc., etc. Ein Teufelskreis. (110)

In Gasser's characterization, a visually and verbally reduced drawing style is a feature of Mahler's comics that places him in the company of German-language independent comics artists whose serious reading matter is appropriate for adult readers. It is not obvious, however, whether all forms of humor must be omitted. The comments raise other questions concerning the appropriateness of ironic, absurd, or grotesque situations that may be colored by humor as well as reasons behind comics being defined in such narrow and contradictory terms.

Gasser's brief biographical and media historical account is joined with the publication history of the comic book in the colophon. *Kunsttheorie versus Frau Goldgruber* was issued and reissued, first with an Austrian and then with a German publisher. The publication information shows that it was printed in Poland and that there has been more than one print run, as already suggested on the back flap by the inclusion of a comics prize after the original publication date. Moreover, the back flap connects the comic book to the author and publisher's websites. Another paratext that connects the author to a theoretical debate on comics can be found in the final pages of the comic. Reference to "further reading" (weiterführende Literatur) points the reader *only* to the other practitioner autobiographies Mahler has published, which invites the continued deliberation of the cartoonist's reflections on media production and aesthetics. Finally, the back cover of the book reveals Frau Goldgruber's hesitant conclusion that comics, or at least those by Mahler, are somehow works of art.

The cover, flaps, publication information on the verso of the title page, bibliography, colophon, Gasser's afterword, and back cover thus reinforce the autobiographical nature of the book. The interplay of these elements in the physical book generates its own self-referential discourse.[7] In a sense, the publication history and paratextual references in which *Kunsttheorie versus Frau Goldgruber* are embedded do not resolve the question about art status that the cover illustration raises. Regardless of whether comics do or do not constitute art, the reissue of *Kunsttheorie versus Frau Goldgruber* in a number of publication formats to an international market seems to underscore the contemporary movement's ever-expanding readership. *Kunsttheorie versus Frau Goldgruber* is hardly a comprehensive theory of art. In his practitioner autobiography, it is the *practice* of making comics (*Produktionsästhetik*) that helps elaborate Mahler's evolving understanding of the status of comics and how they have become serious books after all.

AUTOBIOGRAPHY: ORIGINAL AND COUNTERFEIT

While the book's physical features, described above in detail, shape how we understand Mahler as a successful independent cartoonist, the work's highly referential status can be noted within the body narrative as well. A key element of a practitioner autobiography is the presentation of creative production by an artist. In the opening pages of *Kunsttheorie versus Frau Goldgruber*, the narrative is framed in documentary terms as a "record" or a "sketch" (*Aufzeichnungen*) of a personal nature in which the phrase "*not one word* made up" (*kein Wort* frei erfunden) underscores the authenticity of the subsequent episodes. Around its midpoint, Mahler portrays his character as a visiting instructor in charge of teaching his students how to produce an autobiographical comic book. In these two instances, the narrative draws attention to the work of autobiography, the inscription of the "self" as "written with one's hand," although the artistic production of autobiographical comics is presented as a collaborative activity subject to editorial review in the second case. Here, Mahler discards many of his student's sketches: "The pamphlet will be thinner than anticipated, that means that NOT EVERYONE IS IN IT! You cannot publish every piece of trash OUT OF PITY!" (Das Heft wird dünner als geplant, das heisst, ES IST NICHT JEDER DRIN! Man kann nicht AUS MITLEID jeden Schrott veröffentlichen!; 72). His decision raises a degree of uncertainty about whether the artist alone can control one's authentic personal story as a comics narrative when it is transformed into a self-contained book. Mahler depicts the stack of thrown-away papers (raus-geschmissene Arbeiten; 72) as blank pages in this panel. A comic book is the result of "throwing away" many drafts, pieces, and characters. It is an act of production. In what follows, I will analyze an inscribed version of this same panel-like form—an autograph—which Niki Mahler creates at his desk and likewise discards. For Mahler, comics require a finesse that the artist can only acquire through painstaking and repetitive practice, producing a certain amount of excess that is masked by the final book form. This analysis suggests that this arduous process turns comics into art.

Mahler often draws himself as a character at comic book festivals in his practitioner autobiographies. Held in San Diego, Bethesda, Angoulême, Lucerne, Haarlem, or Lisbon, each international comic book festival represents a nexus of exchange at which cartoonists display original comics pages and interact with fans, translators, and publishers. In Mahler's practitioner autobiographies, reference to encounters with his cartoonist colleagues at such festivals—Jyrki Heikkinen, José Villarrubia, Stefan F. Neuwinger, Craig Thompson, Marjane Satrapi, Patrice Killoffer, Gipi, Reinhard Kleist, Ralf König—map out the dominant players on the European contemporary comics scene. Mahler's autobiographical avatar can be found at a table next to other cartoonists and, without fail, is overshadowed by the popularity and personalities of his colleagues. Fans wait to exchange words with Thompson or Satrapi while they autograph copies of their respective international bestseller graphic novels *Blankets* and *Persepolis*. Mahler's character, however, gains attention at autograph sessions due to his proximity to these cartoonists and not for his own comics. His character reflects on his own insignificance in *Zumutungen der Moderne*. Here, an anonymous Iranian telephone caller from Vienna lectures Mahler about the biased historical portrayal in *Persepolis* merely because the cartoonist had been seated next to Satrapi: "I know that you are in with this COMMUNIST SATRAPI!!" (Ich weiss, aber dass Sie mit dieser KOMMUNISTIN SATRAPI was laufen haben!!!; 2010, 54). The point here is that he has nothing to do with her other than sharing a profession and having benefited from her success as a comics artist.

At times, the autograph session is elevated to reflection on the function, purpose, and production of comics. Italian fans form long lines to videotape the artistic process of José Villarrubia, a colorist for Marvel comics, who smugly quips: "I bet if I get out my watercolors you will REALLY wet your pants!" (2010, 49). The acts of autography and drawing comics converge elsewhere in *Zumutungen der Moderne*: "It is taken for granted much too easily that a cartoonist will produce a valuable original drawing and give it to any old collector" (Viel zu selbstverständlich wird von Comiczeichnern erwartet, dass sie auf Kommando eine wertvolle Originalzeichnung anfertigen und diese an x-beliebige Sammler verschenken; 50). This quotation suggests, much like a scene near the conclusion of *Kunsttheorie versus Frau Goldgruber* in which a "fan" throws a postcard on the table and demands that Mahler's character draw something on it, that the autograph session is a moment in which the writing of the self and drawing comics unite with the comic artist's new status as an author.

In *Kunsttheorie versus Frau Goldgruber*, the issue of hand-drawn authenticity is developed most extensively in an autograph session that occurred in Mahler's youth. Titled "Original and Counterfeit" (Original und Fälschung), the prologue to *Kunsttheorie versus Frau Goldgruber* depicts a childhood tennis lesson. In this flashback, a then ten-year-old Niki Mahler receives an autograph from the Austrian tennis champion Peter Feigl. More than an event common to sports and comic book fandom, this moment sets in motion deliberations in which Mahler's character functions as an "autobiographer," a term Gillian Whitlock employs to describe an "autobiographical avatar [used to] actively engage with the conventions of comics" (971). In Mahler's comic, the use of the autograph session directs our attention to the hand-drawn production of signatures and, by extension, comics.[8] The staging of this event and the reproduction of hand-drawn signs help Mahler define authenticity and originality in the production, distribution, and consumption of comic books and graphic novels. And in line with the chapter title, this definition calls into question distinctions between the real and the fake when we think of autobiography as a genre and of comics as material texts.

One purpose of a tennis lesson, like the autobiographical comics course mentioned above, is the transmission of a set of techniques from an expert to a learner. The promise of an autograph after Niki Mahler and the other youths had played a set with the Austrian tennis player is a gesture that motivates participation in the event as much as it reinforces the champion's own prestige. As such, the scene plays with the expectation that an attempt to duplicate the expert player's swing might confirm improvement in the sport. In the narrative, however, young Niki Mahler misses the ball served to him. Despite the character's lack of skill, he receives a slip of paper signed by Champ Feigl, "an autograph from Mr. Feigl . . . on a flimsy slip of paper" (ein Autogramm von Herrn Feigl . . . auf einem labrigen kleinen Zettel; 9), in accordance with the conditions set out by the gift exchange.

Through his failure as a tennis player, Niki Mahler discovers his talent as a cartoonist.[9] As the next panel transitions from the tennis court to home, the youth begins to copy the autograph at his bedroom desk (figure 9.2). The eight panels on this page and the next illustrate a creative process in which Mahler transforms Peter Feigl's signature from a mere handwritten communicative artifact to a proto-comics panel. It is the character's scene of creative origins. This situation calls to mind that artistic ability in an aesthetics of production is often portrayed as a moment of "enthusiastic inspiration (ἐκστασις, ékstasis, furor poeticus) or as the potential for the acquisition and application of a set of artistic techniques (μίμησις, mímesis, imitatio naturae)" (Semsch 140). Niki Mahler's doodle unites imitation and inspiration, a mimetic drive for its own sake. The reproduction of the autograph within his retreat is described as a type of spiritual exercise that develops into an automatism: "[s]oon I could imitate the signature with my eyes closed" ([b]ald schon konnte ich die Unterschrift blind imitieren; 9). As an "exorcize" of sorts, he extracts something from himself—his creativity—of which he had been unaware and unable to control until this moment. W. J. T. Mitchell has framed such ecstatic moments as an attraction that can be located in myths about the origins of drawing (2014, 24). In this regard, Mahler draws upon a primal experience common to other comics artists.

The cartoonist Ivan Brunetti writes that he began drawing by copying Italian comic books and Mickey Mouse as a child. Brunetti would move on to copy Ernie Bushmiller's *Nancy* as an adult. "When I was a kid," he recalls, "I enjoyed losing myself in these trance-like punishments, half-aware that something other than myself would 'take over' the monotonous task" (Brunetti n.pag.). We might recall W. J. T. Mitchell once again and his observation that writing and cartooning are composite representations that bring together image and text (Mitchell 1994, 90, 95, 113–14).[10] As an exemplary composite representation, the tennis player's autograph card resembles one of the basic elements of narration in comic books: the panel. The act of creating this representational field as an autograph card captures the essence of Mahler's minimalist expressive style—the repetition of panels rarely composed of detailed images or texts—and the embodied labor of drawing and lettering comic book pages.[11] This scene of aesthetic production therefore casts light on the language of comics and points to the importance of creative genius.

Just as there are few indications within the space of the narrative that young Niki Mahler continues to practice tennis or even wants to improve, Mahler's character calls into question authenticity and expertise. His inspiration is not found in other comics or visual arts traditions. The origin of his fascination with comics is found in the act of inscription, the reproduction of handwritten communication in the form of an autograph. Authorship represented in the autograph characterizes his foundational moment as a cartoonist and points to the authenticity inherent to his practice. The youth's act of copying the autograph at his desk presents the work of cartooning as an autodidactic process based on the kind of frenzied inspiration Brunetti remembers. Yet rather than blind imitation of an established mainstream comic strip character or handwriting style, Mahler distances himself from such traditions. Neither Mickey Mouse nor Peter Feigl is crucial at the moment in which his interest in cartooning came into being.

The production of copied signatures at his desk extends beyond repeated handwriting and copying. The act becomes a sculptural craft. Niki

Figure 9.2.   Nicolas Mahler reproduces copies of Champ Feigl's autograph (*Kunsttheorie* 9). Mahler, Nicolas. *Kunsttheorie versus Frau Goldgruber*. 2nd ed. Berlin: Reprodukt, 2007.

Mahler cuts paper with a utility knife to the proper dimensions to match the original autograph card. As he draws and redraws the signatures on these pieces of paper, the reproduction of the autograph and its card becomes inseparable from the work of young Mahler's own hand. These iterative acts of hand-crafting, drawing, and redrawing transform an autograph into a work of art bereft of any value that the tennis player's fame might have granted. Indeed, despite the prologue's title, the copies the character makes are not true counterfeits. Niki Mahler hardly seems to value the autograph and does not intend to deceive anyone by passing it off as an authentic signature.

As the episode continues after dinner, Niki returns to his desk and cannot distinguish the original autograph from the numerous copies he had crafted. The autograph and the copy—the artwork—are seen side-by-side. For the reader, they are indistinguishable in the panel: none bear the original signature's hand-drawn line. The youth selects one slip of paper at random and posts it on his bulletin board. Although he had initially saved this one autograph—not necessarily the original one—the final panel of the chapter depicts how Niki throws away even this piece of paper along with the other copied autographs a week later. What value do these slips of paper have now that Mahler has discovered his own talent as a cartoonist? How can this episode be understood? To find some answers, we must return to the question of the relationships between books and comics.

When one examines the entire narrative, these rectangular forms that Niki Mahler draws at his desk can be found on every page throughout the rest of the book. Although the autograph session foregrounds these building blocks of narration, Mahler positions these first stages of cartooning as a transitional stage leading to the production of books: "The original drawing is worthless. The book is the original" (Die Original-zeichnung ist wertlos. Das Buch ist das Original; 2007, 30). Given Mahler's reliance on irony, we may not take this quote at face value. However, the disposal of the original *and* the "counterfeits" at the young character's desk exemplifies how Mahler understands the production and circulation of comics. Both the player's act of signing the autograph card on the tennis court and the cartoonist's labor in his childhood bedroom are all transformed in the final book publication. Any auratic notion of personality or artistic process is thereby eliminated through the production. Here, a decisive shift is made to the act of reading comics.

This episode therefore sets up an argument for the book as the ideal comics format. Mahler's autobiographical avatar observes in a subsequent chapter that publishers, festival organizers, and curators ask cartoonists at comic book festivals and in museums to display "original sketches." These members of the arts industry (*Kunstbetrieb*) hold up these "bits and pieces of the comics medium" (Versatzstücken des Mediums Comic; 2007, 27), which, according to Mahler, lack any value.

Rather than an interest in books, these audiences seek to elevate interme-
diary forms to the status of high art. Mahler counters that comics cannot
be taken seriously when reduced to a single panel or motif, nor can they
be taken seriously when they are used to address established aesthetic
values and exhibition practices. Comics have their own language and
ideal exhibition format. Adopting Will Eisner's formulation, Mahler asserts that comics narration is built upon the language of sequential images, a notion the arts industry does not want to accept. Unwilling to
ignore the media specificity and expressive form of comics, his autobiographical avatar goes one step further and contends that comics should
be made public in self-contained books that would reach as many people
as possible: "Publication in pamphlet or book form—preferably in widest
possible circulation" (Eine Veröffentlichung in Heft- oder Buchform—in
möglichst grosser Verbreitung; 2007, 30). To do so, cartoonists need the
support of distributors and booksellers so that readers can gain access to
comics.[12] In this regard, the autograph session develops into an instance
of gift exchange that dovetails with the question the signatories of the
Comic-Manifesto raised regarding the cartoonists' need for state subventions to guarantee reaching their readers.

In the subsequent chapters, Mahler chooses a rather absurd situation
that provides only a partial answer to this question. His character appears before the Austrian tax authorities because he wants to be taxed at
a reduced rate. At this office, the reader encounters Frau Goldgruber, the
woman depicted on the cover illustration. Mahler presents evidence of
his successful career as an independent cartoonist to claim legitimacy and
pay lower taxes, as other artists may. Frau Goldgruber responds without
hesitation and rather matter-of-factly that his profession is commercial
rather than artistic in nature. Graphic artists (*Werbegraphiker*) deserve the
subsidy, but not comics artists (*Comicszeichner*) (2007, 17). Mahler defends
his status by drawing comparisons to commercially successful American
and Belgian popular comics. He insists that he does not draw Mickey
Mouse or the Smurfs. He is an artist. Enrollment in the Austrian national
insurance and pension service for freelancers confirms this status. Frau
Goldgruber, however, dismisses his argument out of hand since she
alone seems to determine his status for the tax authorities. Since his evidence of Austrian institutional acceptance failed, he then presents his
books to her. Frau Goldgruber is persuaded neither by comic book editions in French, such as *Le labyrinth de Kratochvil*, nor an exhibition catalog
from the *Centre National de la bande dessinée* in Angoulême at which he
had some of his work on loan. His books provide evidence for previous
international support of his career by the comics industry and members
of exhibition culture. Apart from a document that shows that Mahler had
participated in an exhibit in Krems, all of these signs of artist legitimacy
are insignificant in Frau Goldgruber's mind.

Instead, aesthetic production emerges as the most persuasive reason to accept comics. When Frau Goldgruber's superior wants to go on break, she grabs Mahler to ask what a comics artist (*Comic-Künstler*) is. At first, her boss thinks that she is referring to animators, who are not artists because they do not bring forth an "original creative act" (eigenständige kreative Leistung; 2007, 16). Once her superior understands that Frau Goldgruber is referring to a cartoonist, he immediately recalls a television show hosted by the Austrian caricature artist Ironimus (Gustav Peichl). The program featured the artist's creative process: "and he sat right down without an original or something like that . . . and right out of his head . . . as if he came up with something right out of his head!" (und da hat er sich hingesetzt, ohne Vorlagen oder so . . . und hat aus dem Kopf . . . als hat sich was ausgedacht! aus dem Kopf!; 2007, 17). As in Niki Mahler's youth, *Kunsttheorie versus Frau Goldgruber* makes the production process visible. Here, the remediation of aesthetic production finally convinces Frau Goldgruber, who had, up to this point, only been interested in the question of financial independence, which is a rather odd measure since Mahler is seeking a governmental tax subsidy in the first place. A consideration of aesthetic production thereby transforms Frau Goldgruber from being a bureaucratic gatekeeper at the beginning of the episode to the medium's chief advocate at its end. Mahler's interactions with these tax officials reflects the formation of a rather arbitrary opinion about the status of comics in Austria that cannot be upheld by a single law or ordinance.

CONCLUDING REMARKS

This chapter has discussed ways that the referential nature of autobiographical comics can be used to explore the medium's conventions and the question of artistic legitimacy. Taken as a whole, Mahler's theory of art reads like a head-on assault on many of the values the signatories of the *Comic-Manifesto* agreed to and the validation they seek. His autobiographical avatar questions whether cartoonists should be trained in the fine arts tradition and questions the value of exhibition practices in the lecture circuit. He criticizes the arbitrariness of national institutional support: tax officials do not refer to any volumes of law to ascertain the art status of comics. Instead, they rely on a vernacular notion of genius. As an alternative, the physicality of the book and Mahler's life story indicate that the broader European market is crucial at this moment for makers of comics when their status as artists is still not guaranteed. And more crucially, *Kunsttheorie versus Frau Goldgruber* focuses its readers' attention on the craft of comics, its building blocks, and the earliest creative spark that might lead to a career.

Much like the portrayal of Ironimus's drawing lessons discussed above, a promotional video for the Prize of the Literature Houses (*Preis der Literaturhäuser*) legitimates Nicolas Mahler's comics through the re-mediation of the process of aesthetic production. This short biographical film opens with the cartoonist in his Viennese apartment standing over his desk. In a sequence that recalls Niki Mahler's creative practice as a youth, Mahler reaches for a sketch, balls up the piece of paper, and discards it. The voice-over provides commentary for this scene: Mahler "expands the borders between comics, literature, and art by doing what he does best—throwing things away" (Einer der die Grenzen zwischen Comic, Literatur und Kunst ausdehnt, indem er das tut, was er am Besten kann—wegschmeißen). Mahler's own explanation for this act of disposal addresses how cartoonists pay close attention to ways that graphic narratives tell stories, how they should be read, and how excess is central to the production process: all issues outlined in this study of *Kunsttheorie versus Frau Goldgruber*. In the subsequent scenes of the film, Mahler goes on to claim that he has to make few compromises nowadays. He does not produce comics in accordance with mainstream conventions and, he has always had little in common with high art. His success as an independent cartoonist, he concludes, allows him to take chances on projects without worrying about promising publishers that he will sell thousands of comics. The fact that Mahler won the *Preis der Literaturhäuser*, an award that recognizes outstanding service in the promotion of literature (*Literatur-vermittlung*), underscores that independent comics can be in the service of literature *and* that literature will help their creators sell comics. While comics fans may question recent acquiescence to the demands of the literature industry, comics adaptations of literature have been important for the growing legitimacy of the medium and these works may satisfy those interested in the visual arts, literature, and popular mainstream comics. In short, Mahler is no longer the person whose story he drew in Frau Goldgruber's office; and traditional borders between creative forms may have indeed expanded. The portrayal of Mahler in *Kunsttheorie versus Frau Goldgruber* and in the prize video directs our attention to aesthetic production as a useful criterion with which to consider the value of independent comics authorship.

NOTES

1. *Alte Meister: Graphic Novel*, 2011.
2. *Der Mann ohne Eigenschaften*, 2014.
3. The underground comix movement in the United States in the 1970s established a space in which independent authorship and production sought to circumvent the dominant comic book industry: "Most of the early work in the underground comix movement found its pleasures and its justification in iconoclasm, and in expressing openly topics and fantasies long forbidden (and explicitly outlawed by the comics code of 1954) in mainstream comics and in mainstream society. But in opening up the

form to new ideas, images, and audience, the underground comix movement spawned a new form of graphic expression that would ultimately outlive the movement by many decades" (Gardner 6–7).

4. The publication, reissue, translation, as well as prize-winning filmic and musical adaptation of autobiographical comics help demonstrate that autobiographical comics and graphic memoirs are among the most commercially successful comics genres today. Examples include Henry Yoshitaka Kiyama's *Four Immigrants Manga* (1931/1998), Kenji Nakazawa's *Barefoot Gen* (1972), Justin Green's *Binky Brown Meets the Holy Virgin Mary* (1972), Will Eisner's *Contract with God and Other Tenement Stories* (1978), Art Spiegelman's Pulitzer Prize–winning *Maus* (1980), Marjane Satrapi's *Persepolis* (2000), and Alison Bechdel's *Fun Home* (2006). For more on this subject, see Groensteen 46; Beaty 138–70; and El Refaie's book-length study.

5. In feuilleton, for example, the spatial arrangement on the printed page may lead some German newspaper readers to conclude that comics are closer akin to literature than images. The unique aspects of visual narration in comics are usually not central to these newspaper articles, and the printed page rarely contains excerpted illustrations that are discussed in detail (Ditschke 271–73). Admittedly, the connection between literature and comics is more apparent in some graphic novels. Alison Bechdel's *Fun Home*, for example, refers to works by F. Scott Fitzgerald, Henry James, Colette, and Joyce throughout. Proximity to literature and veneration of literature appear to be a publication strategy when one examines the graphic novel adaptations by Bertolt Brecht's *Herr Keuner* (Ulf K.), Frank Wedekind's *Lulu* (Mahler), Mark Twain's *Huck Finn* (Olivia Vieweg), and Marcel Beyer's *Flughunde* (Ulli Lust), which have been issued recently by the respected literature house Suhrkamp. By the same token, the venue at which *Das Comic-Manifest* was issued, an international literary festival, underscores that the literature industry remains a point of orientation to evaluate and promote a medium whose narrative and materiality attends more to the visual rather than verbal engagement (Harvey 3–4; Groensteen 10).

6. The lettering of Nicolas Mahler's comics will be reproduced in this essay to approximate the original emphasis whenever possible. Lettering in dark, heavy strokes is in a bold typeface; uppercase letters remain uppercase; and expanded character spacing is retained.

7. Such bookish references are not unusual. Mahler routinely plays with the conventions of serious book publication and the question of what constitutes a book elsewhere. His poetry volume, *Längen und Kürzen* (2009), includes a poem titled "*Gesamtausgabe*," in which the volumes ("Band 1 / Band 2 / Band 3") and contents ("Anmerkungen / Dokumente / Bibliographien / Materialien / Korrekturen / Bildtafeln / Register") constitute its lines.

8. Handwriting and autobiography in Alison Bechdel's *Fun Home* is addressed in Jared Gardner's (2008) article.

9. It is difficult for Nicolas Mahler to say when he first discovered the spark for cartooning and realized that he wanted to be a professional cartoonist. He recalls in promotional material for the publisher Suhrkamp / Insel that he began drawing superhero comics at the age of twelve or thirteen. He was never a fan of René Goscinny and Albert Uderzo's French series *Asterix und Obelix*. Instead, Mahler identifies American newspaper comics published in the 1930s, such as George Herriman's *Krazy Kat*, as a possible spark that might have lead to his development as a cartoonist ("Autorenportrait und Gespräch").

10. Mitchell has noted that his philosophical claims about word and image relations are rooted in his childhood experience of reading comics. His observations on writing from *Picture Theory*, he contends, hold true for comics, too (Mitchell 2014, 20).

11. Mahler's style is driven by repetition. *Désir* consists of 328 almost identical images; *Längen und Kürzen*, 234 of nearly identical panels. His character frequently complains about drawing nearly identical panels in practitioner autobiographies to address issues germane to the challenges cartoonists face. The ascertainment of a customs official illustrates how labor of artistic production is misunderstood: "[A]nd

you draw that yourself? Each picture? Isn't that boring? Tiring?" ([U]nd das zeichnen Sie selber? Jedes Bild? Ist das nicht langweilig? ermüdend?; *Kunsttheorie* 55). Apart from the question whether the official's declaration suggests that many assume that comics are produced by other technical means rather than by hand, his disbelief is used in an episode to show how such misconceptions contribute to importation barriers for independent cartoonists. In addition, the repetition of gutterless panels that use dialogue-to-dialogue transitions contribute to visual literacy problems. Mahler writes that his style poses a challenge to readers who do not examine his carefully and repetitively drawn images: "97 percent of people read only the [verbal] text and hardly look at the drawings" (97 prozent der Leute lesen sowieso nur die Texte und schauen die Zeichnungen kaum an; *Franz Kafkas* 97). With regard to legitimacy claims, the labor involved in creating an animated film, a form that bridges Mahler's interest in cinema and comics, requires even more hand-drawn images and faces the same degree of disregard as comics by the proponents of literary and filmic high culture (*Zumutungen der Moderne* 19, 25).

12. Mahler's character recalls one failed attempt in *Kunsttheorie versus Frau Goldgruber*. Distribution barriers helped inspire *Comixautomat*, his short-lived independent way to sell comic books from a repurposed public coffee machine, but profitability for the vending machine owner undermined this venture.

REFERENCES

Beaty, Bart. *Unpopular Culture: Transforming the European Comic Book in the 1990s*. Toronto: University of Toronto Press, 2007.

Bechdel, Alison. *Fun Home*. Boston: Mariner Books, 2007.

Bourdieu, Pierre. *Distinction: A Social Critique of the Judgment of Taste*. Trans. Richard Nice. Cambridge, MA: Harvard University Press, 1984.

Brunetti, Ivan. *Aesthetics: A Memoir*. New Haven: Yale University Press, 2013.

Chute, Hillary, and Patrick Jagoda. "Special Issue: Comics and Media." *Critical Inquiry* 40.3 (2014): 1–10.

"Das Comic Manifest." *Internationales Literaturfestival Berlin*. 2 September 2013. Web. 1 August 2015. www.literaturfestival.com/archiv/sonderprojekte/comic/manifest.

Ditschke, Stephan. "Comics als Literatur. Zur Etablierung des Comics im deutschsprachigen Feuilleton Seit 2003." *Comics: Zur Geschichte und Theorie eines populärkulturellen Mediums*. Ed. Stephan Ditschke, Katerina Kroucheva, and Daniel Stein. Bielefeld: Transcript, 2009. 265–80.

Eisner, Will. *Comics & Sequential Art*. Tamarac, FL: Poorhouse Press, 1985.

El Refaie, Elisabeth. *Autobiographical Comics: Life Writing in Pictures*. Jackson: University of Mississipi Press, 2012.

Gardner, Jared. "Autobiography's Biography, 1972–2007." *Biography* 31.1 (2008): 1–26.

Gasser, Christian. "Ein Mann, sein Humor und seine Klagen." *Kunsttheorie versus Frau Goldgruber*. Nicolas Mahler. Berlin: Reprodukt, 2007. 95–111.

Genette, Gérard. *Paratexts: Thresholds of Interpretation*. Trans. Jane E. Lewin. Cambridge, UK: Cambridge University Press, 1997.

Groensteen, Thierry. "Why Are Comics Still in Search of Cultural Legitimization?" *A Comics Studies Reader*. Ed. Jeet Heer and Kent Worcester. Jackson: University Press of Mississippi, 2009. 3–11.

Harvey, John C. *The Art of the Comic Book: An Aesthetic History*. Jackson: University Press of Mississippi, 1996.

K. Ulf. *Geschichten vom Herrn Keuner von Bertolt Brecht und Ulf K.* Berlin: Suhrkamp, 2015.

Lejeune, Philippe. *On Autobiography*. Minneapolis: University of Minnesota Press, 1989.

Lust, Ulli. *Flughunde Marcel Beyer*. Berlin: Suhrkamp, 2013.

Mahler, Nicolas. *Alte Meister*. Berlin: Suhrkamp, 2011.

————. *Desir*. Paris: Editions de la Pasteque, 2001.

————. *Franz Kafkas nonstop Lachmaschine*. Berlin: Reprodukt, 2014.

————. *Kunsttheorie versus Frau Goldgruber*. 2ed. Berlin: Reprodukt, 2007.

————. *Lulu und das schwarze Quadrat*. Berlin: Suhrkamp, 2014.

————. *Der Mann ohne Eigenschaften*. Berlin: Suhrkamp, 2013.

————. *Pornografie und Selbstmord*. Berlin: Reprodukt, 2010.

————. "Preis der Literaturhäuser 2015 an Nicolas Mahler." Video. Web. 29 December 2015. http://www.suhrkamp.de/mediathek/preis_der_literaturhaeuser_an_nicolas_mahler_939.html.

————. *Von Längen und Kürzen*. Wien: Luftschacht, 2009.

————. *Die Zumutungen der Moderne*. 2ed. Berlin: Reprodukt, 2010.

Mahler, Nicolas, and Max Spallek. "Nicolas Mahler. Autorenportrait und Gespräch." BosePark Productions. Video. Web. 29 December 2015. http://www.suhrkamp.de/mediathek/nicolas_mahler_autorenportrait_und_gespraech_995.html.

Mikics, David. "Underground Comics and Survival Tales: *Maus* in Context." *Considering Maus: Approaches to Art Spiegelman's "Survivor Tale" of the Holocaust*. Ed. Deborah R. Geis. Tuscaloosa: University of Alabama Press, 2003. 15–25.

Mitchell, W. J. T., and Art Spiegelman. "Public Conversation. What the %$#! Happened to Comics?" *Critical Inquiry* 40.3 (2014): 20–35.

Mitchell, W. J. T. *Picture Theory. Essays on Verbal and Visual Representation*. London: University of Chicago Press, 1994.

Rehm, Dirk. "Comic-Verlger Rehm: "Es geht langsam aufwärts." *Badische Zeitung* 15 August 2014. Web. 16 July 2015. www.badische-zeitung.de/nachrichten/kultur/literatur/comic-verleger-rehm-es-geht-langsam-aufwaerts.

Satrapi, Marjane. *Persepolis: The Story of a Childhood*. New York: Pantheon Graphic Novels, 2004.

Semsch, Klaus. "Produktionsästhetik." Historisches Wörterbuch der Rhetorik. Ed. Gert Ueding. Darmstadt: Wissenschaftliche Buchgesellschaft, 2005. 140–54.

Spiegelman, Art. *Maus*. New York: Pantheon, 1980.

Thompson, Craig. *Blankets*. Marietta: GA: Top Shelf Productions, 2003.

Vieweg, Olivia. *Huck Finn nach Mark Twain*. Berlin: Suhrkamp, 2014.

Whitlock, Gillian. "Autographics: The Seeing 'I' of the Comics." *Modern Fiction Studies* 52.4 (2006): 965–79.

TEN

The Perfection of Imperfection

Nicolas Mahler's Alte Meister

Brett Sterling

In 2011, the Suhrkamp Verlag made history with the publication of Austrian artist Nicolas Mahler's adaptation of Thomas Bernhard's *Alte Meister* (*Old Masters*, 1985), the first comic to be published by a major literary publishing house in Germany. This marked a watershed moment for the critical acceptance of comics in the German-speaking world. Not only did it cast light on the fact that high-quality comics were already being produced in German, but it also spurred production by new artists and publishers. Thus, it is fitting that this particular work inaugurated Suhrkamp's graphic novel program.[1] In Bernhard's novel, the central question concerns the value of art—specifically the high art of the "old masters"—and the ability or inability of art to achieve ideals of aesthetic perfection. Adapting a novel that challenges the artistic distinction between high and low helps to break down the divide between comics—historically viewed as low art—and the more established fine arts and literature.

Bernhard's main character, Reger, a music critic and self-styled "critical artist" (Bernhard 52), spends every other day sitting on a bench in Vienna's Art History Museum (*Kunsthistorisches Museum*) dismantling the reverential aura of the old masters in scathing diatribes on fine art's essentials flaws. Key to Reger's critical view of art is his insistence on imperfection, which is caused, on the one hand, by the limitations of human creative ability, and on the other, by the existential panic that the finite observer experiences when faced with the infinite and flawless.

This essay explores Mahler's comic embodiment of Reger's artistic criticism, specifically the ways in which Mahler's use of caricature, fragmentation, obscuration, and repetition depict Reger's challenge to the veneration of high art. Additionally, it investigates how Mahler simultaneously advances an understanding of comics as a medium that can dismantle the high-low binary. The following analysis will demonstrate how Mahler uses the visual realm—all but absent in the novel—to offer a more radical challenge to high art than even Reger espouses.

REGER'S AESTHETICS OF CRITICAL ENGAGEMENT

Thomas Bernhard's *Alte Meister* provides a platform for exploring the thoughts of the curmudgeonly critic, Reger, as he ruminates on art and life in the *Kunsthistorisches Museum*. Over his thirty-year period of visiting the museum, Reger has developed a critical view of art that he shares with Atzbacher, the novel's narrator, in a series of extended monologues. In the novel, Reger expounds at length on his distaste for several topics, notably art, religion, and the Austrian state. But rather than developing and arguing a clear aesthetic theory, Reger merely pontificates. He presents his own esoteric tastes as definitive and normative, as this prime example from the text demonstrates: "And in actual fact [Anton] Bruckner too is nothing but sentimental and kitschy, nothing but stupid, monumental orchestrated sickly ear-wax" (Bernhard 41).[2] At the root of Reger's scathing criticism, though, are serious questions about the role of art in human life, the limitations of art, and strategies of artistic reception. Despite the vehemence of his critique against fine art and cultural institutions, art in general and the *Kunsthistorisches Museum* in particular have a central importance for Reger's existence.

His visits to the museum provide a necessary routine in Reger's life, while the art of the old masters elicits in him a combination of reverence and disgust. *"I have to go to the old masters to be able to continue to exist, precisely to these so-called old masters*, who have long, that is for decades, been abhorrent to me" (Mahler 2011, 37; Bernhard 104; emphasis in original). Reger's hatred is the result of a deeply held belief in the essential fallibility of art, even, or especially, in the works of the old masters. Indeed, Reger returns to the museum time and again specifically to reveal the defects of "great" art. No artwork is ever truly perfect, Reger claims; the most pristine works will always contain a fatal flaw: "In every one of these paintings, these so-called masterpieces, I have found and uncovered a massive mistake, the failure of its creator. . . . Not one of these world-famous masterpieces, no matter by whom, is in fact whole or perfect" (Bernhard 19). The implied expectation that art can or should be perfect has a long historical tradition in Europe, which Reger vehemently opposes.

Reger's entire critical viewpoint is a response to the legacy of eighteenth- and nineteenth-century aesthetics—as developed primarily in the works of Immanuel Kant, Friedrich Schiller, Friedrich Wilhelm Joseph Schelling, Georg Wilhelm Friedrich Hegel, and Arthur Schopenhauer—which established art as an autonomous realm, independent of practical purpose, that could purportedly provide viewers with aesthetic experiences ranging from intense emotion to deeper insight into life, truth, and the universe.[3] This understanding of art has since been used in part to distinguish "high" art, or works considered worthy of aesthetic contemplation, from "low" art, or those perceived to exist solely for amusement and entertainment. The sublime artwork of the former category does not exist for Reger, but it provides the paradigm against which he measures all art and determines its inadequacy. The flawed nature of art, in Reger's view, speaks to the inherent limitations of human ability, as Fatima Naqvi notes in an article on Bernhard's novel: "Experiencing the flaw in beauty, he [Reger] recognizes the fallibility of every human endeavor" (261). Dismantling the concept of perfection, though, actually provides Reger with a way forward in life: "There is no perfect picture and there is no perfect book and there is no perfect piece of music, Reger said, that is the truth, and this truth makes it possible for a mind like mine . . . to go on existing" (Bernhard 20). Indeed, Reger's very survival depends on "the systematic affirmation of imperfection" (die konsequente Bejahung von Unvollkommenheit; Atzert 163).[4] For Bernhard's protagonist, artistic wholeness is a source of distress for the human individual: by virtue of his/her own fallibility, the individual views the perfect whole as a disturbing reminder of its own imperfection: "We cannot endure the whole or the perfect" (Mahler 2011, 47; Bernhard 19). Consequently, while wholeness is irritating and threatening to the human individual, fragmentariness is pleasing: "Our greatest pleasure, surely, is in fragments . . ." (Mahler 2011, 44; Bernhard 18). Therefore, Reger proposes that the only way to deal with supposed perfection in art is to break the artwork into manageable parts. Reger achieves this by first recognizing that there are no complete works, including those by the old masters. The key is to systematically identify the fatal flaw in all works of art, thus reducing them to bearable human creations. In practice, Reger describes this as a process of caricature, of which he claims most people are unfortunately incapable: "When we observe a picture for any length of time, even the most serious picture, we have to turn it into a caricature in order to bear it . . . . Most people . . . are incapable of caricaturing, they observe everything to the bitter end with their terrible seriousness" (Bernhard 57–58). The inability of "most people" to make high art into something ridiculous is in turn a root cause of what Reger sees as the unwarranted, even idiotic, veneration of art by uncritical observers.

Reger claims that, unlike himself, the masses believe in the possibility of perfection in art; and as a result they become lost in veneration of perceived masterpieces. This ignorant worship of art is anathema to Reger, but he is confronted with it at all times via the patrons of the *Kunsthistorisches Museum*: "Nothing repels me more than observing people in the act of admiration . . . . The state of admiration is a state of feeble-mindedness, . . . nearly all of them live in this state of feeble-mindedness. And in that state of feeble-mindedness they all enter the Kunsthistorisches Museum . . ." (Mahler 2011, 76–77; Bernhard 59–60).[5] Reger considers himself more clever and more enlightened than the bulk of society, which is content to settle for the uncritical consumption of kitsch in the guise of the masterpiece, whether it be the work of Albrecht Dürer, Adalbert Stifter, or Martin Heidegger, to name just a few of the figures Reger reviles (Mahler 2011, 66, 82–85; Bernhard 29, 34, 41–46). After the death of his wife, Reger also comes to the realization that, regardless of how highly society values art, it can never replace the love and companionship of another human being. Indeed, art is revealed to be a human—and ultimately futile—attempt to come to terms with the world and the trials of life: "All these pictures, moreover, are an expression of man's absolute helplessness in coping with himself and with what surrounds him all his life" (Mahler 2011, 134; Bernhard 151). Reger considers the thought unconvincing and indefensible that art could provide insight into and solace for humanity's helplessness.

Reger does make one major exception to his "rule" about the shortcomings of art: Tintoretto's *Portrait of a White-Bearded Man* (ca. 1570).[6] This painting alone has survived Reger's withering gaze during the more than thirty years of his critical engagement with the *Kunsthistorisches Museum*'s collection. As such it functions as a priceless existential anchor in his life. Reger's aesthetics, as presented in Bernhard's novel, represents a polemical challenge to the established world of high art and culture. At the same time, for all of Reger's biting critique, his attachment to Tintoretto's painting is symptomatic of his problematic relationship with art. As Stephen Dowden argues: "Tintoretto's *Man with a White Beard* embodies for Reger all that is false and treacherous in great art: the utopian promise of transcendence, of human nobility, of perfection. However, he does not deny art its place in his life . . . . Reger survives by continually rediscovering the flawed element in seeming perfection" (63). Reger's extensive study of the old masters has led him to the conclusion that their works are empty, flawed, and ultimately disappointing at key moments in life: "Everything here at the Kunsthistorisches Museum . . . ultimately means nothing to us, *I mean at the crucial point in our existence*, nothing at all" (Mahler 2011, 130; Bernhard 151, emphasis in original). This insight is partially nullified by Reger's claim that, in spite of the essential meaninglessness of these artworks, "we must make ourselves believe that there is high art and the highest art . . . otherwise we should despair" (Mahler 2011, 136; Bernhard 37). Reger's insistence on a "nevertheless" statement reveals—in contradiction to his vehement critiques—a romantic attachment to veneration and to the concept of high art, an attachment that Mahler does not share. The dichotomy between high and low art is of especial importance for both novel and comic, and a range of assumptions about these categories is at play in each.

HIGH ART VERSUS LOW ART

The distinction between high and low art is an outgrowth of the centuries-long development of a modern art system in the West, during which the fine arts were separated from crafts and valued more highly for producing aesthetic objects, as opposed to works intended for practical use. Despite repeated challenges throughout the twentieth century that the division between high and low art is baseless and untenable,[7] it remains entrenched in contemporary culture, where, in Ted Cohen's words, the distinction seems "indefensible and indispensable" (1993, 152). The separation of low art from high art has been especially important for comics, which still struggles against a reputation as a throwaway medium intended for children and the unsophisticated. While photography and film—initially derided as low art—have been accepted into the pantheon of high art (at least certain exemplary works), the comics medium remains largely relegated to the ranks of low art, especially in the German-speaking world. This has resulted in a sense of insecurity and a struggle for legitimacy among some comics scholars,[8] which Ole Frahm addresses in *Die Sprache des Comics* (*The Language of Comics*): "Although comics have increasingly been accepted as a part of 20th century culture, they have by no means been accorded an equal place alongside literature, visual art, or even film. It seems at times as though engagement with comics demands special justification. As though the seriousness of the comical topic must be justified again and again" (Obwohl Comics als Teil der Kultur des 20. Jahrhunderts zunehmend akzeptiert sind, wird ihnen keineswegs ein gleichberechtigter Platz neben Literatur, bildender Kunst oder sogar Film eingeräumt. Gelegentlich scheint es, als stehe die Beschäftigung mit Comics unter einem besonderen Rechtfertigungszwang. Als müsse immer wieder die Seriosität des komischen Themas begründet werden; 31). In *Comics versus Art*, Bart Beaty attributes the division between comics and the art establishment not to any real or imagined deficits of the medium, but rather to the comic world's own insistence on the distinction. Beaty makes the important claim that "comics have not been recognized as art largely because until recently, with a very few exceptions, they have not actively solicited that form of recognition" (24).[9] Indeed, Beaty explains, many comics creators have insisted on an opposition between comics and the art world, rejecting the latter as overly pretentious (51ff). Frahm and Beaty illuminate related factors that have contributed to comics' separation from art: the competing perceptions that comics are inferior or superior to art. On the one hand, comics were long viewed only as mass products created for short-term commercial gain and immediate, uncritical consumption. This understanding of comics has proven especially persistent, and much comics scholarship, as Frahm notes, still struggles to legitimize the medium. On the other hand, numerous comics artists, such as Art Spiegelman, Robert Crumb, Peter Bagge, and others, have embraced comics' purported deficiencies, including crudeness, simplicity, and vulgarity, as a badge of pride to distinguish comics from an overly serious, self-important art world.

In this context, Mahler's *Alte Meister* enters into the debate over high and low art from two directions: from Reger's vigorous resistance to the veneration of high art, and from Mahler's own creation of a comic (traditionally a low artwork) that questions the persistent existence of the high/ low distinction. In the first case, Mahler adopts strategies and attitudes espoused by Reger to visualize, but also to undermine the latter's critical aesthetics. This leads to an intermingling of both perspectives, with Mahler appearing to sanction Reger's theories in one panel, and to refute them in the next. In the second case, Mahler employs the tools of caricature, fragmentation, obscuration, and repetition, making effective use of the visual dimension unavailable to Bernhard. Indeed, Mahler's *Alte Meister* functions first and foremost as a visual response to, and interpretation of Bernhard's text.[10] In his adaptation, Mahler opted to use only text taken directly from Bernhard's novel. As a result, the comic is shaped by the selection and arrangement of textual material, but even more so by the addition of visual information. The interaction of text and image in Mahler's comic is of further importance given that Bernhard's novel contains virtually no visual description. As Thomas Zaunschirm notes, "Contrary to the book's title and setting, 'visual' art is dealt with only peripherally" (Entgegen dem Buchtitel und dem Ort des Geschehens wird 'bildende' Kunst nur am Rande behandelt; 68). In contrast to the novel, where Bernhard almost never describes artworks or mentions them by name, Mahler makes full use of the comic's setting, using the *Kunsthistorisches Museum*'s vast collection as a reservoir of works to be manipulated, distorted, and caricatured.

CARICATURE

Reger's aesthetics relies on a critical viewing eye that pierces below the supposedly beautiful, masterful surface of art to the underlying imperfection of human creation. For Reger, this requires the use of caricature to reduce an overwhelmingly beautiful image to a laughable version with which the viewer can more easily cope: "We can only stand a great, important picture if we have turned it into a caricature" (Mahler 2011, 73; Bernhard 57). Caricature relies on exaggerating a particular detail to grotesque proportions, passing the point of common ugliness to achieve humor or to advance critique. As David Carrier explains: "Caricature is inherently an art of exaggeration. The Neoplatonic tradition involves creating ideal beauty, finding that perfection realized only imperfectly in actual individuals; caricature (and the comic) involves deformation" (16). Mahler's drawing style, which is not unique to *Alte Meister* (his published works are all marked by a lack of extraneous ornamentation and the use of characteristic meatball and stick figures) combines this deformation with a stark simplification of visual details. As a result, his style is well suited to Reger's program of caricature and the reduction of artworks to a single "serious flaw" (Mahler 2011, 131; Bernhard 151).

Mahler's reproductions of famous works of art in *Alte Meister* straddle the line between ugly and comical. These images rely on the reader's willingness to go along with Reger's theoretical, and Mahler's visual degradation of art to convey the absurdity of human limitations. In reproducing works from the museum, Mahler plays with the proportions of the original images—inflating, elongating, and flattening figures—and thus eradicates any possibility of venerating the artworks he depicts. In one panel, Tintoretto's *Bathing Susanna* (ca. 1555/56) takes on Mahler's typical meatball shape, but inflated to a degree that she fills nearly the entire panel (70). On another page, Mahler gives Peter Paul Rubens's *Helene Fourment* (ca. 1636/38) a sort of Picasso treatment, emphasizing the misalignment of her breasts and the creases on her skin (15). In a later reproduction, Rubens's figure appears as hardly more than an amorphous blob (144). The most striking example of grotesque caricature is a double-page spread depicting the right wing of the Master of the Guild of St. George's triptych *Charles V and his Sisters as Children* (1502), in which Mahler chooses to focus on the detail of a young girl's lips (figure 10.1). The first image displays the lips as two tight rows of vertical brush strokes, complementing the wrinkles on the rest of the face. The second image is a close-up of the face, showing the lips as a disturbingly bloated hole, highlighted yellow, instilling in the viewer the "very bad taste" in the mouth that Reger claims on the same page results from a deeper analysis of any artwork (Mahler 2011, 68–69; Bernhard 32). Viewed against the source painting, Mahler's version transforms a child's face into something monstrous and wizened; even the child's doll acquires lumps that appear tumorous. The sight of such imperfections can result in disgust, but also in relief that the beautiful image is as flawed as the human who painted it. By reducing these artworks to caricature with his exaggerated style, Mahler makes the sublime laughable, and thus bearable to the viewer in conformation with Reger's aesthetics.

The development of caricature within Reger's aesthetic program is connected not only to his fear of perfection and wholeness, but also to his hatred of veneration (*Bewunderung*), which treats its object as sacrosanct and thus unapproachable in its perfection. The act of venerating art is

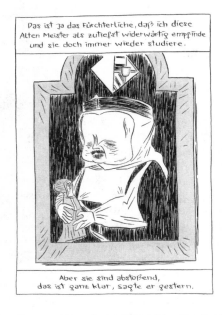

Figure 10.1.   Scene from *Alte Meister* by Nicolas Mahler. Nicolas Mahler. *Alte Meister*. Berlin: Suhrkamp, 2011. 68–69.

anathema to Reger, because it stands in direct opposition to his critical mind-set. Caricature, on the other hand, refuses to take its object seriously, using deformation to render the sacred ridiculous. In Mahler's comic, this includes exaggerated depictions, especially of religious imagery to underscore the gap between veneration and Reger's cynical criticism. Mahler's meatball figures are particularly effective at breaking down the veneer of holy authority. In one scene, Mahler depicts the banal Irrsigler—long-time usher in the *Kunsthistorisches Museum*, as well as Reger's devotee and mouthpiece—nose to nose with the pope, an equally squat and rotund figure dwarfed by an ornate cross more than four times his height. In these proportions, the pope is revealed to be "just as helpless and grotesque a person as anyone else" (Mahler 2011, 49; Bernhard 19). Similarly, Mahler's reproduction of Lucas Cranach the Elder's *Paradise* (1530) removes any possibility of adoration by sending a meatball-shaped angel with a comically oversized sword to expel Adam and Eve from the Garden of Eden (61). Angels, saints, and even the body of Jesus Christ receive caricaturistic treatments in the comic.

These works—and Mahler's versions of them—support Reger's claim that the old masters, far from creating art of genuine insight or faith, only ever produced "state art" (Mahler 2011, 64; Bernhard 29), or art co-opted and corrupted by the religious and political interests of those in power. In the case of the *Kunsthistorisches Museum*, this refers specifically to the

Habsburg dynasty and its conservative Catholic mind-set. In keeping
with Reger's dual critique of religion and political authority, Mahler lam-
poons not only religious paintings, but also those representing the aristocratic elite. The old masters were in Reger's view nothing more than
hypocritical shills for their Catholic patrons: "Religiously mendacious
assistant decorators of the European Catholic rulers, that is what these
old masters are, nothing else . . ." (Mahler 2011, 63; Bernhard 30–31). As
Mahler's scenes follow Irrsigler on his rounds through the museum, he
takes the viewer past distorted busts and enormous portraits of emperors
and dukes. Mahler exaggerates the ridiculousness of the baroque coif-
fures in Velazquez's *Portrait of the Infanta Maria Theresa* (ca. 1652/53) and
Rubens's *Infanta Isabella Clara Eugenia* (ca. 1620), making the portraits'
subjects resemble clowns more than royalty (64, 67). There is no grandeur
left in these paintings once Mahler has interpreted them with his pen.
This is evident in a panel where the sphere-like Irrsigler passes indiffer-
ently by an aristocratic portrait more than eight times his height (138).
The original painting, Hyacinthe Rigaud's *Duke Philipp Ludwig Wenzel
von Sinzendorf* (1728), is only six feet tall. In the comic, the duke in question is portrayed as an oversized wig with rudimentary facial features
atop a corpulent body draped in robes, with no air of regality. Mahler
uses the enlarged Rigaud as an illustration of the empty pomp exemplified by such works of "state art" that fail to impress and command,
even as they tower over a tiny Irrsigler. Through the use of caricature,
Mahler demonstrates that nothing is sacred in his comic and undermines
every attempt at seriousness or reverence in his absurd drawings. In
addition to caricature, he also adopts the use of fragmentation to render
Reger's critiques of perfection and veneration visually.

FRAGMENTATION

In Reger's view, the fragment is preferable to the whole because its in-
completeness is comforting to the flawed human individual. Fragmentation, like caricature, is a method of dismantling monumental, seemingly
perfect works of art into manageable pieces that are pleasing in isolation.
The details of an artwork can be either positive or negative, effectively
outshining the whole in the former case or destroying an otherwise perfect composition in the latter. According to Reger, even the old masters
were only ever capable of moments of perfection that stand in contrast to
complete failures elsewhere in their compositions:

> Quite apart from the fact that of all these so-called old masters each one
> invariably only painted some detail of his pictures with real genius, not
> one of them painted a one-hundred-per-cent picture of genius, not one
> of those so-called old masters ever succeeded in doing that; either they

failed with the chin or with the knee or with the eyelids. (Mahler 2011,
56–57; Bernhard 152)

To illustrate his protagonist's claim, Mahler employs both isolation and
fragmentation of details in his depictions of famous artworks to highlight
the flaws—and moments of genius—that Reger identifies. Mahler's reproduction of Titian's *Madonna of the Cherries* (ca. 1516/18) exemplifies the
combination of isolated genius with multiple failures (figure 10.2). The
left-hand page of a two-page spread depicts a small pile of cherries and a
few leaves—the exceptional detail—alone in an otherwise blank panel.
On the right-hand page is a more complete reproduction of Titian's painting, with Reger's words, enclosed in text boxes, effacing the elements of
the composition mentioned as failures, namely, the chin, knee, and eyelids (56–57). Mahler's depictions of fragmentation fill a gap left in the
novel, where Reger's theory is never shown in application: "A detailed
strategy on Reger's part, of just how the process of fragmentation mani-
fests itself in a concrete example is never mentioned in the text, just as the
appearance or the substantial composition of works is never mentioned"
(Eine detaillierte Herangehensweise Regers, wie sich der Prozess der
Fragmentmachung denn nun an einem konkreten Beispiel manifestiert,
wird im Text gänzlich verschwiegen, wie auch das Aussehen oder die
inhaltlichen Zusammensetzungen der Werke selbst verschwiegen werd-
en; Werkmann 32). Through his renderings, Mahler deconstructs numerous paintings from the *Kunsthistorisches Museum*'s collection in order to
direct the viewer's focus to details that Reger cites as positive or negative.
Mahler's comic simultaneously plays with the positive valuation of the
fragment and the negative valuation of failed details in larger compositions.

In one instance, Mahler presents the Virgin Mary's halo in the Master
of the Bambino Vispo's *Mary with Child* (ca. 1430/40) as a pleasing fragment in isolation, contrasted with the full painting on the opposing page
underneath Reger's words: "the whole and the complete and perfect are
basically abhorrent to us" (Mahler 2011, 44–45; Bernhard 18). Conversely,
the hands in Veronese's *Susanna and the Elders* (ca. 1585) are highlighted
in a blank panel to show their disfigurement (58). In this way, Mahler
shows the isolated detail to be of greater importance in Reger's aesthetics
than the completed whole, whether as the limited expression of genius or
as the fatal flaw, though each plays to the observer's supposed discomfort with wholeness. Yet even as Mahler appears to be affirming Reger's
claim that moments of perfection exist in art, and can be isolated as
pleasing fragments, his drawings remain caricatures. While the comic
purports to depict exceptional details, Mahler actually continues to
undermine the impulse to venerate art, at the level of the whole as well as
of the fragment. In Mahler's version, the "successful" details are as crude
and grotesque as the failures; every image is painted with the same

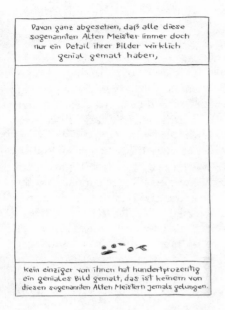

Figure 10.2.   Scene from *Alte Meister* by Nicolas Mahler. Nicolas Mahler. *Alte Meister*. Berlin: Suhrkamp, 2011. 56–57.

brush, so to speak. Mahler's approach thus challenges Reger's conviction that art can ever be perfect, even as an isolated fragment. Caricature and fragmentation undermine the veneration of artworks by making them laughable and destroying their compositional integrity.

OBSCURATION

Another strategy against veneration in Mahler's comic is obscuration, used here to mean the partial concealment or effacement of artworks. Mahler makes frequent use of obscuration as a means of defying the viewer's connection to, and identification with works of art, as well as to further destroy the aura of individual artworks. Obscuration differs from fragmentation in that it does not focus the viewer on a particular detail, whether positive or negative; and the intent is not to reduce an artwork to something ridiculous or to reveal a moment of excellence. Instead, obscuration refuses to let the artwork be considered as a whole. The backdrop of Mahler's comic is the opulent interior space of the *Kunsthistorisches Museum*, and within this setting artworks are featured both as background props and as the focus of entire panels. In the absence of an intricate and active plot, Mahler constructs his narrative from a progression of these artworks in dialogue with Reger's aesthetic monologues.

Rather than allowing these images to be viewed in full, though, Mahler overlays Reger's thoughts on depicted paintings to disrupt their reception. The result is an imposition of imperfection and incompletion onto a perceived complete and perfect masterwork.

Mahler employs this strategy most often using the recurring scene of Reger viewing Tintoretto's *Portrait of a White-Bearded Man*. Reger's monologues are then placed in text boxes at the top and bottom of each panel, as well as directly in front of the white-bearded man's face. Reger describes the Bordone Room, where the Tintoretto painting is displayed, as the ideal space for the development of his own thoughts, and Mahler uses the space as a container for those thoughts. By positioning text over the face of the white-bearded man, Mahler projects Reger's ideas into the object of his contemplation. When text obscures the painting, however, it interrupts the viewer's ability to contemplate the *Portrait of a White-Bearded Man* in Reger's stead. The effect of this obscuration is a challenge to Reger's conviction that Tintoretto's work is a painting worthy of constant study—indeed the only painting in the *Kunsthistorisches Museum* to withstand his criticism. Simultaneously, the scene depicts a veneration of Reger's own words, indicating that the sound of his own voice is more precious to him than the prized Tintoretto.

While the texts Mahler chooses to cover the figure's face are not always directly critical of art, there are scenes where the juxtaposition between word and image explicitly undermines Reger's continued appreciation of the *White-Bearded Man*. In one scene, the narrator recalls his conversation with Reger from the previous day. The narrator is shown observing himself sitting in the Bordone Room, as Reger makes the damning pronouncement, "This art is pitiful, no less" (Mahler 2011, 55; Bernhard 29). This statement is directed at the art surrounding Reger in the *Kunsthistorisches Museum*, but carries over to the concept of art in general. Mahler encloses Reger's declaration in a word balloon that covers the *Portrait of a White-Bearded Man*, effectively including Tintoretto's painting among the other wretched art in the museum and at large. In this way, Mahler reveals the romantic flaw in Reger's aesthetics, which acknowledges a fatal mistake in all artworks *except* for the *White-Bearded Man*. Mahler's view admits no such exceptions, insisting rather on the imperfection of all art.

Beyond the *Portrait of a White-Bearded Man*, Mahler uses obscuration to disfigure a number of artworks considered by the cultural world as masterpieces, further complementing his techniques of isolation and fragmentation. As mentioned above, Mahler's fragmentation of artworks is often paired with text boxes obscuring details of the paintings described by Reger as flaws. In addition, Mahler occasionally inserts critical commentary into the picture plane in the form of banners. These scroll-like text boxes incorporate Reger's iconoclastic words into religious paintings, which can be viewed, on the one hand, as Reger skewering the hypocrisy of these paintings within the paintings themselves, and on the other hand, as Mahler mocking Reger by emphasizing the sanctimonious nature of Reger's own aesthetics. In two separate instances, Mahler inserts the word "falsehood" (*Verlogenheit*), which questions the sincerity of the religious images accompanied by the text (60, 133). Within a reproduction of Jan Gossaert's *Saint Luke Painting the Madonna* (ca. 1520), Mahler interweaves Reger's claim that "These pictures are full of lies and falsehoods and full of hypocrisy and self-deception, there is nothing else in them" (Mahler 2011, 133; Bernhard 151). The painting depicts the Madonna floating with an infant Jesus as he is crowned by a host of putti. Juxtaposed with the painting, the quote reinforces Reger's assertion that generations of old masters—specifically those displayed in the *Kunsthistorisches Museum*—created art not out of a desire to seek the truth, but rather as hired mouthpieces for the powerful interests of the aristocracy and the Catholic Church. Mahler's use of banners embeds Reger's quote within the painting so seamlessly that it appears to be a part of the original composition.

When read as an integral part of the artwork, then, the statement seems to negate itself, as this image, too, would include nothing but falsehood. When the reader zooms out to consider the full panel, however, Reger's quote indicates that Mahler's entire comic (as a collection of pictures) is also full of lies. Within the context of Mahler's project, this statement should be read not as an indictment of the comic, but a tongue-in-cheek moment of self-reflexivity. While Reger presents his theories with the weight of absolute truth, Mahler questions the existence of truth in images. His comic is a satire of satire, subtly but relentlessly undermining any attempt to make absolute pronouncements about art or life. Since Mahler's aim is not to reveal or mediate truth, Reger's accusation has no real force but to emphasize the absurdity of his dogmatism. Indeed, as Reger has established, all human endeavor is imperfect; everything created by humans—and by extension all theories posited by humans—is by nature flawed. In thought as in art, Mahler takes Reger's theories a step further and embraces the imperfection of his own work.

REPETITION

Obscuration responds to claims of perfection by concealing and interrupting the wholeness of an artwork. By contrast, repetition, a technique of central importance for the medium of comics, negates perfection by making the artwork unremarkable as it ceases to be one of a kind.[11] The use of similar or identical images in comics creates continuity between panels, providing the reader with the visual information necessary to recognize characters and settings in a sequential narrative. As opposed to film and drama, where the faces and bodies of actors are generally con-

stant from shot to shot or scene to scene, comics must reproduce characters in each new panel where the characters are featured. The artist may
also need to redraw scenery in successive panels in order to maintain a
consistent setting. While repetition is an essential element for comics in
general, Mahler's use of the technique goes beyond the conventions of
the medium to undermine the conception of art as exceptional and original. In Walter Benjamin's seminal essay, "The Work of Art in the Age of
its Mechanical Reproduction" (1936), the singularity of an artwork is key
to its identity as art. The act of reproduction, according to Benjamin,
destroys the aura of the unique artistic object. The refutation of originality, or at least of the sacrosanct aura associated with it, is programmatic
for Mahler's version of *Alte Meister*. There are two distinct types of repetition to explore in Mahler's comic, namely, the repeated illustration of
specific images and figures, and the reproduction of artworks existing
outside the comic itself. This begins with Mahler's depiction of the narrative's setting: the museum.

The museum is a temple to art, resting on the assumption that the
works it contains are of exceeding aesthetic or cultural value, whether
that value is rooted in beauty, craftsmanship, sublimity, or some other
criterion. Reger rejects the assertion that art has value beyond its function
of providing humanity with the faint hope that transcendent perfection
may exist, thus undermining the museum's foundational principle. In his
graphic novel, Mahler also undermines the museum and the high art for
which it stands, beginning with his use of the museum as a design concept. The bulk of the comic is composed of single-panel pages, with text
boxes across the top and bottom of each panel. This creates a framed
image on each page, giving the reader the impression that the entire
comic is a sequential picture gallery. For extended stretches, the comic
actually does become a picture gallery, as successive frames are filled
only with Mahler's reproductions of paintings from the *Kunsthistorisches
Museum*'s collection. As shown, these reproductions intentionally deform
the originals on which they are modeled, whether by means of caricature,
fragmentation, or obscuration. While these reproductions attack the quality of the museum's collection, Mahler's extensive use of repetition
throughout the comic works against the understanding of the museum as
a repository of unique and exceptional works.

In comics, the differences in visual depictions between panels lead the
reader to assume and re-create a cause-and-effect relationship from one
panel to the next that moves the narrative forward.[12] In Mahler's comics,
repetition with only slight differences is often used to comedic effect as a
reflection of life's absurd monotony. Lino Wirag describes the use of
"especially agonizing repetitions of identical framing, which are often
only minimally varied, or not at all" (besonders quälende Repetitionen
immergleicher Bildeinstellungen, die oft nur minimal — oder gleich gar
nicht — variiert werden; 44), as characteristic of Mahler's work. In *Alte*

Meister, this is most evident in the Bordone Room scene, which Mahler re-creates—with slight to significant variations—thirty-three times. In this scene, Mahler depicts Reger seated in front of the Tintoretto, as viewed from behind. By framing Reger from behind, Mahler projects the reader into the Bordone Room, where the reader views Reger, who in turn views the Tintoretto. As Reger contemplates the *White-Bearded Man*, we contemplate Reger. This scene provides a template that Mahler manipulates to illustrate Reger's various statements while also emphasizing the unchanging nature of his life's routines in the *Kunsthistorisches Museum*. While Reger's thoughts recycle in various permutations, his body remains rooted to the bench in the Bordone Room. The stasis of Mahler's scenes reveals the false dynamism of Reger's theories, which are actually as monotonous and repetitive as his thirty-year habit of visiting the museum. Reger eventually comes to realize that his life is far from exceptional, regardless of how superior he has considered himself to be: "The things we think and the things we say, believing that we are competent and yet we are not, *that is the comedy*, and when we ask *how is it all to continue? that is the tragedy . . .*" (Mahler 2011, 138–39; Bernhard 154, emphasis in original). He is forced to concede that his pretension of insight and expertise is a denial of the helpless inscrutability of human life. Mahler establishes this fact at the outset with visual staging that presents Reger as an unmoving lump in a museum rendered banal by its monotony.

It is also significant that Mahler does not simply copy these images, but rather draws the scene anew, each time presenting a different imperfect reproduction. Monika Schmitz-Emans sees this as a confluence of Bernhard's technique of textual repetition—where ideas and phrases are constantly recycled with slight alterations—and the sequential nature of the comics medium. Bernhard's repetitive style, according to Schmitz-Emans, indicates that there can be no absolute or final statement on a subject. Rather, the imperfection and inexhaustibility of expression drives textual production: "Imperfection is the driving factor behind continuing to speak and write" (Unvollkommenheit ist der Motor dafür, dass es weiter geht mit dem Sprechen und Schreiben; 2015, 27). Even in the comic's highly abridged version of the novel's text, Mahler makes Reger's repetitive thought processes evident in the concentration of passages chosen to exemplify his aesthetic criticism.[13] On the visual level, Mahler's flawed reproductions reinforce the imperfection of the written text, while creating a sequence from a static array of nearly indistinguishable images: "The 'imperfect' drawing thus motivates production, leads to a sequence — and in this respect does the comic's groundwork" (Die 'unvollkommene' Zeichnung motiviert also die Produktion, führt zur Sequenz — und arbeitet dem Comic insofern zu; (Schmitz-Emans 2015, 27). Mahler's imperfect drawings therefore contribute not only to the effect of his caricatures, but also to the creation of narrative progression through

subtle variations on the same image. The extreme reduction of these variations additionally thematizes the overriding monotony of the comic's
(and by virtue of adaptation, the novel's) plot.

Beyond contributing to the monotony of the comic, Mahler's decision
to re-create each image by hand further dismantles the aura of originality
and authority of the source material, specifically of the Tintoretto painting: in each repetition of the Bordone Room scene, Mahler not only reproduces Reger, but also the *Portrait of a White-Bearded Man*. Reproductions
are frequently judged by their faithfulness to a perceived original, where
a successful reproduction would be seen to most closely resemble that
original. By refusing to duplicate the painting exactly, Mahler ceases to
use visual fidelity as the standard for a successful reproduction.[14] And
though hand-drawn reproductions across panels are common in comics
production, the persistent imperfection and lack of defining detail take
on greater meaning within the context of this particular work. Mahler's
skewed versions of the *Portrait of a White-Bearded Man* never try to re-
create a perfect original, and each new reproduction weakens Reger's
claim of the painting's exceptionality by refusing to take either the claim
or the painting itself seriously. While Reger asserts that the Tintoretto
painting is the only artwork able to endure his devastating criticism,
Mahler's portrayal challenges that assertion, reducing it to just another
imperfect painting among many.

From the beginning, Mahler challenges Reger's veneration of the *Portrait of a White-Bearded Man*. In the left-hand panel of a two-page spread,
Mahler introduces the key elements for the Bordone Room scenes: the
centrally located painting with its illegible identification plaque, the velvet rope separating patrons from the painting itself, and Reger seated
squarely on a low, plush bench (figure 10.3). This panel functions like a
portrait in and of itself—a static image devoid of word balloons or any
intrusive text—and establishes the baseline for the scenes that recur
throughout the comic.[15] In the same moment that the Tintoretto painting
is enshrined prominently as the object of Reger's obsession, Mahler
underscores the painting's relative insignificance using Reger's own
words in a heading to the portrait-like panel: "As you know, I do not
come to the Bordone Room for Bordone, indeed not even for Tintoretto . . ." (Mahler 2011, 30; Bernhard 16). The quote continues in the right-
hand panel to explain Reger's actual interest in the Bordone Room: the
bench and the room's climate, both ideally conducive to Reger's thought
processes. As the quote reveals the painting's irrelevance, Mahler removes it entirely from the scene. What remains is an empty bench, the
velvet rope, and a text box where the painting used to hang. From the
outset, Mahler establishes a counter-narrative to Reger's insistence on the
exceptional quality and importance of Tintoretto's painting. In the comic,
Mahler disfigures, conceals, erases, replaces, and reduces the painting to
a sequence of flawed images reproduced until no one true Tintoretto

remains. Mahler thus achieves with the *Kunsthistorisches Museum* and the *Portrait of a White-Bearded Man* what Reger claims we must all do to destroy our idols: we must personally and physically confront them to reveal their hopeless inadequacy as "a tasteless concoction" (Mahler 2011, 48; Bernhard 19).

CONCLUSION

Throughout Mahler's *Alte Meister*, it is difficult to discern where Reger's criticism ends and Mahler's begins. This essay argues for a reading of Mahler's comic as an adoption of Reger's skepticism for the purpose of leveling the artistic playing field for comics. It is no coincidence that in his adaptation, Mahler does away with Bernhard's narrator, the independent scholar Atzbacher, and replaces him with the stick figure version of himself. Although Mahler never names the narrating figure, he uses the same avatar as in his autobiographical comics. In the comic, Mahler becomes Reger's compatriot and mouthpiece, but unlike Atzbacher, Mahler is willing to take Reger's nihilistic artistic viewpoint to its necessary conclusion: all art, as a human construction, is imperfect. There is no such thing as high and low art, only individual artistic expression. In his autobiographical works—especially in the volumes *Kunsttheorie versus Frau*

Figure 10.3.   Scene from *Alte Meister* by Nicolas Mahler. Nicolas Mahler. *Alte Meister*. Berlin: Suhrkamp, 2011. 30–31.

Goldgruber (*Art Theory versus Mrs. Goldgruber*, 2003) and *Franz Kafkas non-stop Lachmaschine* (*Franz Kafka's Nonstop Laugh Machine*, 2014)—Mahler has reflected on challenges to his work from the established art and litera-ture worlds, as well as the skeptical treatment of comics by a public of cultural dilettantes, under-informed about the medium and overly reliant on a binary conception of art.

In *Kunsttheorie versus Frau Goldgruber*,[16] Mahler is faced with the task of convincing his tax adviser that his comics are art, not commercial graphics, and that he should therefore be designated an artist by the state for tax purposes. After viewing Mahler's comics, the disinterested Frau Goldgruber remarks: "Well, they aren't really proper comics . . . because, when you hear 'COMICS', you think about the Smurfs and Mickey Mouse . . . but those look much different than Mr. Mahler's . . . You can't earn anything with that kind of thing anyway . . . . Well, somehow or other that will be 'art.'" (So richtige Comics sind das ja nicht . . . weil wenn man 'COMICS' hört, denkt man ja an die Schlümpfe und Micky Maus . . . aber die schaun schon anders aus wie die vom Hrn. Mahler . . . Mit so was kann man eh nix verdienen [. . .]. Na das wird schon irgend-wie 'Kunst' sein; Mahler 2007, 17–18). In *Franz Kafkas nonstop Lachmas-chine*, Mahler's artistic validity is again called into question, this time by representatives of the avant-garde art set and literary scholars. Each side is stuck firmly in its own medium, and complains about the lack of so-phistication of Mahler's visual art and writing, respectively, which leads Mahler to accuse the artist of "a lack of narrative intelligence" (mangeln-de narrative Intelligenz) and the literary scholar of "a lack of visual intel-ligence" (mangelnde visuelle Intelligenz; Mahler 2007, 55). Mahler re-sponds to these two sides with a problematic argument employed by comics proponents: "We can clearly see, then, that comics are *superior* to art *and* literature, because they represent a complex combination of word and image, and cannot be reduced to one or the other" (Wir sehen also deutlich, dass Comics der Kunst *und* der Literatur *überlegen* sind, weil sie eine komplexe Verbindung von Wort und Bild darstellen und nicht auf eines von beiden reduziert werden dürfen; Mahler 2007, 56). Taken out of context, this statement reads like a hypocritical declaration that, where the artist and the literary scholar were ignorant for declaring their respec-tive media superior, simple addition can show that comics are truly superior. Mahler's work in general is far too self-deprecating for this statement to be taken at face value, and he even questions the assertion a few pages later. Mahler's intention seems much more to be the break-down of artificial barriers between high and low culture, conveying legit-imacy on all forms of artistic expression, but especially on comics. The adaptation of *Alte Meister* is a strong and potentially militant expression of this intention.

Thomas Bernhard's novel presents a damning critique of art and its capabilities, but it nonetheless includes a caveat about art's ultimate importance for humanity. The hope of the possibility of perfection is Reger's defense against existential despair. The imperfection of art reassures us that our own imperfections are natural, while the belief that there might be something greater impels artists to pursue an ultimately unattainable perfection. Nicolas Mahler's comic seems to say instead that imperfection is no reason to despair. Through the use of caricature, fragmentation, obscuration, and repetition, he actively challenges the assumption that perfection is desirable and instead suggests that artists and critics take themselves and their objects too seriously, drawing artificial boundaries between the supposedly beautiful and ugly. In his adaptation of *Alte Meister*, Mahler demonstrates that the ugly can be beautiful just as the beautiful can be ugly, making these categories irrelevant to the individual production or appreciation of art. By giving purposefully crude shape to the critiques of an iconoclastic curmudgeon, Mahler's comic opens the door to a broader discussion about the aesthetic potential of comics and a reevaluation of the nature of art.

NOTES

1. Suhrkamp's graphic novel offerings primarily comprise literary adaptations (Olivia Vieweg's *Huck Finn* [Mark Twain; 2013], Ulli Lust's *Flughunde* [*The Karnau Tapes*, Marcel Beyer; 2013], Ulf K.'s *Geschichten vom Herrn Keuner* [*Stories of Mr. Keuner*, Bertolt Brecht; 2014], etc.), while works such as Volker Reiche's autobiographical *Kiesgrubennacht* (*Gravel Pit Night*, 2013) and Olivia Vieweg's coming-of-age story *Schwere See, mein Herz* (*Heavy Sea, My Heart*, 2015) have expanded the scope of the program. The increasing inclusion of non-adaptive comics is a signal that Suhrkamp has accepted comics as a medium capable of producing exemplary works without reference to canonical texts. Mahler is by far the most well-represented artist in Suhrkamp's graphic novel line, with six comics, the majority being literary adaptations: *Alte Meister* (2011), *Der Mann ohne Eigenschaften* (*The Man Without Qualities*, Robert Musil; 2013), *Alice in Sussex* (Lewis Carroll and H. C. Artmann; 2013), *Der Weltverbesserer* (*The World-Fixer*, Thomas Bernhard; 2014), *Lulu und das schwarze Quadrat* (*Lulu and the Black Square*, Frank Wedekind; 2014), *Partyspaß mit Kant* (*Party Fun with Kant*; 2015).
2. Mahler's text is taken directly from Bernhard's novel, so I have used Ewald Osers's translation of the novel to provide quoted passages in English. In order to maintain clarity about where individual passages occur in Mahler's comic, I include dual citations: first the page number in Mahler's comic, followed after a semicolon by the passage's location in Osers's translation.
3. Please see Shiner (130–51) and Hammermeister (23, 63–64, 91–95, 112–13) for further discussion.
4. All translations from the German are mine, with the exception of Osers's translation of *Old Masters*.
5. Osers translates *Bewunderung* alternately as "admiration" and "veneration." In my text, I have opted for the latter as a stronger term that evokes the connotation of religious devotion.
6. All dates for paintings were taken from the *Kunsthistorisches Museum*'s image database (*Bilddatenbank*).
7. Ted Cohen accepts in his essay "High and Low Art, and High and Low Audiences" that high and low art exist, along with their attendant audiences, but claims that there are no solid philosophical or aesthetic criteria for the division: "What makes the high art high? Is it that its appeal is mostly to high audiences? Then what makes

the audience high? That its taste is for high art? Well, of course, that makes a *circle*" (142, emphasis in original). In *What Good are the Arts?*, John Carey proposes that the only acceptable definition of art is a purely subjective one ("A work of art is anything that anyone has ever considered a work of art, though it may be a work of art only for that one person" [29]), and further that there "are no rational grounds" for assuming the superiority of "high" art over mass/popular art (32). Noël Carroll admits to a distinction between mass art and avant-garde art in *A Philosophy of Mass Art*, but he rejects the notion that one category is inherently better than the other.

8. There is a widespread tendency to align comics with either art or literature as a means of lending the medium greater legitimacy (Hatfield xi-xii). This often involves the use of terms linking comics to other media (graphic *novel*, graphic *literature*, sequential *art*; Frahm 35) or the creation of a genealogy that traces comics' development from exceptional works in other media (the Bayeux Tapestry, Trajan's column, the Lascaux cave paintings, etc.), in an effort to demonstrate a rich history beyond the comic strips of the late nineteenth century (Wolk 29; Ditschke et al. 15).

9. The *Comic-Manifesto*, delivered and signed by over 70 German artists, scholars, and publishers at the *Internationales Literaturfestival Berlin* on September 2, 2013, is an important recent attempt to make the case for comics' status as art, specifically within German-speaking Europe. The signatories declared that comics are art, and further: "No serious critic is in doubt today about the fact that the comic is an independent form of art that has earned its place on equal terms alongside literature, theatre, film or opera" ("Comic-Manifesto").

10. There has been much debate about the nature of comics, and whether it is essentially a hybrid form of literature and visual art, of text and image. Proponents of the hybrid view include David Kunzle (2), Aaron Meskin (234), Monika Schmitz-Emans (2012, 8), Bernd Dolle-Weinkauff (14–15), and Ole Frahm (10), while Scott McCloud (92) and Thierry Groensteen (3, 12, 17) prefer a more image-centered concept. Further, scholars and creators have argued about the primacy of the visual over the textual mode, and vice versa. Kunzle notably states that "a preponderance of image over text" is constitutive for the comics medium (2). Bill Blackbeard also suggests that a comic should have "generally minimal narrative text" (41), while Bart Beaty follows Groensteen (14–15) in pointing out numerous works considered comics that are not even hybrid in form: "Hundreds of examples of text-free comics exist— and a much smaller number of image-free as well—each of which demonstrates the commonsensical observation that hybridity is not necessary in the comics form" (Beaty 20). Undoubtedly, Mahler's comic makes use of both text and image, and in staying so close to Bernhard's text, each mode is essential to the work. However, I argue that the visual dimension is of primary importance to this particular adaptation—without going so far as to claim that this need always be the case in comics.

11. Schmitz-Emans refers to repetition (*Wiederholung*) as "a defining structural pattern of comics" (ein den Comic prägendes Strukturmuster; 2015, 41).

12. Scott McCloud has established this process, which he terms "closure," as essential to the creation and reception of comics (McCloud 60–93).

13. For example: ". . . the whole and complete and perfect are basically abhorrent to us." (Mahler 2011, 45; Bernhard 18); "We cannot endure the whole or the perfect" (Mahler 2011, 47; Bernhard 19); "Only when, time and again, we have discovered that there is no such thing as the whole or the perfect are we able to live on" (Mahler 2011, 52; Bernhard 19).

14. There are many comics that reproduce famous works of art, and each artist approaches the task differently. Some incorporate actual photographs of paintings, which may blend with the rest of the comic or stand out starkly in contrast to the artist's style (e.g., Bernar Yslaire and Jean-Claude Carrière's *The Sky Over the Louvre*, Nicolas de Crécy's *Glacial Period*, Sascha Hommer's *Im Museum* [*In the Museum*], etc.). Others attempt to imitate as closely as possible the style of the reproduced work, striving for the aforementioned fidelity to the original (e.g., Steffen Kverneland's *Munch*, Xavier Coste's *Egon Schiele*, Brecht Vandenbroucke's *White Cube*, etc.). Then

there are artists who reinterpret artworks in their own style, whether to conform to the rest of the comic, as a form of parody, or as an homage (e.g., Barbara Stok's *Vincent*, Hendrik Dorgathen's *Spacedog*, Lars Fiske's *Merz*, and Gerhard Seyfried's *Wo soll das alles enden? [Where Will It All End?]*, etc.). In *Alte Meister*, Mahler belongs to this final category, and while he is not unique in abandoning visual fidelity in reproducing well-known artworks, his consistent and purposeful use of flawed reproductions is key to the project of his comic.

15. Gabriella Catalano points out this same phenomenon within Bernhard's novel, making Mahler's staging all the more appropriate: "It appears as though Reger—posing in front of the picture—becomes a picture himself. Atzbacher is the one who facilitates the transformation, as he contemplates Reger like a portrait" (Es hat den Anschein, als würde Reger—vor dem Bild posierend—selbst zu einem Bild. Atzbacher ist derjenige, der die Transformation vermittelt, da er Reger als ein Porträt betrachtet; 205).

16. See Vance Byrd's essay in this volume for an extensive treatment of *Kunsttheorie versus Frau Goldgruber*.

REFERENCES

Atzert, Stephan. "Von der Kunst als 'Überlebenskunst' zur Kunst des Lebens: Über Thomas Bernhards *Der Theatermacher* und *Alte Meister*." *seminar* 42.2 (2006): 155–70.

Beaty, Bart. *Comics versus Art*. Toronto: University of Toronto Press, 2012.

Benjamin, Walter. "Das Kunstwerk im Zeitalter seiner technischen Reproduzierbarkeit." *Illuminationen*. Frankfurt a.M.: Suhrkamp, 1977. 136–69.

Bernhard, Thomas. *Old Masters*. Trans. Ewald Osers. London: Quartet Books, 1989.

Blackbeard, Bill. "Mislabeled Books." *Funny World* 16 (1974): 41.

Carey, John. *What Good Are the Arts?* Oxford: Oxford University Press, 2006.

Carrier, David. *The Aesthetics of Comics*. University Park: Pennsylvania State University Press, 2000.

Carroll, Noël. *A Philosophy of Mass Art*. Oxford: Clarendon Press, 1998.

Catalano, Gabriella. "'Jedes Original ist ja eigentlich an sich schon eine Fälschung': Zu Thomas Bernhards *Alte Meister*." *Thomas Bernhard Jahrbuch 2007/2008*. Ed. Martin Huber et al. Vienna: Böhlau, 2009. 203–14.

Cohen, Ted. "High and Low Art, and High and Low Audiences." *Journal of Aesthetics and Art Criticism* 57.2 (1999): 137–43.

———. "High and Low Thinking about High and Low Art." *Journal of Aesthetics and Art Criticism* 51.2 (1993): 151–56.

"The Comic-Manifest: COMICS ARE ART." *Internationales Literaturfestival Berlin*. 2 September 2013. Web. 24 November 2015. www.literaturfestival.com/archiv/sonderprojekte/comic/manifest.

Ditschke, Stephan, Katerina Kroucheva, and Daniel Stein, eds. *Comics: Zur Geschichte und Theorie eines populärkulturellen Mediums*. Bielefeld: transcript, 2009.

Dolle-Weinkauff, Bernd. *Comics: Geschichte einer populären Literaturform in Deutschland seit 1945*. Weinheim: Beltz, 1990.

Dowden, Stephen. *Understanding Thomas Bernhard*. Columbia: University of South Carolina Press, 1991.

Frahm, Ole. *Die Sprache des Comics*. Hamburg: Philo Fine Arts, 2010.

Groensteen, Thierry. *The System of Comics*. Jackson: University of Mississippi Press, 2007.

Hammermeister, Kai. *The German Aesthetic Tradition*. Cambridge: Cambridge University Press, 2002.

Hatfield, Charles. *Alternative Comics: An Emerging Literature*. Jackson: University of Mississippi Press, 2005.

Kunsthistorisches Museum Wien Bilddatenbank. Kunsthistorisches Museum Wien, n.d. Web. 24 November 2015.

Kunzle, David. *The Early Comic Strip*. Berkeley: University of California Press, 1973.

Mahler, Nicolas. *Alte Meister*. Berlin: Suhrkamp, 2011.

———. *Franz Kafkas nonstop Lachmaschine*. Berlin: Reprodukt, 2014.

———. *Kunsttheorie versus Frau Goldgruber*. Berlin: Reprodukt, 2007.

McCloud, Scott. *Understanding Comics*. New York: HarperPerennial, 1994.

Meskin, Aaron. "Comics as Literature?" *British Journal of Aesthetics* 49.3 (2009): 219–39.

Naqvi, Fatima. "Of Dilettantes and Men of Taste: Thomas Bernhard's Pedagogical Project in *Alte Meister*." *Monatshefte* 96.2 (2004): 252–72.

Schmitz-Emans, Monika. *Literatur-Comics: Adaptationen und Transformationen der Weltliteratur*. Berlin: De Gruyter, 2012.

———. "Nicolas Mahlers Literaturcomics." *Graphisches Erzählen. Neue Perspektiven auf Literaturcomics*. Ed. Florian Trabert et al. Bielefeld: transcript, 2015. 19–42.

Shiner, Larry. *The Invention of Art*. Chicago: University of Chicago Press, 2001.

Werkmann, Björn. *Auslöschung, Fragmentierung und Projektion in Thomas Bernhards später Prosa*. Marburg: Tectum, 2011.

Wirag, Lino. "Die Fallsucht des Zwiebelmenschen: Drei Meditationen über Nicolas Mahler." *Kritische Ausgabe* 25 (2013): 42–46.

Wolk, Douglas. *Reading Comics: How Graphic Novels Work and What They Mean*. Cambridge: Da Capo Press, 2007.

Zaunschirm, Thomas. "Neues vom Holzfäller: Über Thomas Bernhards 'Alte Meister.'" *Parnass* 6 (1985): 66–71.

ELEVEN

Patterns of Memory and Self-Confrontation in Gerald Hartwig's *Chamäleon*

Lynn Marie Kutch

Following a May 2015 "performative reading" of excerpts from his largely autobiographical graphic novel *Chamäleon* (2013) at the Goethe Institut in Toronto, Austrian graphic novelist Gerald Hartwig faced some tough questioning. An American professor of German literature in the audience critiqued the novel's content, claiming that it consists of a series of unoriginal tropes.[1] Indeed, as the chronicle of a naïve yet ambitious artist who travels to Los Angeles in search of a film career (with experiences in the pornography industry, numerous sexual relationships, and financial loss), *Chamäleon* reintroduces the cliché of the wild artist's life. In a reading of comic autobiography, Yäel Schlick describes the potential of flattening life, art, self, and text into a single surface when placing those elements into the strictures of literature, a flattening that could certainly furnish or support cliché (42). Although the criticism from the post-reading exchange at the Goethe Institut focused exclusively on plot and failed to take the graphic aspect into account, it nonetheless raised some important critical questions about these risks of "flattening" life experiences into set parameters of a subgenre: here the autobiographical graphic novel. The first area of questioning concerns the coexistence of cliché and autobiography in a text that finds its inspiration in an artist's real-life events. The second considers the distinct potential of graphic texts for visually presenting the process of internal self-examination that often accompanies autobiographical writing. Finally, how does the graphic mode of presentation thus succeed or fail in recasting and reinterpreting clichés? By considering these questions and examining the text's visual patterns and thematic repetitions, this chapter argues that Hartwig absorbs clichés of popular art into his innovative artistic gestures.

In particular, the present reading analyzes selected samples in a series of nearly all-black pages found in *Chamäleon* that contrast the otherwise prevalent sepia tone, and that appear at various stages in the graphic novel. Hartwig uses these matte-background pages to present portraitures or caricatures of Jerry, the Americanized first name with which he refers to his protagonist Gerald Hartmann, the pseudonym that Hartwig uses throughout the novel. Recurring reference in the text to markers of the wild artist's existence—sex, drugs, and rock 'n' roll—contributes to what could in fact on the surface be regarded as a hackneyed formula. Reminiscent of the comics tradition of R. Crumb and the American underground comix scene and even the literary tradition of the Beat poets, however, Hartwig exploits and ultimately redefines these outwardly controversial clichés. As part of his autobiographical storytelling, Hartwig must necessarily render Jerry visually again and again against the backdrops that set the scenes for the artist's lifestyle, a requirement that elicits the "public privacy" or "affected privacy" parallel to the essential condition of Beat literary production, and which also centralizes arguably clichéd topics such as voyeuristic interest and the artist's identity crisis (Arthur 227, 229). Jerry's constant pursuit of the right filmic formula that will guarantee his success in the American movie industry does result in a relentless return to the same destructive and superficially clichéd patterns.

Hartwig often depicts the symptoms or side effects of this repetitive process in a very explicit visual manner; and Jerry explains the repetition this way: "Life goes in cycles but not necessarily in a forward moving spiral. Once again I happily disregard my own unpopular patterns" (Das Leben verläuft zyklisch, aber nicht unbedingt in einer Vorwärtsspirale. Ich verkenne wieder gerne meine eigenen ungeliebten Muster; 226).[2] The variations in style that Hartwig employs to mark Jerry's stations of development and discovery in his developmental process "indicate degrees of certainty and nuances of attitude in relation to what is being recounted" (Miller 123). This notion of varying attitudes and even certainty or uncertainty of recall that defines autobiographical writing relates to my reading of Hartwig's manipulation of cliché and autobiographical elements as part of the artist's process of retrospective self-interrogation and self-examination. These outwardly clichéd elements are embedded in techniques of representation that can be categorized into realistic or caricatured self-portrait, self-reflection through others, or self-reflection through aspects of his natural environment. When the artist envelops the clichés in these artistic techniques, a multiplicity of identity emerges: that of the aspiring filmmaker, that of the autobiographer, and that of the graphic novelist who prioritizes and foregrounds technique.

CLICHÉ AND AUTOBIOGRAPHY

Before I move to a close reading of the primary text, I would like to elaborate on the possibility of cliché within autobiography, and also its possible function, by briefly discussing descriptors of cliché in conjunction with chief characteristics of autobiography. In his influential book *From Cliché to Archetype* Marshall McLuhan defines cliché as a "normal" action or phrase used so often that readers become "anesthetized" to its effects (4). When used as a literary device, cliché can result in a disconnection between reader and text where the writer would most likely desire a connection. Relating this to autobiography, on the one hand, many people in the same profession—for example, the aspiring artist, author, or filmmaker—share very similar experiences. These commonalities correspond to the "normal" part of McLuhan's definition. On the other hand, methods that individual artists use to render their recall and later interpretation of those events vary considerably. Personalized artistic presentation and customized style preclude a numb or unfeeling reaction to a text, even if it contains clichéd tropes. Hartwig explains this process of personalizing, customizing, and reinterpreting: "I think that memory recalled in a visually and subsequently literal way does take on a new quality, almost as if the brain tries to install new meaning into a past event, categorizing it with adapted consciousness."[3] Similar to Hartwig's idea of installing new meaning into memory, many scholars have summarized autobiography as an interpretation of memories based on the author's current perspectives, which have been influenced by experiences that have occurred since the time of those past events. As Barbara Prys-Williams formulates it, autobiography is a "past recalled from the lived reality of the present" (172). Fitting that pattern, Hartwig wrote his novel years after he had returned home to Austria following his stay in the United States, and thus had the advantage of both geographical and temporal distance to the material.

In *The Fiction of Autobiography*, Micaela Maftei explains that writing about the past involves the "rewriting of an already completed process" (3). As this analysis of Hartwig's work will demonstrate, the experiences may be over, but the process of portraying and simultaneously assessing those events continues into the present. Because an autobiographer bases his or her writings or rewritings on real-life occurrences, readers often believe and expect that memoirists or autobiographers present "true" and authentic accounts of their lives. Yet discovered inauthenticity of autobiographies and memoirs has fueled numerous debates about accountability and even conscious deception.[4] It would seem much more logical and probable that when vague and hard-to-define terms such as "memory" and "interpretation" come into play, a greater risk for inauthenticity develops. Using terms such as "unsearchable," "unverifiable," "unremembered," and "relying on intuition or emotion," Maftei rightly characterizes autobiography in a way that complicates possibilities for authentication and verification (1). These variable and non-scientific components cause autobiographical narratives to become sites for "investigating the transition from reality to fiction" (Weigand 156). For Hartwig, his lived experience in Los Angeles has turned into an imagined and stylized fictional artistic visual interpretation of that past that finds expression in the pages of his graphic novel.

Despite this creative boundary between the documentable and the imagined, readers of autobiography often expect a clean overlap between the author and the protagonist, or in the case of *Chamäleon*, between Gerald Hartwig and Jerry. Many theorists agree, however, that the intermingling of memory and imagination contributes to the fictive quality of autobiography, and a subsequent sense of disengagement between author and protagonist.[5] As Sidonie Smith and Julia Watson explain: "The teller of his or her own story becomes, in the act of narration, both the observing subject and the object of investigation, remembrance and contemplation" (1). This in fact holds true for *Chämeleon*, as seen in the split that I will emphasize throughout this chapter between Hartwig and Jerry, whose parallel development yet resulting separate identities become the main object of the artist's contemplation. Autobiographers create their material by interpreting memory, but, as mentioned above, the temporal distance that they have to the past makes a difference in recall and rendering of themselves in the story. The unity between writer and narrator is "dismantled because of time elapsed," as well as because of individual changes the author experiences during that time (Maftei 68). For Hartwig, this distance and disconnect is evident through the portraitures and caricatures that he produces throughout the novel. Confirming the unique creative potential of the medium, the visual distance between older-looking Jerry who appears in the beginning and the young artist who appears throughout most of the graphic novel pictorially signals the passing of time.

The range of depictions and evolving interpretations of self confirms to the readers that the autobiographer never presents "isolatable fact" but rather "situated associations" (Smith 24). Roland Barthes, writing about his own autobiographical process, reveals the essence of the oeuvre, suggesting that stories told in the form of autobiography are as changeable as the recollection of the memories on which they are based: "they were not the last word when I wrote them, they are not the last word now and the stories will never be the last word because my self at the time of writing had no advantage over my past, nor any advantage over my present" (120). This changeability stems not only from the author's role as reader and interpreter of his or her own past, but also his or her perceived task both to verify and disrupt memory as part of the autobiographical narrative process.

The questions remain whether autobiography can be cliché, whether *Chamäleon* is cliché, and what implications that may have for its reception as well as the reception of other autobiographical graphic novels. As has been shown in the preceding paragraphs, Hartwig's work corresponds to general definitions of autobiography. For example, it represents a recalled and interpreted past, and exists at some point between fact and fiction. In terms of authenticity, as a retelling of the decade the author spent in Los Angeles, *Chamäleon* in fact exhibits many of the stock elements of a travel narrative featuring intercultural encounters, which are "commonly associated with . . . cliché and one-dimensionality" (Topping 65). In the context of the question of stereotypical themes and plot elements, memory and personal experience necessarily play a role, contributing to the complexity that El Refaie mentions as an aspect of "life writing," her term for autobiography: "life writing has a more complex relationship with the truth than explicitly fictional work" (135). For autobiography in general and for *Chamäleon* in particular, not only does interpretation of memory define the plot, but also external factors, such as knowledge (whether conscious or subconscious) of common plotlines and associations (such as the life of an aspiring filmmaker in Hollywood) can also influence the final product. In *Giving an Account of Oneself*, Judith Butler discusses these uncontrollable and variable outside influences as they relate to the morality of portraying oneself authentically: "And there can be no account of myself that does not, to some extent, conform to norms that govern the humanly recognizable, or that negotiate these terms in some ways, with various risks following from that negotiation" (38). Clearly, Hartwig works with clichéd plotlines in writing about his protagonist who hopes that what is popular in the film industry will lead to his success. For the present discussion, it could be said that Hartwig's reading of his experience and memory through Jerry conforms to the "humanly recognizable" norm of the aspiring and free-spirited artist.

"EIN MITTELDING": THE GRAPHIC NOVEL AS MEDIUM FOR AUTOBIOGRAPHY AND SELF-ASSESSMENT

Chämeleon does in fact have an identifiable story line, but, as Paul Jay argues in his discussion of James Joyce's autobiography, it is important to understand that an "autobiographical text cannot depend on memory alone, but must, rather, rely on the transforming power of fictional art" (144). Jay refers here to prose, but graphic art can also contribute, and has contributed, to a remarkable multimodal autobiographical aesthetic. Having had experience with the process of filmmaking and especially storyboarding, Hartwig sees a number of similarities between film and graphic novel production, but also acknowledges differences between the two media:[6]

> The graphic novel is to a certain degree another term for "comics" that publishers use to attract a different kind of reader. It's essentially a long comic, a story in pictures. In this sense, the graphic novel is closer to film than to the novel. There are many overlaps, such as with the technique of storyboarding. [For this novel] in my head I came up with a movie, with long shots, close-ups, music. Just on paper instead of film.[7]

Scholars have taken similar approaches to positioning the medium in a creative inventory. El Refaie references its multimedial influences, and writes that autobiographical graphic literature "draws on models from literature, but also from art and photography" and "traditional self-portraiture" (19). Douglass Wolk makes just as strong of a statement about the medium by articulating what it is not: "Comics are not prose. Comics are not movies. They are not a text-driven medium with added pictures; they're not the visual equivalent of prose narrative or a static version of a film" (14). In response to a separate question following the Goethe Institut reading regarding the potential of graphic art as compared to prose and film, Hartwig described graphic literature as a "*Mittelding*," or a medium that combines characteristics and the expressive potential of various media, thus implying its narrative capability.

In addition to definitions of the medium, scholars have also, over the last few decades, attempted to devise a single term that encapsulates the notion of a mixed verbal and visual presentation of autobiography. Gillian Whitlock and Anna Poletti's coinage "autographics" seems to be the most appropriate and comprehensive to describe a "[l]ife narrative fabricated in and through drawing and design using various technologies, modes, and materials" (2008, v). Whitlock and Poletti do not limit the definition to the production of graphic texts, but rather they include reception in the definition as "[a] practice of reading the signs, symbols and techniques of visual arts in life narrative" (v). Thus, the graphic novel is especially well suited for autobiography because of the intense visual analysis and subsequent actual visualization of the self that the oeuvre requires of both the artist and the reader. Comics require a high level of involvement from their readers, but the author still decides on the degree and perspective of "focalization," or as Jane Tolmie colloquially explains, "how much readers are allowed in someone's head" (193). Hartwig comments on the choice of medium for providing his audience with this sort of focalization:

> I carried this story, which is largely my own and that against my will ended with getting thrown out of the United States, around with me for a long time. At first I wanted to produce a series of large format storyboards, then a screenplay. Finally, a graphic novel seemed the logical choice.[8]

Although much earlier examples of this technique exist, researchers locate the roots of the autobiographical comic in the 1970s United States, often naming R. Crumb and Justin Green as its pioneers. Many of the qualities of these early works, such as "taboo-breaking subjects, subversive humor [and] irony," and "brutally honest, even exhibitionist accounts" typify much of autobiographical graphic narrative to this day (El Refaie 4, 38). Hartwig's work is no exception.

HARTWIG'S ASSESSMENT OF HIS SELF-STORY

As mentioned in the introduction, this analysis focuses on the black matte pages that contrast the prevalent sepia-toned pages of the rest of the work. Of the 261 pages of narrative, the roughly nineteen nearly all-black pages alternately take on the function of expressing intense emotion or representing a moment of concentrated self-reflection. Similar to other traditional and current graphic autobiography, the episodes that Hartwig isolates on these pages often include irony, frank commentary, and simultaneously visually highlighting clichés and calling them into question. *Chamäleon's* main plot thread does in fact trace the sordid experiences of an artist trying to make it big in Los Angeles, like so many other artists. Although much of the graphic novel displays characteristics of a "hypothetical fantasy" far from the "terrain of actual events," the novel begins with a personal and real impetus: the unexpected death of Hartwig's father (Arthur 236). This private yet universally relatable incident signals the start of the author's personal reflection on his life experiences and identity up to that point.

Hartwig comments on the impact the death had on inspiring the production of *Chamäelon*:

> A drastic event like the death of someone very close forces you to confront your own mortality. I had to examine my own story, engage in a search for clues. Somehow it was also like I was telling my father the story of my life that he had only witnessed from a distance.[9]

Yet, as the closer study of his portraitures and caricatures will show, it also seems that Hartwig now experiences his already-lived life from a distance on his storyboarded pages, supporting my hypothesis that he presents a carefully designed visual interpretation of his memories. The first page of the series of black matte pages mentioned in the introduction marks the starting point for the artist's piecing together of his identity. The primarily black page features a bird with outstretched wings that regards the reader head-on.[10] The bird's left wing obscures the text's first portrait of Jerry, which is half blocked by shadow. In the center of the page, the name "Jerry" appears in white lettering.[11] Just as this black page marks the beginning of the author's examination process, each of the other full black pages contained within the graphic novel functions to mark a specific location in the artist's carefully archived sequences of self-investigation.

Similar to other examples of graphic autobiography that El Refaie discusses, the comic technique, and in Hartwig's specific case the black matte pages specifically, break up the "continuous flow" of memory or autobiographical storytelling with "frozen scenes" (115). The next series of black pages appears physically close to the opening page, and form one large episode that presents the family members' reactions to the father's death. The portraitures or caricatures of Jerry and his family members express Hartwig's present-day interpretation of how he re-members receiving and responding to the devastating news. The artist first shows his own recalled reaction through a caricatured form of Jerry (figure 11.1). On the left side of a double black page, the reader sees the single word "Ja?" (yes) enclosed in a small white box, which refers to Jerry's answering his mother's phone call (10). The right-hand side shows a close-up of the protagonist's face, but with part of his head and the left side of his cheek obscured in shadow. The words "something terrible" (*was Furchtbares*; 11) written in a frantic scrawl begin on the right side of his head and continue across the forehead, ending with a white exclamation point in the black space where the left side of his head should be.

Next, the artist renders Jerry's mediated memory of the actual circumstances through a portraiture of his mother. The top panel, which blends into the page's bottom panel, shows an ambulance with Jerry's superimposed question "What do you mean he's dead? (Was heisst, er ist tot?; 13). Mirroring Jerry's caricature from the previous page, the artist provides a close-up portrait of the mother as well, but her facial features contrast Jerry's shadowed and incomplete head. The verbal aspect consists of straightforward terms explaining what had happened: "He wasn't feeling well, he just collapsed at the theater. . . . I have to go . . . The ambulance is here" (Ihm ging es ganz schlecht, er ist einfach umge-fallen im Theater. . . . Ich muss jetzt rein . . . Der Rettungswagen ist da; 13). These two pages feature the parallel motif of close-up and emotional faces, but the totality of the mother's face, along with the ambulance, suggests that a clinical explanation grants her more emotional complete-ness. The sketches communicate to the readers that her reaction differs considerably from Jerry's, whose partially drawn face with the vague words "something terrible" stamped on it signifies his limited capacity— at that moment and perhaps even when he was rendering it visually years later—for understanding the event both rationally and emotionally.

The third page in this scene covers one and a half pages and depicts the moment when Jerry shares the news of his father's death with his wife. Still maintaining the all-black background, these pages feature a much different layout than those on the other pages. The words "As if disembodied I tear open the bathroom door" (Körperlos reisse ich die

Figure 11.1.   Jerry reacts to the news of his father's death. Gerald Hartwig.
Chamäleon. Wien: Luftschacht Verlag, 2013. 11.

Badezimmertür auf; 14) overlay a rendition of a steamy shower with only his wife's head visible, thus also disembodied. In panels that Hartwig has carefully framed, yet arranged in a disorganized manner on the page, he captures the reaction of Jerry's wife, showing her first from the waist up in the shower, then zooming in two more times to focus on the facial features that expose profound grief. As I will maintain throughout this essay, the framed, more photograph-like panels designate those moments of particularly vivid memory. This does not necessarily mean that Hartwig has depicted these moments authentically. Instead, they represent moments that contain characteristics of the actual moment and the retrospective act of recall and artistic rendering. As Maftei argues, these moments exemplify "unity between two selves" and gain depth from "later learned knowledge" that "changes the significance of certain events" (4). Despite this impression of unity or even closure, the artist points to the simultaneous unreliability of his memory. The phrase "The rest of that night is a blur" (Was von der Nacht noch bleibt, verschwimmt; 15) provides a textual transition between the all-black top half and the white bottom half of the next page. Reinforcing the notion of distorted memory, Hartwig once again employs the motif of the close-up face, this time that of Jerry's wife, but in a much more indistinct form than the depiction of his face or his mother's on the preceding pages. Tears or water droplets frame the face with a very thin, jagged line, and the reader can only see the eyes and nose of someone who has been sobbing. Otherwise, the drawing of the face does not show any dimension or shading, which could indicate Jerry's move closer to the emotionless state that often accompanies shock, and the present non-finalized process of negotiating this highly significant personal turning point.

These three pages reference that one particular moment, but each one blends a series of motifs and techniques to different effect in order to represent Hartwig's retrospective interpretation of this particular memory through Jerry. The designs liken his renderings to instances of "performed authenticity," located between the narrative and the life it represents (El Refaie 137). In a similar vein, Tolmie writes about the "various layered processes of memory and self-representation," but also the "impossibility of direct transmission of lived experiences" (vii, ix). Accordingly, the three portraits impart various degrees of feeling and authenticity, and remind the reader of the undependability, yet deep and enduring impression of significant memories. Throughout the novel Hartwig's process of self-examination involves intimate and, sometimes literally naked, portrayals of other figures close to him, as for instance the shower setting referenced above. At these moments, Hartwig presents an original take on the mirror technique found in many self-portraits. Laura Cumming explains: "[T]he mirror becomes a metaphor for this appalling mutability, its slipperiness reflecting our inability to grasp, or even clearly see, our ever-shifting selves" (148). Looking directly at those closest to him, often laid bare as the result of various circumstances, Jerry is Hartwig's tool for confronting himself; and he embarks on this process by assessing himself through his relationships. Hartwig's figures display full frontal views and establish direct eye contact, or as Cumming describes, the visual equivalent of direct address (38). Hartwig uses the body, whether his own or those of others, in an autobiographical narrative technique that Smith and Watson label "embodiment": "the body is a site of autobiographical knowledge because memory itself is embodied. And life narrative is a site of embodied knowledge . . . because autobiographical narrators are embodied subjects" (49). Hartwig often centralizes the body, and in particular the physicality of other characters with whom Jerry interacts, in order to interpret visually and with brutal retrospective honesty both his development and his persistent return to certain patterns.

The content of the all-black pages vacillates between this mirroring technique, whether Hartwig's intensified attention to Jerry's physical body, or reflecting modes of identity through other people or the environment. The next example in the series of black matte pages draws upon the latter, resides at the site where imagination and fiction intermingle (Weigand 148), and reveals a decisive look inward through the motif of a dream from January 17, 1994, the night of a devastating earthquake in the Los Angeles area (48–49). Representing a combination of imagined memory and documentable environmental influence, these hybrid pages are partially black and partially sepia. With the use of a simple time stamp in the upper right- hand corner of the frame showing Jerry sleeping, Hartwig records the exact date and time (4:30 am) that the earthquake happened. Although the graphic novel includes this detail of the natural disaster that actually took place on that day at that time, Hartwig does not invoke the earthquake in order to provide a newspaper-like account of the incident. Instead, the author mediates the event; and that process is a "highly complex, self-referential system of selection and interpretation, with the artist choosing what to retain and what to discard" (El Refaie 99). In this case through the traumatic event, Hartwig comments on Jerry's tenuous (and as he sees in retrospect, misguided) relationships with other purported professionals in the Hollywood film business. The dream becomes a way for Hartwig to convey to the reader his present acknowledgment that these collaborations with untrustworthy individuals only led to more dead ends in his advancement as a filmmaker.

The earthquake dream sharply contrasts, and ironically reinterprets the mood of the scene that directly precedes the scene. Reflecting on his career thus far, Jerry characterizes the collaborative and creative progress positively, and predicts "nothing would be able to stop us now. The earth would actually have to open up . . ." (nichts würde uns bremsen können. Da müsste schon die Erde sich auftun . . . ; 47). Recalling the filmic technique of a cutaway to a scene that definitively and completely reverses yet also ironically confirms what the protagonist has just pro-

claimed, the scene turns to Jerry's experience of the earth actually opening up (48). At first, the artist invokes the visual metaphor of a train
rattling over tracks that have been laid across Jerry's face as he sleeps.
Falling rock and gravel turn into objects from his apartment, which form
a line to the lower half of the page where a thicker black line runs
through the center of the page in the form of a seismogram. As a visual
confirmation of the sense of precariousness with which he reads this
event in his life, Hartwig sees himself mirrored in indistinct characters
that alternately balance on and fall from the peaks of the recording of the
earthquake's impact.

On a subsequent black matte page, the focus turns back to a portrait of
Jerry, who cowers in the lower right-hand corner, enclosed in a framed
panel. Superimposed white text describes the arrested passage of time:
"after the eternity of a millisecond . . ." (nach der Ewigkeit einer Millise-
kunde . . . ; 49) and a more conventional caption that would seem to jolt
the protagonist out of his dream finishes the phrase: ". . . the car alarms
strike up an eerie concert . . ." (. . . stimmen die Autosirenen ein unheim-
liches Konzert an . . . ; 49). The artist mixes sepia and black in this sequence, and uses these colors to shade the mushroom clouds caused by
explosions in the wake of the earthquake and his envisioned devastation
occurring outside, which he labels "Jerry-View" (Jerry-Blick). The "actual
view" (echte Ansicht) of the city, seemingly untouched and back to normal, appears on the next page. In this sequence, the artist uses an actual
natural disaster as a vehicle for documenting his memory of the trajectory his career had taken at that point in time. Jerry views this enormous
break as a significant turning point. By contrasting Jerry's view and the
actual view, however, Hartwig helps the reader to see the difference
between his memory of an event and his current interpretation. In hind-
sight, he can tell the difference between how he perceived his career at
the time, as shown through Jerry, and a more differentiated view of this
great turning point in his life, as shown through the artist's original
choice of visual motifs that depict his mental state with the metaphor of
an earthquake. His constant return to "old patterns," or the perhaps clichéd elements of sex, drugs, and rock and roll as the subsequent scene
shows, intensifies the irony that also runs through the novel with the
same regularity as the clichés.

The next black matte episode is an example of Jerry's identity as reflected through others. The story turns to one of many described and
explicitly illustrated sexual relationships: an all-black page follows a moment of severe disappointment when Jerry's Italian girlfriend has a decidedly different interpretation of their affair. When Jerry says he believes he is in love with her, she answers "I know" (Ich weiss). He responds "And now?" (Und jetzt?), to which she replies with an Italian-
accented "Nothing" (Nichts; 56). In order to emphasize visually the disheartening sparseness of this exchange, Hartwig has divided the black

page into three main parts. In the left top section, the reader views the scene from over Jerry's shoulder. A white-framed "nothing?" (nichts?) hovers above his head as he views his girlfriend in the distance outlined by a halo of white light (57). The top right shows white text on an all-black background. The disappointing conversation has cued a musical reference that contributes to the novel's "soundtrack," a tool used throughout the graphic novel that contributes to its system of irony: "The rest of the evening and my departure disappear in a deep dark cave far away from me. Beck has written a song about me. 'Sooooy un perdedoor I'm a loser babyyy, so why don't you kill meee?'" (Der Rest des Abends und meine Abreise verschwinden in einer tiefen, dunklen Höhle weit weg von mir. Beck schreibt ein Lied über mich. 'Sooooy un perdedoor I'm a loser babyyy, so why don't you kill meee?; 57). The bottom half of the page, in dark sepia rather than black, switches the setting and changes the scenery, thereby signaling a shift in memory, as shown by a change in geographic location: "We will soon be landing in Graz" (Wir landen in Kürze in Graz; 57). A subsequent quick change of setting sees Jerry back in LA; and one's interpretation of being in love links the earlier scene with Mandy and the current one. This time, Jerry has taken what might be considered the upper hand in a love relationship with a different woman, Irene. Hartwig documents this memory, thus making it more authentic for the reader, by drawing Jerry's handwritten note that proclaims: "I'm not in love with you" (ich bin nicht in dich verliebt; 61). With this gesture, Jerry has seemingly remedied the hurt feelings caused by Mandy's nonchalant "nichts." The visual gesture of including a drawing of the piece of correspondence lends the scene a degree of perceived authenticity.

The next significant black matte page belongs to the category of self-portrait, although this time exaggeratedly caricatured as seen by the bizarre iconography the artist chooses. The pages that appear before and after this page about halfway through the graphic novel mark the titular pivotal moment: Jerry imagines himself turning into a chameleon (figure 11.2). Although the other portraits could be assigned a subversive function, the choice of aesthetic here makes this one a supreme "representation that sets out to subvert the genre [of self-portraiture] and that [does] so in order to underline the positive and productive outcomes of self-portraiture as a process of dissociation" (Kalpaxi 68). The transformation follows a conversation Jerry has with a close female friend after he has told her he has broken up (quite callously as the reader knows) with his girlfriend Irene. The friend offers this piece of advice: "You have to change something within yourself, internally. I don't see any other way" (Du musst irgendwas in dir ändern, von innen. Ich sehe sonst kein Licht; 121). Hartwig again picks up the mirroring technique with an image that depicts Jerry gazing out of the panel in the reader's direct line of sight. This time it appears especially eerie and alienating, as Jerry's eye takes on the reptilian look of a chameleon's.[12] Three larger portrait-like panels display the chameleon in varying degrees of light and shadow. Hartwig shows the stages of the transformation in remarkable detail; and the fact that the reader can discern Jerry's T-shirt on the chameleon's body makes it clear that the creature is a cross between man and reptile. This scene demonstrates the difference that I argue for in this essay between using the protagonist to visually document the memory of a moment, and the artist's retrospective analysis of identity within that memory. His artistic rendition of the subsequent "change" reveals his retrospective realization that he never accomplished deeper, internal change. Instead, he only achieved a superficial transformation into a creature that can instinctively adapt to any situation by changing color.[13]

Taken as a whole, the disparate examples of self-portraiture correspond to a characteristic of modernist self-portraiture, as Gemma Blackshaw explains, with its "emphasis on the artist-individuals and their pain, anxiety, or exclusion as badges of authenticity" (379). Through these depictions, the artists reveal that they understand themselves as "in process" (McDaniel 199). While Hartwig's rendering shows the "in process" (suggesting forward-moving) part, Jerry continues to return to old patterns and behaviors, illustrated through the black matte episodic portraits. Nicole McDaniel applies the adjective "serial" to a character in graphic autobiography "that repeatedly or regularly performs a specified activity" or a "practice performed on a recurring basis" (199). In addition to the protagonist's performing of these serial acts, the artist also performs a "particular practice of episodic introspection that can be defined as serial" (McDaniel 199). Hartwig's portraiture of Jerry in a subsequent episode reveals his serial behavior of trying to find an easy point of access into the movie business. Three portrait-like framed pictures show a washed-out and nearly indiscernible Jerry holding a camera, as if photographing the reader. "Yes, this will turn into something" (Ja, das wird was; 128). The oversized camera lens becomes the top of the showerhead in the adjoining shot, and Hartwig presents Jerry from a bird's-eye view in the shower.

With this acute concentration on the body, the artist is able to "represent identities in ways that reflect [his] own innermost sense of self," using symbolic elements and rhetorical tropes to add layers to this reading of identity (Ef Rafaie 51). Contrasting his expression of earlier confidence, Jerry assesses the situation in the past tense conditional mood, which emphasizes his vulnerability and subsequent failure as signified by his naked body: "Yes, that could have been something. If . . ." (Ja. Das hätte was werden können. Wenn . . . ; 128). The artist switches to a close-up portrait of Jerry as he thinks: "This 'if' has been with me ever since my move here" (Dieses 'wenn' begleitet mich schon seit meinem Exodus; 129). When Jerry turns the shower off, caricatured versions of his face appear in oversized water droplets, a remediation of an earlier scene

Figure 11.2.   Jerry's imagined transformation into a chameleon. Gerald Hartwig.
Chamäleon. **Wien: Luftschacht Verlag, 2013. 122.**

when he moved into a new residence in Los Angeles (68). A carefully drawn ATM reveals that he has only $28, a detail of documentation, like the handwritten note, that could potentially add authenticity, but more strikingly reverses any sense of hope that the bubbles might portray.

Another episode of all-black pages underscores this intense feeling of a lack of hope, and instead accentuates Jerry's vulnerability, weakness, and defenselessness. Also an example of a caricatured self-portrait, this scene magnifies the attention to the physical body and touches on the issue of drug use, often seen as a clichéd and stereotypical part of the aspiring artist's life. Traditionally, the "choice of self-portraiture betrays psychological imbalance," a category into which drug use could potentially fall (Kalpaxi 67). Fortunately, a positive shift has occurred in the study of autobiography since the 1990s, now allowing self-portraiture to be critically regarded as "multiple versions of selfhood," which "crafts an archive as [the author's] various self-portraits and stories are gathered" (McDaniel 201). Inadvertently responding to this critical trajectory, Jerry's commentary on this episode does not allude to any imbalance, but rather gives the distinct impression that he simply cannot avoid drug use given the artist's lifestyle: "How it happened and why: nobody really knows exactly anymore" (Wie es passiert ist und warum, weiss niemand mehr so genau; 201). In this visual rendition of his "self" at that time, Hartwig offers a highly stylized interpretation—much more caricature than portraiture—of his memory of taking cocaine.

Readers face Jerry, but have a view as if they are looking up at him. He has large bulging eyes, but they do not invite eye contact with the reader. From this angle, the dollar bill through which Jerry snorts cocaine appears disproportionately large. The cocaine that spills from the bottom draws a line to the larger picture that takes up the bottom half of the page. The artist has designed the lower picture on the page as a self-portrait, but Jerry's head tipped back suggests the absence of eyes and thus a distancing from the reader as well as Hartwig's own retrospective dissociation with and criticism of the situation. In the lower right-hand corner, the artist provides commentary on the episode, questioning the decisions he once made: "White is the color of innocence? (Weiss ist die Farbe der Unschuld?; 201). The images on the page that follows maintain the theme of innocent vulnerability by featuring a series of portraits of Jerry with a particular focus on his nearly naked body. This concentration on the body recalls the technique of embodiment often used with autobiographical texts: "The ability to recover memories, in fact, depends on the material body. There must be a somatic body that perceives and internalizes the images, sensations, and experiences of the external world" (Smith 49).[14] Here, the artist uses the body, and in particular exaggerated body parts, not only to emphasize his physical dependence on drugs, but also to comment on that time in his life when he felt particularly vulnerable.

Moreover, Hartwig makes his presence known through a process that involves visually stylizing his memory. He returns to his commentary on the persistent drug abuse by captioning another self-portrait with the critical statement: "I imagined self-sufficiency differently. More self and more sufficiency" (Die Selbständigkeit habe ich mir anders vorgestellt. Mehr selbst und mehr standing; 214). In a smaller framed panel overlaying the portrait, the reader sees a mostly darkened street, but with the wide light of a streetlamp in the foreground. Jerry says: "2 grams. That's all the money I have, Sergio" (2 Gramm. Mehr Kohle habe ich nicht, Sergio; 214). These pages are similar in color and layout to other black matte pages, marking "the particular practice of episodic introspection that can be defined as serial" (McDaniel 199). They are also similar in their purpose of advancing Hartwig's process of commenting in retrospect on his own questionable, yet at the time seemingly necessary, life choices.

Another black matte marker a few pages later interrogates the notion of the artist's prototype in general, and exposes a greatly intensified stage of self-confrontation, which fits into both the category of reflection through others, as well as that of intensified caricature. A critical comment by Jerry's then-girlfriend Yumi begins this episode of self-interrogation: "You're so different lately. You're not the artist that I met anymore. So . . . tough. Now" (Du bist so anders in letzter Zeit. Nicht mehr der Künstler, den ich kennengelernt habe. So . . . hart. Jetzt; 217). Jerry and his girlfriend's nakedness, as well as a close-up framed shot of an eye, at first convey intimacy and establish a direct connection to the reader. With a sequential spatial arrangement that reflects that of the chameleon scene, three small, framed panels show the eye as it slowly transforms into the form of a harmless-looking sleeping tiger. Directly below that panel series, a naked Jerry observes the tiger as it becomes transformed into a vicious animal, with both human and beastly characteristics (217). The style of the close-up portrait of Jerry on the subsequent page closely matches the design of the faces after the family has heard the news about the father's death, indicating this moment as a significant turning point. In this case, it is Yumi's direct comment that he has changed, with the implication that is has been for the worst. Hartwig portrays these feelings through close-up renderings of Jerry's pained face as well as a smaller snapshot-sized framed portrait of his eviscerated body.

In a standing position, he peers down at his mangled self, while the reader looks head-on at the naked and disemboweled protagonist. His comment on the next page blurs the lines between this highly fantastic happening and the possibility that it *did* actually happen: "Outwardly, I try not to let the inner turmoil [but also literally condition of being torn apart] show" (Nach aussen versuche ich die Zerrissenheit nicht anmerken zu lassen; 219). This confrontation with the tiger precedes Jerry's experimentation in the porn industry, another decision that may have

seemed necessary at the time, but one that also, like Yumi, calls his credibility as an artist into question. Another all-black page completes this
"episode" about his ultimate failure in the porn industry (and in his
progress as a real artist). Jerry comments on the disappointing and mentally trying end to the project: "Phase 4 means total overstimulation of the
senses and a collapse of all energy reserves" (Phase 4 bedeutet totale
Sinnesüberreizung und ein Einbruch aller Energiereserven; 223). Windows of a dwelling frame Jerry's self-portrait in a long shot; and he takes
on the same look as in a previous portrait, with indiscernible dark features and glowing eyes. Not only does his latest professional failure mark
the end of this episode, but also his breakup with Yumi. The mirroring
and exaggerated caricature techniques correspond to distinctive verbal
and visual strategies of authenticity, which "signal an intention to be
frank about one's own memories, experiences and emotions" (El Refaie
138). After a series of subsequent black matte pages not discussed in this
study, Jerry articulates the point he has reached in the process. "I give up
trying to measure myself against others. . . . Life doesn't work completely
without confrontation. So I'd rather fight against the master of all oppo-
nents. Myself" (Ich gebe es auf, mich mit anderen messen zu wollen. . . .
Ganz ohne Auseinandersetzung funktioniert das Leben auch nicht, also
kämpfe ich lieber gegen den Meister aller Gegner. Mich selbst; 230–31).
With this pronouncement, Jerry also proclaims the beginning of a new
phase.

The second to the last of the black matte pages plays a role in the
system of repetition and episodicity that, as this analysis has shown,
characterizes graphic autobiography. It also belongs to the category of
self-reflection through others. In *Chamäleon*, this means a return to the
recurrent theme of intimate sexual experiences. In contrast to other similar episodes throughout the book, this one does not show the bodies
graphically or clearly. Instead, Hartwig uses a more abstract style, and he
encases it within the visual rhetorical photo frames that reappear
throughout the book as a pattern. Jerry's own sensibilities are mirrored
through this lover, which allows Hartwig to see himself more intimately
at this point in his life. Referring to the mirroring technique described
above, Cumming explains: "Everyone's mirror is the site of repeated
stand-offs between hope and disappointment, confidence, and frank in-
credulity" (148). With this intensified depiction of the body, Hartwig
shows an intensified level of self-interrogation. This scene turns out to be
less about the clichéd theme of yet another sexual encounter, and more
about the artist's reading of the types of emotions and sensibilities that
theorists such as Cumming identify. At this point, the artist looks back at
seven years in the United States with very little to show for it profession-
ally, except the polarities of hope, disappointment, confidence and incre-
dulity. Hartwig's packaging of these memories and reflections in the
physical form of his graphic novel, however, demonstrates a "complex

convergence of past and present, writing and image, the unconscious and the conscious, the raw matter of life and its formed (but not formalized) products" (Tolmie 34). These layers of narrative content and meaning fortify the narrative layers of *Chämeleon,* which comprise its complex aesthetic construction.

The graphic novel ends with three sequential black matte pages that narrate the difficulties Hartwig had with United States Immigration authorities in 2004, as emblematized by white lettering above a pair of oversized handcuffs that appear to float on the page. Jerry explains how he had been arrested because of a visa issue (this actually did happen to Hartwig), which meant he had been in the United States illegally for one day. In the second to the last line of the graphic novel, the words of the immigration officer accompany the last image Hartwig has of his time in the United States: "Why do you keep smiling the whole time? Most people are inconsolable when they leave the United States" (Warum lächelst du eigentlich dauernd? Die meisten Leute sind untröstlich, wenn sie die Vereinigten Staaten verlassen; 258). In a series of portrait-like frames, Hartwig conveys his memory of that last day, ending with the officer's friendly face. In closing, he writes in English "the end is never the end" (261). If one thinks of the entire book as a set of repeated patterns such as the futile search for fame, success, and love in LA, we could imagine returning to the beginning when the artist is back in Europe recalling his years of unsuccessful attempts.

CONCLUDING THOUGHTS

Taken as an integrated arc, the series of black matte pages form an aesthetic system by which the reader experiences how Hartwig retrospectively views himself as an artist at various stages of his development while living abroad. In this chapter, I have shown ways that the reader can observe the interaction of visual and verbal elements as a method of depicting the artist's stations of self-confrontation and self-assessment. Drawing on a longer tradition of graphic autobiography, techniques that contribute to this method often include irony and frank commentary, two techniques that Hartwig employs repeatedly as a way to reinterpret and subvert the clichés that could define him as an artist, but that he vehemently resists in retrospect. Additionally, Hartwig manipulates visual and verbal devices in order to call into question or reverse clichés that often accompany the life of the typical artist. As my detailed descriptions and analyses of a selection of the individual black matte episodes attest, he employs many of the elements of the standard creative inventory of autobiography: multiples modes of media, dreams, albums, photos, objects, family stories, and historical events (Smith 25). His adherence to these paradigms and inclusion of certain autobiographical "criteria" do not, however, automatically render his life story cliché. To conclude, I would like to return to the guiding questions from the introduction. Cliché does in fact play a central and even indispensable role in this autobiographical text. Familiar, common, and recurring topics like sexual encounters and drug use help the artist establish a thematic pattern that carries through the work and underpins it. These elements do not, however, exclusively define his retrospective self-interrogation.

The graphic nature of the text precludes McLuhan's "anesthetizing" effect mentioned in the introduction because, as this analysis has shown, graphic texts—as contrasted with prose or film—allow for the establishment of a parallel visual pattern that the author painstakingly creates and that the audience should, and can because of the medium, read just as meticulously. As I have argued here, any artist's individual style and aesthetics support a non-clichéd presentation of the process of self-examination that accompanies autobiographical writing because it presents a sense of perspective and aesthetic rendering—even if marked by cliché—peculiar to that artist. This distinctiveness of the artist and his/her artistic voice is part of what elevates comics out of the realm of pure entertainment. According to Jan Baetens, the autobiographical turn has signaled a shift from commercial to serious comic art, which is characterized by a "strong narrational presence," marked by a "specific voice and tone" and "specific strongly individualized ways of drawing" (67–68). The narrational presence and individualized style help to express what Prys-Williams describes as the autobiographer's required "encounter with oneself that can involve the need to confront potent elements from one's past, a sort of wrestling with personal dragons" (1–2). Or chameleons and tigers, as Hartwig has shown his readers.

NOTES

1. In particular, comparisons were made with Austrian author André Pilz's *Man Down*, also from 2013.
2. Hartwig's translation.
3. Email exchange, June 15, 2015.
4. Most notably, the controversy that surrounded James Frey's *A Million Little Pieces* from 2004 still gets cited today in discussions of authenticity and autobiography.
5. Hartwig alluded to this phenomenon during his presentation as part of the panel "The German Graphic Novel and (Auto)Biography I" at the Northeast Modern Language Association's (NeMLA) 2015 convention. He found it extremely difficult to talk about an "I" when describing his work and instead settled on using the term "protagonist."
6. The design of Hartwig's multimodal performance mentioned at the beginning of the essay also suggests his awareness of these interactions. The event featured the author reading selected scenes from his graphic novel, accompanied by projected images and live music.
7. Interview with Hartwig, January 2014. For the original German interview, please see https://germangraphicnovel.wordpress.com/january-2014-hartwig/.
8. Interview with Hartwig, January 2014.

9. This is the original German from an interview that I had subsequently translated into English, which appears in the main body of the chapter: "Ein einschneidendes Erlebnis, wie der Tod eines nahen Angehörigen, zwingt einen dazu, sich mit der eigenen Vergänglichkeit auseinander zu setzen. In dem Fall musst ich einfach meine eigene Geschichte durchleuchten, Spurensuche betreiben und irgendwie ist es auch so, als ob ich mein Leben auch meinem Vater erzähle, der es ja nur aus der Ferne miterlebt hatte. http://germangraphicnovel.files.wordpress.com/2014/03/gerald-english.pdf.

10. The same bird image appears again on pages 44–45 when he is describing his new home on Catalina Island. The bird hovers over the deck that looks out over the water. A fragment of a screenplay and Jerry in profile complete the layout. The words "Bohemian. Jerryesque" suggest his state of mind at this time in his life, as well as allude to what the bird could possibly symbolize.

11. Throughout this essay, I will use "Jerry" when referring to the protagonist, and "the artist" or "Hartwig" when referring to the author.

12. This drastic transformation calls to mind the events of Kafka's *Metamorphosis*, with some of the same themes of self-reflection and even self-disgust forming some parallels.

13. When asked during his panel discussion at the 2015 NeMLA convention in Toronto (March 2015) why he chose a chameleon, Hartwig answered very simply that he likes them. My reading seems to dismantle this response, but the reading also shows the depth and dimension that graphic texts can have, as well as their eliciting various responses in different readers, regardless of author's intent.

14. This motif appears in many graphic novels, in particular Chris Ware's *Building Stories* is one story in which a woman muses about her self-understanding and is shown at the center of many pages subsequently "unclothing," finally revealing her skeleton.

REFERENCES

Adams, Timothy Dow. *Light Writing and Life Writing: Photography in Autobiography.* Chapel Hill and London: University of North Carolina Press, 2000.

Baetens, Jan. "Uncaging and Reframing Martin Vaughn-James's *The Cage.*" *Drawing from Life: Memory and Subjectivity in Comic Art.* Ed. Jane Tolmie. Jackson, MS: University Press of Mississippi, 2013. 67–85.

Barrington, Judith. *Writing the Memoir: From Truth to Art.* Portland: The Eighth Mountain Press, 2002.

Barthes, Roland. *Roland Barthes by Roland Barthes.* Trans. Richard Howard. New York: Farrar, Straus and Giroux, 1977.

Beaty, Bart. *Unpopular Culture: Transforming the European Comic Book in the 1990s.* Toronto: University of Toronto Press, 2007.

Blackshaw, Gemma. "The Pathological Body: Modernist Strategising in Egon Schiele's Self-Portraiture." *Oxford Art Journal* 30.3 (2007): 379–401.

Booth, Wayne C. *The Rhetoric of Fiction.* Chicago: University of Chicago Press, 1961.

Butler, Judith. *Giving an Account of Oneself.* New York: Fordham University Press, 2005.

Chaney, Michael A. *Graphic Subjects: Critical Essays on Autobiography and Graphic Novels.* Madison: University of Wisconsin Press, 2011.

Cumming, Laura. *A Face to the World: On Self Portraits.* London: Harper Press, 2009.

Currie, Mark. *About Time: Narrative, Fiction and the Philosophy of Time.* Edinburgh: Edinburgh University Press, 2007.

El Refaie, Elisabeth. *Autobiographical Comics: Life Writing in Pictures.* Jackson: University Press of Mississippi, 2012.

Groensteen, Thierry. *The System of Comics.* Trans. Bart Beaty and Nick Nguyen. Jackson: University Press of Mississippi, 2007.

Hartwig, Gerald. *Chamäleon.*

Hatfield, Charles. *Alternative Comics: An Emerging Literature*. Jackson: University Press of Mississippi, 2005.

Herman, David. "Narrative Worldmaking in Graphic Life Writing." *Graphic Subjects: Critical Essays on Autobiography and Graphic Novels*. Ed. Michael A. Chaney. Madison: Wisconsin University Press, 2011. 231–43.

Jay, Paul. *Being in the Text: Self-Representation from Wordsworth to Roland Barthes*. Ithaca: Cornell University Press, 1984.

Kalpaxi, Elisavet. "From The Borders to Centre Stage: Photographic Self-Portraiture." *Philosophy of Photography* 5.1 (2014): 65–76.

Maftei, Micaela. *The Fiction of Autobiography: Reading and Writing Identity*. London, New Delhi, New York, Sydney: Bloomsbury Academic, 2013.

McDaniel, Nicole, "Self-Reflexive Graphic Narrative: Seriality and Art Spiegelman's Portrait of the Artist as a Young %@&*!." *Studies in Comics* 1.3 (2010): 197–211.

Miller, Ann. *Reading Bande Dessinée: Critical Approaches to French-language Comic Strips*. Bristol and Chicago: Intellect, 2007.

Pilz, André. *Man Down*. Innsbruck: Haymon Verlag, 2010.

Prys-Williams, Barbara. *Twentieth-Century Autobiography*. Cardiff: University of Wales Press, 2004.

Schlick, Yäel. "What Is an Experience? Selves and Texts in the Comic Autobiographies of Alison Bechdel and Lynda Barry." *Drawing from Life: Memory and Subjectivity in Comic Art*. Ed. Jane Tolmie. Jackson, MS: University Press of Mississippi, 2013. 26–43.

Shannon, Edward. "Shameful, Impure Art: Robert Crumb's Autobiographical Comics and the Confessional Poets." *Biography: An Interdisciplinary Quarterly* 35.4 (2012): 628–49.

Smith, Sidonie, and Julia Watson. *Reading Autobiography: A Guide for Intrepreting Life Narratives*. Minneapolis: University of Minnesota Press, 2010.

Ryan, Marie-Laure. *Narrative Across Media: The Languages of Storytelling*. Lincoln: University of Nebraska Press, 2004.

Tolmie, Jane. *Drawing from Life: Memory and Subjectivity in Comic Art*. Jackson: University Press of Mississippi, 2013.

Topping, Margaret. "This Is Not a Photo Opportunity: Verbal/Visual Struggle in Francophone Travel Narratives." *Journal of Romance Studies* 13.1 (2013): 65–92.

Ware, Chris. *Building Stories*. New York: Pantheon, 2012.

Weigand, Edda. "Words Between Reality And Fiction." *Language & Dialogue* 3.1 (2013): 147–63.

Whitlock, Gillian. "Autographics: the Seeing "I" of the Comics." *Modern Fiction Studies* 52:4 (2006): 965–79.

———, and Anna Poletti. "Self-Regarding Art." *Biography* 31:1 (2008). v–xxiii.

Wolk, Douglas. *Reading Comics: How Graphic Novels Work and What They Mean*. Cambridge, MA: DeCapo Press, 2007.

Wortmann, Volker. *Authentisches Bild und authentisierende Form*. Cologne: Herbert von Halem Verlag, 2003.

Index

abstraction, 22–23, 25, 124; mimesis and, 6, 19, 20, 21, 22, 23, 24, 34
aesthetic criteria, 1, 7, 33, 37
"aesthetic education," 69, 84
aesthetic experience, 106, 107, 109, 112, 129, 239
aesthetic production, 11, 217, 223, 226, 231, 232
aesthetic quality, 37, 40, 44, 133, 230, 237, 241, 250, 255
aesthetics, 8, 114n3, 203, 226, 239, 240; autobiography and, 12, 263, 278; critical, 11, 238, 239, 240, 242, 243, 246, 247, 248, 249, 251; didactics and, 8, 94, 100; historical development of in German comics, 6, 19–34
ACTFL. *See* American Council on the Teaching of Foreign Languages
Alte Meister, 11, 237, 238, 242, 243, 244, 247, 250, 253, 254, 255; *Bathing Susanna*, 243; *Charles V and his Sisters as Children*, 243; *Duke Philipp Ludwig Wenzel von Sinzendorf*, 245; *Helene Fourment*, 243; *Infanta Isabella Clara Eugenia*, 245; *Madonna of the Cherries*, 246; *Mary with Child*, 246; *Portrait of a White-Bearded Man*, 240, 248, 252, 253; *Portrait of the Infanta Maria Theresa*, 245; *Saint Luke Painting the Madonna*, 249; *Susanna and the Elders*, 246. *See also Old Masters*; old masters
American Council on the Teaching of Foreign Languages (ACTFL), 122, 140n5, 145, 151, 152. *See also* NCSSFL-ACTFL Can-Do Statements
artists' collectives, 2; *PGH Glühende Zukunft*, 148

Asterix, 39, 50, 52–53, 58, 60n25, 71, 72, 73, 74, 75, 76, 78, 79, 80, 233n9
autobiography, 11, 82, 148, 158, 177, 185, 217, 218, 226, 259, 261, 262, 263, 265, 274; authenticity and, 278n4; cliché and, 11, 259, 260, 261, 263; definition of, 259, 261, 262, 263, 264, 274; history and, 9, 179; practitioner, 218, 224; visual presentation of, 264, 266, 272, 276, 277
autobiographical comics, 11, 147, 216, 217, 218, 222, 224, 226, 231, 233n4, 253
Autorencomic, 38, 47, 48–49, 50, 53

Baetens, Jan, 111, 147, 148, 278
Bakhtin, Mikhail, 192, 197, 201, 205, 207, 208
Basel, Switzerland, 8, 9, 122, 124, 125, 126–127, 128, 129, 131–132, 134, 136, 137
Beaty, Bart, 24, 31, 34, 241, 256n10
Benjamin, Walter, 58n1, 250
Bernhard, Thomas, 11, 216, 237, 238, 239, 240, 242, 251, 253, 254
Bible, the, 7, 8, 41, 93, 94, 95, 96, 98, 100, 101, 102, 103, 104, 106, 107, 111, 112, 113, 127; Action Bible, the, 114n16; Book of Revelation in, 95, 96–97, 98, 104; English Standard Version, 115n26; Image and, 97; King James Version, 113n1, 115n26; Luther's Translation of, 93, 94; visual adaptations of, 99, 115n29. *See also Book of Revelation, The (The Graphic Novel)*
Book of Revelation, The (The Graphic Novel), 93–117
Brunetti, Ivan, 227

281

About the Contributors

Vance Byrd is an associate professor of German at Grinnell College. His research interests include media studies, museum studies, visual culture, and the environmental humanities. He is completing his first book on nineteenth-century panorama entertainments and German literature, and has published on authors including E. T. A. Hoffmann, Adalbert Stifter, and Annette von Droste-Hülshoff.

Matt Hambro is a PhD candidate and teaching assistant in the joint program in German Studies at the University of North Carolina–Chapel Hill and Duke University. He is currently working on a dissertation on German-language comics and graphic novels and has published previously on ethics and religion in literature.

Joshua Kavaloski, who earned a PhD in modern German literature at the University of Virginia, is Associate Professor of German at Drew University. His scholarship concentrates on literature of the twentieth and twenty-first centuries, and he is the author of the book, *High Modernism: Aestheticism and Performativity in Literature of the 1920s*. He has also published essays on Thomas Mann, Franz Kafka, Jurek Becker, Philip Roth, Daniel Kehlmann, Jason Lutes, and others. His current book project explores the way that graphic novels re-imagine history and frame our understanding of the past. At Drew, he teaches courses both in English and in German on a wide range of topics including modern European literature, the German fairy-tale tradition, the history of the Weimar Republic, contemporary German film, and German-language graphic novels.

Antje Krüger is an Assistant Professor of German at Goucher College. Her research focuses on literary realism, the historical novel, text and image relations in literary texts, and graphic novels as a tool for teaching German. She has published on Uwe Timm, Zsuzsanna Gahse, Rolf-Dieter Brinkmann, and Bertolt Brecht.

Jens Kußmann completed his studies to become a secondary teacher (Gymnasium) at Bamberg University, Germany, in 2015, majoring in German, Social Studies, and History. Additionally, he holds a BA in German Studies, Political Science, and Music Pedagogy.

Lynn Marie Kutch received her PhD from Rutgers University Graduate School, New Brunswick. She is currently associate professor of German at Kutztown University of Pennsylvania. In 2014, she co-edited the volume *Tatort Germany: The Curious Case of German-language Crime Fiction* (Camden House). She has also published on German-language graphic novels in *Die Unterrichtspraxis/Teaching German*, and *The Kafka Society of America Journal*, and has written several forthcoming anthology and journal articles on graphic literature and comics. Her article "From Visual Literacy to Literary Proficiency: An Instructional and Assessment Model for the Graphic Novel Version of Kafka's *Die Verwandlung*" received the 2015 Best Article Prize from the American Association of Teachers of German.

K. Eckhard Kuhn-Osius has taught German at Hunter College of the City University of New York since 1984. He received his PhD from the University of Colorado at Boulder with a dissertation on the topic of what it means to understand a literary text. His literary interests include Goethe's *Faust*, the conservative literary reaction to World War I, the works of Heinrich Böll, literary diaries, and graphic literature. He has published numerous articles and reviews on literary and pedagogical topics. He has a strong interest in teaching German at all levels and is the main author of a three-volume series of introductory textbooks. Prof. Kuhn-Osius participated in several projects to improve language and literature teaching funded by NEH and FIPSE. He also chaired the AATG Testing Commission from 1990–2011 and was a member of the German Advanced Placement committee. He received the German-American Friendship Award in 2000, the Goethe-Institut-AATG Certificate of Merit in 2003, and the Duden-Award in 2007.

Julia Ludewig is an assistant professor of German at Allegheny College. She received her PhD degree in Comparative Literature from Binghamton University. She holds a BA degree in Cultural Studies from Europa-Universität Viadrina Frankfurt (Oder) and an MA in European Linguistics from Albert-Ludwig-Universität Freiburg. Her research interests include literary and linguistic genres, foreign language pedagogy, as well as graphic novels.

Bernadette Raedler received her MA from the University of Munich in Deutsch als Fremdsprache (German as a Foreign Language), German Literature and History in 1996. After dedicating almost twenty years to raising her four children and several transatlantic moves, she is now a PhD candidate in German Literature at the University of Calgary.

Dr. Brett Sterling is assistant professor of German at the University of Arkansas. He received his PhD from Vanderbilt University in 2013 for a dissertation on representation and the phenomenon of mass hysteria in the works of Hermann Broch. Dr. Sterling has presented widely on a variety of topics related to German comics, including the history of comics in Germany, the Berlin Wall in comic narratives, and on artists Jens Harder, Flix, and Barbara Yelin.

Jan van Nahl studied in Bonn, Germany (2004–2009), and Uppsala, Sweden (2006–2007), completed his doctorate at the University of Munich, Germany (2012), and was a visiting lecturer at the University of Silesia, Poland (2015). He is an alumnus of the German National Academic Foundation (since 2009) and the Protestant Academic Foundation (since 2012). He currently holds the position of a postdoctoral researcher and graduate teacher at the University of Iceland and the Árni Magnússon Institute for Icelandic Studies. His main research interests lie within the field of Medieval Studies, the History of German Scholarship since the Third Reich, and the Digital Humanities—major book publications: *Snorri Sturlusons Mythologie und die mittelalterliche Theologie* (2013), *Snorri Sturluson. Historiker, Politiker, Dichter* (ed., 2013), *Die Flüchtigkeit der Information. Wissenschaftsgeschichte im digitalen Zeitalter* (2014). In the recent past, both his activity as a translator of modern literature and his position as a managing editor of the German online journal for literature *Alliteratus* (http://www.alliteratus.com) have brought him into contact with the fascinating genre of graphic novels.